Closest Companion

Treasures of the Maharajahs

Before the Trumpet: Young Franklin Roosevelt 1882–1905

A First-Class Temperament: The Emergence of FDR

The Civil War: An Illustrated History
(with Ric and Ken Burns)

American Originals: The Private Worlds of
Some Singular Men and Women

Baseball: An Illustrated History
(with Ken Burns)

Tiger-Wallahs: Encounters with the Men Who Tried
to Save the Greatest of the Great Cats
(with Diane Raines Ward)

Closest Companion
(editor)

Closest Companion

The Unknown Story of the Intimate Friendship
between Franklin Roosevelt and Margaret Suckley

EDITED AND ANNOTATED BY

GEOFFREY C. WARD

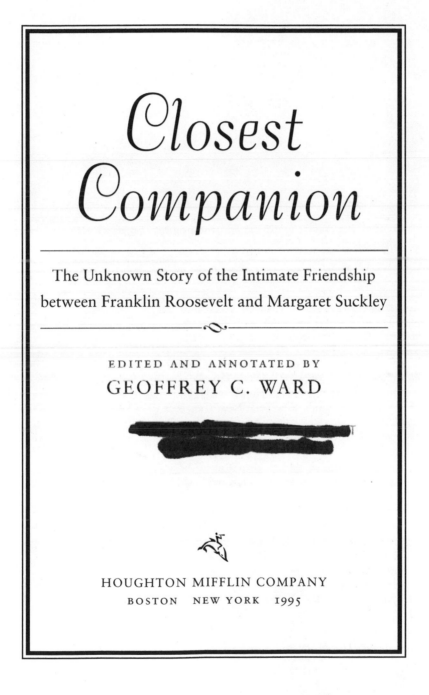

HOUGHTON MIFFLIN COMPANY
BOSTON   NEW YORK   1995

For information about permission to reproduce selections from
this book, write to Permissions, Houghton Mifflin Company,
215 Park Avenue South, New York, New York 10003.

Library of Congress Cataloging-in-Publication Data
Ward, Geoffrey C.
    Closest companion : the unknown story of the intimate friendship
between Franklin Roosevelt and Margaret Suckley . . . / Geoffrey C. Ward.
        p.   cm.
    Includes index.
    ISBN 0-395-66080-7
    1. Roosevelt, Franklin D. (Franklin Delano), 1882–1945 — Friends
and associates. 2. Suckley, Margaret, 1891–1991. 3. Presidents —
United States — Biography.   I. Title.
    E807.W329   1995
    973.917'092'2 — dc20   94-45394
    [B]   CIP

Printed in the United States of America

MP 10 9 8 7 6 5 4 3 2 1

For Diane, again

Contents

$\mathcal{P}$reface

MARGARET LYNCH SUCKLEY was Franklin Roosevelt's closest companion during the last years of his life. No one was more often with him during World War II than the quiet, good-humored distant cousin he called Daisy. She was admiring and circumspect, perfectly content to remain in the background as long as she could be near him, concerned always about his well-being. Hers is a familiar name in the Roosevelt literature — attending picnics; riding in FDR's automobile; working over his papers with him at the Franklin D. Roosevelt Library at Hyde Park or in his White House study; walking Fala, the celebrated Scottie she had given him; and, finally, at the President's side when he was fatally stricken at Warm Springs, Georgia. But she has remained little more than a name until now, and some members of Roosevelt's White House staff, put off by her constant but mostly silent presence, fooled by the skill with which she played what she herself once called "my part of prim spinster," and sometimes alarmed at what they believed to be her dangerous meddling with the President's failing health, even privately dismissed her among themselves as "the little mud wren."

That was pretty much how she wanted it. She told two generations of scholars who came to call at Wilderstein, her family's home in Rhinebeck, New York, that she really had very little to add to the Roosevelt story, had simply been privileged to be a social friend of the President's. When asked whether she had ever kept a diary, she would smile and reply with a question of her own: "What makes you think *I* would keep a diary?"

She died at Wilderstein in 1991 in her one-hundredth year. Shortly afterward, friends cleaning out her cluttered bedroom found a battered black suitcase beneath her bed. In it was a bundle of papers that showed she had not been entirely forthcoming with her visitors. There were in fact thousands of pages of diaries, covering the period from 1933, when she began to see a good deal of the President, until the day he died. And there were scores of her letters to FDR, as well as thirty-eight letters from him to her — some of them running on for pages, all handwritten, many of them more revealing of his inner thoughts than any he is known to have written to anyone else during his years in office.

Daisy Suckley was no literary stylist. She was determinedly reticent and not much concerned with politics or world events. And she was blindly partisan, never veering far from the opinion of FDR she formed the first time he ever took her driving in his open roadster in the spring of 1933: "The President is a MAN — *mentally, physically, & spiritually* — What more can I say?"

But her letters and journals nonetheless provide an invaluable record of Franklin Roosevelt in his off-hours, away from the crises that haunted his presidency. Others close to Roosevelt might have provided an equally intimate portrait — Marguerite LeHand, Louis Howe, Harry Hopkins, Pa Watson, the President's daughter, Anna — but none lived long enough to do so. It will be impossible for any future biographer of Roosevelt, any chronicler of the years through which he led his country, to overlook this entirely unexpected trove.

Daisy's papers provide the most complete surviving record of the sad, steady decline in the President's health that he and those around him successfully hid from the press and public during the last two years of his life. They constitute as well an old-fashioned love story, genteel but clandestine and sometimes distinctly flirtatious, which began on a splendid September afternoon in 1935 on a wooded hilltop at Hyde Park, altered over the years that followed, but never really ended. Theirs was an extraordinary friendship, unexplored until now yet clearly among the most important of Roosevelt's life. FDR truly loved Daisy Suckley, in his fashion. And no one ever loved Franklin Roosevelt more than Daisy Suckley did.

*   *   *

Part of the attraction each felt for the other grew out of the fact that they were both products of the same sheltered Hudson River world. Margaret Suckley — known as Daisy from the French word for the flower, *marguerite* — was born at Wilderstein overlooking the river on December 20, 1891, the fifth child and first daughter of distant cousins, both of them descendants of Robert Livingston, the seventeenth-century first Lord of Livingston Manor, and of Henry Beekman, the Patentee of Rhinebeck. Neither they nor their daughter ever forgot that whatever had happened to the family's fortunes over the years, their ancestors had once ruled the Hudson Valley.

Daisy's mother, Elizabeth Phillips Montgomery, was the daughter of an Episcopal clergyman, the Reverend Henry Montgomery, who presided over the Church of the Incarnation, sometimes attended by the Roosevelt family during its winters in New York. "The Roosevelts and the Suckleys were always friends and neighbors," Daisy told me once. *"Always."*

Her father, Robert Bowne Suckley (rhymes with "Bookley"), was the son of a Hudson River gentleman. He had inherited his father's considerable fortune in real estate at the age of thirty-two, and so had never needed to concern himself unduly with making a living. He had a New York law practice for a time — just as FDR's father did — but, Daisy said, "he never worried much about it," preferring to travel abroad in the summers and ice-boat on the Hudson in the winter. On his passport he described himself simply as "gentleman." Handsome, refined, fond of books and playing the violin, he was "very stylish," his proud daughter remembered. "You could have taken him anywhere for an Englishman."

And, as far as possible, the life he led on the Hudson River — like that led by his neighbors and kinsmen the Astors and Roosevelts, Livingstons and Chanlers, Delanos, Lynches, Langdons, and Montgomerys — was that of an English country gentleman. He inherited Wilderstein from his father in 1888 and almost immediately decided that the comparatively simple two-story Italianate villa in which he had been raised was insufficiently grand for his growing family. He ordered it transformed into a turreted, five-story Queen Anne mansion with thirty-five rooms. A Poughkeepsie architect, Arnault Cannon, Jr., did his best to fulfill Suckley's grandiose aspirations. Calvert Vaux designed the gardens and grounds, along with a gatehouse and a caretaker's cottage. Joseph Burr Tiffany, a first cousin of Louis Comfort Tiffany, did most of the interiors, giving each of the public rooms a distinctive style of its own. The paneled library, dimly lit through leaded panes, was intended to resemble a medieval Flemish chamber. Cherubs and doves pursued a hawk across the ceiling of the formal parlor, whose walls were covered with gold silk, the whole meant to "realize a complete specimen of the Louis XVI period." The adjacent morning room was American Colonial, hung with silk tapestry and filled with ebonized furniture handed down in the Suckley family.

Despite its amalgam of period interiors, the new Wilderstein was meant to be up to date as well: its exterior was painted in a variety of gaudy hues, in the fashion of the day, and a wire ran from the main house to the man in charge of the water-powered dynamo so that Mr. Suckley could signal when he wanted power for the lights turned on or off.

A staff of nearly twenty was required to keep Wilderstein running, and when the real estate market collapsed, following the financial panic of 1893, and more investments went bad four years later, it all became too much. Robert Suckley was forced to close up his new house and take his family off to Switzerland. The family settled into the Hôtel Rosa at Château d'Oex, where they stayed for ten years. The children — three boys and three girls — got their schooling from a Mlle. Blum, who, Daisy recalled, rapped their knuckles with a ruler if they failed to remember their lessons.

It was a comfortable, tranquil life. In the summer there were family outings on the mountainsides, with donkeys to carry the wicker picnic baskets up the slopes, and in the winter, cross-country ski trips. But playmates were few — most of the Suckleys' fellow guests at the Hôtel Rosa were childless Britons — and the high point of nearly every day was afternoon tea, during which Daisy and the other children were seen but not expected to be heard.

Her girlhood was almost as lonely as Franklin Roosevelt's boyhood had been, and, like him, she identified at first more with the previous generation than her own. She returned to America at fifteen, speaking three languages flawlessly but without a single American friend outside the tiny circle of her family. "I think it's a mistake to take children away from their own country," she said many years later. "When we came back we didn't have a friend."

Her parents differed about her subsequent education, as they differed about a great many things: her father, Daisy recalled, often spent the whole day locked in his Wilderstein study, safely out of reach of his wife's voice. He wanted Daisy to go to college. Her mother was against it. "I knew absolutely nobody, no *girl*, who was going to college," Daisy remembered. "My mother didn't approve of it." College made girls "worldly," her mother thought, and, worse, unmarriageable.

Daisy finally proposed a compromise, one of many she would devise to keep peace within her turbulent family over the decades: she would go to Bryn Mawr, but for just two years. Then she promised to return home to help her mother care for the family. "We had so many relatives," Daisy said. "My mother always had people staying with her [who] had to be more or less taken care of . . . Always a lot to do." She was not exaggerating. There were sometimes twenty guests at Wilderstein at one time, so many that sometimes her distrait mother, coming on a nephew or niece in the hallway, would ask when he or she had arrived, only to find that the guest had already been with her for several days.

Daisy would do everything she could to care for her family all her life — until she was the only member left, in fact — and although several men came courting her during her youth, she turned them all away. "We were not especially encouraged to marry," Daisy recalled; of the six Suckley children, only her younger sister Elizabeth ever did so. (Elizabeth's twin sister, Katherine, did eventually move away, into a renovated schoolhouse nearby called the Belfry, where, to the consternation of her family and the fascination of the neighborhood, she lived with a married couple.)

Daisy was attractive, bright and witty, and well read, but she always looked and acted older than she was and dressed in the fashion of her parents' generation. When playing tennis at the Edgewood Club, for example, she wore full-length skirts long after her opponents took to the court bare-legged. And she seemed, as one relative recalled, "adamantly uninterested in sex." She was apparently sympathetic to her mother's attitude: sex was something only men wanted, an ordeal for women so ghastly that Mrs. Suckley invariably wept at weddings at the thought of the awful things awaiting the bride. (The best solution to the problem of overpopulation, Daisy once told a young relative, was to sterilize most men. "It's most efficient," she said, "and I understand it does not affect . . . whatever it is they get out of it.")

World War I served to expand Daisy's sequestered world a little. During the summer she sold war bonds door to door in Rhinebeck and up and down the river, and each morning during the winter she left her family's Manhattan home on Twenty-third Street and Madison, boarded a horse car for the Battery, then took a boat out to Ellis Island, where she worked as a nurse's aide, bringing comfort to the wounded soldiers and sailors hospitalized there.

But the war also marked the start of the family's rapid decline. In 1917, her eldest brother, Henry — the handsome, capable son on whom their father had pinned the family's hopes — was killed when a German bomb hit the plainly marked Red Cross ambulance he was driving near Salonika, in Greece.

Four years later, Daisy's father himself died suddenly from a heart attack, at sixty-five. Daisy, just twenty-nine, was devastated. She had worshiped her father, sympathized with him in his arguments with her mother, considered it a privilege to accompany his after-dinner violin performances on the piano, and treasured all her life the memory of having once climbed a Swiss mountain with him over the objections of her mother, who thought such adventures unladylike.

Now, she seemed to abandon any hope of making a life for herself apart from the family. "I was 31 years old yesterday," she confided to her journal on December 21, 1922, "but it means nothing to me. I don't feel either young or old. I just *am!* I love life, I love people, I don't love myself, but I interest myself because I have a better opportunity of knowing myself than anyone else. I know I am an inadequate creature, that I lack that spark, that fire, whatever one can call it, which I continually complain is lacking in the other members of my family, cousins and all. We are over-civilized and we need some new young blood. I wish I could bring it into the family."

She resigned herself instead to looking after her mother and her surviving brothers, Robert and Arthur. They needed lots of looking after. Her mother had firm views about the running of her household, but was querulous when it came to even brief sojourns into the world beyond her gates. It fell to Daisy to see that the grocer was paid, the pipes got fixed, the runabout was kept filled with gas.

"Her brothers basically did nothing," a niece remembered. "They just sat there and let Daisy do it all." Both attended Harvard. Neither was graduated. Nor did either ever see much reason to leave Wilderstein, though Arthur did manage to build himself a villa in Monaco, where he spent his winters until — to his great annoyance — the Nazis invaded France.

Robert Suckley was eccentric and reclusive; his mother thought him "delicate." He ghosted through the neighborhood on errands only he understood and, according to the late Joseph P. Lash, who once spent a summer next door, devoted much of his time when indoors to perfecting his recipe for Hollandaise. Robert quarreled frequently with Arthur; after one especially bitter confrontation, he moved into the basement, from which he controlled the ancient and complex furnace system that allowed him to punish his brother (and any other family member who crossed him) by selectively withholding heat.

The Great Depression hit the Suckleys hard. As the older surviving son, Robert had been left in charge of most of what remained of the family fortune. He lost a great deal of it investing in German Reichsmarks during the early twenties and all but a little of the rest in the crash of 1929. At about the same time, Daisy's sister Elizabeth, her husband, Littleton C. F. Hambley, and their three children suddenly found themselves back at Wilderstein. Hambley's job on the cotton exchange had evaporated, and he was reduced, as Daisy wrote, to trying to make a go of things "growing vegetables."

Finally, to make ends meet, and to keep Wilderstein going, Daisy took a position as the paid companion of her elderly and invalid aunt Sophie, Mrs. Woodbury G. Langdon, dividing her time between Mrs. Langdon's New York apartment, at 399 Park Avenue, and Mansakenning, her summer home just down the road from Wilderstein. By the early thirties, the Suckleys were without servants, had been forced to sell their family house in Manhattan, and were largely dependent on the small but steady salary Daisy managed to bring in.

* * *

Those were grim times for the occupants of Wilderstein, tense and claustrophobic and made even more difficult by the fact that Littleton Hambley had come to blame Daisy's family for the troubles that had befallen his own.

She found escape through reading, filling the shelves in and near her third-floor bedroom in Wilderstein's tower with books on spiritualism, the occult, Eastern mysticism — anything that would take her away from her pinched existence for a few hours. "I live," she told a friend, "mostly in dreams."

In 1933, one of her fondest dreams came true: her old friend and Dutchess County neighbor Franklin Roosevelt became President of the United States.

She had been dazzled by him since adolescence. She first saw him in 1910, at one of the few dances she ever attended, a New Year's party at Crumwold, Archibald Rogers's monumental Hyde Park château, just down the river from Wilderstein. She was eighteen. Franklin was twenty-eight and married, but she never forgot the sight of him, she once told a visitor, tall and laughing as he whirled one partner after another around and around the dance floor. She saw him again in the neighborhood from time to time, and watched from afar as he won election to the state senate, went to Washington as assistant secretary of the Navy, ran for vice president of the United States.

Then, in the spring of 1922, Sara Delano Roosevelt telephoned Daisy, asking her to come for tea at Springwood, her Hyde Park home. Her son was lonely, she said, and needed company. He had come home to Springwood an invalid — infantile paralysis, contracted the summer before, made it impossible for him to stand unaided, let alone to dance — and his wife, Eleanor, was already busy elsewhere, seeing to the care of their five children, pursuing causes of her own, trying to keep the Roosevelt name alive in the political world.

Even before Franklin's illness, the Roosevelts had been more political partners than husband and wife. Eleanor Roosevelt's bitterness over FDR's wartime dalliance with her social secretary, Lucy Mercer, was the catalyst for their having decided to sleep — and, for the most part, live — apart. She once claimed to have forgiven but not forgotten his transgression, but in fact she was never able to do either.

Still, the cause of the difficulties between them lay deeper. Sara Delano Roosevelt, not Eleanor, was always the most important woman in FDR's life, and it was his wife's bad luck that almost from the first she had echoed too vividly the element in his mother's personality he resented most — her insistence on his doing the right thing — while being incapable of supplying the unqualified adoration that was among his mother's most precious gifts to him.

His illness had brought husband and wife into close proximity again for a time — she bravely nursed him through the first agonizing weeks — but she soon found caring for him as onerous as he found wearying her earnest exhortations to do his exercises. In the spring of 1922 he agreed with his doctors that if he was to improve at all, he would have to do so while living apart from the strains of his crowded New York household.

And so he returned to his mother's big empty house on the river. FDR was so gregarious, so charming, so obviously fond of good times and good company that it is hard to credit that he could ever have been lonely. But he had in fact been a solitary child, and after polio trapped him in his wheelchair, he would be lonely again for much of the remaining twenty-four years of his life.

"He might have been happier with a wife who was completely uncritical," Eleanor Roosevelt wrote after her husband's death. "That I was never able to be, and he had to find it in other people." Over the years, those other people would come to include his secretary and confidante, Marguerite LeHand, Crown Princess Martha of Norway, his daughter, Anna, and, during the last months of his life, in a final irony a novelist would have been reluctant to concoct, Lucy Mercer herself.

We now know that they also included Daisy Suckley, though neither Eleanor Roosevelt nor the President's mother — the latter concerned always with maintaining the appearance of propriety and normally wary of any young woman who showed too lively an interest in her son — seems to have been fully conscious of it.

That is understandable. Daisy appeared to pose no threat. She was ten years younger than FDR, distantly related to him (they were sixth cousins), dowdy, retiring. If Franklin enjoyed her quiet company, that was fine with everyone.

Certainly it was fine with Daisy, who was more than happy to sit quietly on the lawn several afternoons that spring and summer while Franklin pulled himself around a set of exercise bars, telling extravagant stories to keep her entertained and as unaware as possible of his helplessness. "I'm not going to be conquered by a childish disease," he told her again and again through gritted teeth, and her heart bled for him. "My God, he was brave," she remembered.

Daisy longed that year for "light" and "fire" to come into her life. Franklin Roosevelt had enough to warm them both.

They saw each other casually all through the twenties, and about the time FDR returned to politics and ran for governor of New York, in 1928, Daisy began secretly to amass newspaper clippings about his daily activities, the start of a collection that would one day fill a vast steamer trunk in the Wilderstein attic.

Then, in March 1933, FDR invited her to attend his inauguration as President, and the story of their extraordinary friendship really began. As far as possible in the pages that follow, Daisy Suckley and Franklin Roosevelt tell that story in their own words.

G.C.W.

Nagarahole National Park
Karnataka, India
January 14, 1995

Editor's Note

THIS VOLUME contains a little over half of Margaret Suckley's papers and constitutes only a tiny fraction of the huge Wilderstein collection of family papers that stretches back to the eighteenth century.

Most of Daisy's letters to FDR are included here. So are all thirty-eight of his to her, edited only slightly. Daisy sometimes kept more than one journal at a time, and in editing them for publication, I have felt free to mix passages from different volumes in the interest of a clear narrative. Ellipses indicate omitted material within letters or diary entries. I have not indicated the existence of entries left out entirely.

For the record, I have also left out most of the material that does not concern the Roosevelts, the menus for all but a few of the hundreds of lunches and dinners Daisy shared with FDR, and a good many of Fala's amiable but redundant doings.

I have tried to identify everyone Daisy mentions, but failed to puzzle out a few identities. My apologies to the descendants of anyone whose full name I am unable to give. Write to me in care of Houghton Mifflin Company, and should there be a second edition, I'll try to see that they are included.

One question nagged at me as I worked away at Daisy's papers: why did so many of her letters to FDR survive? Her undying affection for him had made it impossible for her to throw away most of his letters — though, as the reader will see, she did destroy some and drastically edited others. But as far as I could tell, her letters to him — always sent in specially marked envelopes through trusted intermediaries — had never been filed among his papers. One would have assumed, as Daisy evidently did assume, that he had thrown them away. Yet there they were, decades later, in the suitcase beneath her bed. Had she found them tucked away somewhere while working as an archivist at the Roosevelt Library, and quietly spirited them home? It didn't seem like her, but I could think of no other explanation.

Then, just as I was finishing my research, I found the answer in a letter Daisy wrote to the President's daughter, Anna, just two weeks after Roosevelt died, in the spring of 1945. Charlie Fredericks, a Secret Service man especially close to the President, had evidently telephoned to say that he and Anna had come across a bundle of Daisy's letters in the box of stamps that had traveled with FDR wherever he went so that he could work over his albums in the evenings.

Daisy wanted those letters. They constituted a large part of the only record she had of the most important relationship in her life. But in asking Anna for them, she was characteristically careful, even after FDR's death, not to seem overanxious or to reveal the intimacy she had shared with him, which, however real, might have discomfited the Roosevelt family:

> I had no idea he had ever kept any of [the letters], but suppose it was just easier to toss them into the stamp box rather than bother to tear them up & drop them into the waste-paper basket! I am wondering if there were any in his desk drawers. Charlie says you & Jimmy [Roosevelt, FDR's eldest son] emptied them. If there were some & you haven't destroyed them I would love to have them — Don't worry about them one way or the other but they would fill in the spaces between his rare letters to me and everything connected with him becomes more & more precious! I wonder if anyone ever before was loved by so many people as your dear father — and, I might add, loved so much in a personal way.

1933–1941

Our Hill: The Years Before the War

1933

[The written record of the friendship between Daisy Suckley and Franklin Roosevelt begins with his first inauguration, in 1933. FDR saw to it that she was invited to witness his triumph, and she eagerly noted her impressions of it in a little green leatherbound book stamped, in gold, "My Trip."]

↬ *Friday, March 3rd, 1933.* Arrive Washington 1 PM and drive to . . . Virginia Hunt's [Miss Hunt was a Livingston and an old friend of Daisy's] at 1155 16th Street. The Roosevelts are at the Mayflower. Right away we go to get grand-stand tickets for the Parade. *Mine is on the President's stand!* "Among the family," as he told Reggie [Robert Reginald] Livingston [a cousin of Eleanor Roosevelt's and chairman of the Democratic Party in Columbia County]. My excitement when I discovered this was such that I told Helen [Brown, the married daughter of Daisy's aunt Sophie Langdon] I thought I should go to a convent after this week-end!

↬ *Saturday, March 4.* Stayed in bed . . . until time for Inauguration. The tickets for [the] stand at the Capitol did not come, & we felt anyway that it would be difficult to get back to the Court of Honor. So we all listened to the radio at the Grafton [Hotel]. Heard the taking of office of [Vice President John Nance] Garner. Then Roosevelt and his excellent speech. He was evidently very serious.

A light lunch and then off to the Court of Honor in front of the White House. My seat was on the President's stand, section B, top row, from where I saw the White House grounds, the parade, & the President's head throughout the afternoon. He had a high chair to sit on, which gave the effect of his standing. Glass on three sides &, I hear, an electric heater so he could be comfortable for the tedious three-hour parade. The first part was dignified, the last part a sort of circus — Tom Mix [a cowboy movie star] cavorting in white on a black horse — Movie actresses on a float — Bands in fantastic feather costumes, etc., etc. Democracy!

In spite of my fur coat, I was cold & thankful when Reggie Living-ston turned up, also frozen, at about 5.30. We went straight around to the East Entrance of the White House . . . The President had come in and gone straight to his study for a cabinet meeting. The Banking situation is his first problem. [Runs, panics, and failures had virtually destroyed the American banking system; banking services in all forty-eight states had been suspended.]

Eleanor Roosevelt received alone in the Blue Room, the visitors walking in single-file around the empty room . . . No crowding and the whole thing *nice*. Delanos & Roosevelts in large numbers. Mrs. James Roosevelt [the President's mother] came, looking tired but "game," and said she was of course "just waiting around to see Franklin."

[Later] . . . the Inaugural Ball in [an] Auditorium. A mass of all sorts of people in an unattractive pennanted hall — More Democracy! Rosa Ponselle sang "America." She had a hard time being heard over a blaring brass band!

᙮ *Sunday, March 5th.* Helen and I went to St. John's Church. Got seats early & the President with all his family sat in the pew across the aisle. He looked very well but never looked to right or left — very serious.

᙮ *Monday, March 6th.* Papers tell us Roosevelt has been in confer-ence all the last two days & closes banks for 4 days.

Hurrah!! For action!!

᙮ *August 1st, 1933.* [Mansakenning, Rhinebeck, the country home of Mrs. Woodbury G. Langdon, Daisy's aunt and employer] *A Red Letter Day: The President of the United States of America called me up on the telephone!* I was at a picnic with [friends]. He said he would call again!

᙮ *August 4th, 1933.* Mrs. Franklin D. Roosevelt called me up to ask Aunt Sophie [Langdon] & me to tea — At a quarter to five we drove up to the house, to find the President being photographed. His wife apologized & flew off to lecture on Euthenics at Vassar. Aunt S. & I spent an hour alone with the President & his mother!

Only one interruption by Marvin McIntyre, secretary, who whis-pered at some length in the President's ear. The P. looks well, but I thought I saw a good deal of preoccupation "behind his eyes." He has such a load on him. Asked me to *drive alone* with him on Monday aft. Haven't told the family yet!!! . . .

~ *August 7th, 1933.* Monday — 3 P.M. at Roosevelt entrance — police[man] asks whom I am to see — "The President."

"The President. Himself?"

"Yes, the President himself!"

Police telephones to the house & lets me by. At house, a man comes forward & asks "Miss Sibley" to park her car "there." Another man at the front door says the Pres. regrets he may be delayed, but will I sit down. I get "British Agent" off the piano & start reading. In a few minutes the coloured attendant comes & conducts me to the study where I spend an hour talking & looking at old books . . .

The Pres. & I drive in his roadster through his woods — followed by 4 detectives in a state trooper car. On the swamp lot we think we see an egret which turns out to be a quart bottle on a stump!

On our return Pres. shows me more books; also illustrations of birds, etc.

Mrs. [Eleanor] R. somewhat surprised to see me!

6 P.M., Miss [Marguerite] LeHand [the President's secretary] & I drive with the President to the "cottage," where the Rs have a picnic for the press. Mrs. Franklin [Roosevelt], Mrs. James [Roosevelt, the President's mother], Mrs. J.R.R. [the widow of the President's half-brother, James Roosevelt Roosevelt], Anna Roosevelt Dall [the President's daughter] all there. I choose a hot dog, potato salad, beer. Ernest K. Lindley [a journalist, author of *The Roosevelt Revolution*] tells me he is writing another book, from March 4th onward. He writes for the *Tribune*. About 8 P.M. I leave with Mrs. James & Mrs. J. R.

The President is a MAN — *mentally, physically, & spiritually* — What more can I say?

~ *September 30th, 1933.* Red White & Blue letter Day! To wedding reception of Alida Robinson [the daughter of his half-niece Helen Roosevelt Robinson] & Kenneth Walker at "Red House" [the home of the late James Roosevelt Roosevelt] in Hyde Park. The Pres. proudly asked me to go to a picnic at the cottage afterwards. It was a perfect day & place for the wedding. They say the bride wanted hers to be just like her mother's. The coach & four had to be given up however . . . A glorious moon, a roaring fire, sausages, corn etc.

Pres. told me to come & *stay* at the White House when I go to

Washington! Just to write him ahead & telephone Miss LeHand when I get there!

◌ *October 2nd, 1933.* Monday — With Ethel [Merritt of Leacote, in Rhinebeck] to Garrison to play our match against Mrs. [John W.] Cutler [the sister of FDR's Republican congressman and archenemy, Hamilton Fish] & Mrs. [William Maxwell] Evarts on [the] Vanderbilt [Webb] tennis court. A glorious day. Fall colours appearing in spots. They beat us 6–2, 6–3 — But it was great fun — Just the joy of activity!

I wonder if the Pres. does not sometimes have moments of despair when he realizes he can never again move without help. It must overwhelm him — Though he never shows anything but cheerfulness. Saturday, he *was* serious, and twice sighed — What a job he has!

[On October 23, the morning after the fourth of FDR's Fireside Chats, in which he declared that "we are on our way, and we are headed in the right direction," Daisy wrote to congratulate him on the speech. She also may have hinted, on paper or in person, that she was in financial distress because of the ineptitude and ill luck of her brother Robert Bowne Suckley, Jr. In any case, Roosevelt responded by hand five days later, offering to help.]

The White House
Washington

Oct. 28 '33

Dear Daisy —

That was dear of you to write me about the Sunday night talk & I'm glad you liked it because that means so much more from a very understanding person like you — When I saw you that hectic Saturday I did not have the chance to tell you that if ever I can help in any way you really must let me know — but that I think you know without my telling you — These are days of so many difficulties and readjustments for everybody — but I truly think we shall all work out of it — & the fine spirit of most people keeps me buoyed up — Your own unselfishness I understand & appreciate —

All the same I miss the River — I had hoped to go up for Election Day — but I dare not leave here — something new breaks loose every few hours! I count on that visit soon —

Affectionately yours,
F.D.R.

∽ *October 31st, 1933.* A letter from F.D.R. on White House paper — He "counts on that visit," & wants me to let him know if there should be any way in which he "could help." I don't deserve such a friend . . .

1934

[In the end, the President's direct intervention was not needed. Daisy's brother Arthur asserted himself in time to save at least a little of Daisy's inheritance.]

∽ *January 3rd, 1934.* Arthur has performed a miracle in dealing with Robin. The properties in town are all practically taken out of his hands, so that he *can't* spend any more money. The problem for the future will be his support, for he has nothing. We have hopes the [Public Works Administration] or other Federal agency will take the Hoboken land . . . I feel Arthur is doing with Robin & the Suckley properties as Roosevelt is doing with the country — My best compliment!!

∽ *January 7th, 1934.* A strange experience this morning in St. James Church: while waiting to go up to communion I looked across at the pew ends, to get the number so that I could find my pew. I saw the number 49; looked at the next pew, saw 38 in a different kind of lettering. Looked back & saw 36, as one would expect. It was a definite "vision" of the number 49 — I could not account for that particular number. On my way home, through 65th St., I suddenly realized 49 is the number of the President's house — [When in New York, FDR and his family occupied a town house at 49 East 65th Street, built for him by his mother, who lived in its twin next door.]
  I can't account for the above, as I wasn't thinking of anything but . . . the Church service. "Take it or leave it!"

[Daisy was fascinated by the occult — numerology, reincarnation, telepathy, astrology, mediums, spirit writing. All of it appealed to her, and her letters and diaries are laced with dubious evidence of its power.]

In late January, Daisy visited Washington again and described in detail what followed in her small "My Trip" book.]

❧ *Sunday, January 28th*. [at the Washington, D.C., home of Virginia Hunt] . . . This evening V[irginia] told me that Eleanor & Franklin Roosevelt evidently don't get on together. She is always off somewhere, though always on hand for dinners or receptions. It is very sad, as they are both such splendid people and must miss a happy married life.

V. says Washington life is so narrow that the gossiping is terrible, and it is unfortunate that there is [so] much ground for it in the case of the Roosevelts.

❧ *Monday, January 29th*. . . . 8 degrees above zero. Bitter! . . . Virginia and I went to the White House to leave a note for Mrs. [Edith] Helm [White House social secretary], asking her if we are to leave before the reception on Thursday, or after . . . On returning to 1155 [the Hunt residence] the maid almost at once announced the White House on the telephone for V: We *are* expected to the reception & will receive a ticket of admission for our taxi!

"Is Miss Suckley here yet? . . . I must tell Miss LeHand. She was asking me just this morning."

I begin to feel I am quite important at the White House!

❧ *Tuesday, January 30, 1934*. The President's 52nd Birthday. . . . A wonderful concert by the Boston Symphony Orchestra, [Serge] Koussevitsky conducting. On our return at about 6.30 P.M., the maid said the White House had called up Miss Suckley. They would give no name but would call again!

Period of intense expectancy for about ¾ of an hour. The telephone rings and the President & Miss Suckley have a pleasant talk with the result that Miss Suckley is to present herself at the Executive Offices at 4.45 tomorrow, see "the whole works" and have tea with the President!!! !!!

❧ *Wednesday, January 31st*. . . . At 4.45 I arrived at the White House, to find the lobby full of smoke and men. After waiting 5 minutes, a man asked me if I had an appointment. I said, "Yes, with the President."

"A personal one?"

I was ushered into Mr. Phillips' office. [He] introduced himself & asked me to sit down. Another few minutes' wait while I had time to notice the busy people in & out, the simple good decorating of the room, an excellent picture of F.D.R. over the mantle.

Mr. Phillips then . . . took me through a short passage into an oval room, hung with ship pictures. At a desk in the middle of the room, the President was sitting. A stack of papers on his desk. Some of the various Birthday presents he has received — [a] beautiful gold plaque from California, engraved, in a red velvet case — a special book gotten up by the Roycrofters, beautifully bound. There was of course no time to do more than glance at them.

He acknowledged that he *does* get mentally tired and that it is terrifying to realize the responsibility that rests on him. He added that he would say that to very few, and that it was not for quotation!

Soon, he called "Gus" [Gennerich, his bodyguard], transferred to his wheeled chair, put on a hat and long cloak, and we started for the White House and looked in at the swimming pool. [Augustus Adolf Gennerich was a burly, former New York policeman who had joined FDR during his governorship and was expert in helping him maintain the appearance of mobility in public. Quiet, genial, unmarried, he was devoted to his boss, who called him his "humanizer" and "my ambassador to the man in the street."]

On the way [FDR] said there were two ambassadors waiting in the East Room to present their credentials. On our way up from the basement in the elevator a secretary showed him two brief abstracts describing the careers of the two ambassadors he was about to receive.

On reaching the 2nd floor we all left the elevator. He called, "Darling, Daisy Suckley is here," and left me to get some tea with Mrs. R. while he put on his braces. Mrs. R. was evidently surprised to see me but introduced me to the Polish Ambassador and gave me tea.

The [ambassador] talked in very halting English of Japan & Siam. He said the Japanese always laugh at kissing in the movies . . . They have no equivalent for it . . .

[T]he aide came to the door and said the President wanted me in the Red Room, to watch through the door while he received the credentials of the Cuban Ambassador [Marques] Sterling and the minister from South Africa . . . "Gus" & I stood in different doors.

[After the ceremony a servant] told the President that Mrs. R. had some ladies to tea. The President said, "Then we will go to the study!" It is another oval room . . . very attractively arranged with the President's desk, many comfortable chairs, & the ship pictures & models one hears of so much.

I was so glad to see the President sit right down in a deep sofa. I've always seen him on stiff chairs before! We talked for about two minutes, when a secretary came from Mrs. R. to say that Sir Frederick White and Mrs. C. [Frances Crane] had been waiting for some time to see him. At first he said that he would see them a little later. The secretary returned with the message that Mrs. R. suggested he see them now, and she would take them away in a little while. I suggested leaving several times, as things seemed a little hectic, but he always said no, wait until the others had gone. One must obey the President!

Mrs. C. & Sir Frederick were then ushered in. Both tall, attractive & good-looking. Franklin evidently knows Mrs. C. & calls her Frances. She has much charm & a gracious smile. The three talked most interestingly about the Far East. There is trouble brewing with Japan . . .

Franklin spoke of a certain prominent Japanese who was at Harvard with him [Otohiko Matsukata] & who spoke rather too freely one day about the plans of the Japanese. They had two policies, the land & the maritime, to be used according to the way events shaped themselves. There would be a war against a European nation, to show they could beat them, a war against an Asiatic nation for the same purpose — gradual expansion over Manchuria & China, eventually to include Siam & Indo-China, *up to* India but not including her. *A foothold,* no more, in Central America.

It is a plan looking a century ahead, a thing we Anglo-Saxons can't do, and in considering what *has* happened so far, since 1900, they seem to be carrying out this plan.

Franklin said that he & [British Prime Minister] Ramsay MacDonald discussed this subject last spring. *They apparently agreed that England & the USA cannot allow Japan to have Naval parity.*

We must watch coming events!

All this conversation took place in about 10 or 15 minutes & then Mrs. R. came in & took the two away because Franklin was to have his swim before dinner! Franklin told Miss Suckley to delay the swim for 15 minutes — which she did. During that 15 minutes Anna Dall [the President's only daughter, then married to Curtis Dall] brought in four people to shake the President's hand, & the two babies Buzzie [Curtis] & Sistie [Eleanor] dressed like Indians. Anna looked very pretty. She has a charming smile.

Also . . . a large thick envelope was brought from the Treasury. It is a wonder the President can keep his head. He is always ready to smile & joke, however. He celebrated his birthday last night by a long session of poker with his partners of the 1920 [vice presidential] campaign. [This Cuff-links Club — so-called because of the souvenirs the candidate gave the men who had worked hardest for him — convened annually on his birthday.]

You *cannot* think of poker & state affairs at the same moment!

At 6.15 I finally collected my things & left, not disturbing Mrs. R., who was entertaining.

〜 *Thursday, February 1st.* Actually, it is 2.30 A.M. February 2nd, but I can't sleep, my mind is so full of the past evening that I might as well write it all up . . .

CLIMAX of trip!

At twenty minutes to seven we went down to the waiting car. V. in black velvet; I in my blue lace with the velvet jacket, blue & silver brocaded slippers, my 10-cent-store star hairpins, "diamond" bracelet — and my star sapphire! White suede gloves! . . .

[An] usher escorted us to the Red Room and asked us to wait there, after finding out which one of us was which. In a few minutes three aides came in & were introduced by the usher. I was so pleased that my name was given correctly . . .

Very soon the rest of the dinner party arrived: *Will Rogers* [whom Daisy and Virginia had seen in a movie earlier that day] with his wife & daughter! This was the beginning of one of the most amusing evenings I've ever spent. Will Rogers is . . . Will Rogers, nothing else! Under his commonness, he is probably one of the sweetest people in the world, to judge by his wife and daughter. Mrs. Rogers is a perfectly sweet, quiet, retiring *lady*. Mary is something of a flapper in appearance, but very sweet & sensible . . .

The President came to the door on the arm of Captain [Walter N.] Vernon and they led the way to the "small" dining room, Mrs. Roosevelt taking Mrs. Rogers' hand to walk in with her . . .

Not being near the President, I had the next best position, almost opposite . . . Part of the time, Will Rogers holding the floor. The President was his usual cheerful, charming self. Anna Dall more quiet & sweet than I would have expected. She looked so young . . .

I finished some of the soup, but only ate scraps of the rest. I was too excited to swallow.

Six coloured men waited on us, so appropriate in that lovely old house with its tradition and southern atmosphere. With all the formalities of their life, the Roosevelts make one feel so very informal. It would be impossible, it seems to me, to do a gauche, undignified thing in that house, but *not* because one would be awed. They are such *fine, real* people, that one unconsciously aims to imitate them.

After dinner we had about ¾ of an hour upstairs in the President's study. I behaved remarkably well, and talked to everyone but him. I arranged to be in a position to look at him, however!

. . . At nine we all went downstairs to the Red Room again, this time to watch the Diplomatic Reception . . . Finally, the President, with Captain Vernon, Mrs. R. with Colonel [Edwin] Watson [the President's military aide and, later, his secretary, often called Pa], came through the room followed by the Cabinet and all walked in a dignified manner to their places in the Blue Room. Franklin looked at me, winked & laughed. I smiled circumspectly! In the afternoon before, he said he was sure I would laugh at him as he went by in the procession, and I said I would *try* to behave properly. I did!

. . . During the Reception, Virgina & I had the most amusing time. Alice Longworth [Theodore Roosevelt's daughter, a famously sharp-tongued critic of her Democratic cousins] spoke to the Rogerses and to Virginia. She certainly has charm, and [an aide] told me she comes to *everything* at the White House. He didn't know how she managed it, but she is *always* there. I had a feeling she might be a sort of eye & ear to the Republican party. Secretary [of State] and Mrs. Cordell Hull, Mr. and Mrs. "Jim" Farley [postmaster general], I recognized.

. . . The whole evening was such a novelty & so thrilling to me that I feel it was a sort of dream . . . We heard some clapping and found the President and Mrs. R. had gone upstairs. It turned out later that Mrs. R. had been feeling sick all the evening. She looked pale but kept right on with her part.

We saw Col. Watson & I asked him if it would be all right for us to go up to say goodnight. He said he thought not, as the President had retired and was expecting a couple of people upstairs. So we made up our minds everything was over and moved down the hall. An usher came to us in the most crowded place with the "order" from the President that Miss Hunt and Miss Suckley were wanted upstairs! *We* were evidently the "couple of people."

He opened the gates at the foot of the stairs and I flew up. V. came along in a dignified fashion and tried to keep me from arriving breathless into the President's study.

We found him with Mrs. [Caspar] Whitney, who was talking California politics to him, & wants him to land at Fresno, on his summer trip, & make a radio address to assure the Californians that he is not expecting to smash all existing institutions. Something like that, anyway. Evidently, [California Senator William G.] McAdoo is giving some trouble.

Mrs. Whitney left, and almost immediately Secretary [of Labor] Frances Perkins came in, seemingly rather put out at finding two nincompoops with the President. She did not know we had been summoned!!

The conversation was fascinating . . . a plan for insurance for labor . . .

Anna Dall came in pyjamas, looking like a little girl, & whispered to her father, evidently about her mother being ill. She kissed him goodnight and as soon as Sec. Perkins left we started to say goodnight & were hurried by [Miss Perkins] returning to the door and asking if she should keep the elevator for us!

. . . When I said goodbye to Franklin, I said, "I'll see you next Summer."

"Oh, before that," he answered in a determined fashion.

Of course, I wonder if it *could* mean that I would be asked to stay at the White House!! He said that as soon as Lent came he would be through with big receptions & hoped to have some small dinners.

I must not forget that I am a working woman!

[Daisy and the President very likely saw each other again that spring and summer, but there is no record of it. Their first documented encounter follows.]

⌁ *September 24th, 1934.* [Mansakenning, Rhinebeck] . . . At 10.15 P.M. the Pres. called on the phone to ask me to tea tomorrow . . . We went for a lovely drive to the [Val-Kill] cottage [the hideaway FDR built for his wife on Roosevelt property across the road from Springwood] for his bathing suit! . . . 2 cars following. Back for tea about 5.30 . . . F.D.R. gave me "The Happy Warrior" before I left. [Presumably an autographed copy of the nominating speech delivered at the 1924 Democratic Convention, in which he hailed Governor Al Smith as "the happy warrior of the political battlefield" and signaled his own return to active politics after his polio.]

I am so spoiled that it seems quite natural to drive with the President of the U.S.A. He goes [back to Washington] tonight.

[Roosevelt took enormous pride and pleasure in driving his open car, which was especially equipped with hand controls of his own devising. Driving provided freedom, relaxation, mobility, and a welcome change of scene for an often harassed man otherwise reliant on a wheelchair. Over the next eleven years, Daisy would be his most frequent and enthusiastic passenger.]

∾ *September 27th, 1934.* . . . . [T]ea at Mrs. J. R. Roosevelt's. [She] always seems lonely & conscious of others' criticism. I like her — and her Scottie & two beautiful police-dogs!

[James Roosevelt Roosevelt's widow had been born Betty Riley, the daughter of a threadbare English clergyman. The President's half-brother met her when she was a shopgirl at Harrod's and kept her as his mistress for many years before they were married. She was always acutely aware that the Roosevelts had been reluctant to welcome her into the clan, and FDR's celebrity seems only to have added to her insecurity.]

The White House
Washington

Oct. 22 1934

Dear Daisy —
    Thanks ever so much for speaking to Helen Crosby [daughter of Maunsell Crosby, Daisy's neighbor and FDR's boyhood mentor as an amateur ornithologist] about that silly little old ornithological diary — if she finds it you will be amused by the enthusiasms of a Dutchess County naturalist at the age of twelve! That was before you had begun to attend dancing class.
    . . . [W]e expect to get to H.P. the morning of Nov. 3rd & stay at least till the evening of Election Day — Do *please* come down one of those afternoons — whichever is best for you — only let me know a little in advance which is the most convenient — I hope to have a real four days without political thoughts — isn't that a grand idea for the period immediately preceding an important election?
    Come & tell me about ships and cabbages & kings — the mythological kind — but not about sealing wax — that would be too much like the State Department — It will be nice —

Affectionately yours,
F.D.R.

[Daisy did go, she and FDR took another drive together, and she evidently asked whether he would look into the background of a friend's fiancé, just the sort of insider's task FDR loved to perform.]

The White House
Washington

Nov. 14, '34

Dear Daisy —

I'm glad you liked *our* day — I did too — very much — Will you
go again in the spring to rediscover some more of *our* County? I think
you added several years to my life & much to my happiness — Don't
forget that it would be nice if you can come down to a party in the
Winter — if you can give me a little suggestion as to approximate
time I can offer you a choice of diplomats — or Congress — or Army
& Navy — or Departments! I think it a very pious idea —

By the way my dear — how do you think I can tell you anything
about the Young Fiancé of the friend of yours if you do not give me
his name or the *kind* of exam he took! Write me *at once* to Warm
Springs, Georgia, by order of the President — Uncle — Cousin — or
just perhaps me — giving the necessary data — And too it is best to
enclose it in another envelope to *Miss LeHand* as otherwise it might
get lost in the general mailing room —

Yours affectionately,
F.D.R.

Yes — the Election was surprisingly good — but — well — I suppose it means more work — [The 1934 congressional elections
were a triumph for the New Deal; Democrats now controlled
better than two thirds of the Senate and of the House.]

*   *   *

The White House
Washington

Dec. 22 [1934]

Dear Daisy,

No news yet from the Civil Service people, but I am jogging their
memories & will let you know soon —

I like our "Earth" enormously [possibly *The Good Earth,* by
Pearl Buck, published two years earlier] — it is a joy to find the rapier
thrusts do not outweigh the vision & the hope — It is like you to like
it & for that I am glad —

The period of rush is upon us here — but I am full of health after

the two weeks at Warm Springs — some day you must see that spot
— you would like the great pines & the red earth — but it's very
different & can never take the place of *our* River. By the way I know
another hill which you & I will go to in the spring —

[During the 1920s, Roosevelt had built a cottage for himself
at Warm Springs, Georgia, as well as a treatment center for fellow
polio patients; he returned to it seventeen times during his presidency.]

It is possible I may spend Feb. 24–28 at Hyde Park — a change
of scene will be in order by then — perhaps you will be in Rhinebeck,
then — But in any event carry through the Washington trip if you can
— it does not have to be a gold lace party unless you demand it! And
in the meantime a Merry Christmas and a Happy New Year — I
know of no one who, as we say in the Navy, "rates it more."

Aff
F

1935

The White House
Washington

Monday [February 18, 1935]

Dear Daisy —

I loved that letter of yours & the "scenes" of the telephone that
kept me — or rather put me — in good humor ever since — You
might practice some snappy lines to use the next time, such as:

"Oh! Mr. Chief Justice — it's just too sweet of you to want me
to come down to hear the gold decision."

OR

"Huey! How thrilling to hear your voice!"

OR

"Why! Dr. Townsend — I'm so glad to hear all about your wonderful plan!"

I shall understand if you talk to me that way the next time.

[It is unclear just what Daisy's telephone "scenes" were, but FDR lists three of his future antagonists here: Chief Justice Charles Evans Hughes, who had recently voted with the majority in *Nebbia* v. *New York,* a case that sustained Roosevelt's decision to take the country off the gold standard, but who would soon turn against the New Deal; Senator Huey Long of Louisiana, already campaigning for the presidency in 1936 on a platform calling on Americans to join the Share Our Wealth Society, and Dr. Francis E. Townsend, author of a popular plan for a national system of old-age pensions.]

I still hope that you can come up early in the week — but in any case why not call me up at H.P. on Sunday — Poughkeepsie 545 — And the Cherry Blossoms sound very, very nice. [Daisy was evidently thinking of making a visit to Washington, ostensibly to see the cherry trees in bloom, actually to see FDR.] Do I know a better reason? Yes — you *know* I do — only be sure it is not till after April 10th, for I may cruise with V[incent Astor] before that, for I hope two weeks beginning March 25. [Astor and Daisy were friends from their youth and almost exact contemporaries; he was just five weeks older than she.] And it will be just as well because I may be piss cross by then. Really though I'm not — just that I need either to swear at somebody or to have a long suffering ear like yours to tell it to quietly!

The gold decision was a boon — but what a crying shame that it prevented me from delivering an impassioned plea on the air that night if it had gone the other way — some day I will show it to you — it was all prepared —

Tuesday — Yours has just come and I do so hope you can get up Tues or Wed . . . — I have to leave Wed night at the latest — In any event call me up Sunday or Monday — best time is about 12:45.

A bientot

Aff.

F.

*   *   *

The White House
Washington

Wed Eve — [March 6, 1935]

Dear Daisy —

I had hoped for it and this morning it came & don't ever leave out the dots & dashes & exclamation points — I love them. It was good that you got those days on the River — only I think you might have taken me with you when you slipped off, hatless, in the wind. There is a hill — in the back country — perhaps this spring we can go to it. Why is it that *our* River and *our* countryside seem so to be a part of us? Perhaps it's the "common" Beekman ancestry! [Both FDR and Daisy claimed to be descended from William Beekman, a Hudson River pioneer who first settled at Esopus, across the river from Rhinebeck. They were sixth cousins once removed. Though Daisy rarely spoke of it, she was actually more closely related to Eleanor Roosevelt, her fourth cousin through the Livingston line.]

By the way were you photographed in the old dress you wore at the Rhinebeck celebration when that [Brigadier] General [John Ross] Delafield person presided? If so the Pres. wants one. [Delafield, not a favorite of the President's, was a wealthy antiquarian, autocratic and self-important, who owned the historic Montgomery house in Barry-town. There was no such picture as the one FDR requested, but Daisy noted that she did send FDR a photograph, one "taken at Bourne-mouth, England, in 1921!"]

It's a little hurricane we're passing through down here and rather risky to the future of the country — but it's worse in other countries & I'm trying to keep a very tight rein on myself — for the time has not come *yet* to speak out.

[March 4, 1935, had marked the second anniversary of FDR's presidency, and he seemed to have lost momentum in Congress: the Social Security bill was being rewritten; a $4,880 million work relief bill had been stalled since January; and Huey Long was continuing his drumfire of criticism from the Senate floor.]

You *do* help — very understanding one — and I am glad.

Aff.,

F.

Entirely forgot to send you this weeks ago — Apparently the young man is safely in a better job! Now *you* owe *me* one!

[The enclosure, which is missing, was apparently a report on the friend's fiancé mentioned above.]

The White House
Washington

Thursday [April 18, 1935]

Dear D —

I'm *so* glad about next week — the only change is that *Thursday* evening is a lot better than Friday because Laura Delano [the President's first cousin] & a lot of school girls will be here Friday & on Thursday evening I think you will have to have a solitary meal with me . . .

So *can* you change to Thursday? Also I hope you and VH [Virginia Hunt] can lunch with us Sat or Sunday — I will get that arrangement made here via the social Secretary!

You might very nicely telephone me Wed evening when *you* get in (about 7 P.M.) or Thursday A.M. about 9:15 (if you are awake). I'm glad you had the party with Henry. [This was probably Henry Latrobe Roosevelt, born in 1879, a distant cousin whom FDR had appointed as assistant secretary of the Navy. The post had already been held by four other members of the family: Theodore Roosevelt, FDR himself, Theodore Roosevelt, Jr., and Theodore Douglas Robinson.] He is an old dear — He's *years* older than I am — two — but I always want to "mother" him!

Next week —

Aff

F

∽ [On April 24th, 1935, Daisy made another visit to Washington, ostensibly to see Virginia Hunt, actually to see FDR.] At seven I called the White House & asked to speak to the President but was told I would be called back . . . 8.45 President called up. Will send WH car for me for dinner tomorrow night!

∽ *April 25th, Thursday.* . . . [Virginia] rather put out with me [for] accepting the President's invitation when she was having a dinner for me!

I wore my striped dress Helen Brown gave me last summer. It is really lovely. My sapphire goes well with it. The White House car was announced at about 7.25. I went down in the elevator and was met by the bow of a chauffeur.

"Miss Suckley?"

I bowed & he preceded me to the car where I found another man at the wheel. Off to the White House! A lovely balmy evening, with spring blossoms instead of snow like the last time.

Two police guards at the foot of the steps. A coloured man came forward to open the car door, another met me at the open door and removed my coat as an usher stepped up, murmuring "Miss Suckley" with a bow. He led me around to the elevator & on the way up informed me that he was taking me to the President. Also, that Mrs. Boettiger [Anna Roosevelt had divorced Curtis Dall and married the journalist John Boettiger], Mrs. [Louis] Howe [wife of the President's closest aide] and Miss Laura Delano would be at dinner.

In the upper hall, Anna met me & I told her how sorry I was that her mother was away . . .

The usher went in & announced "Miss Suckley." The President was sitting at his desk & before I could reach him Anna appeared around the door near him. She stayed for about five minutes while we had sherry & bitters. Laura then came in & followed by Mrs. Howe we all went down to dinner in the little dining room . . .

The dinner we had: soup, shrimp in ramekins, cold tongue with mashed potatoes & cauliflower, salad with crackers & cheese, coffee.

Then upstairs again, two red setters travelling up & down with us [in the elevator]. Laura has four with her for the dog show, & so has been given a third-floor room as she always has them with her during the shows. It prevents their getting too nervous!

["Laura Delano was a law unto herself," recalls a member of the Delano family. She was the unmarried daughter of Warren Delano III, the staid master of Steen Valetje at Barrytown, and showed her independent streak early: she was known as Polly all her life because as a small child she had refused to drink anything but Apollinaire water.

A niece remembered her as always having been "years ahead of her time." She collected Erté before his work was fashionable and was the first in her circle to wear red nail polish. "Polly, dear," her sister said the first time she tried it, "have you been disemboweling a rabbit?" And when her hair went gray early, she began to dye it — blue, then purple — and carefully painted a knife-sharp widow's peak in the center of her forehead every morning.

She dressed like no one else. "Rope upon rope of pearls," a member of the family remembered, "a silk blouse open to the waist, gold bracelets clattering up and down each arm — until we all wondered how she could lift it — a ring with a huge stone on every finger, and brooches everywhere — in her hair, at her hip, on her bosom. She also wore masses of rouge and lipstick, which she replenished constantly in midconversation no matter where she was."

Her clothes delighted her small nieces, who begged to be allowed to watch her put them on, and she once sent one of them to a formal event at Springwood wearing balloon pyjamas, fastened at the waist with diamond brooches. Eleanor Roosevelt, sensing the little girl's discomfort, hugged her. "Don't worry, dear," she said. "We all know you're staying with Aunt Polly."

Her private life was as distinctive as her dress. She bred dogs and lived alone in Rhinebeck, in an imitation Tudor cottage that swarmed with insects on summer nights because, she explained, "screens ruin the view." As a young woman, she had wanted to marry FDR's Harvard classmate Otohiko Matsukata, a Japanese nobleman's son. Her father was willing to entertain this foreigner at Steen Valejte — he was his son Lyman's roommate, after all — but would not hear of his daughter marrying a Japanese. His opposition turned out to be a largely empty gesture, since Matsukata's father had already forbidden his son to marry an American and a commoner.

No American she met thereafter seemed to suit her. "She was too selfish to marry," a niece remembered hearing from the grown-ups. But she did conduct a lifelong liaison with her large, good-natured, mostly silent chauffeur, who went everywhere with her — except into the drawing rooms of her friends and family. When she began to travel the country to show her dogs — Irish setters first, then long-haired dachshunds — he became one of America's finest dog-handlers.

"She could be incredibly rude if the company bored her," a family member recalled, and her private disdain for Eleanor Roosevelt was said to have been withering. But, like Daisy, who was otherwise her polar opposite, she adored FDR, and he delighted in her lively, unpredictable company.

No one in Roosevelt's circle remotely resembled Laura Delano. No Delano was much like her, either, and there were members of that conservative and overwhelmingly Republican clan who believed the real attraction between the President and his resolutely flamboyant cousin Polly was that each had an ego that found its match in the other's.]

When we got to the 2nd floor hall, Anna informed me I was "to go with Father to his study." The others would go in another room!

I had a delightful evening, talking about everything from Dutchess County hilltops to politics . . . I asked him how he felt about a second term. He said in effect that he had already had enough of it, but that "when you have started a job you want to go through and finish it."

He will doubtless run next year & what the result will be is in the lap of the gods.

At 10.30 I said goodnight & was shown downstairs . . .

✑ *April 28, Sunday.* We planned to go to church . . . but instead we are meeting the President at 11.45 at the White House and driving down to the Navy Yard with him for lunch & a sail on the Potomac.

. . . We [she and Virginia Hunt] were taken in through the South East Gate into the grounds to the South Portico. [We] waited . . . in the basement and at about twelve the President appeared.

In the meantime . . . the yachting party had arrived: Mr. and Mrs. Harry Hopkins [Hopkins was one of the President's closest aides, administrator of the Federal Emergency Relief Administration], Raymond Moley [an economist and member of the Brain Trust], Joseph P. Kennedy [chairman of the Securities and Exchange Commission], & a Mr. [Edward] Moore, who is working with him . . . Jimmy Roosevelt [the President's eldest son], Miss LeHand, Virginia & I. All sorts of ushers, aides & what-nots around, which makes it rather confusing as you don't know who you are supposed to talk to.

The faithful "watchdog" Gus Gennerich was of course on hand. He always seems glad to see me. Franklin is going to take me to see Gus's new farm east of Rhinebeck "in the spring," perhaps when he comes up for Decoration Day. [Gennerich had bought a farm east of Rhinebeck so that when his boss eventually left the presidency he could remain near him.]

. . . We shook hands with the President & then "the ladies" — Virginia, Mrs. Hopkins, & I — were told to get in with [him]. I sat next to him on the back seat with Mrs. H. Virginia sat on the little seat.

Four motorcycle police in pairs went ahead . . . Quite a crowd was gathered at the Gate and cheered enthusiastically as we went by.

The President looks wonderfully well & very cheerful. He certainly has the most wonderful disposition and is unfailingly thoughtful of others. Mr. Moore told us that during the 1932 campaign he was with Franklin for two weeks continuously, & that when others were tired, F. *never* once failed in his consideration of others & his patience & good humor.

. . . [W]e followed the President on board the *Sequoia.* He has to wear his braces to walk on & off the boat, the gangplank being too narrow for a wheelchair . . .

The *Sequoia* is a delightful little boat, with accommodations for six people. Just a good size for a *peaceful* weekend.

We sat on the main deck & set sail . . . down the Potomac, trailed by the Radio Ship.

. . . Gus appeared with a wheelchair & took F off to get his braces off for lunch.

Mrs. Hopkins is a sweet little woman, quite intelligent . . . Harry Hopkins is one of the most unattractive people I've ever met . . . A strange, weak-looking face, thin, slouching, untidy — impossible socially.

Ray Moley is strange & unattractive & impossible socially, but he has a strange depth in two black, piercing eyes, and his mouth is scarred & twisted to one side when he smiles.

Conversation was rather difficult up at my end [she was seated at the far end of the table from FDR]. "Missy" with "Joe" & "Harry" were talking about some clubs they were forming for fun, but you could see that they were all thinking of other, very serious things, & were probably working out the President's speech for the evening. He writes his speeches himself but they all go over it & make sugges tions . . .

[This is not the view of many of Roosevelt's most recent biographers, but Dorothy Brady, who often acted as the President's stenographer from 1933 to 1945, confirms it, at least in part. "Some of them say he didn't write his speeches," she says. "They don't know what they're talking about. First, before anyone would say a word, FDR would ramble on and I'd take it all down. *Then* they'd go to work. Sometimes we did sixteen drafts before he was satisfied."]

After lunch we left them & they must have worked together for two hours in their shirt-sleeves before coming out to join us again on deck.

Franklin can shift his mind at a moment's notice. The rest of them are weighed down by their worries & their problems. They all have the most terrific responsibilities on their hands but what a heaven-sent blessing that F. has such a buoyant nature. He could not survive without it . . .

During lunch we passed Mount Vernon & those of us who were "new" had to go out & stand at attention while 21 bells were struck. It is a nice custom.

Jimmy, on my left at lunch, was very agreeable but he looks delicate & abstracted. He worked with the others over the speech & is evidently working up to a political career, though he is *not* going to take Mr. Howe's place as secretary — in spite of the newspaper accounts! [In this case, the newspapers were not wrong, only premature. James Roosevelt became his father's secretary in 1937.]

I had a nice talk with Franklin before we reached the dock. We then drove back to the White House but Mrs. Hopkins sat next to him & put me in the farthest corner! On the way lots of people clapped & cheered & boys whistled & shouted. One fat woman waved wildly & called out, "You're a grand person!"

It was refreshing to see that spirit after listening to the Republicans who talk continuously of impending CHAOS, not to speak of personal abuse against the Roosevelt family. F. says the Chicago *Tribune* is coming out with a series of articles attacking F. through the foolishness of his children. Such a petty game!

"Monty" [Montgomery Snyder, the President's personal chauffeur] brought us home in the President's own car!

[That evening, Daisy and Virginia Hunt returned to the White House at 9:30 and were shown to the Oval Room.] Here we found the most amazing sight: the President sitting at his desk . . . Facing him from every direction were the strongest electric lights trained on him. The floor was covered with batteries, radio sets, coils of wiring. At a table to one side several men sat in front of queer instruments with ear-phones at their heads. Directly opposite the President, mounted on tripods & covered with padding, stood half a dozen movie cameras, looking to me more like a battery of machine guns. All this for making a movie of a speech.

It was a formidable thing to face & when we arrived he was smoking hard on a cigarette.

Anna & her husband, Henry Morgenthau [Henry Morgenthau, Jr., the secretary of the Treasury, was the President's long-time friend and Dutchess County neighbor], and a few others were sitting along the wall & we did the same. A sort of hush fell on the room as ten o'clock approached. Finally, we heard the announcer say, "Ladies & gentlemen, the President of the United States."

He spoke just under half an hour, leaning on his arms at the desk & turning over the pages with one hand. It must be an ordeal, even for F.D.R. [In this Fireside Chat, FDR declared that "fear is vanishing, confidence is growing . . . faith is being renewed in the democratic form of government."]

We said goodnight in the midst of the electric wires & he handed me a brown envelope which contained my goose — for Good Luck. He points UP and Out! I've christened him "Excelsior." [This carved wooden goose, the first of many small gifts the President gave Daisy, would remain her most precious possession all her life.]

⌁ *April 30, Tuesday.* . . . Tea at Miss Owens': Somebody Wilmerding who knew Betty [Hambley, Daisy's sister] at Tuxedo, a very attractive young married woman, Mrs. Makle(?); Dr. & Mrs. Oliver Hart, the new rector at St. John's Church, & three or four others. All belong to (or seem to!) the Conservative Republican group. One of them gave me her latest news from the White House — that F.D.R. has gone to pieces and is having a regular breakdown and will probably have to resign! She was a little nonplussed when I told her I had seen him on Sunday and that he never looked better in his life!

⌁ *June 11th, 1935.* [Rhinebeck] A perfect afternoon driving with F.D.R. on back roads, to see Gus Gennerich's farm just east of the Wurtemburg Church road — A car with 4 detectives & Gus, and a state trooper in another followed us. At the gate when I arrived, the trooper told me the Pres. was going out at any moment — "Yes," I said, "I am going out with him!" A sheepish grin, an apology, & I sailed up to the house!

June 12th

Dear Franklin —

What fun it was yesterday — I loved it, and you're *so* nice to give up an afternoon to being so kind to a *Beekman cousin!*

. . . Someday, when there's more time, I really would like to have some instruction on politics and economics — but a paltry *three* hours is just too short for such subjects!

We are off to Poughkeepsie — & I have to miss the West Point broadcast! Oh my!

Thanks *so* much, again.

Aff —
Daisy

P.S. Tell Gus I *loved* seeing his house, & I know it will be *very* attractive.

* * *

Thurs. Night [June 13, 1935]

Dear Daisy,

Thank you — my dear — for that *bestest* of afternoons — I told you there were a million things I wanted to talk about and I think I only talked about a dozen — so if you will work out 12/1,000,000, you see how often you will have to come again — does it horrify you? Don't we live in the nicest part of all the world — and am *I* a Fortunate Person?

Wednesday at West Point was a really very perfect little ceremony because of its simplicity & brevity and I hope you liked what I said. [FDR had told the 1935 graduating class that "the greatest need of the world today is the assurance of permanent peace — an assurance based on mutual understanding and mutual regard."]

On the train I dictated and had conferences — & found Wash. as usual a bedlam — last night the Parade was a fiasco [FDR had watched as some fifteen thousand Nobles of the Mystic Shrine splashed past the White House] — rain and more rain and I got wet and the old sinus is "acting up" today making me cross to everybody — I don't think that I *could* be cross to you.

Yours affec,

F

Is it all set for the 22nd? Is it a big party? Can you stay after lunch? *Such* a lot of answers required —

~ *June 28th, 1935.* . . . . F.D.R. *is* stirring things up in Wash. D.C. I wonder if he is making a mistake to demand more, serious, legislation — I am afraid so.

[Responding in part to pressure from the left and frustrated by the Supreme Court's hostility to much of the New Deal's most important early legislation, Roosevelt had launched a second series of bills — Social Security, tax reform, an attack on public-utility holding companies, compulsory collective bargaining. And on June 29 FDR had called for an inheritance tax and big levies on fortunes, just the sort of legislation that most appalled the wealthy river families with whom Daisy had tea.]

July 20 — '35

Dear F.

I had a vague idea that July 20th was *possibly* to be a special date of some kind! But it's turning out to be simply a hot Dutchess County Saturday and I am going to a movie with Elizabeth Lynch [an elderly cousin]! *Such* a way to spend a hot day!

I really think I am owed a letter, after those voluminous clippings — too! What do you think? (I really know you're busy!) I was very fresh the other day — please forgive me — but an old friend of my mother's — a perfect dear — asked me what I talk about when with you — "Do you talk politics?" she said — "Oh no," I answered, "not much — we play patty cakes!" Facetiously. My mother was horrified. "*Daisy, don't* be so undignified when talking of the President — he wouldn't like it!" Forgive me — but the idea of you & me playing patty cakes is funny.

I do hope "Things" will get wound up soon in Washington, so that you can get a real vacation — You must need it — though possibly you are cooler in your office than we are with all our windows open! —

Reading all the hot-headed explosions in the paper these days; it is a blessing to be a little aloof from it all — the wonder to me is that *you* seem able to keep an "aerial" view — That's what I've tried so hard to get, all my life — It is very difficult at times, and it is at those difficult times that the beloved "hill top" [Wilderstein] is such a blessing.

George Washington should have included a real mountain when he started thinking of plans for a capital city!

Best Wishes from "Your affectionate cousin,"
Daisy

* * *

Saturday — the 3rd Aug. [1935]

Dear Franklin —

Your letter has just come, & I am particularly thrilled because you corroborate what *I* think *you* think! One always loves to find out one is right!

I was trying to put into words, yesterday, what I feel you are trying to do, something to this effect: these extraordinary changes are taking place all over the world, with Communism, Fascism, Dictatorships, etc. as the natural results — You are trying to *meet* these changes, and to go along with them, and to control them so that *this* country will not have to live through some of the horrors that others have had — Am I right? I always emphasize the fact that these are *my* opinions, for of course we haven't really discussed these things. It's amusing how many people ask me what you think about so & so! and what you are going to do about so & so! — and I *am* such a dumbbell and find it so hard to say what I mean — It's probably a punishment for having been a nagging wife in a previous incarnation!

There is one thing I'm not sure about, though, and that is, whether you are not trying to go *too* fast — that is, faster than "we" can keep up with you; or do you feel that the government is lagging behind what is actually happening?

. . . The world is so full of fascinating uncertainties that I should like to live forever — Or perhaps coming back from time to time will be more restful!

Do you know Beverly Nichols's books? If not, I must give them to you to read — they are like that first crocus you saw in the spring on the White House lawn! You'd simply *have* to forget Congress *et al.* when reading them! They tell of his life in a thatched cottage with a garden, in a tiny English village.

Would you like some news? *It's raining!* and rumbling in the distance — that bowling alley in the Catskills seems to be open 24 hours of the day — and practically *every* day!

. . . When I get my little house on a hill, I shall have my garden & a never-drying well, & the parched will be watered, & the drowned will be drained off down the hill and into the Hudson — And I'll have a dear dog, & lots of books and a seat for dreaming on. Twilight [presumably a Suckley cat] didn't seem to take to the idea at all. Friday, Star-time (Dark — all's well, and asleep!)

I really didn't mean this to grow to 8 pages — but you'll forgive it, as it was so ordered by our Chief Executive!

At times I think I'm getting quite politically minded — but at bottom, I know I'm just not temperamentally suited to party politics — I get too furious at personal attacks on people I think are right, and it's quite impossible to remain impersonal! So there we are — and Daisy Suckley had better remain in her retiring niche where she belongs, & not attempt to argue about things she knows little about — I think the *real* thing that bothers me is people's *limited* point of view — An *intelligent* opinion is so rare! I do welcome one where I find it — which is so seldom — whether I agree or not —

Your dear mother was at E[lizabeth] Lynch's [country house]

yesterday, looking quite well, but it seemed to me she is far more "bothered" about all this political talk than she will let any one know. [Opposition to Roosevelt continued to climb among members of his family's class.] She's a wonderful person and must miss you so dreadfully — I wanted so much to tell her that, after all, the only thing that matters much is that you are — well — *what you are!*

Letters are distracting things to write, for you *can't* say a thousandth part of what you want to say, & what you do write down is so inadequate & stilted that "you" really means "I"!

It's hard to realize we are almost in August — days getting shorter — there should be lovely cool afternoons, which *don't* have to end at precisely 5.30, and *of course* a drive would be quite appropriate on such a day. Or, shall we say, on *any* day! How lucky we've been to have all nice days — only one drop of rain, if I remember rightly!

I wonder if you ever sit under the trees in your "back yard." This *must* stop — *no ninth* page!

Aff.

D.

✧ *August 16th, 1935.* Friday — F.D.R. up from Washington — Called me up for a drive after lunch — 2.30 to 5.40. We went to Gus' farm to see what progress has been made. Complete set of dining & living room solid mahogany furniture, made in Haiti — Good lines & well made. He paid $250.

✧ *August 17th, 1935.* F.D.R. lent me Haiti book [*Voodoo Fire in Haiti*] by Richard Loederer, just out. I told him about W. Seabrook's [*The Magic Island,* also on Haiti and written by a new and colorful neighbor; see below, page 40].

[FDR had been fascinated by Haiti ever since 1917, when, as assistant secretary of the Navy, he undertook an inspection tour of U.S. Marines stationed there. Just a year earlier, as President, he had ended the American occupation of the island.

The afternoon drives continued, so many of them evidently that Daisy heard there was talk up and down the river and worried that the President's wife and mother might be upset by it.]

Saturday — the 17th Aug. '35

Dear Franklin —

I won't send this off until I return the Haiti book — but *so* many things were not said yesterday that I'd like to have said, that perhaps I can add a few words — I fear that on these drives my mind takes the changing directions of those winding roads & I can think of at least a half dozen topics that were just mentioned but not pursued!

On the subject of petty gossips, I should like to say that it isn't of any importance *what* they say, under ordinary conditions, and *I* certainly can laugh them all off, as far as I personally am concerned! — But the real point is that it wouldn't be wise or *fair* to you and your "madam" to give them any kind of a handle to use against you both — they make too many out of whole cloth for political reasons, anyway!! (Slightly mixed figures of speech — but "you know what I mean"!)

I got back to Helen's house yesterday in good time; I don't *think* the speedometer registered over 69⅞ths at any time — You see how obedient I am! It was *such* a nice afternoon — Shall we say a "P.D."? Perfect Day!

. . . I am feeling very guilty at having taken your Voodoo book, for you had not finished it — I'll read it quickly and send it to you — It's one of those I most wanted to read of the new books —

Another brilliant idea! If you *really* think those *valuable documents* we were speaking of *should* be destroyed — how would it do to preserve only the *very last* one? There simply *has* to be *one* on hand!

[It is impossible to be sure what these "valuable documents" were, but they were probably FDR's letters to Daisy written that summer. In them, he may have set forth his continuing plans for the New Deal in language so forthright that he felt anxious about them in retrospect; FDR disliked putting on paper plans he might soon have to change. He may also have expressed his growing affection for Daisy too openly. In any case, she did eventually destroy many letters to which only her responses survive.]

Tuesday [August] 20th —

I've just finished [*Voodoo Fire in Haiti*], & found it very fascinating, & so vivid that I feel almost as though I'd been there — "We" civilized people seem to be somewhere between those naked savages and those highly developed, rare souls we read of who are great spiritual leaders — Both extremes still have a far greater knowledge of the deeper things of nature. "We" have lost much of it temporarily through our concentration on purely material comforts & pleasantnesses —

The Redwoods have come! But in the form of an envelope full of seeds! With instructions as to their care! [Roosevelt loved trees of all kinds and had convinced himself that sequoias from the Pacific Northwest could somehow be made to grow in Dutchess County. Daisy volunteered to conduct the experiment at Wilderstein.] They should appear above the ground within 17–20 days! I'll start them right off! . . .

Aff —

D.

◇ *September 9th, 1935.* Drive in pouring rain with F.D.R.! TO OUR HILL! ETC.! We saw the same egret-bottle we saw Aug. 7th 1933! [During this drive through a downpour, Roosevelt and Daisy took shelter beneath the dripping trees that grew on Dutchess Hill, the secluded hilltop on the Roosevelt property which from that day forward the two friends would refer to as Our Hill. Part of their delight in remembering the afternoon was that the drive had gone virtually unnoticed. See the entry for September 22, below.]

Sept. 12th Thursday — 6.04 P.M.!

[Daisy to FDR]

An event of National Importance has just occurred: I've found *six (6) Sequoia sempervirens!* . . . It's too thrilling! . . . [P]resto, up went two tiny green arms towards the sky! This particular one is going to be called F.D.R. and should, I think, be given special winter care in the Hyde Park greenhouse, if you agree!

Monday, the 16th

. . . You were so nice to call up last night, and it is most delightful *of your mother* to ask us down for tea next Sunday! — My cousins, the Andersons, will be thrilled when they hear of it. A letter will *go right off* to them today!

. . . I am afraid I am getting myself in very deep! Almost like an intrigue and it's so completely foreign to my nature!

I am particularly anxious for you to meet Rupert Anderson [the husband of Daisy's first cousin Margaret, known as "Peg"] since he has his job *as your friend!* No one knows this, of course, and the family thinks your mother is the *only* arranger of this tea party! She *did* tell Peg Anderson to go to see her — so I'll be glad when the meeting is accomplished — I never *could* be a diplomat or a politician or an intriguer — It makes me feel too guilty, and I can't tell a lie very easily!

It's all very well for me to tell you not to get mad at the papers — I get frightfully mad myself! The *Herald Tribune* is positively childish in its political attitude, and as for James Paul Warburg [a Wall Street banker and one-time Roosevelt adviser turned critic] — judging from two or three of his articles, I should think his attack on you, which is obviously hypocritical, would do no one but himself much harm. Just within the last two weeks, two life-long staunch Republicans have taken the trouble to tell me that they are disgusted with the Republican party and admire you more & more for your courage!

Forgive me for bringing these disagreeable topics into this letter — I'm just slightly exploding!

By the way, if it does you *any* good to "explode" to me — you know you can feel perfectly free to say *anything* to me — I don't have to tell you that — do I?

I have worried a good deal over your being depressed during those last weeks in Washington — there are certainly enough things piled on you to make you depressed; being tired, alone, can do it, & that's why I urged you to take more rest, & *sleep* above all — But *don't* get discouraged at other people's blindness — for that's what it really is. "We see through a glass, darkly," and as far as the responsibility of each one of us goes — we are certainly accountable only for our aims — Even the twelve disciples only half understood what their master said to them —

[Roosevelt's depression that summer had several causes, among them the noisy public quarrels among his advisers, a barrage of criticism from both ends of the political spectrum, and a Gallup Poll showing that only 50.5 percent of the American people now approved of his presidency, his lowest rating since taking office. Others had noted his unaccustomed testiness. Walter Lippmann found him "dangerously tired," so exhausted that "if he were confronted with difficult decisions at this moment his judgment couldn't be depended upon."]

[Secretary of Agriculture] Henry Wallace's little book [*America Must Choose*] is quite wonderful. I only wish it were written in a less "deep" way, for the average person won't take the necessary trouble to think out what he says — As an older person, my aunt [Mrs. Langdon] feels the same way about it — We are re-reading it.

You had better fill in the HIGH SPOTS on this map! [Daisy enclosed an illustrated map of Dutchess County, perhaps so that FDR could mark the precise location of their favorite secluded picnic spots and send it back to her.]

You were right, that I would like seeing more people than I do, but *how* did you know it! For I live in a sort of dream so much of the time, and love quiet and a fireside and the open air and a few individuals — I *like* almost everybody   but a very few go very deep — and crowds, particularly *social* crowds, bore me to death —

On the other hand, people are always interesting, and places, and travelling — and books, which means people's thoughts —

But even *all* of these put together, plus a lot of other *nice* things, don't make up for one true friend — n'est-ce pas?

Read Emerson on Friendship!

In his sermon last Sunday, young Scaife [the Reverend Lauriston Scaife] spoke of "Faith, Hope & Love, which is Friendship." I had never before heard it used in that particular way — It seems rather a good way of putting it, in these days when the word love is so mis-used and seems to mean so many different things!

Two of the Sequoia have had their heads bitten off by some villain! There are six other whole ones though, & I hope for more every day!

They seem to come very quickly out of the seed at a certain moment, they then apparently decide just as suddenly to start on their 3,000 year *slow* growth! The first one, F.D.R., has hardly changed since his first release! *Thursday night*. This *was* a surprise evening and a *nice* one! [FDR had evidently called unexpectedly.]

᪲ *September 22nd, 1935.* I took Sophie & Joan B[rown, young granddaughters of Mrs. Langdon] & Monty Anderson [the son of Rupert and Peg Anderson] to Hyde Park Church St. James' to see unveiling by the President of memorial tablet to Jacobus Stoutenburgh [one of the town's founders] — As friends of Mrs. [Maud Stoutenburgh] Eliot we all sat next to the veiled tablet . . . The Pres. made his little speech within 6 inches of Monty, & then walked up to his own pew.

[Later that day, FDR took Daisy for another long drive, following winding back roads through the beautiful Hudson River country, then stopping to park again on the crest of the forested ridge that he and Daisy had named Our Hill.

Something happened in that place on that afternoon that neither of them ever forgot. Three years later, FDR was still calling it the beginning of "a voyage." Perhaps they simply kissed. A poem clipped from the newspaper and carefully pasted by Daisy into her diary suggests that they did:

Eros
by Leslie Grant Scott

You flamed like orange lightning in the sky,
Rending the quiet Summer clouds apart,
And set your fiery seal upon my heart,
Which had grown slower and weaker than a sigh,
Not wanting much of life nor asking why,
Until a blazing god with winged dart,
You swiftly pierced the small deep wound to start
The flow of ruby blood by which men die.
And now your head lies softly on my breast
While close within my arms your heart beats wild,
Your groping lips in need like any child.
I in whom life had ceased can give you rest,
For love is strong where death has so beguiled
And tragedy and pain are but a jest.

Perhaps they merely confessed to each other the loneliness they felt. Certainly they talked of a special bond of friendship and agreed to share some of their secret thoughts, by letter and long-distance telephone and in person whenever they could arrange to be together.

Impetuously, Roosevelt tried to persuade Daisy to come along with him that very night, on a train trip that would take him across the country to dedicate Boulder Dam, then a fishing voyage off Baja California. Mrs. Roosevelt was to travel with her husband as far as the Pacific Coast, but she was not going aboard his ship.

Daisy gently turned him down. But back home at Wilderstein, moments after he boarded his train, she started a long letter to him.]

Sunday, Sept. 22nd

To be read *first!*

P.S. This started out to be a perfectly good "steamer-letter" or "train-letter," and has turned instead into a formidable collection of the meaningless meanderings of a wandering mind!

Forgive it — and drop it into the open mouth of the first shark who shows any interest in humanity. It will, at least, give him a pain!

All the best of luck in the world on your trip, and come back rested and *impervious!*

Aff.

D.

Do you realize the amount of will-power that was necessary to refuse a certain invitation this past week? A slightly *righteous* feeling, I find, gives *no* satisfaction whatever — only irritation!

My Dear Mr. President —

May I call your attention to a very important matter which has occupied much of my time in the last two days — since, in fact, the rainy afternoon of Sept. 9th — (I read in the *Herald Tribune* of Sept. 10th that: "A light rain fall during most of the day, discouraging any attempt at a presidential outing"!! *Who* writes up your "daily doings"!!)

But to return to the serious matter under consideration: After much deep thought, I have come to the very definite conclusion that OUR HILL is, quite without exception, the nicest Hill in Dutchess County! The only problem remaining is as to how it should be spelled. Just plain OUR-HILL, or OURHILL, or Owahill, or even OW-WA-HILL!

I know you will welcome suggestions!

But, really, it *is* the *nicest* of *all* hills — and entirely worthy of Excelsior's upward looks — (By the way, said Excelsior is doing a *little* better — I tried to explain to him just what his duties are and he seems to be improving!)

You remember the little verse by Maria [indecipherable] on Friendship? On the blessing of being able to *talk* freely to one's friend? Shouldn't there be another verse, on the silent moments, where often more is said — *without* words than with them — I suppose Mendelssohn's Songs Without Words meant tremendous things to him, and to the person for whom they were written . . .

Today, my sister Katherine took me for a heavenly drive in her 1929 open DeSoto — the engine is perfect, but at any moment *some-*

thing may break somewhere in a hidden corner and one walks miles to a telephone and usually ends up by being towed in, ignominiously, amid the charitable grins of the "populace."

However, on this particular occasion, nothing happened! I drove, and chose all the roughest, narrowest and hilliest roads. (*So* good for the car!) And came out, at last, near Smithfield, and took my mountain road, up a valley, 'til you suddenly come up over a little rise and find the gorgeous view of the Catskills in the distance — You *must* see it, *some time!*

. . . We came down the mountain on a *very* steep road! I almost wished for your emergency brake once or twice — but we managed it safely —

To return to your new hill-top for a moment! Are you going to put up any kind of a log cabin? It would be such a perfect place for you to write your detective stories, when you can get around to them —

[Ever since 1933, FDR said in a brief memorandum dictated in 1942, he had been thinking of "building a small place (atop Dutchess Hill) to go to escape the mob" that pursued him whenever he came to his mother's house. He had already discussed it with Missy LeHand, who, according to members of her family, believed she was to share it with him after he left the presidency. He now evidently began to talk about it with Daisy, too.

Roosevelt, an inveterate reader of detective tales, enjoyed coming up with elaborate plots and liked to say that he would write some after he left the White House, just to show how easily it could be done.]

Maunsell [Crosby] had a log cabin 'way off in his woods [near his home, Grasmere, in Rhinebeck]; just one room with a large rough stone fireplace, and he used to study the birds out there for hours at a time.

Such a nice picture in the paper today, of you, "roasting your own" hot dog! *Was* there a scrambled egg too — I wonder! [The picture was taken at a picnic at Eleanor Roosevelt's cottage. Scrambled eggs were often the sole item on the menu when she was doing the cooking, and Daisy's question may be a gentle joke about the famously dreary Roosevelt fare.]

. . . It seems strange that I probably *won't* have a chance to talk to you again — *really talk* — for *ages!*

. . . *Don't* let them get you angry by what they say in the papers! It takes half the wind out of their sails if you don't answer back; and only talk constructively — You'll think I have a certain amount of nerve in making any kind of a suggestion on political matters — but I am quite certain I am right in this particular case, for, you see, you *are* a *gentleman,* and everyone knows that, and it means a definite thing and a very high standard of behavior to even the lowest; though they might not acknowledge it. The fact is, that they expect just about *perfection* of you, and don't want you to be even capable of losing your temper!

It's pretty hard on you, *I* think!

Arrangements are already made for my coming up for Election weekend. I'll be at "me own home!" —

When you read Beverly Nichols, will you mark anything that happens to strike you? It will be the next thing to reading it with you — I *think* you'll like him, but if you don't, & he bores you — I'd like to know that too!

[FDR to Daisy; this is all that remains of a longer letter now lost but written from his train the day after their memorable encounter on Our Hill.]

September 23rd, 1935

You are so very right about not answering attacks no matter how provoking — I found this the other day — by A. Lincoln during some of the difficult days of the war: "If I were trying to lead, much less answer all the attacks made on me, this shop might well be closed for any other business. I do the best I know how, the very best I can; and I mean to keep on doing it to the end. If the end brings me out all right, what is said against me will not amount to anything. If the end brings me out all *wrong,* then angels swearing I was right would make no difference."

All the same — no matter how philosophic he was in public — those attacks did hurt A. Lincoln — not because they were attacks but because they were repetitions of false or twisted statements. But he kept his peace — that was and is the great lesson — and you have sensed it in another case, as I knew you would and that helps a very great deal — Do you know that you alone have known that I was a bit "cast down" these past weeks. I *couldn't* let anyone else know it — but somehow I seem to tell you all those things and what I don't happen to tell you, you seem to know anyway!

* * *

Sept. 26th '35

Dear Franklin —

I left a box of Crax for your mother this morning at a house which seemed strangely silent and deserted — none of my detective friends except the one who is usually at the gate. He was sitting "at ease" in the booth nearest your study — Your study door was wide open (it's almost 80), and Buzzie & Sistie [Anna's children] were playing at a table near the garden hedge. The setters came out and barked hopefully at us!

. . . This evening, "Dutch Houses" [*Dutch Houses in the Hudson Valley before 1776,* for which FDR had written an introduction]. It's so interesting — but I can't keep those names straight — much less pronounce them — What do you do with MARRITSE — or ARIAAN-TJE. Poor Ariaantje! Do you remember her story? A repressed old maid at 44 when her father died, she was not happy with her 20-yrs-younger husband whom she married at 51 — Her only two compensations seem to have been a "full-length portrait in the most elegant of gowns, and in her hand a rose, up-lifted," and her handsome house at Coeymans — It is now occupied by several Italian families!

. . . How *much* water has run over the dam since you wrote the introduction to this book in 1928! The amount you've done is almost miraculous . . .

I mailed the letter to San Diego [the port from which FDR was to embark on his fishing trip] this morning — and felt quite sure that everyone in the P.O. knew just what I was doing! They didn't though!!

[The need for absolute secrecy made the relationship between FDR and Daisy both more difficult and, I suspect, more exciting. The thrill of almost being found out is a theme that runs through many of their letters to each other.]

I *hope* you & Sec. [of the Interior Harold] Ickes & Harry Hopkins will not spend your whole time discussing WPA & PWA!

[Ickes and Hopkins, two of FDR's ablest and most trusted advisers, had been feuding for months; their joint presence aboard ship was meant to help make peace between them.]

Friday the 27th Lunch at Ethel's today — She's such a real person & a loyal friend — Michael Pym [a woman novelist and the long-time companion of Daisy's friend Ethel Merritt] started telling me about the cost of a glass of milk! *I know* it costs *us* more to produce than it would to buy — She "questioned that statement," however, so I veered off to other subjects: tennis & cats & puppies — You should get her into your cabinet — make a new post "advisor-in-chief to the president." She can sit at your elbow and tell you *just* what to say & do! (I'm *afraid* I'm a *cat!*)

. . . I wonder if, after these long months of hard work & responsibility, you can still feel something of the romantic excitement of your position! The accounts of your "retinue" & your progress across the country really is thrilling!

Saturday — The 28th — Did you get my scribble via Albany? It wasn't mailed until 1.30 and I hope it caught a plane in time!

Your Washington letter came this morning, just as we were starting for "Beaverwyck" [the old Dutch name for Albany] and there are so many things to answer and talk about that I can only make a beginning.

[Since Daisy destroyed all but one paragraph of this letter from Roosevelt, it is impossible to know what it contained. Perhaps FDR expressed concern that his sudden invitation to Daisy to sail with him might have alarmed her. Certainly, her response was meant to reassure him.]

You know the French saying: "*Tout comprendre c'est tout pardonner*"? [To understand all is to forgive all.] I would change it to: "*Tout comprendre c'est n'avoir rien a pardonner*"! [To understand all is to have nothing to forgive.]

P.S. This does *not* mean that good resolutions can be thrown away!

I did "get" that feeling of yours, & wanted so much to do something to help — But I'm sure it's gone now, or will be, entirely, the minute you get on the water — I'm glad you found that quotation from Lincoln — It's always a help to know how others have taken the rocky roads. But I don't think it's ever worth getting hurt at what others say — for if they intend hurting you, they are automatically putting themselves in the wrong, and if they don't intend it, there's no point in getting hurt anyway — With a man in public life, it's a question of selfish politics or fear — isn't it? I'm being theoretical too! I'm glad you can keep your peace of mind most of the time —

. . . If you are told of L.H.'s getting something (in AAA or elsewhere) *would* you let me know? It *might* be good for me to know directly — [The President had agreed to help relieve the crowding and tension at Wilderstein by finding Littleton Hambley, Daisy's unemployed brother-in-law, a job with the Agricultural Adjustment Administration in Washington.]

... Monday, Sept. 30th

A strange sign of the times! William Seabrook, the author who lives down near the gate here, has just announced in the paper his marriage to Mrs. Seabrook *last February! Last November,* "Mr. & Mrs. Seabrook" came to tea at our house! *The Suckleys — Rhinebeck — Dutchess Co.!!* He has evidently been a drunkard & certainly "unconventional" — and has come to the conclusion that old-fashioned ideas have their value — He's perfectly honest about himself, and very quiet & retiring & shy, & I can't help admiring him for that very honesty. He *loves* Rhinebeck & hopes to live here always —

[The writer William B. Seabrook was best known for highly colored travel books — *The Magic Island, Jungle Ways* — and for a vivid account of his own treatment for alcoholism, *Asylum.* He and his wife, the novelist and biographer Marjorie Worthington, lived for a time in a cottage adjacent to the Langdon estate.]

I'm *furious!* I accepted a lunch party, & won't be able to listen to you at Boulder Dam! Tomorrow I'll read it, though, as I have your others — But no engagements *tomorrow,* & I *will* listen in then — at whatever hour!

Not tomorrow — but *Wednesday!* I'll be so relieved when you get off!

This may be my *last* epistle until, oh — *weeks!* Though there may be another by air on the 10th *if* I can get it off! It's been such fun writing & I've been *really* good in not making them more voluminous! You don't know *what* you've been spared!

I'm so inspired by studying old houses that I am making plans for my own new-little-old-house — Why not architecture too! I'm a very much Jack-of-all-trades, & a master of none whatever, unfortunately!

Such marvelous weather here! No frost yet, but the maples & sumac are "turned" already, and the air is *thrilling* & makes my nose cold!

Monday evening — I didn't mention that your farms speech [at Fremont, Nebraska] was *wonderful* — Leila's lunch today was most impressive! [Mrs. Lyman Delano, born Leila Burnett, presided over the vast Steen Valetje at Barrytown; her husband was an implacable political foe of his cousin Franklin.] 14 ladies! We were all quite overcome at our own importances! Your mother & I felt terrible at missing your speech at Boulder Dam, but we were eating delicious fat food instead! I don't need to tell you which I would prefer! As soon as I got home my mother & aunt told me it was wonderful — your talk at the dam — and you sounded perfectly fine, and vigorous — etc. etc! *Great* enthusiasm all around!

Your mother said you had given her your P.O. list, & she'd written you to San Diego — I think — I'm silently proud of my own itinerary!! [FDR had given Daisy a far more detailed itinerary than the one he gave his mother, along with meticulous instructions as to which mail pouch to catch to be sure to get her letters to him in the shortest possible time. His letters to her were now delivered in envelopes personally sealed and addressed by him.]

* * *

[FDR to Daisy]

Monday Eve, Sept. 30th [1935]

I wish so much my dear that you could have been at Boulder Dam today — Nothing I could say would give you a picture of the *immensity* of the whole canvas — A huge peak — bigger than a hundred other peaks near by — was clear at seventy-five miles. The colors marvelous — yet not a tree or grass in sight — Do you know the pictures of Gustave Doré illustrating Milton's *Paradise Lost*? — I love the desert and the rocks — but not to live among — still true to Dutchess!

Some day though you must see this country — It has been a successful trip — really happy crowds of people — even bigger than last year — and there is no doubt of the great great gains in prosperity. My difficulty is in having to keep on my "braces" from early morn till nearly midnight — because at every stop — even a water tower — a crowd surrounds the rear platform & I cannot disappoint them by refusing to go out and say "Howdy" —

This P.M. we took a glorious drive up a canyon on a new narrow road, which greatly alarmed the newspaper men but was really not dangerous. [FDR, over the objections of the Secret Service, had insisted on visiting a Civilian Conservation Corps camp near the dam. When the chauffeur tried to turn around on the narrow gravel road, he came so close to the edge that the President's frail secretary, Marvin McIntyre, got out and tried to push it back from the precipice. FDR, immobilized in the back seat, just laughed at the danger.]

Tomorrow a day in Los Angeles — a huge gathering in the Coliseum — 110,000 people — and I am to appear, drive slowly around

& say a few kind words — I can't make out if I am the lion in the Roman Arena or the Early Christian Martyr — I have a new sympathy for both.

I will add to this tomorrow in San Diego — but in the meantime there is no reason why I should not tell you that I miss you *very* much — It was a week ago yesterday — [September 22, the day they had visited their hill together].

Allowing for three hours' difference in time you are now very soundly asleep at 3 A.M. in Rhinebeck and I hope you are having very happy dreams. I look forward so to my letter on the ship —

Tuesday midnight! Safely here at Coronado Beach (San Diego) and *both* your letters are here & constitute the real news — It is a long long road to Panama.

[Daisy to FDR, continued]

. . . *Tuesday* Oct. 1st The papers have just come, telling about your trip up that mountain road — *please* don't do such things again! There's no point in being frightened after it's over — but I really feel that way — the idea of whoever was responsible getting you into a thing like that! It's awful — But perhaps the papers made the most of it — I hope so — Boulder Dam must be most inspiring — Someday I'm going to tour *all* the big dams & mountain tops: I loved your speech there — the whole tone of it — ["To employ workers and materials when private enterprise has failed," FDR told the assembled crowd and his radio audience, "is to translate into great national possessions the energy that otherwise would be wasted. Boulder Dam is a splendid example of that principle."]

Oct. 1st Evening — I'm still frightened about that mountain road! You'll really have to get some more responsible person to manage your trips! They shouldn't *allow* a Pres. of the U.S. to get into such a dangerous position! And at least they should have made you get out of the car when they turned! Now — if *I'd* been driving you — oh my — I fear I might have wanted to go up that road too!

— Let me see — (denotes deep thought!) — San Diego tomorrow — Speech at about 5 P.M. E.S.T. — Sails right afterward — A letter *may* have been mailed there during the day — *Should* get to the East *within* a week?!?

We go to 399 Park [Mrs. Langdon's New York apartment] on Oct. 10th —

Shall I confess something? These trips of yours — in crowds — on trains — near precipices — *really* worry me — I'll be relieved when I know you are safely at sea —

Aren't we humans something like the pieces of a jig-saw puzzle? Each one touches others at small points, & they in turn touch each other at entirely different points. When we touch at several points we are friends. The tragedies are where no points seem to fit! Dr. Carrel [Alexis Carrel, a French scientist and mystic, was the author of the best-seller *Man, the Unknown*] claims *everyone* has a certain amount of telepathic power — our sixth sense — perhaps — It would account for Friendships that can live & flourish even when people see little of each other.

The picture in the paper of you & Anna at the Pawling games is perfect — "looking out" at one, as I like a photograph to do — It's you, at least as I see you — it's you —

Early this morning I had a *very* serious talk with a Certain Person. [In their letters, FDR and Daisy each often used "Certain Person" (C.P. for short) as a code name for the other. Here and elsewhere Daisy also used it to create imaginary dialogues with herself.]

I told her she must come to earth, attend to her job, and stop looking at the moon (there is a particularly silvery new one) — She took it *very* nicely — agreed with me *perfectly* — said I was *entirely* right — She will reform for at least for about two weeks *after* Oct 10th [when FDR was to be at sea], and then for an indefinite period *after* Nov. 5th [when FDR was evidently expected to return to Washington after a visit to Hyde Park]! I really *had* to speak to her rather severely, for she spends entirely too much time writing letters.

Wednesday — *Oct. 2nd* 5.45 P.M. Eastern Standard Time: You have *just* left the San Diego Stadium; *do* you realize how wonderful and inspiring your speech was — I wish I could tell you how I loved the spirit behind it. I sat in a western window watching a brilliant red sunset, & realizing that that same sun was high up over San Diego. I think *you* are the best example of "the good neighbor" — and of countless *other good* things — This must *really* end! This letter —

Au revoir & good luck,
D.

[At San Diego, FDR had warned that the best way to offset the twin threats of "malice domestic and fierce foreign war" was to follow the policy of "the good neighbor," at home and abroad.]

Sat. the 5th
Nearing Cocos Island

Oct. 1935

D. dear — [FDR to Daisy]

This doubtless will turn into a stupid diary — or a dissertation on fishing or the delights of the bounding wave — so if you become bored toss it into the fire — I wonder if you have a fire at 399? — I would say kitchen stove — but probably that is an electric contraption — Oh the horrors with apartments!

First of all — why have I only just discovered that you paint and draw adorably? Why hide such a delightful light under a bushel? Even if I return the books, the markers stay with me — and before you know it you will be doing sketches and maps of Cocos and other enchanted spots. [Daisy's steamer letter, beginning September 26, included a tiny watercolor sketch of sailboats at sea and one of a number of hand-painted bookmarks she presented to friends over the years.]

I'm in the midst of a village in a valley and it is perfect for this mood of pushing away all the dreary facts and actions of many months — It gives me a mental peace and a sense of proportion which is much needed. [Daisy evidently also sent FDR a little sketch of a house to be built on Our Hill.]

Yes — I like it much — and I can understand the garden if I translate the flowers in part at least in terms of trees — But, you know, you and I, because we are we, can't quite ever think in terms of a garden only — perhaps it's because of a good many generations in a Big Place — that we like the Hill Top and the distant view — The intimate wood or garden is a part of our bigger whole — and that is where we have a distinct advantage over B. Nichols — He would not be truly happy to sit with us on the porch after sundown and look at the Catskills and all the things between.

You said once "log cabin" — But I don't think so — even [the naturalist] John Burroughs's — across the [Hudson] River — looked very artificial. They all do unless they are a hundred years old — & then they are full of . . . crawly bugs — No, I think a one-story fieldstone two room house — just like the one William (or was it Gerardus?) Beekman lived in (without doubt) when he (or they) first went to Esopus — one with very thick walls to protect us against the Indians and a little porch on the West side. Do you mind — *then* — if I tell you fairy stories till it gets very late?

Yes I know the house below Poughkeepsie very well — but it has been added to — and some day you shall do me a water-color of the house on the Hill — In the Old Houses book there are some pictures that are a little like what I mean —

Now to fish! Wednesday after the really wonderful gathering in San Diego — we went on board and out of the harbor and went through the tactical fleet exercises till sundown — a battle where the "enemy" was most of the time invisible behind the horizon or behind artificial cloud banks laid by planes or destroyers — very dull for spectators unless they understand that in modern naval warfare one fleet might easily be totally destroyed before it had even seen the other fleet from its decks —

That night we steamed south and reached Cerros Island Thursday noon — and got into the small boats for three hours' fishing — Two people in the stern of each launch — each with a rod and huge reel — and you troll with a "feather" or "spoon" which drags just under water about 200 feet astern — When the fish grabs it, or "strikes," he runs with it a short or long distance depending on his size and then you stop him by putting the brake on the reel and slowly, with many another "run" or "sounding" on his part, you work him up the boat where a sailor "gaffs" him and pulls him in to the boat — It is a real battle — and often you lose him — We got four or five apiece — The largest about 20 pounds — various kinds — yellow tail, tuna, seabass, groupers, mackerel —

(October 4th) Friday we got to Magdelena Bay, 300 miles further south — a wonderful spot with great bare mountains 4,000 feet high — more excellent fishing — Col. Watson the "high man" with a 55 pound Tuna.

(Saturday Oct. 5th) Today we have fished off Cap San Lucas, the tip end of Lower California — again great mountains and marvelous colors especially at sunset — It was a bit rough and the fishing not so good, but between the four boats from this ship and two from the "Portland" — our escorting cruiser — we landed about 50 fish. I have been sleeping much and have begun to get very brown — and I think my nose will peel —

By the way do you know that a certain unselfish Person has had no trip since Wyoming — 2 years — 3 years? ago — and needs another one — Did *you* know *I* knew that? [Daisy had accompanied her aunt on a visit to the Barrett Tylers, her cousins in Wyoming.]

Tuesday 8th — Storm at sea! Sunday we all attended Church service on the "well deck" — simple and short sermon and ending with one of my special hymns "Eternal Father" — about 300 of the

officers and men there. Then it began to blow — Sec'y Ickes suc-
cumbed & is still laid low — It blew harder and harder and last night
was blowing a "fresh gale" — 46 miles an hour — so we slowed
down as the water was coming over the bow and things were rather
uncomfortable and wet. Today is better but we fear it will be so rough
at Cocos tomorrow that we won't be able to get into the small boats
and fish. Last night I attended the "movies" given on the well deck,
after supper but in the middle of the show the top of a wave came on
board and drenched the audience!

I have been getting an honest to goodness rest — the only excitement my strenuous efforts to get the State Dept. to see that war is
war — and to agree with me that we should say so without waiting
for Europe to acknowledge the unfortunate fact.

[Italian troops had marched into Ethiopia on October 3. The next day, FDR
telegraphed to Secretary of State Cordell Hull his belief that whether or not
war had formally been declared, the fighting within Ethiopia's borders was
enough for him to invoke the Neutrality Act and cut off American arms and
supplies to either side, an act that would in practical terms have affected only
fascist Italy. Hull urged caution, and later, when the League of Nations failed
to call a halt to Italian aggression, the United States also backed away from
confrontation.]

Heavens! The cruise is less than a week old and I have written
more than you will ever want to read! — We have gained back two
of three hours of time difference — it is now 4 P.M. which means you
are 5 P.M. — I wonder what you are doing at this moment?

In case I forget it — we expect to land in Charleston about the
23rd — you will know by the papers — and if we do will you send
me a letter marked "Personal" c/o The Commandant, U.S. Navy
Yard, Charleston, NC — send it air mail 36 hours before I am due —
I want to be welcomed home!

Sat the 12th — What a four days! Cocos Island is all that I
remembered — the most enchanting spot in the tropics. We had three
days of the best fishing I have yet had — and enough fish for the
1,300 or 1,400 men on these two ships — Trolling along shore one
gets the smaller varieties — running however up to 20 or 30 pounds
apiece — but the real thrill is further off shore among the big sailfish
— I have tried for them before — many times — off Florida and here
but never got one. On Wed. I hadn't been out in the launch for an
hour before I hooked one — 110 lbs and 9 feet 6 in. long — and it

took me 40 minutes to get him alongside and into the boat. Yesterday I got my second — two hours and twenty minutes of constant fighting and he turned out to be 134 lbs and 9 feet long. Three others were caught — the biggest of all by faithful Gus [Gennerich] — 148 lbs!

The net result is that I ache in every muscle — very good for one — and I think my figure is improved.

We picnicked on shore on Thursday and there should be some good photos — and we talked with the Treasure Hunters — 15 Englishmen and their Costa Rican guard of about 20 soldiers under a Colonel. I think no treasure will be found!

Last night we got under weigh and soon will be in Bahia Honda on the Panama Coast about 150 miles West of Panama — I really must get you a good atlas if you like to follow these peregrinations — It looks now as if we shall transit the canal either the 18th or 19th and get to Charleston the P.M. of the 23rd.

[Although Daisy had decided against voyaging with FDR in the Pacific, she yearned to be with him, and on the morning of October 10, reading the New York *Evening Sun,* she came upon a poem that seemed almost uncannily to describe the longing she dared not express even to herself. She carefully copied it on the typewriter, perhaps because she wanted no one else in the family to wonder why she'd cut it out of the newspaper.

Some Day
by Charles Oluf Olsen

Of all my dreams, I like the best
A little, lonely dream
That never gives me rest.

It takes me to voyaging lands
That lure and beckon me, and gleam
With wave-girt reefs and sands.

Some day, perhaps, when time is kind,
I and my wayward dream shall find
A way of joining hands.]

[FDR's letter continues]

There is a chance that a plane may bring us mail tomorrow and perhaps there will be a letter — and I will send this off. Day before yesterday I thought of you leaving R[hinebeck] at about noon and lunching below Poughkeepsie and getting to 399 about 4 — Do you know that I don't like to think of you in NY, especially for such a long winter — Neither of us belongs in a city — Don't you think perhaps Feb. and March in a city — just to "freshen up" on the latest which a questionable "civilization" and a distinctly questionable "society" have to offer?

No — you are years too young — I truly want you to see lots of people and do lots of nice things in town — and perhaps some day find just the right kind of "Gentle Man" who will take very good care of you — and even then will you remember that your old Country Cousin from H.P. is to be counted on and leaned on very much — *always* — almost we can say "allways," which is a nice name — even if the Flower Man writer [he may have meant Beverly Nichols] thought of it before we did.

I suppose this trip is good for one — but do you know that I feel a long long way away here in the Pacific near the Equator?

Sunday the 13th — Another service this morning for the officers and men of both ships in this very lovely landlocked harbor — only a few Indian thatched huts on the shore — everything very wild and tropical — The destroyer will take this from the Pearl Islands in the morning — and I will write again from Panama the 18th or 19th — but that will reach you about the same [time] I land in Charleston.

Today we are back to the same time as NY so I can think of you as keeping the same hours as I do — Don't forget to take very good care of a very Special Person — because it means a great deal to lots of people — but I think most [to] —

Your affec
F

It is, I take it, three weeks to Election Time — and I hope you'll vote!

* * *

United States Ship Houston

Oct. 16 [1935]

D. dear —

Now we are at anchor in the Atlantic Ocean after a hectic day of formalities, salutes, and uniforms — and I am glad that at 7 P.M. the Pres. of Panama [Harmodio Arias] and sundry dignitaries left the ship and that I was able to shift into *very* old and rather scanty clothes again — I will write no more tonight except to tell you once more that I loved *your* letters.

Oct. 17th — A grand day! We left Colon at 6 A.M. and got to Porto Bello at 10 and went on an exploring trip in the launches to see the old forts which were captured by Sir Harry Morgan — He was rather a mean old Devil because he knew he couldn't get his men close enough to the walls to put up the scaling ladders so he took all the nuns out of the Convent in the town and made them go ahead as a screen for his troops — A small sum would restore the very extensive ruins — The rest of the party visited the village and the Church which has in it a Black Christ.

At noon we went on again to the San Blas Lagoon & had time to visit one of the Indian Villages — They are wholly independent of Panama control — a friendly shy people who have the good sense to keep *all* outsiders away, except for a little barter with occasional boats — Their huts are tightly packed on 2 acre islands — Several families to each hut & as many as 4 or 5 hundred people on a tiny island which is not more than a foot or two above the lagoon —

Oct. 18 — A day of exploring among the islands and their villages — a little barter for "embroideries" & arrows & spears — & a visit of the "King" & "Queen" to me as I sat in great State under a canopy in the stern of the whale boat — One young man had a little English so we got on well & I gave them cigarettes & candy & soap! I have *longed* to have you with me — you would have loved every minute of this amazing contact with *pure* Indians who I imagine have changed very little since Columbus was here about 1498 —

Oct. 19 — Homeward bound after a day in the fishing launch with a soaking shower every twenty minutes — a few fish but not large ones — a few very runny meat sandwiches — & a close view of two "white Indians" — albinos, of which there are many in these tribes —

Oct. 20 — Sunday and very wet and squally at sea — too much so for Church Service & too much so for the Sec'y of the Interior — Perhaps that is a fitting title for him. Three more days and Charleston —

Tues. the 22nd — We have had a rather bad two days — Yesterday we got radio news of a hurricane just astern of us in the Windward Passage between Cuba and Haiti — but we have kept ahead of it though we slowed down to make it throw us about a bit less — I have been clearing up a lot of papers I brought along & have read two detective stories & a life of Mary Queen of Scots & two volumes on economics — all this since Saturday! Also I am very *proud* because my figure is definitely *improved* & I hope you will *approve* — *next week* — isn't that grand —

I can't tell till I get to W. about actual dates but — I will hold this & add to an altogether . . . [The rest of this letter is missing.]

[There were more drives on empty country lanes that autumn, and at least one happy visit to Our Hill. FDR had brought home gifts for Daisy — including a pair of wild boar tusks from Cocos Island and a straw hat from Panama.]

∾ *December 10.* Arthur Krock in the *Times* thinks F will get in next year "*unless*" he gets overwhelmed by a wave of unpopularity like the one which swept out Mr. Hoover in '32. How strange that such a thing should be written down — and yet *his* mother said, in '33, when he was being praised to the skies: "In six months he may be the most hated man in the country."

She is wise — knows what public opinion is — So does he — but still it can hurt. I pray he may not have to suffer that — For a cripple, who can't even pace the floor of his own room, it would be just so much harder to bear.

[The following fragments from the President's letters to Daisy were found in a separate envelope she'd marked "rather interesting." We will probably never know why they were saved or what caused her to destroy the rest of the letters from which they were cut.]

Dec. 23, 1935 About Haile Selassie [Emperor of Ethiopia, then fighting Mussolini's forces] — Let me put it this way as my conception — he and the other feudal Rexes or Chieftans are probably in very much the stage of civilization as the small Kings & Barons were in Europe in the 12th Century — extraordinary cruelty — slavery of sorts — dirt — horrors — yet with it all a great patriotism and a strange deep spiritual undercurrent — as in the Crusades. Ras Dista Dentu visited me here in 1933 — the Emperor's Son-in-law — Now in command on the Southern front — he had the beautiful eyes — perfect features & poise of the Arab — tho' of course much darker —

I don't believe for a moment that Selassie is a scoundrel (perhaps I am prejudiced, for he keeps my photograph on his desk!). He is six centuries behind us — but he is a Christian — & the Coptic Church was founded by St. Mark six or seven years before St. Peter turned up in Rome —

I am however getting really worried over this flirtation you are carrying on with Ernie Gurza. Do you think it is nice — especially to use *my* Ambassador to aid you? Ernst is the *only* recourse I have. There is a very comfortable little jail about 2 blocks from here — it is kept for international intriguers and desperadoes.

[This presumably was Jaime Gurza, author of an enthusiastic study of FDR's leadership, *Logic, Roosevelt and the American People*, published in Mexico. Roosevelt hoped it would be brought out in the United States, too. He teased Daisy about her enthusiasm for the author as well as his book.]

1936

∾ *January 9.* — F's Jackson Day Speech — The tone of his delivery was too political — He is evidently in fighting trim! What an awful year of partisan mudslinging it is going to be . . . [FDR's Jackson Day speech merely echoed the fighting spirit of his annual message to Congress, delivered six days earlier: "We have earned the hatred of entrenched greed," he had said then, "discredited special interests" that foster only "poisonous fear."]

[New York]

∾ *Monday, January 20.* A thrilling & unexpected weekend. Mrs. James Roosevelt came to the reception at 4 & told us the news that her dear Franklin was arriving at the house at five & we must excuse her if she said anything queer! Her cheeks were pink and she looked better and handsomer than I have seen her look for a long time. When she was leaving, she put her arms around me, and said: "Would you like to come in this evening for the broadcasting?"

("Would I *like* . . . !")

. . . [G]ot through all the police in 65th street & I started up the steps when a plainclothesman came from somewhere & towered over

[Franklin Paris, Daisy's escort and a friend of her brother Arthur] & asked our names, in the most courteous manner. "Miss Suckley & Mr. Paris," said FP. That did not seem to be enough . . . I turned around & the detective . . . smiled & bowed at me. "Oh! Miss Suckley." All doors opened without a question after that.

Dinner was not yet over, so we went upstairs to the drawing room, where the ladies came pretty soon — When the President came up he went into the library where he was to broadcast — It was very tantalizing to be way off, where I could see but couldn't talk to him . . .

About 10.15, Mrs. [James] Roosevelt asked all to go up to her bedroom to hear the speech on her radio! So we all trooped upstairs & sat around the room — on bed, chairs & sofa — Almost *anyone* else would have apologized for taking us up to her bedroom!

Afterward we all went in to say goodnight to the Pres. & to then go down for refreshments! F asked me to stay & have ice cream with him. F. Paris & Count Fleury [another friend of Arthur Suckley's] were beckoning violently for me to go downstairs, evidently thinking I was being simple-minded & staying behind all the others. When I explained that *I was invited* there were raised eyebrows & "ohs" & "ahs."

— In the P.M. [on the 19th] to the Roosevelt Memorial dedication — The President made the first speech. Governor [Herbert] Lehman & Mayor [Fiorello H.] LaGuardia. All very good & the mayor struck some sharp notes on the Constitution! He evidently thinks "Teddie" Roosevelt would have backed up his cousin F.D.R.! The young Theodore showed what he is by making a very stupid speech, and by not knowing enough to open it by addressing himself to the President & the other important people there — He almost certainly did it on purpose to avoid addressing his cousin Frank.

[On January 19, 1936, FDR dedicated the Theodore Roosevelt statue in front of the American Museum of Natural History on Central Park West. It was a tense occasion, since the Oyster Bay and Hyde Park branches of the Roosevelt family remained at daggers drawn. Theodore Roosevelt, Jr., who had always hoped to occupy the office his distant cousin now held, was the last to speak and made a point of sarcastically saluting those orators — FDR included — who were now willing to say kind things about his father but had not been with him when it counted, during his independent run for the presidency in 1912. Daisy's indignation may have been slightly misdirected. At least in the printed version of his remarks, TR, Jr., did, in fact, address the President and the other assembled dignitaries before he began.]

❧ *January 27.* I've been thinking over Al Smith's speech of Saturday "blasting" the New Deal & Franklin Roosevelt — The real tragedy is not the political effects, or the accusations, be they true or false — the Tragedy lies in the bitterness of spirit which must have [inspired] such an attack on an old friend . . . No man could have been a better friend to Al Smith than F.D.R. and F.D.R. has repeatedly held out the olive branch in spite of Mr. Smith's vindictive attitude —

[On January 25, 1936, Smith spoke to the anti-Roosevelt American Liberty League at a dinner in Washington and mounted an all-out attack on his old ally. "Let me give this solemn warning," he said. "There can be only one capital, Washington or Moscow. There can only be one atmosphere of government, the clean pure air of free America or the foul breath of communistic Russia." The shrill speech later backfired on Smith, the Liberty League, and the Republicans.]

Madison Grant is another of the "*violent* ones"! [Grant, a fixture in New York society, was the author of virulently racist books about the supposed evils of immigration, including *The Passing of the Great Race* and *The Conquest of a Continent.*] Yesterday he made a wild statement: Mr. James Roosevelt was "all bad," Mrs. Roosevelt "all good," Franklin a "strange mixture of good & bad." He summed up thus: "The whole thing is, Daisy, that he has *betrayed his class!*"

I prefer [George] Cardinal Mundelein's description: "He has had the *courage to go against* his class."

But the funniest thing was Morton Eustis [grandson of Vice President Levi P. Morton, who had owned a nine hundred-acre estate next to Wilderstein] setting out to *prove* to me that the President is a scoundrel! He led up to his accusation at great length: "This *couldn't* be denied — it was well known — Daisy you can't explain *this* away," etc, etc. And then, all I got was: "He & Mrs. Roosevelt *only* gave $100 to the Community Chest after urging others to give to it."

[Fragment of a letter from FDR to Daisy]

Sunday Jan. 29th [1936]

How did you like Al Smith's speech — He did himself little good I think — but it is a queer thing that I can't hate him in spite of the things he has said & done —

* * *

Jan. 29th '36

Dear Franklin —

Your letter came just a few moments ago, and I am so terribly glad (and *not* surprised) that you can't hate Al Smith — One couldn't blame you if you did, but it's so wonderful that you don't, and it just confirms one of the many things I already know about a C.P.

Disappointment and difficulties seem to do such strange things to people's minds and to their spirits; and perhaps one can't blame them any more than for the physical diseases that attack them — I so often think of cataracts over people's eyes. So many people seem to have cataracts over their *minds* . . .

I'm glad you find Fides [a toy penguin] congenial. It's the *nicest* kind of a name, and matches so beautifully with Excelsior in its general "tone"!

. . . Kindly give Fides a message from me: He was *not* sent to Washington to encourage conversation in the middle of the night — but to demand a certain required number of hours of sleep! [FDR had apparently called Daisy very late at night.]

I am getting so fond of Jujube, and really feel a deep sympathy with him — You see — it really *is not* ferocity or anger — it's just that he is *very* young, and he *can't* make out what it's all about, and he's really crying for enlightenment from Excelsior — [The penguin was evidently given to FDR by Daisy as a reminder that he was to take good care of himself and not get overtired. He gave her another toy bird to go with the goose Excelsior; Daisy named it Jujube. Precisely what signals this figurine was meant to send to her is unknown.]

Feb. 5th — Did you know that Excelsior is a magic bird? He *is!* Last night, he carried me on a delightful journey through "The Blue." We covered *thousands* of miles — First we flew over a lovely white city by a gentle river — then we stopped at Boulder Dam, and looked across the desert at the mountains, rising clear-cut, 50 miles away — then up a rocky canyon where the party were all terrified of the precipice — all that is but the occupants of one car! Excelsior & I were *not* afraid, for we soared over the peaks and down into the depths — free of the risks of the narrow road and crumbling "shoulders." (We *were* a tiny bit worried for the party on the road.)

On to Coronado, and then, southward on to the Pacific — to tropical paradises — big & little fish — (How we laughed when one got away!) Tall mountains and rocky coasts — some good-sized seas — *and a* Panama hat!

Over the canal we flew — A few more days in warm waters —

white Indians — old ruins — and then a race before the storm — northward — the spray in our faces!

And tonight — it's sorting books — and . . . back to a nice letter —

And Excelsior — calm and imperturbable as ever! *Can* it be anything *but* magic?

I had a funny time getting F.P. [Franklin Paris] to promise to give that message [see FDR's letter to Daisy of February 2, below] — I told him so often that he began to protest, and I said he didn't have to give it as *often* as I had mentioned it. At which he said I was losing my nerve!!

He seemed to think it might be difficult in front of [New York Representative] Sol Bloom or whoever might be there. I said I didn't mind who was there! He's more discreet!

I hope the plans for the Exposition [the New York World's Fair, then three years away] are satisfactory — It would be nice for it to mean something, & to be more than a glorified side-show!

[January 30, FDR's birthday, was celebrated annually in cities and towns all across the country with birthday balls to raise money for the March of Dimes and the fight against polio. Daisy attended the New York ball at the Waldorf-Astoria, at which Sara Delano Roosevelt presided. She and FDR had evidently arranged to send each other mental "messages" at a specified time during the festivities.]

Do you know, I *did* "get" that message at the Ball — We were all listening attentively [to the President's broadcast remarks], and then I suddenly realized *I* was getting something special! Like the flashes Marceline the clown used to get in the funny papers — Do you remember?

And they played "the President's Waltz" and I had a marvelous dance — Harry went home early with a tooth out — He's the *kindest* person. [Harry Hooker was an old friend and former law partner of the President's who would often, over the years, act as Daisy's escort to presidential occasions at which her presence might otherwise have sparked gossip.] . . . Don't tantalize me with dates in February and April! I really don't think there is a chance for either time. And I'd rather not think about there not being a chance! But after what

happened two weeks ago — I'm *always* prepared for *anything!* [FDR
had evidently made a surprise visit to Hyde Park.]

* * *

Sunday, Feb 2

[FDR to Daisy]

A quiet day — lots of clearing up of things to be put away — &
I found the enclosed rather gruesome letter from an old friend of
mine, Wyant Hubbard — telling of what modern war is like when
conducted by a "civilized nation" against "barbarians." [The letter
evidently chronicled Italian atrocities against the Ethiopians.]

It all makes one's heart ache. Will you send it back to me — I
mean the letter, not the heart?

Monday — F. Paris was here today with Sol Bloom — a short
visit about expositions — & at the end he stepped over & whispered
"Daisy sends you her love" — and that was very very nice —

Gus has been buying rugs for his house — We simply *must* work
out some system by which you or I — or better both — pass on his
decorations first — Those rugs may be *terrible* — What to do?

I am at my desk in the oval room — & [Executive Clerk Rudolph]
Forster has just called out that it is 1 P.M. I'm off! Such an intelligent
and yet understanding & gentle hand — He actually grinned when I
stayed up till 1:30 A.M. playing poker the night of Al Smith's speech —

[Daisy's February 5 letter continues]

Thanks for sending Mr. Hubbard's letter — Whatever is to happen to that poor little country, and when will this human race get
some sense of decency? . . .

Feb. 8th Saturday A package came, two days ago. Do you *really*
suppose these little books are going to be "thrown away"! In the first
place, I know I'll like many things in them — Secondly, there are a
couple of inscriptions in strange handwritings. In the third, and biggest, place, each one contains a 3-letter inscription, and one contains
a 6-letter inscription: FORMLS!

By the way, I quite casually invented a monogram today:

It came of itself! —

... What an interesting description of Haile Selassie in Mr. Hubbard's letter — Thanks again for sending it on — and so much, again, for the books —

Aff.

D.

[Fragment from an FDR letter]

Jan. 30th '36

Will you not worry about all the horrid and unnecessary things of this political year? You are so right about them — but *we* must bear with them & while we try not to add to them still we must get the truth brought out — And if we carry on and lose at least we will have tried honorably — And there are lots & lots of other thrilling things to do in this life —

✎ *February 12* — Lunch ... at the Knickerbocker Club [with] Mr. and Mrs. Kenneth Miller Simpson & their daughter ... I talked to Mr. Simpson for perhaps 2½ hours and found him very broadminded & unbiased — He is Republican — worked under General [Hugh] Johnson in the beginnings of NRA [National Recovery Administration] & has not many illusions about human nature — He is in Wall Street — belongs to the "Bankers Group" who, incidentally, are coining money these days, and he says it was incredible to hear those men, who are our "best people," educated, charming socially, etc., saying the most awful personal things against F.D.R., the kind of things you might expect from a slum dweller who has *no* education!

Feb. 12th '36

Dear Franklin —

I've maligned my nice room [in Mrs. Langdon's Manhattan apartment] and its *big* patch of sky! It shows how little time I spend in it, for I remembered that there was one hour of sunlight on the 3rd floor, where we used to be, but I discover that up here, on the 6th floor — a thin slant comes in at about 10.30 — works around on top of various roofs & chimneys, & finally disappears behind the next building on Park Ave. after 2 P.M.! So you see, my little garden of agaves and ivies really are *bathed* in sunlight for *hours!*

... I've just read Lincoln's speech after his re-election — It's just about what you say to me when I rant against politics and people! Perhaps when I'm *very* old — I'll learn something? Do you get out at all in this kind of weather? You're much more snowed in than we are!

... *Feb. 14th* Such a Valentine as I got this morning! It's *lovely,* and I know it's beautiful — just from looking through the pages quickly — We will read it aloud in the evenings (inscriptions just right!) — Shouldn't you and I belong to the Society of the Men of the Trees [an organization dedicated to the preservation of forests]? *You* certainly should, and perhaps I should too, just because I love them without knowing much about them — I had a little rock garden [at Wilderstein] a few years ago and had long arguments with Ethel & Maunsell [Crosby] as to where it ought to be. They insisted it should be in the open — with all possible sunlight — I put it in a little grove, with trunks of trees framing the river view — It was lovely, and even now, though it's been neglected since I have been with Aunt Sophie, there are still lovely blossoms in the spring, and periwinkle covers most of the stones, and my tree trunks are a little thicker, and my shade a little deeper —

What can I say to you to make you stop sending me such fascinating things! You know, I really *can't* have you receiving a letter from me every week! And yet I *must* be polite and thank you! You see, you are really putting me in a *very* awkward position!

One of those boys on the streets, who rush and wipe off your car when there's a red light, said to my friend Muriel Gordon — "I think there's no one like President Roosevelt — He's the *first* one who has ever given a thought to people like me" — She agreed with him perfectly, and he wipes her car regularly whenever she parks!

... My niece "Roly" Hambley is down for the night, and she & I are going on a series of "bats"! [Margaret Beekman Hambley used the nickname Rollie. Her aunt always spelled it "Roly."] When I asked her what she wanted particularly to do, she said at once that she wanted to go to a burlesque show, where "ladies are not allowed"!! Eleven years old! But she is a *perfect dear* — Can I bring her to see you sometime? ("En famille," we always say she's a "regular Suckley"!! — She's just like her mother, as a matter of fact.)

I see you mastered the technique of that monogram

/ ⎯ ⊃ \

Sunday the 16th — No — I have no cold, and I am perfectly fine & have been right along! Don't let yourself have "feelings" about anything like that, for I'm *very* healthy and haven't had a cold all winter! (I'm knocking violently on wood!) And as for the weather, I don't mind *any* kind, for the simple reason that I always go out into it! Yesterday was lovely, *overhead!* —

. . . Last night, at almost eleven P.M. when we had *all* gone to bed! — the doorbell rang for a Special Delivery! I am thankful it wasn't mailed any later! But *don't* send "Special Deliverys"! I love to get them — but unless there's something specially important, an ordinary letter comes in more quietly!

I'll remind you right now! Tell me about the pink lighthouse on the beach in the Bahamas! [FDR had thought warmly of Daisy while gazing at a pink lighthouse somewhere in the Bahamas, had even imagined what it might be like to share it with her; then, in part of a letter now missing, evidently teased her to ask him about it when he got home.]

There's really no chance of my going up on the 25th so don't even think about it except to let me know how the redwoods are! (And anything else you can think of!)

. . . It may seem strange, but I really think Al Smith has done you some good! He must be an unhappy man, to have his present viewpoint, and perhaps some day you & he can be friends again — when you become a private citizen again.

Now — and *this is serious* — I think I'll write you a *steamer* letter next, when you go for your fishing trip — That'll be about the middle of March, *n'est-ce pas?* That does *not* prevent the mail carrier from being kept occupied *from* Wash. *to* N.Y.!

I'm glad Fides is doing his duty, and with a *little* effect — anyway —

Thanks *so* much for the Tree book — One doesn't expect sentiment from the English but I think they have a more genuine kind than the temperamental Latins —

Aff.

D.

* * *

[New York]

Feb. 20th '36

Dear Franklin — *What* do you suppose that wretch F. Paris did this afternoon! He actually came in during the Chess Club Tea, and taunted

me with the information that he was going to Hyde Park this week-
end and *why* wasn't *I!!* I almost turned Jujube on him!

And, on top of everything, and after all my boasting, I *have* a
cold, since yesterday — pride goeth before a fall — Its only 9.30, but
I've "retired" with large doses of orange juice — and it will be all
gone in a day or two — I foolishly ate a *very* delicious and huge lunch
today: two helpings of the most rich things, so it serves me right!

You wouldn't think the death of Gen. [Billy] Mitchell [the controversial advocate of air power] would affect me in any way — I've
never even seen him — and yet it does, in a rather personal way, too,
for years ago my brother Henry was very much in love with Betty
Miller (Mrs. Mitchell). She was one of those rarely fascinating and
lovely looking girls who always had at *least* a dozen men in love with
her at one time. It is hard for girls like that to know which one they
prefer over all the others, and Henry went to Albania at the head of
an ambulance unit in an unhappy state of uncertainty. While [he was]
there, however, Betty wrote to him, promising to marry him, and he
wrote home about it at once. A few days later he was killed by a
German airplane bomb. We received his letter some three weeks later,
and I have always felt profoundly grateful to Betty M. for giving him
those really happy days — Of course there was never any announcement, and I don't quite know why I tell you all this, excepting that it
is a very human story. I suppose you know the Mitchells well — I
hear they were very happy together — I wonder if Betty is still as
fascinating, perhaps even more so, as an older woman . . .

In the "front parlor," I think I told you, we have that picture of
you out of "Today" [a magazine] with the inscription at the bottom:
"To Today from Franklin D. Roosevelt." This afternoon, two people
picked it up with a remark to me: "Does he call you Toddy?" That's
what I get for my honesty in leaving the magazine inscription!

. . . By the way, do you have any trouble disposing of C.P.'s
"volumes"? [By this, she seems to have meant to ask whether FDR
had found a way to dispose of her long letters without their being
read by anyone else. The answer — though evidently she did not ever
hear it from him — was that he did not throw them away, and in fact
kept at least some of them near him even when he traveled.]

*   *   *

[Hyde Park]

Mon. Feb. 24

M.M. [FDR to Daisy]

A series of Tragedies & plans gone wrong! As you will see by the papers I go back tonight because of poor Harry's death [Henry La-trobe Roosevelt had died on February 22] —

Never have I seen so much snow here since the blizzard of '88 — which *of course* you remember! The stone walls are merely slight longitudinal ridges in a white expanse. It is *lovely* & I do wish you could see it — Nothing but the main roads open — & difficult even to get to the cottage — & of course geting into the woods is impos-sible — Prof. [Nelson C.] Brown [of Syracuse University, the Presi-dent's adviser on his trees] came to lunch yesterday & we couldn't even see the tops of trees put in 3 years ago —

Our road must wait till the end of April or May. [FDR and Daisy had discussed building an all-weather road through the woods to their hilltop.]

I need a young woman — resident of Dutchess Co — experi-enced in gardening and trees & hill-tops to help me to try it out — perhaps by then one will apply for the job — There are other quali-fications I have in mind — so difficult — yet I hope & really believe just the right kind of applicant will turn up. Luckily I am to be the sole judge —

[Daisy's letter from New York continues]

Sunday the 23rd — I'm so sorry about Col. H. Roosevelt — Do you remember he was at the movies that night, last summer?

I loved your talk in Philadelphia — You put things so clearly, and I've been thinking a lot about your "three qualities of education." Concerning the second, "The sense of equality in connection with things of the mind," so many people in our "class" still object to more than the minimum of education for the mass of the people, for that very reason that it *does* give them the sense of equality, and they lose the sense of subservience to — shall I say — "us"! I've had lots of arguments on that subject!

I'm wondering if you laid out the new Hill road today, and if it was a gorgeous day, as it was even here, and if you went to see the Redwoods [in the Springwood greenhouse], and if they are still thriv-ing . . .

Your speech at Temple, *I* think, strikes exactly the right note for your speeches this year! We all laughed at your "precedent breakings"! [On Washington's Birthday, February 22, FDR received an honorary degree from Temple University in Philadelphia and said he would like to break two precedents: he would not quote from George Washington, nor would he pretend to know what Washington would have said "if he had been alive today."]

How are you? in *every* way? Cheerful?

I'm *really* stumped by the "M.M." at the beginning of your last letter! *What* does it mean?

Tuesday — the 25th Well! It was evidently *not* meant to be today!

Was there anything said about not "writing"? I think not! It must have been "not mailing" letters! There really *is* a great difference!

March 1st Sunday — There are *so* many things I want to talk about, *so* many questions I want to ask, that it seems quite useless to even *try* to get started! Are you really getting off [for another fishing trip] about the 19th? You *must* have that trip in the sunlight & the salty air — and *perhaps* there will be one small cloud of spray to splash you and remind you of your friends in the north!

We go to Rhinebeck for a week on March 28th, then back here until we go up for the summer about May 15th — I shall be with Aunt S. again this summer . . . Is there *any* chance of seeing you up there at any time before Election Day? You'll be speechifying all summer, I suppose! — Are you getting a fishing boat for the New England coast? ? ?s ?s ?s ?s

The spring has a most disturbing effect — you want to be moving — moving *out* — out of yourself — out of that house — out into the country! Every place seems narrow & constricted, and here, in these [big-city] canyons, there's not a sparrow left to chirp the good news to you; and your winter clothes look shabby in the new spring sunlight, and — all in all — you just want to get out to *the top of a hill!*

And, for all your wanting to get out of them, you stay right in the canyons!

Are *you* in canyons? And do you want to get *out?* I'm sure you do! And you must need to, too — It's a long time since your last holiday — to Warm Springs — for those flying trips to N.Y. & Boston & H.P. couldn't have been much of a rest!

Do you know, I have a very definite conviction (an intuition, if you wish) that "things" started going "up" a few weeks ago, and will keep right on going up, in spite of set-backs — Somehow, it's in the air; and the *only* thing that worries me is lest you won't follow Fides' *very* sound advice, *most* of the time! It's *so* important that you do, especially when you start active campaigning!

Just now, it's 11.40 Sunday morning, and I am having a grand feeling of being alone, with the "family" in Church, the sun shining on this page, and just about an hour before numerous uncles and aunts start arriving for lunch!

I've been reading some interesting things in the paper — Knowing things gives one such a strange mixture of contradictory feelings: a great humility, because you realize how little you do know and understand; and also a sort of insight into what marvelous things are in the world, to be known, and to be understood if only the mind can be kept open and expanding.

Generalities are very unsatisfactory, but it seems to me that the only classifying of human beings that doesn't fail at many points is that which divides them into the two groups of the open-minded & the closed-minded —

———

I have a *very* strong suspicion that this *will* be mailed *before* the 19th, with some lame sort of excuse that it is *getting* too voluminous!

Don't think I'm staying home from Church for any reason except that I felt like it! My cold vanished *days* ago! and I feel perfectly fine. I *do,* however, need some news from the capital! There hasn't been any for weeks — except, of course what the papers give — and *that* kind is only 2nd rate! It's just about two weeks, and that is twice as long as one week! (*Very* relevant!)

. . . I didn't congratulate you on your new grandchild! You must be very proud to have six of them —

I'm going to send this off, *now!* It's a compromise between one & four weeks! You stayed in the W.H. Saturday — Are you *all right allways?*

Aff.

D.

* * *

[New York]

Tues. March 3rd

Dear F.,

I'm *completely* green with jealousy! I've just been hearing about a visit to the *W.H. attic,* where a certain person in shirt sleeves was sorting out books — Lucky Gus there too — and later, I'll be hearing of another visit, I suppose! It's just too tantalizing and I think life is treating me *very* badly, for all *I* can do is to read meager accounts in the papers and try to fill in the gaps with my imagination — I must acknowledge the imagination is a great help, but it's only a *temporary* help!

. . . *Please* tell me how you are — if you are getting out in the sun quite often? If it's something of a nuisance to go out driving, couldn't you get up to the roof in some way?

. . . Weren't you thrilled when you touched off the key to the dam the other day — [On March 4, the President had dedicated the Norris Dam, the first in the Tennessee Valley Authority chain.]

There's something so perfectly wonderful in all those huge projects, and the effects they will have on millions of lives. My very first trip — when (and *if!*) my ship comes in — will be to visit Tennessee & Boulder Dam, & Washington State, etc, etc. — And Alaska, en passant, & perhaps the new highway to Mexico and some tropical islands, and *more* etc.s!

But, after all, though one talks so much about the interest & beauty of things & nature, the real interest comes from the personal contacts one makes — the people one meets on the Broad Highway (you remember that *very* romantic book we all read when we were growing up) — One finds, it is true, "sermons in stones" and one finds God in the forests and open spaces, but far more convincing than Nature, is what we find in the heart of a friend — And beside that, comforts and surroundings mean very very little, in contrast — (I *do* like the comforts also!)

I've been counting up the books belonging to the Ourhill Library! Can you guess how many there are? *13!* The first and earliest one is dated 1926 — And the 13th has inscribed the name of the Library, and so it's the most valuable of all! Some others have *very special* inscriptions, which make *them* terribly valuable, but, I think, perhaps, the *last* will always be the *most* valuable! [These volumes, enjoyed by both FDR and Daisy, were meant to be housed in the cottage Roosevelt planned to build on their hill.]

Saturday, March 7th — Well! This has been a particularly nice day, because I got some good mail this morning! It really didn't make the slightest difference about the Special Delivery! It was just amusing, and I just couldn't help imagining what embarrassing questions I *might* have had to answer, *if* anyone but the maid & I had been waked up! They evidently forgot to mail it that evening and so put on the special stamp — It was postmarked that morning at, I think, 11 A.M.!

It's too bad that trip was so disappointing. But you *did* see our lovely country covered with snow, and all that snow is a blessing to growing things, besides being beautiful to look at — It's too bad also about the Redwoods — however it might be interesting to try some more this summer — I still have a small package of last year's seeds and will try a few in a cigar box, right here in my room. You never can tell what miracles Nature will perform, if you give her a free hand! It seems strange those Sequoias died — possibly some germ got at them — the remaining one will be doubly precious — Do you mind bothering about it? It belongs to you anyway — *What* is your gardener's name: PLOG? [William Plog, pronounced "Plow," cared for the Springwood grounds for more than half a century.] As to the "young woman" specialist you require for laying out your Hill road, I know *just* the person — only she's *not* so young, and she won't be available until after May 15th [when Mrs. Langdon planned to move back to Rhinebeck] — Also, she is not so *very* far from remembering the blizzard of '88! Perhaps the best thing would be for *you* to lay out the road, earlier, and then get her to approve — It won't be difficult I'm sure! And I'm *quite* sure she'd *love* the job! Somehow, I don't see any trips for April, except that first week to Rhinebeck . . .

I'm upset about [Major] General [Johnson] Hagood. [Appearing before a House appropriations subcommittee, the commander of the Army Corps Headquarters at San Antonio, Texas, had unwisely denounced WPA funds as "stage money" and complained that it "is harder for me to get 5 cents to buy a lead pencil than to get $1,000 to teach hobbies to CCC boys." For this outburst he was summarily removed from his command, over the gleeful protests of Republicans in Congress who accused FDR of muzzling dissent. Daisy tactfully chose to believe that someone other than the President must have approved the dismissal.]

After reading everything I can find about it, it seems to be nothing in the world but the satisfying of a personal grudge by a superior officer — Can't you do something about it? — It seems so terribly unfair —

The Service strike [of New York apartment house personnel] has its funny side! Every time I come home, I peer through the bars of the glass doors, and find a young giant (who should be the hero of a mounted police movie!) peering through at me, to be sure I am quite a safe person to admit! As a general thing it's all pretty peaceful, but the isolated cases of intimidation by union men of the non-union men make one perfectly furious, and I want to get a blackjack and stand guard at the front door — I almost feel like inviting them in to do something, so that they could be properly dealt with, and sent to jail! I'm quite sure that much of our trouble with gangsters could be eliminated if the average man had more courage to meet violence with violence — (How brave I am!! — but I know I should run like a rabbit if I came up against it, myself!)

Monday morning — the 9th — This is no. 14 in the O Library, and I have worked out the proper marking — to be put in the upper left-hand corner of the first page: so:

There should be a very special and significant book-plate — One can be designed to contain all sorts of legendary and symbolic animals, vegetables, and even minerals!

Wednesday the 11th A *real* March day — raining and blowing — But you should see my garden of five little flower pots! They are on the window ledge — against the law — but they are having such a good time shaking their heads in the warm wet wind, that I haven't the heart to bring them in, just yet —

[Pasted to the original letter is the following newspaper clipping:

BARS ONE ARM DRIVING

Lee, Mass., March 6 AP. Police Chief Frank T. Coughlin does not tend to interfere with Cupid but he insisted today one-arm driving must cease. Swains can park and spark right on Main Street, he said, and police will not bother them. But when the cars are in motion *both hands must be on the wheel.*

Daisy had underlined the last seven words in pen.]

This clipping will make you realize that people really *are* trying to prevent motor accidents! I'm *sure* you approve of such a ruling and that it should be strictly enforced —

You must be looking forward to the new boat! [A new yacht was being fitted out for the President. He was about to embark on a two-week fishing trip.] Just forget *everything* that's on land during your short vacation, and *don't* let your secretaries pursue you with mail bags telegrams & radios! — It would be an excellent opportunity to write a very complete description of a Fishing Trip to the Bahamas, in the form of a letter or diary — And you might leave instructions with Congress to use the time of your absence for all the *un*necessary conversation they have to indulge in, so that they can get down to sensible business when you return! Only put in your more tactful way!

Sunday the 15th On the side of a hill in N.J.! At a moment's notice, yesterday afternoon, I packed a toothbrush, some note paper and a book on the flight of birds, and came out here with the [Rupert] Andersons for two nights — A woodpecker was dashing up and down the trunk of an old tree, and some green shoots are pushing through in the flower bed, and this morning I awoke to the gentle chirping of something very sweet outside the window —

Your letter came Saturday morning with breakfast, and oh, I *hope* you can get off next Thursday —

Do you really want some advice about your itinerary this summer? That's not difficult — It can be very simply worked out in a little picture of the U.S.A. There is *one* particular starting point and the finishing point is the same — You can fill in the cities on the way! Isn't that simple? [See next page.]

Monday morning — [T]his is to wish you the best of Bon Voyages!

Aff.

D.

* * *

March 8

[FDR to Daisy]

— Here I am wondering what you are doing — & wishing you had been at the [National] Cathedral with me this morning [for the special service held on the anniversary of his first inauguration] — It is going to be by far the most lovely Cathedral in this country some day — & I'm so glad they are building it a little piece at a time — it ought to take a full century — I have always wished that [New York Bishop William T.] Manning had not been in such a hurry with St. John's!

I'm glad you told me about Mrs. Mitchell — & glad too that Henry knew [her] and was happy — I have only seen her once, but she seemed a really lovely person — Billy M. had enormous charm but was a very difficult person — full of enthusiasms and wild ideas and isms —

toothbrush, some note paper and a book on the flight of birds, and came out here with the Andersons for two nights — A woodpecker was dashing up and down the trunk of an old tree, and some green shoots are pushing through in the flower bed, and this morning I awoke to the gentle chirping of something very sweet outside the window —

Your letter came Saturday morning with breakfast, and oh, I hope you can get off next Thursday —

Do you really want some advice about your itinerary this summer? That's not difficult — It can be very simply worked out in a little picture of the U.S.A. There is one particular starting point and the finishing point is the same — You can fill in the cities on the way? Is it that simple?

The news from Germany is bad [on March 7, German troops had marched into the Rhineland] — & tho' my official people all tell me there is no danger of actual war I always remember their saying all the same things in July '14 (before you can remember, my blessed infant) —

The Tragedy — deepest part of it — is that a nation's words and signatures are no longer good — If France had a leader whom the people would follow their only course would be to occupy all Germany quickly up to the Rhine — no further — They can do it today — in another year or two Germany will be stronger than they are — & the world cannot trust a fully rearmed Germany to stay at peace —

* * *

[New York]
        Sunday — a real *Sun* Day — the 22nd, I believe. [March 22]
Dear F.
    . . . [T]he only place I can write at the moment is near the parlor radio! This sounds peculiar — but the bedlam in the apartment is complete! My cousin from Wyoming & her 16 yr boy are here for the holidays — I *have* a bed to myself, but nothing else, and, in fact, I'm partly packed & living in a suitcase, ready for Rhinebeck next Thursday!

    [The radio announcer] is talking in the intermission in the Philharmonic [concert], and three ladies are discussing I-don't-know-what in the other room, and the *comparative* quiet of a moment is already broken by the sounds of teacups preparing to come in —

    And I'm wondering if you are getting off today — the sky *is* so blue —

* * *

Mon., Mar 23

[FDR to Daisy]
    Safely on board the Destroyer U.S.S. *Dale* — after a long day beginning at Rollins College — The "Chapel" is lovely — Spanish type — very Catholic in pictures, statues, etc. — & Hamilton Holt [president of Rollins] told me without a smile that it is all low church Baptist!

    Every College President of the State of Florida took part in the honorary degree ceremonies — I sometimes think that each time I get a new degree I know less — Perhaps Doctorates are merely a symptom of an inquiring and receptive nature —

A long drive brought us to Coast & the Train — & I had a long talk with Gen. Hagood. He will get a new post — *but* he is an awful bumptious unbalanced idiot! I had never seen him before — He should *never* have been a general — perhaps a South Carolina Congressman — not even a Senator. [FDR received Hagood aboard his special train and evidently offered to reinstate him; in the end, just twenty-four hours after being awarded a new command, the general resigned from the Army.]

We are underway — i.e. there is way or headway on the ship — but when a ship is at *anchor* she gets under*weigh* i.e. she weighs (or hauls up) the anchor — That's the best explanation — I forgot to tell you last autumn — one of those thousand things I want to tell you about all the time —

[Daisy's letter continues]

Monday —

I was so excited to read in this evening's paper that you quoted from "The Life of Pasteur." [In his remarks at Rollins College, FDR had recalled a line from this film, spoken by the actor who played Joseph Lister: "My dear Pasteur, every great benefit to the human race in every field of its activity has been bitterly fought in every stage leading up to its final acceptance." That, Roosevelt said with a grin, was true of "politics" as well as science.] I have brought it up a dozen times, not with the words of Lister, but as an example of the lack of vision, the blindness of the educated, controlling classes. The "Tale of Two Cities" shows that also. And haven't all violent revolutions been due to just that same thing?

What does "M.M." stand for??

I am so glad you are off on the briny deep — It will do you a world of good, & how lovely the coral beaches must be, & the pink lighthouses — But — holding back the log is *most* unkind!

I shall start my remaining Redwood seeds in Rhinebeck — It sounds more promising than a window box in this dusty atmosphere! The President & the First Lady must both be proud of those tributes at Rollins College — no one deserves it more than they . . . [Eleanor Roosevelt was on the platform when FDR received his honorary degree. She heard him praised and was praised herself.]

And I am so glad about Gen. Hagood — He must be very happy, for after a long useful life it would be terrible to end it in disgrace —

And it must be a difficult thing for you to go over the heads of others. But you have harder nuts to crack than that, haven't you?

Rhinebeck Thursday, the 26th — A "soft" day for our drive up [to Rhinebeck for the summer] — And can you guess who were the most important passengers . . . The answer is without doubt: Excelsior & Jujube! And I am wondering if Excelsior gave me the right message! It was a *nice* one, anyway, for *he* wouldn't deliver any other kind! The quiet is wonderful — and so full of meaning — One stops to listen to it, consciously, and one hears a million small voices —

My sister [Elizabeth Hambley] brought over the three children soon after we had arrived — My nephew, Bobbie — just under 6 ft. and dreadfully shy — & I had quite a talk about his future — He hasn't, so far, shown any particular bent, and the problem is to know what to help him get into — I wonder if there is much opportunity in some sort of conservation work — The Forestry Service for instance — I want very much to ask you about it when I see you — It might be good to send him to Cornell rather than attempt an ordinary College course first —

[Bobbie Hambley was not merely dreadfully "shy"; he was eventually diagnosed as schizophrenic, though the diagnosis took a long time coming, and his father would never accept it. Helping her nephew was one of the quiet causes of Daisy's life, one in which she eventually enlisted FDR's help.]

The Spring fever will make it very difficult to get settled in town again, and I *shall try* to get up for a weekend *at home* during April! Perhaps the weekend of the 25th will turn out to be convenient — It will be just about between now and May 15th, when we come up for summer —

It *would* count for a lot —

Friday — pouring, pouring, pouring! . . . Lots of green things on branches and poking up from the ground. In late April [when she hoped to meet FDR in Hyde Park] there will be lots of blossoms! I think *almost surely* I can get up then — probably with a little friend of mine who adores Dutchess Cty & is looking for a small house with a view of the river or the mountains — [Daisy is here coyly referring to herself.]

We both love going out to tea on Sunday afternoon — *perhaps* we could think up some place to go — Can you suggest any nice place for tea? That is *if* I can make it turn out as I wish! Probably we would take a Friday night train up, and we would plan to return to

N.Y. Sunday evening (she works), *but — if —* something *very* important turned up for Monday P.M. I *might possibly* manage to stay over;
for there are *really* lots of important things for me to do at the house!

I want so much to hear how you like the "Potomac" [the new
presidential yacht, evidently named by Daisy; see the entry for March
25, below] — perhaps there will be a picture of her in the papers
before you return to Washington —

[FDR's letter continues]

Tues Mar 24 —

We anchored off Cat Island & got out the fishing boats & gear
but had very little luck though we tried two different anchorages —
It is too rough to stop at Long Island this P.M., as the wind is wrong
— but I saw our pink lighthouse through the glasses — I do wish I could
draw — perhaps someone will give me lessons. [See opposite page.]

The point looks out to the South — Spain is the next land across
the point.

Wed Mar 25 — This A.M. we anchored off Matthew Town, Great
Inagua Island, & found the *Potomac* — She came alongside & we
transferred ourselves & much baggage & gear — She looks nice —
successful planning & more room than the old *Sequoia* — She awaits
your inspection next month — very necessary because you are responsible for her name.

We have had fairly good fishing, both trolling & bottom fishing,
& Pa Watson got a big Barracuda, about 30 lbs.

Thurs. Mar 26 — Here we are at the Deserted Village [on] West
Caicos Island — several ghostly white ruins close to a steep beach
that looks like a 5-mile rampart of coral rock — We have all had
marvellous fishing — the best I have ever had in the West Indies —
good I suppose because as far as I know no white men have ever
trolled here before & the natives only catch small fish on hand lines.
No one seems to live on this island now and we feel far from civilization — not a bad thought on occasions. The charts also are primitive so our navigation has to be cautious and our speed slow.

Fri. 27 — More fishing this A.M. but we have to meet a mail
plane & must head back to the Westward — actually homeward
bound though we are only a few days out. We had a rough sea
running to Mariguana Island & the Potomac behaved well — she
rolls rather fast — six seconds — & I was up on the bridge & the
spray came on board — nice warm spray — soft spray — a special

Tus. Mar 2 —

We anchored off [...] Island
& got out the fishing boats &
gear but had very little luck
though we tried two different
anchorages — It is too rough
to stop at Long Island this
time, as the wind is wrong —
but I saw [...] point lighthouse
through the glasses — I do
wish I could draw — perhaps
someone will give me [...]

the point looks out to the
South & [...] is the next
land across the point.

kind. [This "special kind" of spray was to remind him of Daisy; see her letter to him of March 1, 1936, above.]

We fished just before the sun went down — & I got an amazing big Mystery fish — 27 lbs — can't identify it — so it goes on ice for the Smithsonian & I hope it will arrive there two weeks hence without "offense."

Sat 28 — All day at Mariguana — & we got some crawfish . . . from the Natives, but they were too big — too tough — & I had to apologize for I have been saying that crawfish are at least the equal of lobsters on the Coast of Maine.

[Daisy's letter continues]

Saturday — This will be a scribble, for I am writing on the corner of a tiny table! Yesterday, we were living in a world of dripping wetness — today, it's been heavenly and drying sunshine, and I didn't do anything but please myself all day — specially this P.M. when the family left the house for some four hours! I listened to "Carmen," while crocheting an afghan, and read that quite wonderful little book by William Jordan "The Majesty of Calmness" — which you sent me. (No. 16 — O Library!) I find in it so much that I should like to be myself — and so much that I know in certain persons — I'd like to start quoting — but it would mean too much to be copied — But I like this: "God commits to man ever only new beginnings, new wisdom, and new days to use the best of his knowledge." Have you read the book through?

It is strange to live in someone else's [Mrs. Langdon's] house — strange: even after two years of being treated like almost a daughter — You always have your own home in the back of your consciousness. The wind in the trees, even, is a strange wind, whereas there is an intimacy with the wind that sighs through the branches of the pines outside my tower room at home — the creakings in the floor, the way the sun slants through the windows — no matter how often you've heard them, they are always strangers compared to the creakings and sunlight at Home — Everything is strange, and perhaps for that reason interesting, in this little world — "excepting thee & me — and is thee a little strange too?" (With apologies for plagiarism!)

Or is it simply a matter of where the heart happens to be? Most certainly, a large part of mine lives permanently over there [at Wilderstein] — but there is another *very* large part that does a lot of travelling, and makes long "hops" with the greatest of joy! Oh well — it's all a great adventure — with plenty of tragedy mixed up with the comedy of it all! Not to forget the pure drama.

And L[ittleton Hambley] has a job in Washington! And I am so *very very* thankful — It means so much more than just the salary involved — Self-respect is perhaps the best word — and not only for himself, but for his wife and children — You can imagine how it is, after four years of "growing vegetables" up here! I so hope he can make himself really useful, so that it can be a permanent thing, or at least a step ahead — Need I say I am grateful? More than I could possibly express —

[FDR's letter continues]

Sun 29 — We got to Crooked Island this morning & the mail planes arrived from Miami — & I cleaned up mail & dispatches & sent them back with many official signatures & memoranda — We have been blessed with clear weather & an even temperature & I'm getting brown without much burn.

Mon 30 — We have been off Little San Salvador Island — poor fishing but it has given me a chance to read all kinds of reports — I hate to have to do it — but if I don't the accumulation on return is overwhelming — & so far I am up to date. Some day C.P. is going to see all these islands — & the ones "Down the Islands" — all the way to Trinidad — some I know & others need to be explored — in *fact must* be.

Tues 31st — Nassau this morning and Sir Bede Clifford & wife & staff came to lunch — also 15 newspaper men who flew over from Miami. Nothing very exciting or interesting & now at 4 P.M. I'm back in old clothes as we proceed South into the Tongue of the Ocean — a very deep spot about 70 miles long & 30 wide & 1 mile deep — all surrounded by coral reefs.

April 1 — We are at Green Cay & it is very muggy & I have a headache & wish I were at H.P. at this particular time. *Why I wonder? NO, I DON'T WONDER.* [Crossed out by FDR but meant to be legible to Daisy]

Most all of the men on all three ships have gone over to the beach & are swimming & looking for some great big lizards I told them about — My uncle [Frederic A. Delano, a railroad executive, city planner, and philanthropist] left us yesterday — He is a dear & you would like him.

April 2 — Another muggy day — spent in water from the Dale,

swimming, & running 30 miles to Middle Bight — I horrified all hands by taking the Potomac way into the Bay — 2 feet of water under our keel & the Navy had a collective fit.

April 3 — What a day! Off at 8 A.M. & back at 8 P.M. All day in a whale boat or a flat bottomed punt — way up the "creeks" — & into 6 inches of water — then casting a line with a crab on a hook & sitting silent — waiting for a bone fish — Imagine me sitting silent for hours! Jimmy [the President's eldest son and secretary] got one fish who dashed three times around the boat — great fun on a very light rod — We were guided by two very gentle black men — one of them, in our boat, Mr. Albert Moxey is a preacher when he isn't fishing for sponges — He gave me a plant — but alas, it won't live as he cut the roots — I wish I could bring it to you. Dr. [Ross] McIntire [later Admiral McIntire, the President's physician] got the only other fish.

Sat 4th — Last night the wind rose I got out of our rather doubtful anchorage & we have been rolling our way to Great Stirrup Key — All of our muscles are sore — & we are recuperating from yesterday. This time we really are headed for home.

Sunday 5th — Storm warnings are out (by radio) & the sky looks bad — Too rough for me to get into the boat — so the others fished for our supper.

Jimmy left on the *Monaghan* tonight — bearing much mail for Washington — I would have sent this . . . at Nassau & today it seemed best not to — I count on a letter on my return — I would have given you the Nassau address but there was no USN there —

[Daisy's letter continues]

Monday the 30th — Such a happy day! But first I must explain that I have what people call two "weaknesses." It's a complete misnomer, for these two "weaknesses" are really my two greatest sources of strength & should be called "Forces" — Be that as it may [the first "weakness" is FDR; the other] is my long, lanky shy nephew, who is at the threshold of life and does not know what lies before him — well — he and I are great friends, ever since he shrieked his first protest on coming into the world — Today we spent the entire afternoon from 1–5 wandering around the place — shooting at bottles & tin cans which we threw into the river from the dock-that-was — shooting also at a cracker box which he has set up in the field as a target — I've only pulled a trigger about six times in my life before, so I felt quite proud at hitting anything at all — I hit the cracker box from *90 yards* — was that so bad?

. . . I also moved some iris, and found my first wild flower, a periwinkle — which I enclose as a proof that even way up no'th we have Spring with us . . .

[FDR's letter continues]

Mon 6th — Out of water on board most of the day but tonight at Great Isaac Key it has been smooth enough to go alongside Dale & fill the Tanks — Good fishing & the general feeling of "only one more day" —

Tues 7th — Last day! — A good cruise & a real [rest] — & very nice comrades — quiet, good fun & no rows! I sometimes feel in Washington like murdering some of my official family — they want to "grab" or "bite" or ridicule —

Tomorrow we land about noon, spend Thursday at Warm Springs & get to W Fri. morning.

P.S. Days later — I will tell you about M.M. — it's something very nice — but I have the great idea that you won't be the least bit surprised — I have decided that somewhere subconsciously I knew about it a whole century ago — But I must explain it *very soon* —

Aff.

F.

* * *

Thursday April 9th New York again

[Daisy to FDR]

To cover the last few days I'd have to write *several* volumes, & they would never get written, & you'd *never* have time to read them! Suffice it to say that I loved being in my own tower room, with *my own* pieces & *my own* mountains — *and my own* floor creakings!

We were very busy at a thousand things & I am back in town up to my head catching up on the "left-undone" things of two weeks. Just as you will be tomorrow! (Excepting that you are running the country!)

Please don't get tired again!! Early to bed and not too many conferences!

I had a good laugh at myself last night, for I was *certain* of a special piece of mail — absolutely *positive* it would be here — and everything else one could think of was there but the special one!

You must have had a wonderful vacation, I'm *so* glad — and also that you are back again —

Aff. —
D.

* * *

At sea

Tues. [April] 7th

[FDR to Daisy]

Tomorrow we land at Ft. Lauderdale about noon & then to Warm Springs to spend Thursday — The report of a very bad tornado has just come & I *may* stop in damaged areas to see if the relief agencies are all functioning properly & together. All has gone well thus far & I'm slept out & much tanned, tho' the glare has given several of us occasional headaches — Today we are anchored close to Great Isaac Key — in the shadow of a very tall red & white striped lighthouse — not *our* light — fishing is good — so I am told, though I won't go out in the boat till 4 this P.M. Here we are only 54 miles from the U.S. & it will be a really comfy feeling to know I'm back in the same continent with C.P. *What* a long time I've been gone! We have NY papers up to 3 days ago & at least there is no disturbing news.

Wed Eve. on Train — A 5 minute stop — it is too jiggly to write while the train is going over these rough rails. There are floods in Georgia & the Gainesville disaster grows — I stop there tomorrow night. The distance lessens.

Thurs. night — midnight — I haven't been up as late as this for nearly 3 weeks — We have just left Gainesville — All the relief work goes on well but the tornado levelled everything over a two mile strip two blocks wide — over 200 killed & 1,200 injured. I'm always very thankful that we have no serious tornado or flood history in Dutchess!

I have missed you *ever* so much — in spite of *very* nice messages from a Penguin. And I hope so very, very much for some good news about the 25th — & for pages when I get to the office tomorrow afternoon —

Affectionately,
F.

* * *

New York —

Dear Franklin —

   . . . *a.m. [April] the 13th.* This morning some very welcome mail . . .

   The Deaconess [Daisy's private name for her aunt and employer, Mrs. Langdon] is getting out annual reports which depends on my books; and I've been away from there three weeks! What a week of "figuring" before me! I start at 10 this morning!

   Wed. 15th To Knox this morning with a package in tissue paper! From Knox to a "little man" on 6th Ave. & 49th, who does all their [hat] blocking — the "little man" opened the package and took out a C.P.'s panama — and his eyes literally shone as he handled it and stroked it and exclaimed over and over "Beautiful straw, beautiful hat"! I began to feel King Midas must have had something to do with weaving it! He made me write my name inside, so I would know I was getting back the same hat; and, it will be finished next Tuesday! I am *so* delighted with it — and *no one* knows where it came from excepting two people — two C.P.s!

   It will appear as part of my "spring outfit"!

   What a struggle we women have keeping up to date in hats! This spring there is little to choose from excepting flat dinner plates & the spoonbill platypus hat! With a bunch of flowers hanging on!

   Dinner (of vegetables!) with Harry H[ooker] the other night. He appears two or three times in succession; then vanishes for months; until he suddenly pops up again as casually as though he had just gone out for five minutes — You don't know how hard it is to discuss *every* subject *but one!* The *One* subject never fails to creep in at least once an evening, however!

   The "Treasure Chest" [evidently a gift from FDR] is now constantly open, and read at odd moments — One should know *all* its selections — And how characteristic that the two choices of Mrs. F.D.R. are Corinthians 13 — & the 121st psalm —

   . . . Excelsior and Jujube are flapping their wings with spring fever to get out and over the treetops!

   Did I mention that *new roads* and *new hills* and *high woods* all looked — oh — *very* enticing, in Dutchess County last week?

   . . . *What* does "M.M." mean? *Honestly,* I haven't an idea!

Saturday, April 18th

   . . . I missed your Conservation speech (adding for the Deaconess) but I loved reading it afterward. [On April 16, FDR dedicated the new Department of the Interior Building in Washington.]

As for the Baltimore speech — I think the Republican reaction to it was quite delightful! There wasn't anything for them to attack so they had to make up something. Walter Lippmann's article was the best summing-up of their lack of ideas that I saw anywhere — I've found even a few Republicans who agree about it! [On April 13, the President had addressed the Young Democratic Club of Baltimore, saying, among other things, "There are counselors these days who say: 'Do nothing'; other counselors who say: 'Do everything.' Common sense dictates an avoidance of both extremes. I say to you: 'Do something,' and when you have done something, if it works, do it some more; and if it does not work, then do something else."]

I'm going right out to get some of J[ohn] Buchan's books — and I'll tell you about them — Though I haven't much confidence in myself as a Literary critic!

Later — I have J.B.'s "The People's King," about George V. How *very* obedient I am! [This is the first instance of many of FDR's assigning Daisy the task of reading the latest books and then telling him about them so that he could dazzle dinner guests with all the reading he had somehow managed to do.]

But on another subject, I see I shall have to be *very* firm! Re Monday and Tuesday, it must without any question whatever be "either — or" — and, perhaps, 2:30 would be a better hour!

. . . You might let me know as early as possible *by telephone,* (Next week at Rhinebeck of course) about our survey of Dutchess! *Early* Monday morning would probably be the best time — Or, if at some time on Sunday, when I am out, you could leave a simple message, that is, naturally, if you find you will have the time to spare for a "country cousin"!

I'll mail this now, *Sunday morning* . . .

Aff —

D.

P.S. *Please* don't forget to tell your family who is coming to the house!!! Though I have no more trouble with the men at the gate! P.S. Wednesday the 13th Friday —

[FDR did come up, they spent time together, and Roosevelt explained that MM meant "My Margaret." Daisy then signed this and many subsequent letters YM — "Your Margaret."]

[New York]

May 1st [1936]

This mass of scribble leaves today! We go to Rhinebeck Friday! Good luck — Y.M.

Dear F. Do you mind if I do a little thinking aloud — on paper? The subject is Friendships, and the way they start and grow — An introduction, a shake of the hand, a few casual words to begin — and then, by various stages, sometimes slowly and sometimes remarkably quickly, the friendship is established — That's the usual way, and the friendship is tested in its different stages, and usually finds very definite limits not so far from the surface.

On rare occasions, however, it seems to *start* in the deepest depths, where the important elements are — and in these rare cases, the superficial elements are completely unimportant. They can be, however, a source of *interest* and *amusement* — a never-ending voyage of discovery to strange and distant lands — with never a feeling of fear, because of the safe & solid ship one *knows* is underfoot —

How badly expressed! I'll try again sometime with a new combination of words — I never *was* made to be a talker!

Politics! — for a moment! It *is* a fact that everything started "going up" after [Al Smith's] Liberty League speech — and they *will* keep on up — if you keep on as you are doing now — facts — and figures — and — principles. What *can* be said against them — And you then put your campaign on that "higher level" you spoke of — And then your second term will be all the more effective & inspiring — You won't have to think of politics then, will you? Or at least only to a much smaller extent. Four years more of hard work! It seems awfully long when you look ahead — but it passes very quickly when there is *so* much to be done.

Ten times a day, I think of subjects, just touched on, which one could have carried on for hours — But either a lovely tree, or a distant view, or the "fret" [fretwork] on an old house, would turn one's mind away — But just *being* was the important thing — wasn't it —

. . . Monday morning
. . . The week-end was lovely, and, strangely enough, *no one* asked me *why* I was there!

This morning, with the paper — some awfully nice mail!

[Another fragment carefully preserved by Daisy seems to fit here. The front represents one of the rare instances in which FDR admitted in writing to frustration and even a measure of self-pity at the demands of the presidency; the back is evidently part of a long litany of subjects they hadn't had time to talk over during their last brief visit. The "grand trip to the Azores" must be a reference to another of their drives through Dutchess County.]

[*Front*]

April 29th

Thurs. What a week — why did I come back — why this endless task — why run again — why see the endless streams of people — why the damned old basket of mail which is either full & hanging over my head or just emptied & ready to be filled

[*Back*]

the book work you've been doing & the O. Library — & solemn political problems — & Louis Howe [FDR's closest adviser, who had died on April 18, after a long illness] (I wanted to tell you about him) & enough other things to take 365 days a year for 50 years —

But — wasn't it a grand trip to the Azores, etc., etc., etc., & weren't . . .

[Daisy's letter continues]

I'm *so* glad you had that weekend on the Potomac — with the nice Murrays [Lieutenant Colonel Arthur Murray, an old friend of FDR's, was a prominent member of the British Liberal Party, assistant military attaché in Washington during World War I, and one-time parliamentary secretary to Foreign Minister Sir Edward Grey] . . .

I have *not* read Lord Grey's book — the O. Library would *love* having it — I *know* — And *I* wanted, also, to talk about Louis Howe — I am sure he was a great man, and I've cut out a good many accounts of him —

Speaking of the Knob, at Warm Springs — the same thing has happened in Dutchess! Usually in a wooded road and *once* on the top of a Hill! You didn't know that did you!!

[Dowdell's Knob near Warm Springs offers a splendid sunset view of the Georgia countryside. If a polio patient seemed about to give in to despair, Roosevelt once told a fellow survivor, he or she was to be brought up to Dowdell's Knob right away; one look at the glorious view would provide the will to go on. The site was also a favorite necking spot for local young people. It is impossible to know for certain to which use of the Knob FDR referred. Perhaps a little of each.]

I really have to keep *some* things out of sight — at least — where I *think* they are out of sight!

Wed–Thurs.!!
May 6th–7th
    . . . That basket of mail! I'm sure it *does* hang over your head — It's rather symbolical of the *routine* side of your job! But what you are *really* doing through the medium of that mail basket & those endless conferences is *so* wonderful — Gov. Lehman [Herbert Lehman succeeded FDR as governor of New York] is having *his* troubles! You wouldn't think they would pick on a thing like the Social Security to fight against — would you —
    Poor F. Paris — I'm *so* sorry for him — He is in such a state of nerves & unhappiness over his wife — his boy — and his own loneliness — At the moment he is swamped by the World's Fair meetings, and conferences, and more meetings, & more conferences — and he's just getting himself more & more tired out, and so, more & more unhappy — I tell him to take a trip, or go abroad for a year or so, and get away from everything for a time — but he seems to feel he has to keep *doing* something, every minute — Couldn't you send him as an Ambassador to Monaco or Liechtenstein or Andorra?
    Or, do you think *I* should take your mother's suggestion and marry him? He might not accept the suggestion, for I can assure you that he has never even hinted at such a thing to me! But "they say" that when a man is in his condition of mind — a woman can do *anything* with him.
    Not so long ago, you yourself said that I should get someone to "look after me"!

Friday.
    . . . [T]he future is full of possibilities of adventure, no matter what its dangers — the only thing we must *not* lose, is our capacity to meet what comes with a free spirit and an open mind — A free

spirit — that implies somehow the wind blowing in your face on a hilltop — and through your mind and your heart — blowing away all dust & cobwebs — and leaving a memory of itself, even when you have to come down to the crowded dusty streets —

If one could only bring down that clearing wind to the crowds in the dusty streets! But no — one can only *tell* them about it; they must climb the hill of their own accord —

Saturday
. . . This morning at about five A.M. I awoke with a start at the zooming of an aeroplane overhead — One leap took me to the window and there, far up, over Long Island, her green & red lights shining brightly in the dawning sky — was the *Zeppelin!* She moved quickly, and disappeared behind the water-tank on the next roof! It was really thrilling and she had such a beautiful clear morning to land —

This morning, sewing furniture covers & making bags for E. Lynch [Elizabeth Montgomery Lynch, Daisy's much older cousin and benefactress, was the proprietor of a New York business of her own] — And, accompanied by the whirr of the sewing machine was an argument between M. & D. [an internal debate, between Margaret and Daisy].

"If you get through that work quickly — you can get home early, and there *may* be a letter —"

"Nonsense, there won't be any letter this week —" "Well, there *might* be —"

"Of course not — the wretch (!) *expects one from you*"!

"He said he did, but I said 'not for weeks' — But you scratched out the *s* and put a question mark — that certainly might be taken to imply . . ."

"Well, anyway, he knows I simply can't have Missy receiving one every week —"

"Well, anyway."

— Repeats — Repeats!!! Etc. Etc.!!

And so it goes — entirely too often — !!

Monday — Thank heaven — it's cool again — Quite perfect, all day Sunday — the streets in their Sabbath quiet — Couples, and families, and old ladies with pet dogs — strolling around, with a peaceful look on their faces which they lose in the hurry of everyday life — Lonely people, too, who don't know how to make a contact with other human beings — I think those are really the people to be pitied most — don't you think so — and how surprisingly many there are —

Are you having a little more free time these days? I see there were *only two* appointments Saturday! That sounds quite miraculous! The mail basket must have been actually empty for some hours!

You spoke, the other day, of the thousands of transient workmen in the country — wouldn't the Swiss system be a solution? As I remember it, many many years ago *every* adult had to have his "papiers," which showed where he belonged — At the first sign of vagrancy — begging, etc. — the police asked for his papers, and, if he needed help, shipped him straight back to his own village, which *had* to take care of him — You rather hinted at such a system, but the first step would be to make every one *have* a settled home somewhere —

Would Mr. Winant be a good president? I've been surprised that they haven't brought up his name before — or are they keeping him back as the dark horse, or for 1940! He is a wonderful person, isn't he? [John G. Winant, a businessman and former Republican governor of New Hampshire, was named by FDR to head the Social Security Board. He resigned that post to counter GOP attacks on his program and later succeeded Joseph P. Kennedy as ambassador to the Court of St. James's.]

A most mysterious thing has happened! On my mother's desk, on Saturday, I found a "Natural History" magazine, addressed to me, and brought it to my room. This morning, I opened it, to find that the first article is on "Canvasback Ducks in Northumberland" by Viscount Grey of Fallodon!

And among the pictures are two photographs of Sequoias, planted respectively in 1845 & 1862!

Did you by any possible chance send me this? It is the Sept–Oct. copy, of 1932 —

Or, is this one of those strange coincidences? The magazine may have been lying around on a closet shelf all this time — no one knows anything about it in this apartment —

Speaking of mysterious things — could I, some time, see those "messages" of Lincoln & Washington etc? I'd so love to, if you had no objection —

[Daisy reveled in this sort of not-so-spooky coincidence. FDR may have, too. Someone had evidently sent him "spirit messages," allegedly from Washington and Lincoln, and he thought enough of them to mention them to Daisy in a part of his letter now missing.]

. . . We are off on Friday morning — a car-load of three ladies (back seat *thoroughly* filled!), a mass of bags in the front seat, and your humble servant on the little seat — clutching some plants and a fragile hat box — for their respective safeties! Excelsior travels *inside* the crown of a hat in a mass of tissue paper — that pointing beak of his is very dangerously placed on his long neck —

[Fragment of letter from FDR]

May 11 — Sat night the Press Club was fun — & I actually made a good speech because it wasn't prepared! & I didn't really give a D — because it couldn't be reported — Think of its being lost to posterity! I hate my speeches — so I took myself completely by surprise & was quite cheerful all day yesterday, even though I had to . . .

* * *

[Rhinebeck]

Friday — May the 15th, 1936

Dear F.

We're here! And I for one am exhausted! I've been packing & unpacking since 6.30 this morning — With lunch and the 3-hour drive between —

Such a beautiful day — with a warm sun and bracing cold breeze — Just perfect Dutchess County Weather — and only *one* thing missing to make it all complete! Can you guess what that "thing" is? . . .

Saturday — Another gorgeous day — And I got out all my summer clothes — including *my panama* & my tennis racket — Also, I pushed the cultivator down two long rows of beans, while waiting for the car — So good for the shoes which are supposed to be driving with Mrs. L[angdon]. (*Can* one be a farmer & a lady-of-leisure at the same time?)

Are you going to Brazil after Election Day?

Monday A.M.! MAIL! [This letter from FDR is missing.] And I am feeling *so* much better — I was rather distracted & harassed too and to the point of feeling rather sorry for myself — and — you gave me a resounding (mental) slap on the back — told me what an *idiot* I am, & made me realize that *my* troubles are *nothing* compared to yours — So I am feeling strong again — and ashamed of myself — thanks *so* much —

And I've just finished my figurings for this fiscal year for the Deaconess — and torn up *pages* of calculations which were caused by *one* mistake, months ago — I haven't told the Deaconess — but it was *her* mistake! Poor woman — *She* is harassed by a million things all day & every day, too — and she *should* have a daily secretary, instead of one who comes intermittently, as I do — However — it all "balances" in the end.

In case you've missed this *valuable* clipping!! No wonder we ordinary citizens are in a state of panic — when we realize what sort of a man is in the White House! [Enclosed was a shrill letter to the editor, denouncing FDR as a dangerous radical.]

Seriously, however, there *are* people who take a letter like this literally, and I suppose *they* have to be reassured, too!

Couldn't you tell them, just as you might explain it to me — if I were thinking you too radical, etc. Of course you *do*, but it has to be repeated, over and over again, for they hear *so* much on the other side, constantly —

Tuesday . . . I'm sorry about the Guffey decision, & wonder what you're going to do about it — As you said about the AAA decision, "it's a nuisance"!! [The Supreme Court had recently invalidated the Agricultural Adjustment Administration. Now it had destroyed another central piece of New Deal legislation, the Guffey Bituminous Coal Act.]

I do hope these conservative opinions of the Supreme Court are not going to prove to be too reactionary, with serious results. I certainly believe in working things out carefully & thoroughly, but not to the point where you drive people to violence — And various comments of labor groups look rather ominous — Let us pray they will use peaceful means —

Aff.

Y.M.

* * *

49 East 65th Street

Oct 31st '36

> 6 tickets enclosed for
> Democratic Rally at Mad. Sq. Garden

Dear D. [FDR to Daisy]

Here are six tickets. You should get there by about 6 to 6:30 P.M. — What a long wait.

Can you call me *now* before 10:40 at Rhinelander 7890 — or between 2:30 and 3 P.M.? *Very important*

F

⌒ Election night — I was invited to Hyde Park & sat in the dining room for a while, just to see how the thing is done: From the next room, the typewritten telegrams came on long strips to the President as fast as he could read them. This continued until 3.30 A.M.

I joined the 80-odd people in the Library & at 10 we had a buffet supper — Harry Hooker was there — Fannie Hurst, the writer — [journalist] Stanley High and his wife — the Governor of Bermuda & his wife — all the family, of course — On leaving at 12.15 midnight — I looked into the dining room door — F was still poring over the figures! Everyone else was exhausted — he was still as strong as ever . . .

Such a triumph for F.D.R.! [Roosevelt had won the greatest popular landslide in history up to that time, carrying every state but Maine and Vermont.] And he is quiet & rather humbled by it. He thinks only of the added responsibility on his shoulders — I feel he will proceed very cautiously. He said he would have to do some very heavy thinking on his trip to S. America. It will be an opportunity, when away from innumerable people with ideas & advice.

U.S.S. *Indianapolis*
Sat. Eve.

Nov. 21

[FDR to Daisy]
I wished so this morning that mail might come as fast as radio — We got in to Port of Spain, Trinidad, at six, & I found a few official documents which had left Washington the day after I left — I signed, then had breakfast, then received the Deputy Governor, the Am. Consul & their wives & the press, & went fishing while the two cruisers took on fuel oil — We travelled about 25 miles escorted by a British Colonel — he may have been a good colonel, but he didn't even get one bite for any of us! It is always thus — if we take any local guide who-knows-all-about-it with us, the fish disappear — & when we go alone, with no local knowledge, we always do well — I blistered my nose and we got back on land at 1:30 & left on the long voyage at once — 3,279 miles to Rio — longer than across the Atlantic.

Tonight I signed documents & did lots of oddy endy things — Isn't it grand to do that! I have few chances in this type of life — & I begin to think the electorate made a grave mistake Nov. 3 — for it does not help one's *happiness* to think of four years more!

However there is compensation and that helps *such* a lot — Doesn't it?

Sunday–22nd — Church services this morning on the well deck — but the Chaplain's sermon was very long & the sun very hot — He did not have the Navy hymn "Eternal Father" — I wish some day you could hear it sung on one of our ships — I sunned on the top deck this P.M. & sorted some stamps & Capt. Hewitt came to dine. Out of a clear blue sky he mentioned that he knew the Hudson — for he had married a Hunt & stayed with the Tom Hunts at Tivoli — His wife is a cousin of Virginia's — Isn't the world small? [The Hunts were Dutchess County friends and cousins of Eleanor Roosevelt's.] I felt like saying "Do you know a friend of Virginia's etc" — Why is it that I want to talk about a C.P. & have to bite my tongue to stop doing it?

Every night there has been a very clear moon & it is now almost overhead — & I tell stories to the stars & the messages go like this: [See above.]

And then in the middle of it C.P. says that isn't the least bit necessary because here we both are & it's a very poor movie anyway & we might just as well start telling some of those million things we haven't got to yet —

This afternoon was nice because when I was up under the guns

of No 2 Turret right by the canvas windbreak a black squall came on
us with sharp rain — sunshine one minute — then stinging drops for
one minute then sunshine again — & how C.P. loved it. We were dry
again in no time — Here is where I sit [see above].

Monday 23 — All is preparation for the Crossing of the Equator
— I am the Senior Pollywog & this afternoon I set "watches" on top
No 2 Turret & on the bow, two officers & two enlisted men changing
at ½ hour intervals (all of them also Pollywogs) — dressed up in
ridiculous costumes — watching for Davy Jones or Peg Leg to come
on board over the bow — Sure enough at 7:30 tonight there was a
loud beating of drums and blowing of bugles & they appeared with
their retinue in splendid costumes & all of us witnessed the ceremony
of announcing that at noon tomorrow Father Neptune & his court
will come on board to initiate all Pollywogs into the mysteries of the
deep & make them into Shellbacks!

Tues. 24th — At last YF [Your Franklin] is a Shellback! Are
you duly proud of him? Are you still going to take care of him as you
always have? Really quite very lucky that I am — for when you
"cross the line" I will try to make the initiation easier for you by using
all my influence with the other Shellbacks —

As a matter of fact I got off very lightly — The King, Queen,
Royal Baby & a large Court retinue appeared in the most gorgeous

costumes, were duly seated on a platform & then the fun began — I
had to make a speech in defense — but the others were ducked in a
tank, put in a coffin, "electrocuted," spanked, tickled, etc — over
200 of them & it lasted from noon till 4 —

We dined with Capt Hewitt & Com. Badger, the Executive Officer.

Wed. 25 — All on board have settled down to the usual routine
after the "show" of the past two days — and I slept till ten this
morning — We are back in the more crowded ship lanes — & have
passed 8 or 10, including an old German battleship which fired 21
guns as a salute to my Flag — Tonight the *Graf Zeppelin* flew over
us & around us on the trip from Rio Pernambucco & thence home.
She was most lovely in the moonlight & lights blinked from her cabin
1,000 feet above us — I sent a message of *"glückliche reise"* [happy
journey] in answer to her greetings.

I spend spare moments signing the King Neptune certificates — big
colored affairs — for the whole ship's company — about 700 of them!

Thurs. 26 — Thanksgiving Day — Church service this morning
& I offered up a *very special* little prayer —

We are busy with many dispatches about plans for tomorrow in
Rio — Later — 11 P.M.–9 P.M. in N.Y. All set for tomorrow ashore
— I must be on the top deck at 7:30 — to see the wonderful harbor
— Ambassador [Hugh] Gibson boards us at 8 & I will show him my
speech for final check-up — I finished it this P.M. It will be very hot
— (*not* the speech) & I have to appear in 3 different costumes —
What a relief when I get back on board at 10 tomorrow night —

I count on a letter in the A.M.!!!! but I fear there will be no chance
to answer it before we sail — You should get this in about 6 days &
another from [Buenos Aires] about 5 days later —

Bless you

F

* * *

Sat. Nov. 28 —

[FDR to Daisy]

What a happy day was Yesterday! And all because in my inside
pocket was something that came in the morning — as soon as we tied
up to the dock & before we went ashore: The 4-leaf clover [evidently
enclosed in Daisy's letter] is within 5 inches of C.P.'s heart — I meas-
ured it.

I'm glad you like the floating ladies — and I will tell you about
the suggestion for a Constitutional Convention at length *very soon*

— It is too dangerous to try in these jittery times — I hate Mark Sullivan [a newspaper columnist] because he is such a solemn patronizing idiot!

"Some day" I want you to see Rio — the amazing harbor — the city — and above all the orchids — You will have read all about the day's events — but the country place we lunched at was fantastic in the beauty of its surroundings — a lovely house filled with marvelous old furniture & paintings & below the Terrace a wide lawn going down to a lake — & the whole surrounded by great hills lush with tropic trees & flowers — Our host had picked 250 orchids outdoors to decorate before we came —

But they weren't O.H.'s — and it wasn't the Hudson — And something much more vital was missing, too —

The crowds were tremendously enthusiastic & all of the official things beautifully done — I was loaded with presents — but I did manage to get your Birthday present — If you can't explain it to the family you will have to wear it on your "undies" — So much for your Puritanical up-bringing! Which I nevertheless adore — at the correct time and place! Now will you be good!

Today we all slept late & I've been sending messages of thanks to half of Brazil, & also writing my [Buenos Aires] speech — It is difficult to avoid merely repeating what I said in Rio.

Sunday 29th — Church this morning and again a very long & tedious sermon — then more work on the speech & at 3 P.M. the Argentine fleet hove in sight & there was much saluting, manning the rail, etc & I was on my position forward for *more* than an hour — We are being escorted in by them and now at 11 P.M. we are all headed in to the wide estuary of the Rio de la Plata —

We dock at 1 P.M., are meeting Pres. [Augustín] Justo & being driven through crowds to the Embassy — What a 3 days we shall have!

I will have this ready to mail when we land because I *think* there is a plane in the afternoon, & I will *try* to send another line from Montevideo on Thursday the 3rd —

And I *hope* something is waiting for me tomorrow when I land — with news up to about the 23rd — It is going to be a long *gap* on the way back for we go without stop to Trinidad — getting there the 11th

Goodnight M. —

F

Mon. 30 — 11 A.M. We are entering the channel — Word came

that there will be no mail for us till Wed. P.M. or even Thur. A.M. at Montevideo — But I will send this, anyway.

[At Buenos Aires, on the evening of December 1, the President's companion Gus Gennerich suffered a fatal heart attack. ". . . [I]t has been a real shock and a real loss," FDR wrote to Eleanor. "Good old Gus was the kind of loyal friend who simply cannot be replaced." Roosevelt apparently wrote to Daisy about it, too, but more emotionally, in a letter now lost.]

Mailed Miami, Fla. Dec. 13th 6 P.M.
Sat. Dec. the 5th, '36

It is three busy days since I "scribbled" on Wed. eve on our way to Montevideo — and I fear it was a very doleful scribble — but you will understand as always — & though I tried talking to a very wise little bird and it helped, still it was only proxy help — & only C.P. could really answer — The more I think of it all, the more I dwell on poor Gus's love of the farm — he was so utterly wrapped up in it — all of a happy future was placed there — all kinds of enchanting vistas — not only of a happy life in Dutchess, but of all kinds of new adventures — gardening, trees, blueberries. And with it all I am certain that he thought much of the days when he would live there and at the same time be near to you and to me — He would so have loved the things he was buying — in Rio a "bargain" — always a bargain — a collection of horrible plates & saucers with butterflies and butterfly wings under the transparent surface — and some huge artificial flowers made out of bird feathers —

What shall we do about the place? — We can not tell yet of course till I have seen the nephew — The boy should probably sell it & put the money in trust for himself with Gus's life insurance — about $5,000 I think — That, with the value of the farm — say another $5,000 — would give him an income of $400 a year — But I hate to see that place just sold to anybody — don't you? Should I buy it — & you & I manage it? I long so to talk it all over with you — and I can't with anyone else & wouldn't want to if I could.

Thursday at Montevideo was really nice, for on landing I drove for over two hours with Pres. [Gabriel] Terra — all through the city with its waving, cheering crowds. Then out along the wonderful beaches & rocky promontories, back through the country to his villa — Then a formal lunch, his speech & mine, then a reception, then back to the ship & a dramatic departure with 75,000 people on the quay. The last time Pres. Terra entertained a visiting president [Getulio Dornelles] Vargas of Brazil last year), he was shot through the shoulder by an anarchist — & we got word they might try to get him again but would take precautions not to hit me.

I *must* learn Spanish — Why don't you move to W. & learn it with me —

Thursday night was an asterisk moment for me (very quietly) — at 11 P.M. we turned out of the Rio de la Plata & headed *North* — do you know whither that leads? This afternoon we passed Rio & at 3 anchored at Cape Frio for three hours, got into the launches & fished — not very successful, but lovely scenery and enough "groupers" for a couple of good chowders!

Sunday 6 — A long sermon in a baking sun — (& I wore my hat all through it) — & I have been filing papers & answering many election letters — also getting tanned again — I'm so thrilled about the coronation — of course you must go — it's a grand chance — & I so hope today's news of the king does not cast doubt on the *Ceremony!*

[British friends had arranged for Daisy to attend the coronation of Edward, Prince of Wales, as King of England. The "news" was that he was determined to marry the American divorcée Mrs. Wallis Warfield Simpson, a decision that would swiftly bring about his abdication.]

Tuesday 8th — A very interesting searchlight drill between this ship and the *Chester* just after dark tonight — The two ships 5 miles apart abreast of each other — each picked up the other's & the problem was to blind the "enemy" gunners by keeping the searchlights on the target in spite of changes in course and the roll of the ship.

At 7:35 P.M. we crossed the Equator! & now I'm back in the Northern Hemisphere where incidentally I think I belong. It has been muggy & sticky all day — a following wind.

Wednesday 9th — We hear that at Port of Spain on Friday we shall get 2 pouches and in them I count on a letter — I hope two — Also we hear that Col. [Edmund] Starling [chief of the Secret Service detail] will fly home from there that day — so I shall send this to be mailed by him in Miami — He should get there by Sat night or Sun morning — so perhaps you'll get this Monday — the day before I land — We plan to get to W. Tuesday evening late — too late I fear for me to telephone you — but I hope to find a letter awaiting — & I will call you up Wed. eve about 6:30.

I am having a simple service for Gus at the W.H. Wed. morning early — Then the body will be taken to N.Y. for the interment & Jimmy will go with it. I do want to go myself — but there are several things that make it absolutely necessary to stay in W. & settle them.

Today we have been quiet — amusing ourselves by making a "pool" on what the King Edward situation will be on Jan. 1. We wrote it down & all agree he would still be King — & I think he will make the lady "Duchess of Cornwall" — not Queen — & marry her & keep the throne — So you will go to his Coronation!

Thursday 10th — All wrong! He did abdicate & right in the middle of our lunch! Nevertheless, I suppose the Coronation will take place — "as usual" — only with a different victim — I hope much you & Virginia [Hunt] have arranged for rooms in London, for I hear that they are very hard to get.

We get in to the Port of Spain at 4 A.M. so I must close this — without even seeing your letter. It is such a long time since 3 weeks ago last Monday — Goodnight

Aff

F

1937

January 3, 1937

[FDR to Daisy]

I do not *exactly* know what a *Boiled Owl* feels like, but I think I have felt like one yesterday & today — just cold id by doze & general aches — nothing serious — & by staying in bed each morning it's nearly cured — Also it has *given me* a chance to work on the Message [State of the Union address] for next Wednesday — so far a very poor job but I begin to have "inspirations" & my dictation tonight was distinctly more logical! It will cause quite a sensation I think for the theme of it is that is if Democracy is to be successful it must function in all its parts — & the Supreme Court must do its share to keep up with the needs of the times just as much as the Congress and the Executive. Don't you think that is common sense?

I like your new stationery — the color goes with C.P. — When you get a summer dress, get a white one with blue trimmings & a big wide hat — I don't like the peanut affairs of this era!

Thurs. eve — The Annual Message is all done & I hope so that you will like it — Cold is nearly well & I think my voice will not show it tomorrow. It is a "long-range" message & I think good tempered but firm —

[Filled with confidence after his smashing victory, and still fuming over Supreme Court decisions that had undercut much of the New Deal, FDR sought to streamline the executive branch of government in his message to Congress on January 3. He followed up a little over a month later with a still more revolutionary proposal to change the judicial branch, as well. Under his proposal the President would have been empowered to add a new judge to the Court whenever a ten-year veteran waited more than six months after his seventieth birthday to resign or retire, for a total of six new justices.

There was a national outcry, in which even some of FDR's admirers joined. Daisy, too, was a little bothered, and asked Roosevelt to explain the proposal to her. He did so, in the loftiest possible terms.

"Don't you mean," she asked him when he had finished, "that you are *packing* it?"

FDR blinked a bit, then roared, "I suppose you're right, Daisy! I suppose you're right!"]

Did you know that I am a very firm person — except that where C.P. is concerned I'm not firm at all — & I'm being very obedient in listening to Fides — it's only 11 P.M. now — & I'm taking very good care of myself & trying not to get back the 9 lbs. I lost on the trip — You would almost be proud of my figger — I have a horror of getting really fat — but at my advanced age it means very constant supervision!

Aff

F.

*   *   *

[The White House]

Wed. 11 — [Aug. 1937]

Dear Daisy,

How very strange! But as we have both remarked it is in many ways a queer world — and really a very nice world in spite of its surface and some of the people who inhabit it — and it all depends on *understanding* —

What a time I've come back to — My *time* at H.P. made *all* the difference and I felt so much more cheerful & rested by Sunday and perspective returned — and calm — It looks like Sept. 1 before adjournment, but it's silly for these people to stay in their present frame of mind & I hope I get them out by the 21st — and to get back a few days later —

Sun. 15 — I'm down the [Potomac] River — just couldn't stand the heat & the rows & I've sat & read & fished & declined to talk to the people on board — & my mind has been miles away — Why, on a boat, should one's *mind* be on a hill with no water in sight — only a place where one knows there is another River?

It is hard to write here as people keep popping in & out of my room. We get back this P.M. Yesterday, like you, I gambled & won all these pools. $7.50 1st fish, biggest fish (2 and ½ lbs) & most fish (seven) — So the guests paid for their board & lodging!

Tues 17 — I'm off tonight for Roanoke & speak at 3:30 tomorrow — I have to fight this thing through — for it's queer that the mass of the people understand the spiritual values, & so few of our friends do — Remind me to tell you of 2 millionaires who came to see me — I should like some day to pick out 10 or 15 pages of what Christ taught & put them in a pamphlet to hand to society people & business men & lawyers — & some labor leaders.

[Roosevelt lost his struggle to enlarge the Supreme Court when the Senate voted down the proposal on July 22. Although changes of heart and personnel on the existing Court soon brought it more into line with his thinking, he did not forgive or forget those who had opposed him. On Tuesday, August 17, at Roanoke, he denounced them as favoring "the conduct of government by a self-perpetuating group at the top of the ladder." The next fall he would attempt to purge the Senate of Democrats who had voted against him — and would fail disastrously.]

Thurs. 19th — A very wonderful day yesterday & especially the pageant in the evening — Betty [Hambley] has told you of it — But

all the way through I *felt* the ground — The *exact spot* that Lost
Colony of men, women & children lived on until just before their
tragic end. [Captain John White left a colony of 117 persons on
Roanoke Island in 1587 and sailed home to England for supplies.
When he got back, in 1591, they had vanished, virtually without
a trace.]

Adjournment comes Sat. night — just as well — & I think I must
stay till Thurs.

Aff

F

* * *

Hyde Park, N.Y.

Thurs., Sept. 3rd '37

Dear Daisy —

This is an interesting letter from Arthur Murray & I think you
will like to read it. Let me have it back on Wed. & also those clippings
you said you would show me.

I think if you will all be here at 12 noon we can be on board [the
Potomac] & started up the River by 12:30 — I hope six of you can
come — Cousin Alvey (?) and Reggie [Livingston] are coming too —
also my Uncle Fred (who is a dear)

I am off in an hour — expect to *sleep* most of the time — will get
back Tuesday —

Aff

F.D.R.

[In the late summer of 1937, FDR took time out from his campaign to purge
the Senate of his enemies and draw up serious plans for the small house on
the hill he and Daisy loved.]

Monday, early! It is a beautiful day! [September, 1937]
Dear Franklin —

I've just had the most dreadful thought: I never got up at tea, on
Monday, when the President came into the room! You really *must*
remind me about such things! To myself, there is the excuse that I had
been spending pretty nearly 4 hrs. sitting in a car next to Thenicest-
personintheworld. But that would not go with outsiders, would it —

Wasn't O.H. lovely? And just full of dreams!

And this evening I roasted some chestnuts before the fire, & one of them exploded like a cannon ball —

Friday — I have the plans here, and pictures of the house too! And perhaps I shall *have* to take them down to show to the architect! Who knows?

Sunday — Until Wednesday! And thanks *so* many times for finding out about Katherine Davis [an old friend of Daisy's] — I am so awfully relieved.

Do you know that it is a constant wonder to me that I ever got along at all, before I came to *really* know C.P.! He is *such* a 24-hr. help in all ways —

Au rev —
YM

* * *

Sept. 21st P.M.

[Daisy to FDR]

. . . Do you suppose that Happy Times really do pass more quickly than unhappy ones? It certainly seems so — And I am so worried about your overworking — please don't run any risks — for everybody's sake and specially (very selfishly!) for the sake of YM — And — you see — if you don't take care of yourself — those rhododendrons, & azaleas, & laurels, & cypresses, & yews, & tulip poplars, & dogwoods, etc. won't be attended to — not to forget the Sequoias & the "fireplace." *All most* important! That plan you made has tremendous possibilities — I wonder if you have thought out any details — such as where the front door is — where the fireplace — What to do with that 3-sided space in the back!! I can think of lots of things! In fact, I have the furniture *placed!* Subject to change!

You know — you are really very bad, for you take advantage of a weak woman's yielding tendencies — but I must confess that there's no one to blame but herself & she hasn't *any* excuse to offer in her own defense! — She's just *weak*, & she's weak for the one & only reason that she wants to be weak. No dates — like the 21st being so near the 22nd, etc! (How fantastic!) — has *anything whatever* to do with the subject! This sounds somewhat like a confession! [September 22, 1937, would mark the second anniversary of the start of their new, fond relationship.]

I told the family at home I was lunching with you — and I am glad *your family* was there — It is much better so, & does not raise so many eyebrows! So I told Aunt Sophie all about who was at lunch, & the redwood — and then enlarged on my activities at home. I really accomplished a lot today — I mowed the circle & the edges all around the house — I fixed an old bicycle up — if the tires are still full of air tomorrow I'll know they are good, & will probably ride back to Aunt Sophie's on it.

. . . I find a tiny variety "Cornus Canadensus" only 6–8 inches high, which grow in close patches, "forming a perfect carpet" [suitable for surrounding their hilltop cottage] —

A spring "carpet" of English bluebells would be beautiful, too —

The nuttali or pacific Dogwood has, so far, refused to grow in our Eastern climate — It reaches 60 ft. in British Columbia! *Just* the thing for an experiment on O.H. . . .

Wednesday the 22nd You're going to find me a very contradictory person, for, on thinking it over — The 22nd did have just a *tiny* bit to do with it — but only a tiny bit — It was almost entirely just plain weakness.

Thursday . . . Do you suppose you ever could come to tea on some Saturday or Sunday, so that I could get a few more friends & relatives to meet you? I could perhaps "do them all up" at once! *So* many have been begging for *years* to meet you!

C.P. is feeling rather hectic this week, for she is not only carrying on in her role of Daisy Suckley, at Rhinebeck — but she is also travelling at high speed across the continent *24 hours a day* [FDR was campaigning across the country] — and just now, she must be approaching Omaha with its handsome modernistic station! Four years ago Aunt S. & I spent about four hours there, between trains, in a hotel room — and as the water was piping hot, and the radiator equally so, it seemed a good opportunity to wash my hair! Aunt S. thought me a little off — but it worked beautifully —

I remember that Omaha seemed to be the real beginning of the "West." Ten-gallon hats — and huge handsome cowboys! We sat at dinner with two of them & next morning had to get out of the train for breakfast in a typical "goldrush" village, and the lady of the restaurant firmly made us sit at a table for four with two more cowboys — they all of them were so nice & so friendly that Aunt S. very soon lost her look of terror, & talked most intimately with them!

Then we got off at Casper Wyo. and were driven by Barrett [the Reverend Barrett Tyler, Daisy's cousin, married one of Mrs. Langdon's daughters and was an Episcopal missionary to the Indians] 150 miles in just three hours, to the mission — What *are* you going to look at in Casper! There seemed to be nothing there but a few streets, & oil-wells! Beyond that point, I have never been — but I can imagine the greatness and *bigness* of it all — Your trip sounds really nice — I do so hope it will prove to be a *rest* — Don't forget that you *promised* to take up that question of a *rest after lunch!*

Tuesday Sept. 28th — Gracious, it's almost a week since I wrote last, and it's been such fun travelling [in her imagination] through Wyoming & the Yellowstone & Idaho, and now up north through Washington! One of the interesting things about it has been the impressions of the correspondents — These trips must do them a lot of good in the way of broadening their outlook.

It all seems to show what last year's election showed, that *most* of the people of this country do their own thinking, and do it rather intelligently — Isn't that the greatest possible safeguard against "issues" of all sorts? It's really very thrilling, & I see from your speech at Boise (I think that's the one) that you are getting real rest and inspiration from the "open spaces" — I am *so* glad . . .

Wednesday, 29th P.M.

. . . *Friday* — Judge [Hugo] Black is going to make a speech tonight — I am so glad, for he will surely justify himself. [Supreme Court nominee Black's early membership in the Ku Klux Klan was proving an embarrassment to the administration.] I may be all wrong — but I've felt from the beginning of all this Klan talk, as Senator [George W.] Norris seemed to feel, that perhaps he did belong to the Klan — but that did not necessarily mean that he might not make a very great Judge on the Supreme Court — *On verra!*

Another thing which there was no time to discuss among *far* more important ones! But I felt you were worried over it —

Saturday — I wish you could have heard the speech last night — I shall from henceforth stand up for Judge Black no matter *what* happens!! As for the *Tribune* editorial today — well — I am glad I do not know Mrs. Ogden Reid [publisher of the New York *Herald Tribune*]. That paper is a disgrace.

Aunt S. & I had the nicest day — all by ourselves — this morning we did letters & bills & painting — this afternoon we sat in the sun on the porch reading aloud & working — then tea & more reading by the fire.

. . . Part of the time — whether or not induced by the open fire, I don't know — I was some 12 miles from here, on a Hill, sitting before a fire also — very near the corner of a sofa. Someone was reading aloud — two french windows on each side of the fireplace, opened onto a porch — Outside — it was dark under the trees & a wind rustled what remained of autumn leaves — Across the length of the back of the room were book shelves right up to the ceiling — In the middle, a door opening onto a terrace facing East!

Sunday night. I made a quite perfect floor plan — but suddenly realize that the chimney will stick up in a very queer place — [See opposite page.]

*   *   *

Thursday — [October 7, 1937]

Dear F.

It was *so* nice to have a little talk with you this morning — and to hear at *first* hand that you had a good trip — It certainly *seemed* "good" from the accounts in the papers. I have voluminous clippings for you, which I'll give you when I see you, on a thousand subjects!

. . . I *hope* to get down to the ceremony next Wednesday [FDR was to lay the cornerstone for a new post office in Poughkeepsie] — the *following* Monday or Tuesday would be the best for a drive, I think — If you could call me up, perhaps on Sunday, around 2 P.M. is the best time, as I am apt to be reading the paper then, while the rest of the household "rests"!

It is just too tragic about Mrs. Hopkins [Barbara Duncan Hopkins, Harry Hopkins's second wife, had died of cancer that same day], for they were very happy, weren't they, and she was such a sweet person — You remember that I sat between you & her on the way back from the Washington picnic and liked her so much —

Are you remembering that you *promised* to plan for that after-lunch rest?! Even 15 minutes would help — with your *eyes closed!* That's an important point, as you can't *completely* relax if you are reading or talking — *please!*

Hoping to see you soon —

Aff.

D.

Friday, Oct. 8th

. . . Is it awfully silly writing these letters which should go off on their respective dates, & should be answered every day!! Instead — I'll give you this when everything is obsolete. Oh my — it just is rather distracting. But you needn't bother to read through — for I just love to talk along, & say nothing — &, under the circumstances,

induced by the open fire, I don't know —
I was some 12 miles from here, on a
Hill, sitting before a fire also - very near
the corner of a sofa. Someone was
reading aloud — Two french windows
on each side of the fireplace, opened
onto a porch - Outside - it was dark
under the trees & a wind rustled what
remained of autumn leaves — Across
the length of the back of the room were
book shelves right up to the ceiling - In
the middle, a door opening onto a
terrace facing East!

Sunday night. I made a quite perfect (?)
floor plan - but suddenly realize that the
chimney will stick up in a very queer
place

It wont do at all!

View from the south!

road

How's This?

other wing behind

road

Kitchen porch

View from the West.

it's the best we can do — Quite "by the way," we "do" rather well,
I think!

Oct. 13th A.M. Your [radio] "chat" last night was *splendid* —
But have you a cold? There was one cough!

The Crowleys [Mr. and Mrs. E. Chase Crowley of Rhinebeck] are
taking me down to the cornerstone in a half hour & I'll be looking
at you with an eagle eye to see if you are feeling all right!

Your letter came by *special delivery* yesterday, right after lunch,
& with my frequent luck, the man happened to come to the house
with the station wagon, & I jumped in & went to the P.O. for the
letter! Only the maid, who took the telephone message about a "special delivery," was any the wiser about it!

. . . Aunt Sophie & I discovered a fascinating wood road yesterday,
between Clinton Corners and Pleasant Valley! It is almost straight —
very overgrown, & follows the Wappingers Creek for what seemed
several miles! Do you know it? A wonderful road on which to get
lost — for it looks almost deserted — It was marked "Creek Road"
at Pleasant Valley —

P.M. Well — it was rather unsatisfactory this morning, for we
could not get anywhere near the platform, & several people stood on
a sort of ramp right in front of the speakers — so that we could not
see one thing — meaning any one *person* — not even the top of his
head! It was also hard to hear, though we did hear you would claim
the credit for what was liked, etc!

[Some citizens of Poughkeepsie had objected to FDR's having taken part in
designing their new post office. "Let me straighten out this matter of my
being the architect," FDR told the crowd before he lay the cornerstone. "I
think the easiest way to put it is this: if, when this new post office is completed and the murals are in place and you good people of Poughkeepsie have
had a chance to look at it, if, then, you like it, I will take all the credit in the
world. But if you don't like it when it is finished, why, I had nothing to do
with it whatsoever."]

As soon as you finished speaking we rushed around the block to
the car which was parked just where you would drive out! I stood on
the running board & waved & called, but got no sign of recognition!!
Very humiliating!

Friday — How happy your mother must be to have you with her.
I just couldn't get a car to go to see her this week — In fact, my winter

coat has been in Poughkeepsie two weeks & I can't get down to get it! I wonder how I'll manage on Monday!

Through some accident, I find I haven't the Chicago Speech, & I *do* want it, *so* much [presumably a copy of FDR's 1932 acceptance speech at the Democratic National Convention in which he pledged "a New Deal for the American people"]. Would you by any chance have an extra copy? Or perhaps you'd send me a copy for Christmas! *With* a note!

Sunday night — I wonder why it is that tomorrow promises to be one of the really nice days of the year!! *Can* you imagine why? [They were to take another drive together to their hill.]

I walked down to the gate in the moonlight — such a moonlight — but there was a pinkish glow all around the moon — & I fear bad weather tomorrow — not that it really matters at all! We might take another drive in the rain . . .

À bientôt!

YM

* * *

Wednesday P.M.

Dear F. A lot of the glow of tea time is still about me — which means that I am "actively engaged in" being very happy! I've read again that wonderful speech, and, since, I've been studying the plans [for the cottage on their hill], & longing to discuss certain variations from mine — I think that "porch recess" is a splendid idea — also those little corner fireplaces — in fact I must confess that it all seems *better* than mine!

You have made the wings much bigger than I, & we've both planned for lots of book space! Do you think it might be a good idea to have windows on the north & south ends of the living room? There would be such lovely vistas to look through!

Just one thing *really* worries me! And that is the angle of the attic floor!! The trunks will be continually coasting down to the eaves . . . But that is probably just a minor detail which can be easily arranged! I'll bring all these plans down to W. We can argue about them, & I can be just as facetious as I wish — You won't mind — will you!

Oh my — we *were* so happy this P.M. — but I must go to sleep — Goodnight & God bless you —

Friday P.M. Yesterday, I drove to Brattleboro Vt. in pouring rain both going & coming — *And,* with the thought of C.P. in my mind, I was *very particularly* careful! I really *do* drive carefully & well, so there's not much to worry about — And I love to drive myself — excepting with One person — as I believe I said before!

Were you a little dazed when we all told you at once that you were coming to tea at both Suckleys & Langdons? You see, Aunt S. is a little deaf, & she understood that I was asking you to tea, & that naturally she must say something as I am with her — I am disappointed as I did want you at *our* house — but perhaps next spring we can have another tea!

I've spent ages on the plans, & *think* I have the south wing perfected. We'll see if you agree, or if I'm all wrong! It's all done to scale too!

[Rhinebeck, too, needed a new post office, and FDR hoped that it would replace the dilapidated town hall that stood next door to the handsome old Beekman Arms hotel and be made to look as much as possible like the long-vanished fieldstone house of Henry Beekman. That simple seventeenth-century dwelling, built by an ancestor whom both he and Daisy claimed, had burned to the ground in 1910. But even this matter could not be freed from politics, as Daisy quickly found out when she began doing research on the President's behalf.]

About the Beekman house: [John] Newman [the Suckleys' former chauffeur, who still lived in their carriage house apartment but was now a driver for hire and a Packard dealer] said no one had thought of putting it next to the hotel — Miss [Evelyn] Oliver [a registered nurse who ran a charitable institution called Holiday Farm, supported by the Hudson River families] tells me that all the "best" people in Rhinebeck *do* want it *just there,* and that last year, a petition was signed to that effect!

Saturday 10 A.M. — Well!

. . . I've just written Betty [Hambley] that I *hope* to go to her [in Washington] for a weekend in Nov. *possibly* the 19th, and that you said something about our all going to Church with you *if* & *when* I should go to Wash.

I do hope you will find time to see them soon — & then you might ask when I am coming down? etc. etc.! [FDR and Daisy still had to invent pretexts to meet.]

Monday —

. . . Of course I won't get a word with you this P.M.! Please do not call me up in N.Y.! Perhaps you were not thinking of it anyway! The [Barrett] Tylers will almost certainly be there off & on — mostly on — If plans should become more certain, I'll let you know — Aunt S. [and] Marie [Mrs. Langdon's personal maid] & I go to N.Y. Tuesday the 9th . . . and I am planning for Washington the week-end of the 19th.

Its been a very wonderful Fall — with far more *happiness* than I am entitled to!

Please, please take care of yourself —

YM

* * *

[November 1937]

Dear Franklin —

. . . I've been wondering if, after all, it might not be interesting to have historical murals in the P.O. because, no matter what the architecture may be *outside,* the *inside* will be a modern P.O. [Daisy's notion evidently struck FDR's fancy; the murals, depicting the town's early history, and painted by their mutual friend and neighbor Olin Dows, still decorate the interior.]

Aff —

D.

* * *

Thursday
Nov. 4th

I'm pretty well fixed up for moving to N.Y.: Things sorted out for here — for Wilderstein — and to go to town — Only Excelsior goes with me — for I'll have the little room this winter, with the Tylers coming and going —

Tomorrow you'll be having the Hambleys . . .

I've *such* an exciting book: "Northwest Passage" by Kenneth Roberts, about the French & Indian Wars . . .

Sunday P.M. I'm sitting on the end of the sofa where you sat; the fire is crackling; my feet are on a stool, and I'm thinking of *such nice* things!

Monday — . . . I had a long talk on the village street with New-man which is important, I think — He talks to everybody, and gets the opinions of Democrats & Republicans, as he has no political interest in what is done — He says there is strong opposition to the Town Hall site, in a certain group of Republicans, *because* Benson Frost [a prominent lawyer and head of the local Democratic Party, therefore anathema to the Republicans who ran the town] is being consulted — Apparently Jacob Strong [the publisher of the Rhinebeck *Gazette*] is considered more of a Democrat than a Republican, so that his being consulted also is no help! These people are saying it's evidently all politics — and they are even asking how much benefit the Dows family are to get by improving the approach to the hotel!! [Tracy Dows, who had recently died, had remodeled and run the Beekman Arms after losing most of his fortune in the Crash.] Right after Newman left me someone said to him: "I suppose the Suckleys will get a large amount for the stone"! [Roosevelt planned to use the actual old stones from the ruins of the Beekman House, which lay on a parcel owned by the family in Rhinecliff.]

I suppose you are quite accustomed to that kind of thing! Well — I asked Newman to go around & get all the most antagonistic opinions he can find & write them to me. I will send his letter on to you.

On the other side, the majority of the people seem to want the plan to go through, & the Town Board, most of them Republicans, seem to be all for it. *But,* the present Town Board goes out of office next January — Newman thinks the Post Office Department should take up the subject directly with the Town Board headed by Harry Pottenburgh, and *not* through Benson Frost. Also, it would be best not to mention the Beekman house or anything *to do* with the type of building, until the site is settled by a special election. Harry Pottenburgh is the Republican leader up here, and according to Newman, about the only one — He's an awfully nice man, too.

Of course this is only Newman's opinion after talking to many people, but it sounds sensible to me . . .

By the way, were you rather surprised at the amount of "service" you had at tea last Monday? I told the maids I could hardly see you, for they were passing things to you over & over again. Usually there is only one on hand at a time, but they got out their best uniforms & aprons, & they say the cook would have come too, if there had been a uniform big enough for her!

Monday, still later! S. says they surely won't be in town this week — probably not until after Thanksgiving. So — *if* it's convenient, I shall be ready to answer a call. Don't worry, though, if you can't put it through for any reason — I shall be reading the paper, as well as I can tell at such a distance, between 8.30 & 10 A.M. on Sunday!

I'll get this off now —

Aff —

D

* * *

Sunday —

Foxhall Village [the home of the Hambleys in Washington, D.C.]

[November–December 1937]

Dear F.

We've just come from the little chapel and a sweet, simple little service. The sun is shining half way across the floor of this house — and outside, on a green, some boys & dogs are chasing a football & each other — It's a dear little house, so easy to run and so convenient in every way, and warm & comfortable — a perfect example of what this country stands for, for the "average man" — But, upstairs in my bag, are plans for a Dutch house — just as comfortable & convenient and cheerful — but surrounded by trees and distance and peace and a glow of an open fire. Did you think the south wing plan good — really? Of course, the middle room has the bigger closet — and the eastern room is the larger — But, you see, the occupant of the middle room would probably spend a *lot* of time in the eastern room & she *needs* a big closet! How is this for a name: "O. House on O.H." and for that entrance, there could be quite a large glass square room which could be used in the mornings as a sun porch — [It seems clear from this letter that Daisy thought she would one day be living at least part of the time with FDR on the hilltop she still considered theirs.]

. . . I wonder how you are — & wish so I could help — I know you have many things on your mind & of course they *are* your job — but the rest of the government have *their* jobs too — and you must let them do their own — & not try to do it all yourself —

On the train [back to New York] today I read quite a lot of [Harold] Laski's *Freedom in the Modern State* & found it intensely interesting: the product of real thinking — & such a relief after the day-by-day bickerings of people like Lippmann and Mark Sullivan — (I don't read Sullivan anymore! — he annoys me too much.) Perhaps you'd like to take Laski's book with you on your trip — I'm glad you are going but wish you could get right off now — [Roosevelt was planning another fishing vacation, to the Caribbean this time.]

I put a few "gentle" marks along the margins, do you mind? Just when there seemed to me to be a particularly interesting point —

Tuesday — These last lines show what happens to C.P. in the evening! *Even* when writing to HF [Her Franklin]!

I was about to say that V[irginia Hunt] would be *delighted* to go to the Vice-pres.' dinner! M.L.S. would too!

. . . Do you *really* think you could take that trip to Endless Caverns next spring? Margery [Mrs. Benjamin] King came to Betty's on Sunday and it appears that the Caverns belong to her brother [Edward Brown] now and he & his wife have this rambling old house — the center of which was a log cabin originally, & is now the dining room —

. . . Margery made up this plan to give you an idea how conveniently it is planned — You & your "retinue" could have that suite all to yourselves! And the S.S. can be on the porches all night — the rest of us would be disposed of on the second floor.

Would McDuffie sleep on a trip like this? [Irvin McDuffie was the President's black valet, essential to his getting dressed and undressed but not easily housed in that segregated time.]

M. says there is a little cabin nearby where she is sure he could be installed — Oh my! We have *all* the details arranged! I suppose the cars & chauffeurs could go into the town for the night —

Thursday Don't eat too much Turkey today! The papers the last two days have been really interesting — and perhaps that toothache of yours is a blessing in disguise (very *much* in disguise) [FDR had an abscessed tooth, which would finally force him to cut short his fishing trip] because it has made it possible for you to stay quiet & see only a few people instead of the mobs you have to listen to each day. And I'm sure that more can be done in one or two conversations a day than in endless ones —

It's a real Thanksgiving day — My patch of blue is *very* blue, and when I put up the shade, there was a bright quarter-moon shining right at me!

Saturday Nov. 27th — When you're reading an interesting story, do you sometimes skip ahead, and then have to *turn back* the pages? *To get a proper perspective?* It's easy enough to do, with a book, but far more difficult to do in life — and I wonder so often just how much of worldly *un*-wisdom is allowed by the True Wisdom — What I *want* so easily beclouds what I am entitled to.

Letter last week!
Letter Dec. 4th! [Neither of these letters from FDR survives.]

Dec. 5th Sunday —
   What an excellent idea, for you to have a "Retreat" on the top of your wooded hill — I have worked out a possible plan which would allow of future improvement & enlarging — & would lay pipes where they might be most useful — Doors, also, in three directions —
   "Exploration of the Terrain" would show where a cellar could be dug, without disturbing the most important rocks — Perhaps you would need only a small cellar under part of it —

[FDR's plans for his hilltop had steadily changed. He first thought merely of building a terrace on his hilltop and adding a primitive lean-to that would have included a fireplace and kitchenette; he then thought to construct a large living room so that he could visit in cold weather. Now, he thought he'd build a full-fledged cottage in which he could work away at his memoirs after 1940 without interruption.]

   . . . You *couldn't* have expected another letter at Dry Tortugas, after getting one before leaving and another on your return! Now *really* — I *thought* it was to be an average of perhaps 12 a year — that is, from New York *to* Wash. or "points south," and here is already the third since two weeks ago!! That *should* mean only one between now and Jan. 15th — A Christmas Extra *might* be allowed!
   Friday Dec. 10th
   Your letter came this morning, and I'm so glad to hear all about the trip and the interesting Fort Jefferson. It sounds lovely for a sort of resort, with golf course & tennis court & swimming pool etc in the middle, and bathing and fishing on the outside!
   I'm sorry you were worried last week, but — well — you understand (or *should!*) I *was* tired last week, but am fine now . . .
   I'm *so* glad the tooth is really almost well — You've had a horrid time of it.
   It's very interesting that Joseph Kennedy is going to England, but don't you need him here? [Joseph P. Kennedy had just been appointed ambassador to the Court of St. James's.]
   . . . TAKE CARE OF YOURSELF!!

                                                            Aff.
                                                            YM

1938

[In February 1938, FDR sent a sketch of his proposed hilltop cottage to his architect friend Henry J. Toombs, who produced finished drawings with only slight modifications of the President's plan. There were to be three parts to Top Cottage: a central living and dining room with a high, curved ceiling and an opening onto a western porch with a serene view of treetops, the slow-moving river, and the Catskills, far beyond; a set-back service wing to the northwest that included a kitchen, pantry, and bedroom for a full-time care-taker; and a southeastern wing with two bedrooms and a bath.

Building began that summer over the protests of the President's mother, who is said to have extracted a promise from her son that he would never spend a night in it so long as she was alive. It was bad enough, she is said to have told friends, that her daughter-in-law had insisted on a cottage of her own at Val-Kill. Now her son was threatening to leave her side, even though he had a perfectly good home at Springwood.

But there may well have been more to it than that. Like Daisy, Missy LeHand hoped someday to share the new cottage with FDR, and his mother may have got wind of it. She professed to be fond of the woman she called "dear little Missy," because of her obvious devotion to her son, but she had disapproved of Missy's close proximity to him during long cruises aboard the yacht *Larooco* in the early twenties, and at his Warm Springs cottage after that. Whenever Missy came to Hyde Park while the elder Mrs. Roosevelt was in residence, it was thought best to house her elsewhere. The prospect of the gossip her presence in the new cottage would surely inspire up and down the river may have forced Mrs. Roosevelt to take a stand.

Whether she knew that Daisy also hoped to share the cottage with FDR, whether Missy LeHand knew of those hopes — whether Daisy knew of Missy's, for that matter — no one now knows, and Roosevelt's decision to run for an unprecedented third term in 1940 would soon make all the questions moot.

And there was still another complication: Dorothy Schiff, the vivacious granddaughter of the financier Jacob Schiff and the new publisher of the New York *Post,* was then living apart from the second of her four husbands, George Backer, and FDR had talked her into building herself a cottage next door to his.

Had FDR not decided to run again in 1940, his would have been a very crowded hilltop.

In any case, he said later, "I did not personally expect to occupy the bedrooms, but thought that they could be used by the children in case any of them wished to move there for a holiday or a summer."

The cottage was completed in June of 1939, and as far as anyone knows, Roosevelt never did spend a night under its roof.

In late April of 1938, he undertook still another Caribbean cruise.]

U.S.S. *Philadelphia*

Sat — April 30th, 1938

Dear M —

So far so good — A perfect day — getting off from the Navy Yard at 9:30 and the run down the River past Charleston with its "Battery" & the old house and the slave market is always fascinating — Then past Fort Sumter — the walls are much lower than during the Siege — Fort Moultrie is on the left — firing a 21-gun salute as the C in C proceeds to sea. Outside it is smooth & even the destroyer "Fanning" escorting us does not roll or pitch — There are six in our party — Capt. Woodson [Walter B. Woodson was the President's naval aide], Col. Watson, Dr. McIntire, M[arvin] H. McIntyre & Rudolph Forster.

After lunch I slept for two hours & then went on the forward deck for some sun — and tonight played with stamps — Now it is 10:15 & I'm in bed and . . .

Sunday — Service on the quarter deck under a huge awning & the Chaplain is OK! Much better than that unfortunate solemn idiot who was on the So. Am. cruise — As a result there was a good turn-out of the crew — about 250 instead of the handful that used to go to service on the Indianapolis.

A quiet P.M., more sun & stamps, & so far I haven't done *any* work — One detective story nearly finished — Movies tonight & now it's bed & 10:20 . . .

Monday — This A.M. we anchored on Silver Bank — a formation under water about 30 miles each way with from 20 to 50 feet of water on it, & on all sides it is surrounded by water a mile or more deep. The charts show four or five places on the N.W. side where the coral heads are supposed to come to the surface & I figured it out that there would be fish — but we looked for them in vain — & any way the sea was too rough to lower a boat for trolling. So we ran down to Samano Bay at the N.E. end of Santo Domingo & anchored for the night close to marvelous mountains 3,000 feet high — with very thick vegetation. It is I think by far the richest of the Islands — even more so than Cuba or Jamaica & "only man is vile" — 3,000,000 of them — *all* a problem — The Haiti end (Western 1/3 with 2/3 of the population) is *all* black — The Santo Domingo end (2/3 with less than 1,000,000 people) is a potpourri of Spanish & negro with traces of French etc, etc. They live with comparative happiness next to nature & in complete poverty. Why disturb them?

Tuesday [May 3, 1938] — off bright & early in the whale boats & trolled for 5 hours — Very few fish but a real sunburn — rather painful at this minute on my shoulders & neck — We passed close to a tiny town amid coconut palms, tin houses, tin roofs — but lots of color & lots of dirt.

This P.M. we are steaming for Sombrero Island far to the East & now we are just North of Puerto Rico. We get mail at San Juan on Thurs. A.M. & I will post this there & you will get it either Sat. P.M. or Mon. morning.

I am glad about July, but don't you think it would do you good if you could stay at Nantucket for a week & get a change of air? Or you could go on there a week before Aunt S. returns & bring her back — I had as you know thought of going on the cruise about July 7th for 28 days but I can put it off & go as late as the 20th — What do you think?

Wed. Eve. — A good day, or rather morning, at Sombrero — a flat mass of coral a mile long with a lighthouse — It is almost 30 feet above water & the sea breaks on the windward side & sends fountains of spray high in the air — Nothing between it & Africa —

Now we are on the way home! Tomorrow early we get a pouch at San Juan & this will go via many hands & planes — I'm sorry not to be back Sunday morning early — It has been very nice out on the bow & tonight there was a sunset — and some spray.

Affec.
F.D.R.

* * *

Rhinebeck

May 18th Wednesday
Dear F. Yours did not leave N.Y. until 12.30 P.M. yesterday, & reached me this A.M. here! It is lovely, and the drive up the Bronx River Parkway

was wonderful — but I'm ashamed to say, I was yawning all the way up, and all last evening, 'til I thought I must be getting sleeping sickness, & put off my light at 10 last night, quite exhausted! When I woke this morning I couldn't think where I was — the four windows were quite unfamiliar — and for one brief second thought I was on O.H.! *Very* strange — and perhaps rather questionable!

Unpacking all the morning — my room a perfect mess — and the floor is only just cleared — but all my pictures are out, and a shelf is over the desk, with quite a menagerie of pigs (3) elephants (2) — dog (1) bear (1) — candlestick (1) — on the mantlepiece are Excelsior and Ichthyosaurus & Donald Duck — (whom you don't know). He winks with one eye & looks askance with the other . . .

By the way — I hope you had a good sound sleep Saturday morning!! I was startled at 20 of 8 by the telephone & flew down the hall, very much "*en négligée*," forgetting for a moment that it was only 20 of 7 by DST!

It was Peg [Anderson] — all set for a long talk from Plainfield, N.J.! At 8 I took my breakfast tray into the parlor & turned on the news for 15 minutes — having no paper . . . Nine — our time — was somewhat disappointing — but I'm sure the extra sleep was much needed . . .

Monday. Well! This time I have it on you!! Your note has just come and you evidently forgot all about Saturday morning at 8!! How very humiliating for a poor "girl," sitting at the telephone table endlessly correcting numbers!

. . . I go to N.Y. Thursday A.M. by train, spend the night at 399 — stay in the apartment *until 9 a.m. Standard Time, on Friday morning* — drive back here . . . on Friday P.M. — Saturday & Sunday are completely free, and I won't be off the place until Saturday P.M. in any case — 10 A.M. for a telephone would be very good — but *please* — *if* I'm to be invited to anything, at least let your mother know I'm coming, if you don't get her to invite me, which would be even better!!!!

Are you feeling cheerful again? I was rather "low" myself, last Friday — I hope the Potomac helped . . .

Tuesday the 24th — You will be glad to know that it's raining again for the little trees — It'll probably clear up for your week-end —

If you find things are too much involved over the week-end — You know I'll understand perfectly — and, again, it might be "just as well." But — without fail, enjoy the country, with all its loveliness — and be *happy* over it! I'll be mailing this in Appokipsing this P.M.!

[Appokipsing was said to be the old Indian name that evolved into Poughkeepsie.]

As ever
YM

* * *

U.S.S. *Philadelphia*

Thurs. 5th [May 1938]

[FDR to Daisy]

— The pilot has come out from San Juan harbor & taken our mail & brought a lot of newspapers & official mail which I have glanced thru' with a feeling of complete boredom & laid aside to do on the train on the way back from Charleston — That proves that the trip has been a complete success for the more fit I am physically & mentally the more I incline to put off things that should be done — & the more tired I am the more I insist on keeping up to the minute & driving myself to all the official tasks — That sounds completely "cuckoo" as the children say but I know C.P. will understand —

My face is quite badly burned from yesterday's fishing — too much so to shave today! The Capt & Exec. Officer come to dine tonight — both nice — We are to have a peaceful P.M. en route to Caicos Island whence I have scribbled scribbles to C.P. on two former trips — once on the Potomac in I think 1936 — Spring — & again from the Indianapolis returning from [Buenos Aires] in Dec. '36.

Fri. Eve. — A wonderful day of fishing in the whale boat — 18 fish in my boat & 40 in the other 3. I got 8 in all — the "high-line" & also the biggest fish — so I won both pools & will return $12 richer than when I left — It is toward a captain's Navy cape! [After Daisy died, a Navy captain's cape, very like the one FDR enjoyed wearing, was found in one of her closets. It was his birthday gift to her in December 1938.]

The sea was calm & the air perfect — but the sun did not help my face. We got back on board at 4 P.M. having picnic lunched in the whale boats & now we're headed for Charleston & M & letter.

I am worried about the weekend of the 22nd for I *doubt* I should be away then for four days — but the situation *may* allow it — and if not then it will be the 29th — but it is *such* a long time.

Sat. — Real excitement tonight! Just as we were going to the movies at 7:30 we intercepted a radio from a Norwegian freighter saying she had a man on board with a piece of steel in his eye — two days — bad case & asking help — We got her position — 30 miles S.W. — turned, speeded up & got to her at 8:30 — lowered boat with the Doctor & sent him on board — He found the piece of steel, operated, got it out & was back on board by 10 P.M.! It was a wonderfully inspiring thing — think what radio has done — and all hands watched our boat lowered & its lights moving over the sea to the other ship — Our searchlights made every move clear — The man's eye was undoubtedly saved.

Sunday — 4 P.M. We are entering Charleston harbor — All well & tomorrow I will be back within telephone — & 225 miles — By the way can I telephone you next *Saturday* at 8:30? For I may go down the River Sat P.M. for the night & take the three girls [Betty Hambley and her two daughters] —

Take *very* special care of M.

Your aff
F

[In June, Daisy wrote to her sister Betty, she attended a picnic with the President and First Lady and afterward felt relieved that Mrs. Roosevelt seemed to be "warming up" to her at last. The following month, FDR was back at sea, fishing off Baja California.]

Sunday — July 17, 1938

[FDR to Daisy]

— So the voyage begins — I remember so well the last one from San Diego — the one that really began Sept 22 '35 — and the many happinesses of these years. A difficult departure yesterday — and to-day the same — But to the diary — in faith and hope.

I looked out of my cabin at 9:30 and found we were anchored off Cedros Island — just where we were 3 years ago — its mountains of brown rock pushing up jaggedly in the sky — Church service at 11 — a nice chaplain — not much of a sermon — but better than the So. American padre — Lunch then into the boats to fish till 5 P.M. We old timers — Pa Watson, Ross McIntire & I instructing the neophytes — Basil O'Connor [FDR's law partner and director of the Warm Springs Foundation], Fred Adams [Frederick B. Adams, son-in-law of FDR's uncle Warren Delano III], Steve Early [Stephen T. Early, the President's press secretary] & my new aide Com. Dan Callaghan — how to use the reels & rods — We got enough fish for chowder for supper & mackerel for tomorrow breakfast — and every body started a tan, tho' it was not really hot.

Monday 18th — Putting the date down will be the only way I can keep track of the calendar — It is a long way to Cocos Island! — This is Magdalena Bay Day — & we have fished twice — Excellent this A.M. — Col. Watson got a 60 lb grouper which with the other fish will give the crew of 700 men a chowder tomorrow — they like the change from Navy fare —

Tonight's sunset the most amazing I have ever seen — Do you remember Maxfield Parrish's paintings? Turquoise blues & aquamarine blues close together & then oranges and every shade of pink & deep red — Those pictures with mountain backgrounds — I thought him an impostor till tonight — But they were all there — and the colors were almost as wonderful in the East as in the West —

It got very rough at 6 P.M. as we had to go 8 miles to get back to the ship & we were all soaked to the skin, & tired in the right way. Bed at 10 P.M.

Tues 19th — Another interesting day — way out in the gulf of Lower California inside of Cape San Lucas — Huge mountains — no O.H. there — a forbidding desert country — but my companions were interested — We have kept off politics by common consent. F.B.A. & B.O'C. are like children seeing the circus for the first time — 3 rings and something happening every second — I love to have them so enthusiastic — & they are all good comrades —

Wed July 20th — Today we are at a place I have never seen before & indeed very few others have — Socorro Island, part of a little bump called Revilla Gigedo, far out to sea & really submerged mountains with only tops showing — The extension of the Coast Range up the Californias (Alta and Baja) — An amazing little Island 3,000 feet high, but *green,* covered with a small cactus that makes walking impossible.

Did I tell you that I brought along Dr. [Waldo L.] Schmitt of the Smithsonian — a most delightful naturalist? He is making collections at each place & takes ashore a dozen or so volunteers from the crew, tells them what to look for among the rocks & seaweeds & comes back to the ship laden with bottles & nets and literally dozens of specimens in them — Tonight he is thrilled by the discovery of a new variety of burrowing shrimp — a colored kind — The previously known being white — So we are becoming more shrimp-minded than usual. You & I know lots of shrimp — but they had only 2 legs — tho' their brain capacity was similar to the ones discovered today!

[Dr. Schmitt brought home specimens of thirty new species including *Roosevealtia frankliniana*, a new kind of royal palm, *Thalamita roosevelti*, a crablike creature, *Octopus roosevelti*, and *Merriamium roosevelti*, a species of sponge.]

The fishing was so good that we had enough by lunch time & started for the Galapagos soon thereafter.

Thurs July 21. Really at sea — getting well out into the Pacific — At 10 A.M. we sighted Clipperton Island which you remember we [FDR and his party that is, not Daisy] stopped at for a few hours in '34 en route from Panama to Hawaii — or *do* you remember that?! It is generally too rough to get into small boats — but today we were fortunate — and we fished for 5 hours. But the sharks were everywhere & as soon as you hooked a tuna or grouper the sharks seized him before you could get him into the boat — This meant also that we lost yards of line & hooks & "spoons" — and we finally gave up in despair. Meanwhile Dr. Schmitt had gone ashore & with his crew got a fine collection of all sorts of marine life & some birds — all for the museum — also they shot a little wild black pig — which we shall eat . . .

Friday July 22. A peaceful day — much sleeping & sunning & reading — So far I have confined myself to three detective stories & a book on Latin America — What a comfort to get away from the damn newspapers ('scuse me) — I wish I had enough money to start a *news*paper — confined to *news* without interpretation, coloration, twisting or down-right lying — I think it would be a financial success!

I have been rereading two very interesting letters written to the *Houston* in 1935 — & someday I will show them to you! [These were Daisy's old letters, written after their momentous day together on Our Hill.]

We get no mail or paper of any kind for over a week to come & here we are a whole week out of San Diego.

By the way lest you think there is any danger in fishing for, or where there are, sharks, don't ever, for the only possible danger is in a boat swamping & being in the water a long time. Even then with 7 or 8 men in each boat sharks would probably not attack anybody in such a big splashing group — And near my boat there is always a guard boat & each boat carries a marine with a rifle. I am "handed" into the boat at the "well deck" & she is then lowered into the sea by the seaplane crane, & the process is reversed when I come back on board ship.

The Round things in the water & whale boat are my head & shoulders. [See opposite page.]

Sat. 23rd Another quiet day, though we old shellbacks put the pollywogs through their first "devoirs," standing watch on the fore turret dressed up in fur lined aviators clothes, etc. etc. — the same ceremony I went thro' in Nov '36 — & essentially handed down through merchant ships & navies from the days of the Phoenicians — therefore if for no other reason it must be kept alive — As you have discovered by this time I break precedents & start new things — but still believe in the old traditions — and live up to them.

The air & water are getting colder, we are approaching the Humboldt Current and make one forget one is close to the Equator — Tomorrow we cross.

Sunday 24th Tonight we are actually "South of the Line" — This morning we anchored off Tower Island at the mouth of Darwin Bay which is horseshoe shaped & is the center of an old volcano — very deep water inside. It was too rough to lower the boats, so after church service we moved south about 50 miles to Sullivan Bay on the Easterly side of James Island — an amazing sight — You get the feeling that you are still in the Pleistocene Period — great craters & small ones on the sides of the big ones — Black lava flows that might have run a year ago — queer blacks and red & browns — and every shape of rock & pinnacle rising on the shores & out of the sea — No wonder it is here one finds the most ancient forms of animal life in the world today — The big land and water iguanas & the huge land tortoises — The small penguins and the flightless cormorants — We fished successfully before supper & Dr. Schmitt with a landing party got many rare varieties of shrimp & crabs & one marine iguana about 3 feet long.

Tonight we dined in the ward room — & we shellbacks were entertained by the pollywog officers — Steve Early, Adams, & O'Connor also being made to make speeches & sing. After supper we had the ceremony of welcoming Davy Jones & his party on board, to notify us of King Neptune's arrival in the morning — The costumes & the handing out of summons was well done & the 418 pollywogs duly impressed.

Mon. 25th We got up anchor at 8, recrossed the Equator at 9 (going North) & recrossed again (going South) at 11 A.M. — 3 crossings in 24 hours! This in order to go round the North end of Albemarle, the largest of the Galapagos — Meanwhile the Neptune cere-

into the boat at the "well deck" & she is then
lowered into the sea by the graysham crane,
& the process is reversed when I come back
on board ship.

The usual things in the
water what boat are my
head & shoulders —

——— water line ———

Sat. 23rd Another quiet day, though we old shellbacks put the polly wogs through their first
"divaics" — standing watch on the fore tussit
dressed up in fur lined aviators clothes, etc etc.
— the same ceremony I went thro' in Nov '36
— & essentially handed down through merchant
ships & navies from the days of the Phoenicians
— therefore if for no other reason it must be
right a live — As you have discovered by this time
I break precedents & start new things — But still
believe in the old traditions — And live up to them.
——— The air & water are getting colder, we
are approaching the Humboldt Current and maybe
one forget one is close to the Equator — Tomorrow
we cross.

monies were held — you know all about them — The pollywogs have all survived & all that remains is for me to sign all their certificates —

This P.M. we anchored in the famous Tagus Cove — called the most wonderful spot in the world — but I was dreadfully disappointed — It is a deep indentation with steep cliffs & hills around it but no vegetation except scrub brown grass and bushes — In fact the whole island — 70 miles long — is uninviting for it looks *dead* — a thing that is [a] volcanic sea with no relief — Tufa, pumice, volcanic ash, lava folds — a place I do not propose to live in — or, I think even visit! — The fishing however was excellent & we got several 30 or 40 pound Tuna & many smaller fish — What surprises me most is the temperature — between 65 & 75 degrees — blankets at night — here on the Equator itself! It is caused by the Humboldt Current which runs North from the Antarctic off Chile & Peru, hits these Islands & bounces off into the Pacific. The water too is cold — about 65 and that makes the fish very good eating —

Tues. July 26 This A.M. we went around Narborough Island which is even more forbidding than the others — a very high volcano which exploded & erupted in 1824 — & are at anchor in Elizabeth Bay. Many seals playing around us, though we have seen no "giant manta" — a huge ray 12 feet across — and another survivor of a prehistoric age. A week from today we hope to be at Cocos where a destroyer will meet us from Panama — in touch again!

Wed July 27. We anchored early off Charles Island — Post Office Bay — where there is a barrel on pole for mail to be left or received by passing ships . . .

Later the party went to a nearby cove & contacted an Ecuadorian family & a Mr. & Mrs. Conway who have been here 10 months — They have a little patch of garden & shoot wild cattle & hogs for meat. I stayed on board but Pa & Doc & Fred & Steve had a grand time ashore — They are all good comrades — one could not ask for a more cheerful group & they are all most enthusiastic.

Now we are on our way to Hood Is., the most southerly of the group & when we leave there tomorrow noon we head Northward at last.

Thurs. 28th — We came here by luck — V[incent] Astor [whose yachting voyages had taken him often into the region] had never come but Dr. Schmitt said there were supposed to be albatross nesting here — and there were! He photographed several nests & birds — The fishing was *excellent* — big tuna & wahoos, running up to 55

pounds — got some & then went to the little cove & caught some
little fish that were as brilliant as butterflies — and some little mauve
fish that are quite rare. Everyone rates this our best day & all are duly
tired. I think I have taken off at least five pounds but can't weigh till
I get back — Tomorrow early we turn northward — bow headed for
Pensacola & points North.

Friday 29th — A cold day — anchored off Indefatigable Island
— and a rough sea and not much of interest or sport — I spent 6
hours in the whale-boat & ran out to Daphne Island, a weird rock,
not more than 1,000 feet long — perfectly round & rising 500 feet
from the water — One side of the top is partly broken & the middle
is the old crater — now full of nesting birds

— Same lovely pure white Tern & small birds with one feather
— more than a foot long extending from the tail. I was soaked to the
skin when I got in.

Sat. 30th — This A.M. early we came up to James Bay on James
Island & I sent 100 men to the Beach to try to find Lieut. Cowan's
grave. He was with old Commodore [David] Porter in the "Essex" in
1813, went ashore with a brother officer & was killed in a duel &
buried back of the beach. We found no trace, but if we had I should
have tried to find some of his family (*he* was unmarried) & have a
proper marker put up.

There was a small flock of pink flamingo flying over us — very
rare — The only ones I have ever seen — The fishing was poor —
very rough — again I got soaked by the salt water which broke over
the whale boat — A little smoke is coming out of one of the big
volcanoes on Albemarle Island to the west of us, the only sign of
activity we have seen . . .

Later — 10 P.M. . . . It was rough when we got to Sullivan Bay,
so I did not fish, but signed the "Neptune" certificates for the officers
& men who crossed the line for the first time — They are big lithographs
with pictures of Neptune & Davy Jones & mermaids & McDougal
lobsters etc — I did 350 today for the personnel of the Houston &
there are 300 still to come.

Sun. July 31st — We stopped at 9 at Tower Island where we
could not land just one week ago, but again the water was too rough,
so we are headed North for Cocos & hope to get there tomorrow
A.M. & to find two days without the usual heavy rains that abound
there — A quiet day — Church service at 10:30 — then some reading & stamps, then a nap for an hour, then sat forward on deck &

looked at sea — a lovely sea but a lonely sea — very far from "any-where" but very close to "everywhere" — Tomorrow Cocos, & the destroyer with mail arrives Tuesday A.M.

Mon. Aug 1st — I had hoped the destroyer might arrive tonight, but she won't be in till the morning. We are safely anchored at this loveliest of lovely islands & have been ashore & fished successfully. No treasure party this time. Dr. Schmitt has gone up 1,500 feet & brought out samples & seeds of a lovely palm which grows only here — a kin to the Royal Palm & we shall try to grow it in the Agric. Experiment station in Miami.

Tues Aug 2. Mail is in — all is well —

Aff,

F

[While working as his father's secretary after the death of Louis Howe, James Roosevelt had developed gastric ulcers. On September 9, surgeons at the Mayo Clinic planned an emergency operation. Both FDR and Eleanor Roosevelt hurried west by rail to be with their son.]

[Rochester, Minnesota]

A.M. 11th Sept, 1938

— It has been a trying day — but all is well so far — this A.M. as soon as I put in an immediate operation was decided on — began at 11 — & ended at 1:30 — very difficult but J. came through all right — and though it was touch & go several times they seem very hopeful since —

I'm living in the car at the station, & it's easier than going to hotel. All the doctors are *so* nice — I was here (remember?) several years ago — [Roosevelt was never himself a patient at the Mayo Clinic but he spoke there as President in October of 1934.] Young Gray who did the operation is the son of my old friend Carl Gray, Pres. of the Union Pacific —

Wed. 14 — All has gone so well that I am off — They really are sure that J is making a perfectly normal recovery, that it is safe to go — & he can actually talk a little & smile at my poor jokes. Oh! I wish so that C.P. were here — I am so upset because I must go to W[ashington] instead of the River —

The situation in Europe is full of world dynamite & I don't dare be off the scene because it needs hourly watching. [Adolf Hitler had demanded that Czechoslovakia surrender the Sudetenland or he would take it by force.] At least on this trip I have had a chance to catch up with a mass of official stuff which had accumulated —

I think of you as moving the last things to R[hinebeck] today & closing the [New York] apartment. [Mrs. Langdon, old and frail, now preferred to spend the whole year at Rhinebeck.] — I wish so you could have kept it — just as your own — & been there in days to come to give at least a cup of tea — and then it all had to go — Well, there are other places for the days to come aren't there — and they can be made to suit — Some how, some way — And it's *good* to live a bit in the future.

[White House] Mon. 19th — Such a nice but tiny chat this A.M. — but I wish I could be C.P.'s nurse & compel a real and long rest — For I think I know what this summer has been and the many problems — The difficulties that had to be solved alone — & I wanted so to help, & I haven't been able to —

Wed 21st — Your letters tell me so much I want to know — and I love them and all the details — don't even dare to leave any out. Can't XYZ be sent to a nice parish in Australia? [The identity of XYZ is unknown.]

When I can leave, I don't know "at all at all" — Things are worse abroad & while of course a war does not mean us in it, it does change so many things — hate — all our "economics" — industry, agriculture, etc. And I go about those hectic days with a vile cold in my nose — nearly well every morning then comes up again in the P.M. Tomorrow I'm going to stay in bed —

Sat. 24th — Things are still worse — tho' cold is better — It looks like war in a week —

Mon. 26th — Did you hear Hitler today? His shrieks, his histrionics and the effect on the huge audience — They did not applaud — they made noises like animals —

Last night at 1 A.M. I sent a message — waited for what I hope is the *right* moment — it may help but I doubt it.

[In his appeal, FDR invoked the Kellogg-Briand Pact, whose signatories had pledged to solve conflicts through peaceful means alone. Britain, France, and Czechoslovakia all responded favorably, but Hitler sent an angry eighteen-page reply: Czechoslovakia must give up the Sudetenland, or there would be war. Secretly, he had already decided to attack Czechoslovakia on September 30.]

Tues. 27th — Very late — no, Wed 28th 2 A.M. — I've made a final plea — at 9 tonight — direct to Hitler — & sent one to Mussolini at 3 this P.M. & to *all* other nations asking them also to plan for renewal of negotiations —

Wed. Sept 28, 1938 — At 10 your note — & five minutes later the news that Hitler asks a conference! Could anything bring a more perfect morning! — It is too early to tell but it *looks* like no war —

[Hitler had stepped back from the brink of war and called British Prime Minister Neville Chamberlain, French Premier Édouard Daladier, and the Italian dictator Benito Mussolini to meet with him at Munich on September 29. There, Hitler promised, he would agree to settle all future disputes with Britain through negotiation. In exchange for that dubious pledge, Chamberlain agreed not to intervene as the Germans seized the Sudetenland.]

Another two days, "incidentally," but most important, may let me go to H.P. And when I get there I'm going to telephone —

Fri. 30th — I'm going! Get there Sunday A.M. but I can't wait till Sat. for the tea — anyway that weekend is uncertain — & there must be a view of the cottage & perhaps [you'll] come too & perhaps — all kinds of things — I'm getting a little incoherent — so would you if *you* were *I* — But it's a nice feeling and has lots of possibilities just like the European situation at this moment! But all of the C.P.s are nice ones.

Mon. Oct. 3rd '38 — H.P. — I'm still incoherent & will be tomorrow — will you mind? Let's both be — it would do us such a lot of good.

I hope the lunch people will let me get away by 2:50 & then I might give 15 minutes at 3:30 — And I can't write what I'm going to tell C.P. but I don't have to.

Ever,
F.

[Although it is known that FDR came twice to Wilderstein for tea with the family, there is otherwise no record of his relationship with Daisy during the rest of 1938. Daisy was not well for the better part of the year. Pale, weak, and having lost an alarming amount of weight, she finally visited a Manhattan doctor in November. He discovered what she later reported was "a perfectly good tumor, the size of a grapefruit."]

1939

[Daisy decided to have the tumor removed, but first she needed to get her things in order in case she did not survive the surgery. On January 2, 1939, the eve of her operation, she wrote to her brother Arthur from 399 Park Avenue, making him her executor.

Items inherited from Cousin Elizabeth Lynch were to be distributed equitably among the family, she told him, but Betty, "having a family," should get the largest share. A debt to her cousin Barrett Tyler was to be repaid and what little money was left should go toward making sure that her nephew Bobbie was well taken care of, preferably in a place less institutional than the one where he presently resided.

Members of the family were to divide up her mementos of FDR: ". . . the black navy cape F.D.R. sent me for my birthday this year" was to go to Rollie Hambley; Robert was to get her copy of *Old Dutch Houses;* Arthur was to have all five volumes of FDR's speeches.

And she wished to leave three articles of furniture to the President: "The firebench, which is in Wildercliff garage [Wildercliff was a neighboring house owned by the Suckleys], I promised to him for a Christmas present this year — It is for his new cottage — You might ask him if he would like that folding table which is at the foot of the stairs in Wildercliff — and also the wing chair he found so comfortable when he took tea with us in Wildercliff. He spoke of both these things and they might be useful in the cottage."

But one concern dwarfed all others. She was haunted by the knowledge that beneath her bed, tied in a bundle and carefully locked inside the battered little black suitcase she'd once carried with her to Europe and back, were all her letters from FDR, letters whose true nature she had managed to keep from her family. She still felt she could not tell her brother of her feelings for the President or of his feelings for her, but she was haunted by what might happen if his letters fell into the wrong hands.

The safest thing would be to send the parcel, unopened, to FDR. But to see that that was done, she felt she had to misrepresent its contents to her brother.

"The other thing," she wrote to him, "is a package of books, papers &

pamphlets *lent* to me by *Franklin Roosevelt*. They are done up, all together, in a dark blue package, inside the suitcase under my bed. I would prefer it if you deliver them in person — The procedure would be to write him a letter enclosed in a separate envelope to 'Miss LeHand, the White House,' with a little note to Miss LeHand asking her to give him your letter —

If you don't want to do it this way, you could send the package addressed to Miss LeHand, and write her a separate letter telling her the box is coming & that it contains the books from me. Insure it for $100! The reason for this is that there are 30 mail clerks working in the White House and they open & examine everything that comes for the President, & Franklin says books sometimes get lost that way. Of course I am very anxious that these things should get safely back to him, as they have historical value."

There was one more bit of unfinished business, its importance again carefully masked from the family: "As a token of appreciation of [the President's] great kindness and friendship to us all, I wish you would give him the miniature shelf (here, in my room, on the wall) with all the loose animals, etc."

The "loose animals, etc.," of course, included FDR's gifts to her and were therefore her most precious possessions. She wanted no one but him to have them and the three little portable hanging shelves on which she had displayed them wherever she went.

(In September 1994, after reading this passage, I went to Daisy's house and, with Raymond Armater and John McGuire of the Wilderstein board, climbed the three flights to her tower bedroom. There, hanging on a nail from the cracked plaster wall, were the three shelves, still decorated with dusty knickknacks — a thimble-sized vase FDR had once owned, two miniature seals, a tiny bell. And next to the shelves, carefully kept behind the glass door of a secretary, were more toy animals, including a wooden goose, its long neck stretched upward — "Up and Out," FDR had said when he gave it to her. On its base, in Daisy's neat hand, was "Excelsior!" and on the bottom:

Wash., DC.
April 28, 1935
MLS from FDR
Given at the White House!)

The next morning, a Manhattan surgeon removed Daisy's tumor, along with her appendix and left ovary. The growth turned out not to be malignant, but she remained in the hospital for twelve days and was on her back at Mrs. Langdon's New York apartment for several weeks after that. The experience did not improve her opinion of doctors, especially surgeons.

FDR kept careful track of her convalescence.]

The White House
Washington

January 6, 1939

Dear Margaret,

Betty [Hambley] has telephoned & I'm so glad all goes well — I must give you the usual advice from an old operatee [Roosevelt had undergone surgery for acute appendicitis in 1915] — to yield peacefully to the Doctors & rest, even when in a few days you will want to stand up & run around & later when you leave the hospital to avoid trying to lead your normal life for 3 or 4 weeks even if family & friends urge you to do things — As a matter of fact Betty & I think you will do well to come to Washington — where no one will disturb you & Betty's bedroom is ready for you —

I am sending you a [toy] watchdog. He is very watchful & faithful & won't bite anyone except intruders — It's grand to know that the operation is successfully over.

Affectionately yours,
FDR

[The watchdog, too, would be found in Daisy's bedroom more than half a century later.]

Georgia Warm Springs Foundation
Warm Springs
Georgia

Wed. April 5 [1939]

Dear Daisy

I find that in all probability I can go to Charlottesville and Endless Caverns either Friday & Sat. April 21 & 22, or Sat. & Sunday April 22 & 23 — It would be grand if we could make up a "caravan," visit Monticello, I spending the night with F[ranklin] Jr. [then studying law at the University of Virginia] & all of you joining me to the Caverns, where I would join you the next day for lunch. I am visiting Betty — & I do hope you can come down — Down here we are having real spring & yesterday I picked a lot of honeysuckle out on the Knob — I get back to Washington Monday at noon, in time to supervise egg-rolling from the South Porch.

Happy Easter.

Affectionately,
FDR

[Daisy was not yet well enough to travel to the caverns, but by June, when the Roosevelts entertained the King and Queen of England at Hyde Park, she was able to attend. The royal visit was the first in American history, meant in part to foster American sympathy for England in her struggle with Nazi Germany, and the village of Hyde Park was frenzied with excitement.]

～ June 11 was a red letter day!! I left [home] in a car of Newman's & drove to the Hyde Park Church, arrived with a card of admission, which also entitled one to a special parking space in the field to the south of the church. I was so early that the police knew nothing about it & [I] drove all the way to the village & back before they would let me in!

Even so I was at the church at 10 of 10, & the doors did not open until 11! In the meantime, Mrs. [Frank R.] Wilson [wife of the rector] introduced me to various H.P. villagers . . . She was shaking with excitement.

I got a good seat, 2nd from the aisle, & for an hour enjoyed the comments of villagers on important people who came in! When Helen Astor came in, the girl on my right, overcoming her reticence, leaned toward me and whispered, "Do you know who that is? It's Mrs. Vincent Astor!!!"

I answered: "Oh-ooo-ooo!!"

Eleven finally came & on the dot the Royal-Presidential party! Mrs. James Roosevelt & the Queen walked up together, followed by the King & Eleanor R. The Pres. followed on Jimmy's arm, with Tommy [Qualters, Secret Service agent and successor to Gus Gennerich as the President's walking partner] at his elbow. The Pres. walked with great difficulty & told me later that only one side of his right brace was fastened & if it had broken, he would have collapsed in the aisle!!

. . . The Queen looked so pretty with shining brown eyes & a lovely skin & very beautiful expression. Though she did not actually smile & bow as she walked up, she nevertheless had a very definite look of being in the public eye . . . The King looked very serious & unconscious, as the Roosevelts all did —

The service was simple & very appropriate . . .

At the close . . . The King & Queen walked out together, smiling from side to side — followed by the R. ladies & F.D.R. "stumping" along, as he puts it, as fast as he could . . .

[Daisy also attended the picnic lunch at the newly completed Top

Cottage, remembering to bow to the royals but not to shake their hands, as FDR had directed.]

As it was a hot day, a cold lunch of ham, chicken, salad, also beer & bottled drinks. But one dish of "hot dogs" was served on the porch [on a silver tray], probably so that their majesties could see what they were like. "It is said" that the King asked for a second one!

There was only one jarring note, and that was the way "certain individuals" took advantage of the permission to take photographs, & snapped the poor guests right before them — Mrs. R said about one of them, "She does not know any better!" I am quite sure the *maids* themselves "would know better"! [The offending photographer was Nancy Cook, co-owner of Val-Kill, and an old friend of Mrs. Roosevelt's.]

After lunch there was an interesting Indian program, by a man & woman in lovely full-dress Indian clothes — beaded & feathers, etc. A *little* long, perhaps . . .

It was a memorable day, and since then F has told us details of the visit. He says the King is "*grand!*" with an almost American sense of humor — He never seemed to miss the funny side of anything . . . showed an extraordinary knowledge of this country, the people, and important individuals, and always said something appropriate on meeting them — He was completely natural and put all the "royalness" aside when in private —

The Queen, on the other hand, could *never* quite forget she was a queen, & is a little lacking in humor, though a fine person. Both are extraordinarily kind & considerate of everyone — When they were going on their train [from] H.P. they both turned back & shook hands with Monty Snyder [the Roosevelt family chauffeur] — They gave him a pair of gold cuff-links with the royal coat-of-arms, I think, on it.

F said he tested out the king's sense of humor with two of his oldest jokes, which he can't laugh at himself! The king rocked back & forward with laughter, repeating over & over, "It *can't* be true — It *can't* be true"!

At the two "small" informal dinners at H.P., F broke several precedents. After the usual toasts, F was going to do something about which he had not consulted protocol, or the State Department, or even the British Ambassador! Sir Ronald [C. Lindsay] looked at him with his mouth open, evidently thinking: "What is *he* going to do *now!*"

Then F proceeded to propose a toast to the Queen, a thing which is never done in England. The Queen was so overcome that she drank to herself.

When the dessert had been passed at lunch or dinner, F would catch the King's eye, or call out: "Sir, may we smoke?"

Sunday night before F did this, the King from the other end of the table called out: "Mr. President, it's my turn now, *may* we smoke?"

F told us the most amusing story of four "accidents" at HP, all in the 26 hours the King & Queen were there. In Washington, everything went perfectly, the servants are accustomed to important people. But in HP they evidently all had the jitters! Just a week before, F had received from the city of Limoges a perfectly beautiful 120-piece set of . . . china. It was decided to use them for the K. and Q. In the middle of dinner, on Saturday, 24 of these plates were standing on a little old serving table, & without warning the table & 24 plates crashed to the floor!

Later in the evening, a butler carried a tray with 6 ginger-ale bottles & a few tall glasses. He caught his heel on the top of the steps leading to the library, lost his balance & the whole tray went flying into the room, with him after it.

The King remarked: "That's number 2, what will be the next?"

Sunday morning, the ladies-in-waiting & the aides came down to breakfast & told the butler how they liked their eggs, etc. The butler soon appeared with a large tray laden with freshly cooked eggs, toast, etc. He bumped into the mantelpiece and dropped the entire thing on the floor!

The fourth thing happened Sunday afternoon: The Roosevelts & their guests were sitting around the pool — Franklin on the grass — He wanted to move back into the shade, no one was paying attention to him at the moment, so he started to propel himself backward on his hands — He was doing beautifully and gave himself a final big heave — right onto a tray of glasses & bottles!

The Queen told Mrs. R that they had not the *slightest* idea that F could not walk — They knew he had to use a cane. They have asked him to spend a week with them, at Windsor or Balmoral, where they can be quite informal & not surrounded by people.

On July 3rd, F telephoned Amb. Kennedy in London about the European situation. Mr. K had seen the King who told him the visit to HP was the nicest day on their whole trip . . .

The K told F in Washington that he, like his father, George V, hates garden parties where you have to meet hundreds of people & walk, "smirking" at everyone on the lawn — that should be a comfort to

Mrs. James R., who wanted so much to have a lawn party instead of a picnic!

[On September 1, 1939, Nazi armies drove deep into Poland. The world was at war, and Roosevelt's plans to retire from the presidency after two terms were cast in doubt. It gradually became clear that Daisy's dream of living and working with FDR at Top Cottage would have to be deferred. Her growing disappointment must have been great, though she left no written record of it and she may already have made her peace with the fact that she would never have exclusive possession of the man she loved. From then on, she was always careful to refer to the retreat she'd once called "Our House on Our Hill" as "your cottage."

On November 19, she attended the laying of the cornerstone for the Franklin D. Roosevelt Library in the middle of his mother's front field at Springwood. It, too, had been meant for his retirement years, and warm memories of his tranquil boyhood on the place filled his remarks — he recalled the old pear tree he'd once climbed, the beds from which he'd plucked sun-warmed strawberries, watching with his dogs as woodchucks slipped in and out of their holes. The world was very different now, he said, but his new library was dedicated to "the spirit of peace — peace for the United States, and soon, we hope, peace for the world."]

1940

[There is no diary for 1940 and only a single letter from FDR; whether Daisy kept no journal and exchanged no letters with him, or decided for some reason to destroy all traces of their friendship during that year, it is impossible now to know.]

U.S.S. *Tuscaloosa*

Sat. [February] 17th [1940]

From: C. in C. [FDR to Daisy]
To: M.L.S.

All well — we just got off in time from Pensacola — a big storm there the next day — It has been a bit choppy, spray over the bow, but nice & warm & the stars are out tonight after three days of clouds — Tomorrow I "do" the Atlantic defenses of the Zone — & then some "observation" work on the Pacific side —

We have all been laughing at the complete ignorance & gullibility of the Press! They "fell for" the visit to the Andaman Islands (Indian Ocean) Celebes (No. Pacific) & South Hebrides (Antarctic) and, believe it or not, the Cherable Isles from Edward Lear's *Book of Nonsense!* [Actually, there were no such islands in the works of Edward Lear; FDR seems to have invented them.]

Just before I left I managed to have the big room in the South Wing of the Library (downstairs) plastered for the sleigh and the very grand old carriage & we must work up a sign & a history to go on it — To write to someone in Phila. to ask about William Rogers.

[FDR had persuaded the Suckleys to donate to his library a venerable and stylish enclosed carriage. William Rogers was evidently its maker. Daisy loved to tell of the day FDR came to get it. The Secret Service tied it to the bumper of one of their cars and towed it in a slow-moving caravan all the way back to Hyde Park.]

— I hope to get home again the end of March — Then in April if you are not at Rhinebeck will you act as eyes & legs for me & look at old farm implements in Ben Haviland's barn attic back of Hyde Park? [Ben Haviland was an elderly resident of Hyde Park who shared Roosevelt's love of local history and his fondness for collecting old things of every kind.]

I hope Aunt Sophie is entirely well again.

Affec.
FDR

[In August of 1940, Daisy presented FDR with a gift, a four-month-old Scottish terrier pup that the President named Fala — after toying with the idea of naming it Wendell, for his Republican presidential opponent, Wendell Willkie. Lovingly trained by Daisy, the dog quickly became the most celebrated presidential pet in history.]

1941

Sunday [May 25, 1941]

Dear F. I've been living with a heavy feeling of guiltiness at bothering M.F. [My Franklin] about our [Suckley] affairs — (It's bad enough to do so about *others'* affairs) & that guilty feeling mixed with constant worry about C.P. has been *dreadful.*

But just now — 9.20 A.M. — I've talked to Arthur [Suckley], & he had such a completely satisfactory visit & found C.P. *looking* well & such a *tremendous* help in calling up the right people — and being so *awfully nice* — most important, of course, is his "looking well" — though I can't entirely take Arthur's word for that, as men don't often see "beneath the surface" on such matters as "looking well." But anyway, I feel C.P. looks & *is better.*

Yesterday, I . . . spent about 1 ½ hrs. with Mr. [Fred] Shipman [first director of the Franklin D. Roosevelt Library] looking at everything & talking about the exhibition etc. etc. [The library was to be formally dedicated and opened to the public on June 30.]

I thought the arrangement of things in the big hall excellent, very harmonious & well placed and interesting, etc. with the exception of one small picture of a country schoolhouse, which he acknowledged had no special point there & would be replaced by something more suitable as to colour & subject. *Me* — suggesting things for the F.D.R. Library!! *Very* presumptuous! But he asked me for suggestions & criticisms — and that was the only thing I could find definitely wrong — The "oddities" room is an excellent idea, don't you think, and is dominated by the sphinx of you! It needs a little more arranging & spacing, & I suggested that Gus' lighthouse should have a central position, and be going on & off when on exhibition!

[The "oddities" room — FDR privately called it the "chamber of horrors" — housed some of the more bizarre gifts FDR had received over the years. The "sphinx" was a mammoth papier-mâché caricature of Roosevelt that had featured in a 1940 Gridiron Club skit on the President's reluctance to answer questions about a third term. The late Gus Gennerich had evidently once fashioned a flashing lighthouse for his boss.]

Wednesday — that was so wonderful, last night — everything about it — The way it worked up to a climax & all the many things that you should say — I can't think of anything you left out — Also, the way you spoke was quite perfect — and I realized all the time how *alone* you stood, speaking to the world — and what it must have meant to you — you, at one time a small boy lying in the grass over a woodchuck hole —

[On Tuesday evening, May 27 — alarmed at the appearance of the powerful German battleship *Bismarck* in the west Atlantic and the possibility of a Nazi attack on the Azores — FDR proclaimed "an unlimited national emergency." He vowed to "resist any attempt by Hitler to extend his Nazi domination to the western hemisphere" and to "give every possible assistance to Britain and to all who, with Britain, are resisting Hitlerism . . . with the force of arms." That same day, the British sank the *Bismarck*.]

I seemed to see the unfinished pyramid, with the millions of mankind looking up and straining, most of them with unseeing eyes, to get the stones to the top for the finishing — And on the top a handful of men, placing the stones, with *one* of them showing them how —

Since reading Mr. Wallace's little book, I think so often of that unfinished state of the pyramid — Shouldn't the idea of the *un*finished state of the world be more emphasized in educating the young? They have too much the idea that the world owes them security — without their doing much about it.

. . . *Saturday* — I'll just finish this with a few words *en attendant Lundi!* What heavenly days! But I'll hear *all* about them!

In case I forget to tell you, I'm *trying* to write a "true story of Fala"! I say "trying," for if it turns out to be very dull, I won't do anything with it — but if I *could* make it interesting, I would offer it for publication! That *would* be thrilling! Do you happen to know who does children's stories?

À bientôt!

Aff.
YM

[Scribner's eventually offered Daisy and a professional writer, Alice Dalgleish, a contract to write a children's book, and FDR gave the go-ahead.]

June 8th

Dear Franklin —

Just a week ago tomorrow afternoon, you asked me to remind you about the "praying girl," and about the "Barkers for Britain" medal [given to dog owners who contributed to British war relief], & Fala's license tag, to be sent to the Library for the "Fala Exhibit"!

Here is the reminder!

[Touring the Panama-Pacific Exposition at San Francisco as assistant secretary of the Navy in 1915, FDR had loudly admired a life-sized kneeling bronze nude by Ralph Stackpole, called "Praying Girl" and done more or less in the style of Rodin. When he and Daisy were discussing the landscaping for Top Cottage he suddenly remembered it, and asked friends in California whether they would track down the artist, whose name he'd forgotten, and see if he could purchase a copy. For the result, see page 222.]

. . . I am getting all worked up about my Story of Fala! *If* it's any good, I thought perhaps the outside of the Book could be just the Title:

"The True Story of Fala"
by [Daisy] and underneath
"This *is* the True Story of Fala"
F.D.R.

Katherine Davis says that [the novelist] Stark Young knew Fala as a puppy, & she is quite certain he would write a foreword!

One wouldn't need any more publicity than that!! Would you consent to it, *if* the story is worth publishing?!

I hope the Dr. is still being strict with you!

À bientôt,

Affectionately,
M

It *was* so nice to see you last Monday . . .

*   *   *

Rhinebeck —

July 5th [1941]

Dear Franklin —

It *was* nice seeing you twice this week, but neither time gave me much chance to tell you how much I appreciated my *very* honorable place at the Royal Table on Monday! [Queen Wilhelmina of the Netherlands had visited Hyde Park.]

And on top of it all, (or underneath) was that very sweet puppy-dog, licking my ankles at intervals! I *really* think I should live over a doggery — somewhat like Debby [Dows, a young neighbor who bred and trained horses] — except that I would concentrate *mostly* on dogs, or *a* dog — & —

Then — the ceremonies were awfully nice, except that a friend of mine did not look quite as spry as I should wish —

Also — Tuesday P.M. the garden was lovely & the drinks & food delicious, and the company very agreeable — but there was another "except" there too, in that I need some advice & suggestions on my manuscript, and had no opportunity to discuss it. Altogether, though showered with the good things in life, I'm complaining!

I never realized how much work there can be when one tries to put some thought into words, on paper! I believe I'm working almost as much on my "True Story" as you do on a speech! Though I'm not up to the 23rd draft yet! After I feel I have a reasonably good *first* draft, if there is an *odd* hour you could spare me, it would be wonderful —

. . . Your 4th of July talk was much to the point — how I wish you could go ahead faster with it all — but I understand perfectly why you don't — One would like to put a snowplow on the road, & shovel all the objectors, et al, to one side!

["I tell the American people solemnly," Roosevelt had said, "that the United States will never survive as a happy and fertile oasis of liberty surrounded by a cruel desert of dictatorship. And so it is that when we repeat the great pledge to our country and to our flag, it must be our deep conviction that we pledge as well our work, our will, and, if it be necessary, our lives."]

I don't want to harp *on* one string always, but *please* remember that you are going to be needed *more* & *more* with every passing month. *And still* more when the period of reconstruction comes!

It's a lovely clear day — on Monday I go to Westport for K.

Davis car! I will feel luxurious, & quite spoiled after 6–8 weeks of it!
Let me drive you in it!! — M

A hug to dear Fala — & even a kiss or two on the top of his head!

P.S. I see Miss LeHand is in the hospital, but hope she'll be back
soon. You must miss her. I wonder how you'll get this! Give her my
kindest regards and best wishes.

[Missy LeHand was in Doctors Hospital in Washington, incapacitated —
and silenced — by two strokes from which she would never recover.

On August 3, Sophie Langdon died after a series of strokes. As always,
the details were left largely to Daisy, who arranged for the funeral at the Church
of the Messiah in Rhinebeck and for the burial in Morristown, New Jersey.
FDR expressed his sympathy from aboard his train.]

Aug 3, 1941

[FDR to Daisy]

At the Penn Station in NY a few minutes ago came a wire from
Rudolph [Forster] repeating your telephone — I'm *so* sorry — She
was such a really grand person and so truly understanding — I wish
I could do something to help but after all there will not be many
difficulties, I hope — Only I think of you — for it does make real
differences for you after these years with Aunt Sophie — So many
things I meant to talk to you about — Save any problems for the
broad shoulders of

F

[Daisy genuinely mourned for her sometimes demanding aunt. But she was
now without a job. Although working for Mrs. Langdon had often been
trying, it had paid the bills at Wilderstein, helped feed her mother and brothers, paid the taxes, and contributed to the care of her sad nephew Bobbie.

Unmarried, nearing fifty, with little work experience beyond that of a
paid companion, what was she to do? FDR might be able to think of something, but she would now have to wait to talk it over with him until he
returned from a journey so clandestine that neither the secretary of State nor
his wife was told of it in advance: a meeting with Winston Churchill off the
coast of Canada. As always, FDR reveled in secrecy, and it is evidence of his
utter trust in Daisy's discretion that he shared so many details with her.]

S.S. *Augusta*

Tuesday Aug 5

M. [FDR to Daisy]

Strange thing happened this morning — suddenly found ourselves transferred with all our baggage & mess crew from the little "Potomac" to the Great Big Cruiser "Augusta"! And then, the Island of Martha's Vineyard disappeared in the distance, and as we head out into the Atlantic all we can see is our protecting escort, a heavy cruiser and four destroyers. Curiously enough the Potomac still flies my flag & tonight will be seen by thousands as she passes quietly through the Cape Cod Canal, guarded on shore by Secret Service and State Troopers while in fact the Pres. will be about 250 miles away.

Even at my ripe old age I feel a thrill in making a get-away — especially from the American press.

It is a smooth sea & a lovely day.

Wed. Aug 6 — A bit of fog during the night, and our paravanes (anti-mine sweeps on each bow) made a lot of noise — This P.M. we are off Halifax and in the submarine area — Tho' there have been no reports of them in these waters recently. We are lucky in having good visibility.

This A.M. we got word of a "leak" in London, but it seems to be pure guesswork. I went up to the deck above — alone in the bow & the spray came over as it has before [again reminding FDR of Daisy] —

Thursday — We got in to Argentia, Newfoundland, safely at 11 A.M. preceded by mine-sweepers, & found several destroyers & patrol planes at this new base of ours — one of the eight I got last August in exchange for the 50 destroyers. It is a really beautiful harbor, high mountains, deep water & fjord-like arms of the sea. Soon after we anchored in came one of our old battleships accompanied by two destroyers — & on one of the latter F Jr. is asst. navigator — so I have ordered him to act as my Junior Naval Aide while I am here. It was a complete surprise to him & to me to meet thus.

Elliott had just returned from a survey flight to Baffin Land from Gander Lake, the army base 80 miles from here, so I have ordered him to join me as Junior Military Aide. Again, pure luck, but very nice.

I fished with F Jr. this P.M. & looked at the work on the Naval Station.

Friday Aug 8 — A quiet day. Sumner Welles [assistant secretary of State] & Averell Harriman [defense expediter to Great Britain] came by plane this P.M. & we had a "dress rehearsal" conference including Gen. [George C.] Marshall [chief of staff of the U.S. Army],

Gen. [Henry H. "Hap"] Arnold, [head of the U.S. Army Air Corps], Ad. [Harold R.] Stark [chief of Naval Operations] Ad. [Ernest J.] King [commander of the Atlantic Fleet, and others.] All set for the Big Day tomorrow. I wish you could see this scene. By the way don't ever give any times or places or names or numbers of ships!

Sat. Aug 9 — The huge new H.M.S. *Prince of Wales* came up the Bay with two escorting corvettes & anchored alongside of us at 9:30 — After exchange of "boarding calls" by officers, Winston Churchill came on board the Augusta at 11, accompanied by his staff, headed by 1st Sea Lord [Sir Dudley] Pound, Gen. [Sir John] Dill [chief of the British Imperial General Staff], Air Marshal [Sir Wilfred] Freeman, & Under Secy of State [Sir Alexander] Cadogan. We all met on the top deck and were duly photographed & then Churchill stayed on board & lunched with me alone.

He is a tremendously vital person & in many ways is an English Mayor [Fiorello] LaGuardia! [the short, chesty, voluble chief executive of New York City]. Don't say I said so! I like him — & lunching alone broke the ice both ways.

Sun. Aug 10 eve — To go back a ways! Last night I held the official dinner, 16 of us — very grand — in my cabin — All the head Americans & British — toast to the King by me and to me by Churchill — Then I asked him to sum up the war & later called on Pound & Dill & Freeman to say a few words — A very good party & the "opposite numbers" are getting to know each other — We broke up at 11 P.M.

This A.M. at 10:30 I crossed to the deck of the destroyer, went alongside the *Prince of Wales,* was received with "honors," inspected the guard & walked aft to the quarter deck — & then the service was held — 300 men from our ships had come over for it — A British & an American chaplain did the prayers, Capt Leach [of the *Prince of Wales*] read the lesson — and then we were all photographed — front, sides & rear! Next I inspected the P. of W. in my chair, then sherry in the Ward Room & then a "beautiful" lunch of about 40 — Toasts followed by two speeches.

This P.M. a military & naval conference in my cabin — & now I'm ready for bed after dining Winston Churchill, his civilian aides & mine.

Mon. eve — Aug. 11 — A day of very poor weather but good talks. My staff came at 12, lunched, & we worked over [the] joint statement. They went and Churchill returned at 6:30 & we had a delightful little dinner of five: H. Hopkins, Elliott, F Jr., Churchill & myself. We talked about everything except the war! & Churchill said it was the nicest evening he had had! I so wish you could have been at the Church Service yesterday & at the little dinner tonight! How easy it is really to do big things if you can get an hour off!

It is the first bad day — raw & misty & typical Newfoundland weather. The Governor of N. lunched on the P. of W. with W.S.C. & came to call on me at 3 P.M. W.S.C. came on board Augusta with approval of statement by his Cabinet & the King — & after a few minor changes we gave final OKs & drew up the letter to [Marshal Josef] Stalin, & arranged for release dates etc. The various officers came after dinner & we are satisfied that they understand each other & that any future needs or conversations will meet with less crossed wires.

Tues. Aug. 12 — Still misty — W.S.C. to lunch with Lord [William Maxwell] Beaverbrook [minister of supply] who landed by plane this A.M. at Gander Lake from Scotland. They left at 3:30, their whole staff having come to say goodbye — It was a very moving scene as they received full honors going over the side. At 5 P.M. sharp the P. of W. passed out of the harbor, past all our ships. All crews were at quarters. She was escorted by her two corvettes & 2 Am. destroyers. F. Jr. on board one of the latter. Elliott left on a different secret mission, flying over Greenland's ice cap to Ireland.

Ten minutes later we too stood out of the harbor with our escort, homeward bound. So end these four days that I feel have contributed to things we hold dear —

Wed Aug. 13 — At sea — off Nova Scotia

All well & a bit of a let-down! But the afterthoughts are good & we hope the country will approve. It is still relatively smooth — very lucky both ways — I slept 12 hours!

Thurs. [Aug. 14] — At 11 A.M. we picked up the high hills of Mt Desert — Our new experimental ship the "Long Island" appeared & went through her exercises. At 2 we anchored off Blue Hill Bay, the little Potomac came alongside, we said goodbye to the Augusta, transferred, a run in to the mouth of Eggemoggin Reach, safe from submarines & are anchored in a protected cave trying to catch some flounder & buy some lobsters.

The radio talks & talks of the conference & the commentators are mostly very silly or very mendacious! Why can't they stick to facts? It was funny to [see] a paper again — borrowed from a fisherman!

[Roosevelt and Churchill issued the Atlantic Charter, pledging that "all men in all lands may live out their lives in freedom from fear and from want."]

Fri. — Aug. 15 We came slowly thro' the Reach, saw the new bridge P.W.A. built from the mainland to Deer Isle, fished, caught nought & anchored tonight in Pulpit Harbor [island of North Haven], the loveliest tiniest "hole in the wall" on the whole coast — Tomorrow we have only a dozen miles to Rockland where we take the train — I fear that 50 newshawks will meet us. That part will be harder than the conference itself —

Aff

F

[When he returned, Roosevelt turned his mind to Daisy's problems. On September 6, he came to tea again at Wilderstein, she noted, and "announced to the family that I am to have a job in the F.D.R. Library in Hyde Park! ½ time — beginning Oct 1st! *Just* what I want!" She was to be made a junior archivist, assigned to sorting the President's personal and family papers, at a salary of $1,000 a year.

Daisy's relationship with the President had gently shifted since they first began to talk together of one day sharing the cottage atop Our Hill. Roosevelt had been re-elected; there were to be no memoirs to work on now for at least three more years, and possibly longer.

But the new position would at least legitimate her frequent presence at his side; she and FDR no longer had to come up with pretexts for her visits to Washington or Hyde Park. There were always papers for them to pore over together.

The following day, the President's mother died in her home at Hyde Park. His secretary and confidante Missy LeHand had been immobilized in August. Faced with the likelihood of American entry into a world war, FDR was now more alone than he had ever been before. Two of the most important women in his life had been taken from him.

Daisy would soon find herself trying to make up as best she could for their loss.]

Rhinebeck —

Nov. 7th '41

Dear Franklin —

. . . What "headaches" you are having — I *wish* I could help — you know I *do,* with thoughts, and understanding —

I do so love my job — every minute of it — and I can't yet realize that it is I, M.L.S., who drives in there every day, who has her own

bunch of keys to "secret places," and who has the right to go in &
out all doors. The Pres.'s room looks so comfortable and cheerful and
attractive as I walk by the door!

Affec —
YM

[December 20, 1941, was Daisy's fiftieth birthday, and FDR invited her to a
quiet dinner at the White House. Afterward, in his cluttered study, they
photographed each other, he in evening clothes, she posed on a leopard skin
given to the President by Haile Selassie.]

1942

The One Focus
of Everyone's Eyes

～ *Jan. 20th 1942* —

Following is a sort of Diary of F.D.R. written from the angle of an old friend who has opportunities of seeing him "off the record." It will attempt to show the P. from a personal side which does not appear through the papers, and will not attempt to describe political or world conditions, except where these things are reflected in F.D.R. "by the way."

M.L.S.

[Hyde Park]

～ *Feb. 4th, 1942.* Pres. has been here since Sat. night . . . I am going down on the Presidential Special tonight with him, to work on . . . manuscripts.

Pres. developed a cold during the morning. Temperature a little under normal. All day he insisted on going to our [office] party for supper though Gen. Watson, Mrs. [Dorothy] Brady [one of the President's secretaries], & I tried to persuade him not to attempt it. The difficulty is that he thinks he is too heavy to be carried out to the car in his coat, so they put the coat in the car & carry him out in his house clothes — I think it's absurd! It certainly isn't right in winter weather — [Though he did not say so, FDR also feared that a thick coat made him harder to hold on to, increasing the risk of his being dropped.]

After lunch, he lay on the sofa & read . . . manuscripts until he got sleepy — then I left, promising to return at 4.30, to find out what was to happen.

When I returned, he had just waked from a sound sleep in front of the fire, was very cheerful & relaxed, but the cold was still there(!) so he sent me to tell Gen. Watson to cancel the train at Albany & to bring the thermometer & a corisa tablet.

We found temp. still sub-normal, & Gen. Watson got in touch with Adm. McIntire in N.Y. who was to come up —

They certainly take care of him as far as he will let them, and they are all sweet to him.

That big house without his mother seems awfully big & bare — she gave him that personal affection which his friends & secretaries cannot do, in the same way — He was always "my boy," and he seemed to me often rather pathetic, and hungry for just that kind of thing. His wife is a wonderful person, but she lacks the ability to give him the things his mother gave him. She is away so much, and when she is here she has so many people around — the splendid people who are trying to do good and improve the world, "uplifters," the P. calls them — that he can not relax and really rest. On this visit & the one before, in January, he has relaxed. He has had a few hours of work a day, the rest of the time he has busied himself with Library affairs & the place — and has played cards with the secretaries in the evening. It has been a real rest . . .

∾ *March 3rd.* . . . I went over for lunch with him & Harry Hopkins & Miss [Grace G.] Tully [the President's secretary, successor to Missy LeHand, usually known in Daisy's diaries as GGT]. The conversation is casual — not much about the times. He tries to stay away from the terrible problems of the day during the short hours he can spare for the Library & his books & collections . . .

He asked me to come to supper — I said I'd better come about 9 P.M. before going to the train. His answer was rather pathetic. "No come to dinner at seven — The others will play cards all the evening & I shall be lonely" — So, under "Royal Command," I (not *too* reluctantly!) accepted the invitation for dinner — Monty came for me in the presidential car — Rainy cold night — After dinner we went into the Library before the big fire. Mrs. [Sara Delano] Roosevelt's chair so very strikingly empty — I was conscious of it all the time, & feel he is, too — H. Hopkins & Miss Tully settled down to their gin-rummy. F.D.R. took up a little book and read it to me. It would be good for "morale" read by him over the radio — I am to shorten it for him. About 10 P.M. we started for the station —

Drove through rain to the station at Highland — the train standing waiting — guards everywhere — the P. walks up a ramp — Fala out of the car & into the rain before anyone . . . [W]e all sat in the observation saloon, & had orange juice & delicious canapés — a large variety — and then went off to bed — The President's car consists of a row of staterooms with the observation saloon at one end, the kitchen & dining saloon at the other — most comfortable staterooms with even a little door through which you put your shoes to find them polished the next morning!

. . . This train is so very smoothly run — no jerks & bumps — I must have at least dozed a little for I missed two of the scheduled stops! —

⮞ *March 4th*. Washington — We had breakfast on the train at 8.30 A.M. The P., though rested and cheerful, was beginning to think of his harassing schedule for the day.

. . . Reached Union Station at 9 A.M. and drove to the W.H. As soon as we got there all ushers, aides, Secret Service, etc. crowd around & the procession goes to the elevator where it thins out! The P., Harry H., Capt. [later Vice Admiral John R.] McCrae [the President's naval aide], Fala & I go up — others scatter.

Pres. goes to his desk where they bring him the latest news & tell him what his day consists of. I can see the "relaxation" vanish, & concentrated intenseness take its place — I sit on the sofa looking & listening — Several [are] waiting, each to have his say, all of them evidently on intimate terms with him, but all equally respectful and anxious to help him, too — He has a smile and a joke for each — He takes time to tell the telephone operator to get Betty Hambley on the phone to tell her to meet us for the [ninth inaugural anniversary] service at St. John's —

At 10.15 we go downstairs again. The Pres. sits on the front seat, next to Monty, who has on ordinary clothes — this is an "incognito" trip — I sit on the back seat between Gen. Watson & Capt. McCrae much impressed at myself! — At the Church, a guard of the Marines salutes — the Pres. walks up, Capt. McC. takes charge of me & whispers that "we will sit right behind the Pres." I whisper & nod, "yes!" The Pres., looking very serious, gets into the pew & Tommy Qualters whispers that I am to sit with the Pres. I whisper & nod "yes," step over the Pres's feet & sit down next to him. Harry Hooker & H. Hopkins step over the Pres's & my feet & sit to the left of me —

The service is lovely — short & impressive about 20 minutes — Betty Hambley joins us in the aisle as we move out. She & Capt. McCrae & I drive back to the W.H. on the back seat, Pres. in front.

Upstairs again to the Pres's study — It is about 11. He goes off to his office, looking worried . . .

At 4.30 I leave in a taxi & go to Betty's. Bobbie [Hambley] comes for supper — I haven't seen him for months — He has improved — looks thin as usual, in spite of a huge appetite. Young Rosser [a tutor

and companion, hired by the family] has been splendid with him &
seems fond of him. Only once for a few moments did Bobbie look not
quite right. He looked from one side to the other as though hearing
or seeing something — For the first time in 6 yrs he spoke to me by
name, both arriving and leaving . . .

∾ *March 5th.* According to "orders" I arrived at W.H. gates at 11
A.M. I don't know the guards, who telephoned to the house & let me
through — Inside the doors, I know several & feel relief at smiling
faces — Go straight to work in Pres's study — Soon, in comes Fala,
followed by the Pres. He looks harassed, & says he will have several
bad days "catching up" on top of bad news from the Far East —

[The news could hardly have been worse. Singapore had fallen to the Japanese. Just since the first of the month, the Japanese had landed on Java and
New Guinea and were about to complete their conquest of the Philippines.]

Goes off to his office . . .
At 2.30 I hear Mrs. R. arriving. During the afternoon, I hear her
at intervals, making arrangements, giving orders, receiving people —
No one comes into the room, but with one ear cocked I know a good
deal through the open door! —
At 5.50 I am "woozy" from work & go to the Lincoln Room, where
Malvina Thompson [Eleanor Roosevelt's tireless secretary throughout
the presidential years] has established my hat & coat — I close the
two doors & lie down on the sofa — *Just* beginning to doze off when
a loud knock & [White House usher] Mr. [Wilson] Searles's voice tell
me the Pres. wants me down in the Doctor's office for a moment — I
know at once what it means: My eyes and glasses are to be tested
against my wishes! — I *try* to think, but *can't* think of an excuse, &
go down with Mr. Searles — Find Pres. having his sinus treated, &
laughing at my helplessness — I tell him he is *the* most obstinate man
I have ever known — much to the amusement of the Dr. & Capt.
McCrae.
The Doctor tests my glasses & says in a low tone "I think we have
the laugh on the President." He finds the glasses just right, & I take
great pleasure in telling the P. so, in a loud voice. He says he is very glad
& we all have a good laugh! I am then told to go & "resume my nap."
It's too late to settle down again, so I brush my hair, wash my
hands & face, & go into the P.'s study — Mrs. R, with Miss van Loon
[daughter of the writer Hendrik Willem van Loon] & Joe Lash

[Joseph P. Lash, former official of the National Youth Congress and close friend of Eleanor Roosevelt] both of the "Youth Movement," come in — we have sherry, then go for dinner into Mrs. R's sitting room — (end of hall).

Miss V.L. very earnest, nice & quite attractive — J.L. quiet — Mrs. R. has sheaf of papers on the table beside her plate: Things to "take up" with the P.

The P. wants to relax — looks tired — tries several lighter subjects of conversation, which, however, are invariably turned to some "problem" by the others.

Dinner over, Mrs. R. & two "youths" depart for a meeting of "Flaming Youth." The P. & I get to work on his old manuscripts — they require much time — each to be read for subject, period, associations, writers, etc. . . .

[On March 6, Daisy traveled south to visit her young cousin Rolly Brown Maury and her husband, Jack, then working at the Newport News shipyards.]

ᴗ· *March 6th.* I take 4 P.M. train to Newport News — Lots of very young soldiers & sailors on board — very crowded — a bunch of sailors slightly drunk, talk a lot & try to pick up every young girl — I watch a pick-up of two people of *my* age — *Very* young girl sitting in front of me — her coat bunched on the seat next to her — a *very* young sailor stops & asks if that coat is going to stay there, she nods yes — He returns several times, finally she removes the coat & he sits down! They are both nice young things — Conversation *very* proper & uninteresting! At Richmond he & I get onto a C. & O. train for Newport News — ten minutes later he has found another girl, & they are drinking water together — nothing more happens except that 3 other very young soldiers get boisterous right behind me — started rough-housing & the elbow of one lands on top of my head — no harm done — I straighten my hat . . .

ᴗ· *Sunday March 8th* — . . . [The Maurys] took me to the station for the 3 o'clock train back to Wash. Having arrived after dark on Friday, I was surprised to find the station at the water's edge. A fantastic story they told: Our submarines come into Norfolk to refuel — Some young people were watching them — An English officer remarked that one of them must be one of our very newest models — he didn't recognize it.

This new model took its turn with the others & started out to sea — It turned out later that she was a disguised German! She was recognized down the bay — her crew taken off & she was sunk — A few other cases have occurred at different Southern ports. Pres. says he inquired about this. It did *not* & *could not* happen.

When I arrived at Richmond, I remembered that I was to telegraph the Pres. the hour of my arrival — he insisted on having me met so that I could do some work on R. [Roosevelt family] papers that evening. So, I went up to a very young Western Union boy, wrote out my telegram: "The President — The White House — Washington, D.C. Will arrive at Union Station 8.45. Signed M. L. Suckley" — Cost: 45cts —

Then, with many others, I settled down on first one foot, then the other, to wait for the train which was an hour late. While [I was] still standing near the gate, the telegraph boy came back, showed me the telegraph, & asked, embarrassed, if it was really meant for the President!! I reassured him & he went off & I thought no more about it.

My train finally came — very crowded & hot — We stopped at every woodpile & crossing, *unscheduled* stops, all the way to Wash. & finally reached Union Station at almost ten P.M. I stood, waiting, & the chauffeur appeared, very polite, & took me & my bag to the car — I was much embarrassed arriving so late & suggested to Mr. [Charles K.] Claunch [second assistant usher at the White House] that I had better go right on to Betty's house — Mr. Claunch said no, the Pres. was expecting me, & at the moment, watching a movie — So up we went, & I slipped into the empty chair next to the P. in the dark —

The movie was "Arsenic & Old Lace" — I was too late to appreciate it or have an opinion about it. Franklin Jr. & Ethel [Du Pont Roosevelt] were there . . . attractive nice young people.

The Pres. took me into the study & with much laughter told me that I had almost been arrested in Richmond & "put in the jug"! I missed an experience! It appears that some dozen people each week send telegrams to the P. that they are arriving at such & such a time. Most of them have definite illusions that they are important people — Most of them end up in St. Elizabeth's [a psychiatric hospital near Washington].

My telegram was received by Mr. Hutchinson who "does" the [Secret Service] identification cards. He had never heard my name — neither had another S.S. man who was with him, so he put in a call for Richmond to have me followed & watched — Just then Mike Reilly [Michael F. Reilly, head of the White House Secret Service detail] came in, was shown the telegram, was horrified at what *might* happen to me — The call was cancelled & I never got to the jug! If I'd only known, I could have enjoyed the excitement, & having myself gotten out of jail by the P. himself — perhaps! . . .

∾ *Monday March 9th.* . . . Mr. Searles came in & asked if I had time to get an identification card — I was delighted though I wouldn't have been able to use it on this trip! So off we started — Mr. S. was substituted by the tall negro — we walked over to the Executive offices & there I met Mr. Hutchinson who had *almost* put me in jail! He told me the complete story & we all had a good laugh about it.

He made out my identification card — age, color, etc., took the print of my right index finger, & introduced me as the lady who sent the telegram! I find he has given me *black* hair!

It was something of a rush to get all the old papers and ledgers packed into boxes & taken downstairs to a car with *two-men-on-the-box*, by 3 o'clock — The second man was to help get the books out & upstairs at the National Archives — It turned out to be quite unnecessary, but I enjoyed the rare experience of *looking* important. [The National Archives was to oversee the collections housed in the FDR Library, and it was part of Daisy's job, under the immediate supervision of Fred Shipman, the first library director, to coordinate her work with that of Dr. Solon Buck, the archivist of the United States, to make certain the President's manuscripts and books would be properly cared for.] We plunged down into the depths of the Nat. Archives bldg. where I was expected — The boxes taken out, & I escorted upstairs to Dr. Buck's office — I felt very important being the emissary of the President, and discussing just what kind of containers should be used, etc. I hope the boxes will be right & attractive looking. They are to be blue with gold lettering & marked "*Roosevelt Family Papers.*" I told Dr. Buck about my two-men-on-the-box, & he escorted me to the car, to see them — quite intrigued!

. . . [W]hen the P. took Gen. Watson & Dorothy Jones (Mrs. Brady) up [to Hyde Park] a month ago — Dorothy had what was probably the *first* experience of her life, of staying in bed & having her breakfast brought up to her! At dinner tonight, the P. was telling us about it & getting real satisfaction out of the pleasure Dorothy had had — He also told us about Gen. Watson & his breakfast of pheasant hash with *three* poached eggs! His wife only allows him coffee & orange juice, because he has a decided tendency towards corpulence!! The P. told us that Gen. W., when at home, tells his wife he is going for a walk after breakfast — there is a convenient diner near by, & the General gets a satisfying snack en route — sausages & pancakes perhaps? . . .

At 8.30, the Pres. said we must get to work at the last pile of papers. After 10 minutes of work, Mr. Claunch appeared: "Mr. Pres. they are waiting for your broadcast." We jump — the P. grabs his speech, fortunately prepared beforehand, gets on his chair, and we literally dash to the elevator, across the hall into the room where broadcasts are given. *Just* in time for Mr. [Claude] Wickard [secretary of Agriculture] to begin *his* little speech! . . .

I hated to say goodbye to the P. [and return to Rhinebeck]. In these dreadful days one never knows what to expect next, and these few hours when I see him peaceful & relaxed are few & far between — I know they do him good & are the reason he goes to H.P. when he can — He gets some real rest, while his secretaries play cards together . . .

[Rhinebeck]

᭙ *March 21st.* Pres. called up from Washington . . . He sounded well. Said he had had a "bad nose" but was all right again. Said Littleton [Hambley] is being transferred to another part of Agriculture — Will come up here next week, if possible.

I wrote him about going with [Alan] Frost [a fellow archivist at the library] etc. to hear the "Bird Chorus" at Thompson's Pond on May 10th! He is *thrilled,* but we must not even breathe it to anyone! [Birdwatching was one of the many pleasures that polio had forced Roosevelt to abandon; Daisy had hatched a scheme that would allow him on his next visit to see and hear a host of wildfowl without leaving his automobile.]

᭙ *Friday — March 27th.* The P. came from Wash. last night — Came to the Library about noon today. Looks well & not so worn as the last three visits. I wish I could remember all the interesting things he says — His mind is so full, so active, so sympathetic, so interested, so human —

I drafted a letter for him to thank J. Sterling Bird for the model of the ice-yacht he sent him. Miss Huber typed it & brought it in to be signed — no pen — Pres. takes up a pencil, & scribbles "F.D.R." & underneath: "This is the first time I have used Library paper," or equivalent words — Mr. Bird will cherish that —

I take up the question of the "gate" at his [office] door — the present one is ugly & heavy & awkward. Pres. takes pencil & paper

& designs one to be "like a fire screen" — Thin steel wire with a narrow brass top — Another important "document," for he signs it in the corner!! F.D.R. — *facit (faked)* 1942 . . .

✑ *Saturday March 28th.* A busy morning at the Library doing lots of odd jobs connected directly with the Pres. — It is always a little "hectic" when he is here! At 12.40 he drove up, Harry Hopkins sitting next to him with Fala in his arms, Miss Tully & Diana [daughter of Harry Hopkins, for whom Mrs. Roosevelt had agreed to act as guardian after her mother's death] in the back — I get in with them & Mr. H. hands Fala over to me!

Off we go to the Top Cottage where we have a delicious lunch — First I get out the tea cloth & napkins purchased by F.D.R. himself at Panama, I think, on one of his cruises — It is like Italian embroidery. I put it on the card table in front of the fireplace. A low glass top table is in front of the P. who sits on the sofa — Miss T., Diana & I unpack the picnic baskets (2) & out come: clam broth — hot — A large Kentucky ham, tomato salad — cheese — fruit — coffee — bread — Mr. Hopkins slices the ham & the P. shows us how to butter two slices of bread — spread ham on one, *cheese* on the other, mustard over both, & put them together! Delicious!

I leave about 2.30. They are all having dinner at Mrs. R's cottage [so] no more relaxation, as Mrs. R. has so many things to discuss with & ask the P. about . . . I must look up history of two gavels for him to choose from, for the [new president of the White House Correspondents Association].

✑ *Monday, March 30th.* Get the gavels, wrap up both — take them to Big House at 9.50 A.M. We know nothing about either except that one is marked "F.D.R. 1937."

Pres. says: "Which do you think I should give them?"

I say: "Well the brown one is the best — the one we would rather keep at the Library, because it is marked 'F.D.R. 1937.'"

Pres. says: "All right, I'll take that one, they would like it best, too" —

So off he goes, driving to New York with Miss Tully (H. Hopkins & Diana & Mrs. R. went down last night) to choose things out of his mother's house to be sent up here. [With the death of the President's mother, the twin Roosevelt houses in Manhattan were to be given up. Eleanor Roosevelt rented herself an apartment, but FDR now had no New York City base.]

I wave them off from the Big House steps with the other wrapped-up gavel — Four police and S.S. cars fall in line behind his car — Monty not in uniform — It is less noticeable —

~ *April 17th Friday* — At F.D.R.L. The P. called me up about 10.15 this A.M. He said, "Hell's a-poppin'," to express the general world situation, & he has had a bad week — This morning, from his arrival at 9, telephoning to Washington. Now must write a speech on inflation to be given a week from Monday . He drove over with Miss Tully, Judge [Samuel E.] Rosenman [presidential aide and speechwriter] & M. McIntyre. I got in front & pulled Fala up beside me.

The P. said he was in a bad humor — needed fresh air & a change — We spent an hour climbing up & down his narrowest, most winding wood roads, looking at the lumber they are cutting out for the govt. I went over to lunch at 1. found him finishing a "basket" & listened for a few moments while he & Judge R. discussed policy . . . The P. seemed more relaxed — Everybody in a "pun-ish" mood. M.M. got off a few during lunch! The P. is so accustomed to *not* letting himself go, that one gets only occasional fleeting glimpses of his real worry over the world in general & this war in particular.

[One of Roosevelt's worries about the war that evening was that Colonel James H. Doolittle's daring raid on Tokyo, set for the following day, might fail. Never before in wartime had B-25s, fully laden with bombs, taken off from a carrier. They made it, however, and dropped their loads on the Japanese capital, striking a psychological blow against the enemy and providing America with its first good news from the Pacific theater.]

~ *April 21st.* I returned to my files at the W.H. A little before 4 P.M. Mrs. [Mary] Eben [one of Roosevelt's secretaries since his days as an executive with the Fidelity & Deposit Insurance Company] suggested I go to P.'s press conference. Thrilled! Outside of the little one at H.P., this was my first. The P. had told me at breakfast on the train that he was going to tell them that "Shangri-La" was the base of our planes that bombed Japan! Just about ½ of them "got it," & laughed — [Shangri-La was the mythical Himalayan kingdom in James Hilton's novel *Lost Horizon*.]

~ *April 22nd.* Went to W.H. for four large packages to take to the National Archives. The Filipino Caesar who wrapped them for me said he knew all the Roosevelts well, after six years in the White

House, & he would "go anywhere to serve a Roosevelt." The P. came through the room on his way to his office. Always anxious that everything shall be easy & comfortable. He said he felt well & rested & ready for a heavy week preparing his fireside chat & message to Congress. That means more exhaustion next week! . . .

[Rhinebeck]

⤳ *May 7th Thursday* — I remember a little story F.D.R. told me in Washington. At the [home of Crown Princess Martha of Norway, who had developed a close friendship with FDR] one day, little Harald was told by his mother to do something he didn't want to do. He turned around & slapped her face — She just said, "Don't do that," etc.

When things had calmed down a bit, the President beckoned to Harald & said, "Come over here a minute." Harald came, & the President took him by the shoulders & said to him: "You know, old man, you are getting to be a really big boy, and there are some things a big boy & a gentleman just doesn't do, no matter who he is — Just remember that!" A few days later, when Harald had gone to bed, the Crown Princess went in to say goodnight to him & found him crying. He put his arms around her neck & said, "Mummie, I'm trying so hard to remember I'm a *big* boy."

When Bobbie Delano [a young cousin of the President's] was growing up, & he & the Roosevelt boys were all running around together, & at times drinking a bit too much, the Pres. on one occasion gave Bobbie Delano a talking to. He & Franklin Jr. had given a young girl too much to drink. Bobbie told the Pres. later that he was grateful for the talk & that he wished *his* father would talk to him that way — he would be a better man.

[Hyde Park]

⤳ *May 9th Saturday*. Lunch at Big House. Harry Hopkins drove up from N.Y. with Paulette Goddard [a film star whom some on the President's staff believed Hopkins planned to marry].

Paulette G. *very* pretty — a studied ingenue with an innocent smile 'til you see her in repose, when it's a hard, disillusioned face. Perhaps I am wrong! They shouldn't bring people like that to the house . . .

⤳ *May 10th*. Got up at 2 A.M., prepared coffee, dry cereal, boiled eggs, for breakfast at 2.30 for Ludlow [Griscom, author of *The Birds of New York City Region*] and me. At 10 of 3 we left the house. Went to J. Whitehead's. Got into his car & picked up Alan Frost & Ray Guernsey. [Whitehead, Frost, and Guernsey all worked at the Roosevelt Library.] Went to the President's house. Alan, Ludlow & I got in with him in his big open car. Drove to Thompson's Pond where we heard the bird chorus at dawn.

. . . The P. left us about 7.30. He seemed to really enjoy every minute. It is the kind of thing he has probably given up any idea of ever doing again, so it did him lots of good. In that far-off silent place, with myriads of birds waking up, it was quite impossible to think much of the horrors of war . . . [Roosevelt did enjoy it, carefully filling out the checklist in his bold hand: "Total for day 108 species. Franklin D. Roosevelt."]

⟶ *May 11th.* Pres. seemed very cheerful. He is so fond of [Crown Prince] Olaf & specially Martha whom he calls "Godchild." He drove them to Stockbridge to look at a house for the summer. A perfect day with trees in bloom.

[Some in the President's entourage believed his feelings for Crown Princess Martha may have been stronger than mere fondness; he clearly enjoyed himself in her company. Tall, slender, and always elegantly turned out, she was deferential to him but high-spirited, too, and she blushed easily when teased. She was also married and the mother of three small children, whom he had adopted as his godchildren, and whenever she was eager to reach her exiled husband, Crown Prince Olaf, in England, it was the President who personally put through the calls. Daisy, who spent a good deal of time in Martha's company and might well have been expected to be jealous, does not seem to have thought the Princess and the President were ever more than friends.]

⟶ *May 12th Tuesday* — The P. stopped by for me at 1.15 & drove to the Big House for lunch . . . I had a lovely time alone with the P. You can say *any*thing & ask *any* questions of him when alone, but when others are there I am always afraid of saying something I shouldn't or asking what he doesn't want to answer — I think he feels more hopeful about the outcome of the war, though we may have many bad times ahead, specially this summer . . . He was tired from his weekend, said [this] was the first moment he had had to relax — The Norwegians . . . [and the] "young people" left last night. I am proud that he *does* relax with me, & makes no effort. He misses his mother. The house has no hostess most of the time, as his wife is here so rarely — always off on a speaking tour, etc.

I forgot to write above that he came for me, driving up the Library road. I was waiting at his private entrance & was rather surprised to see him suddenly dash across the grass, S.S. & police cars after him! Everyone laughing, including visitors in the Library looking out of the windows — Before seeing me he tooted his horn, under my office! When I got into the car, he said he loved to drive on Govt. grass once in a while!

◈ *May 26th.* Called me up last night from Wash about the weekend. He can't get away until next Monday or Tuesday . . . "Someone" is coming from England by air, & he will have to spend three days on conferences. He said he was very tired & all alone & was going to bed at 10. He said Fala was very sweet — jumped into the front seat of the car beside him & went to sleep . . .

[Rhinebeck]

◈ *May 30th.* . . . F.D.R. called up last evening. He is very busy with a "visiting fireman" whose name will be announced in the papers in about a week. The "visiting fireman" came from "across the water," doesn't speak a word of English, "comes from Shangri-La & speaks nothing but Mongolian," says F.D.R. He then proceeds to tell me that they talk through interpreters: one, a Russian who talks perfect English, the other, an American who has lived for years in Russia! 2 & 2 = 4!

F.D.R. has never seen the "V.F." before, but hears he is *not* very pleasant, and *never smiles.* Perhaps F.D.R. will make him smile!

F.D.R. is sending Roly [Hambley] her graduation bouquet: red, white and blue, with a white satin ribbon. He wants me to draft a letter from him to Helen Morton [daughter of Levi P. Morton and a Hudson River neighbor] to thank her for the Ellerslie papers [concerning the Morton estate, Ellerslie, donated to the library].

He is having a hectic month! He has to find summer places for Queen Wilhelmina [and] Princess Juliana [of the Netherlands] & Princess Martha, & this next week Peter of Yugoslavia & the King of Greece and the Duke of Windsor are all coming to Washington. He says he hopes for a quiet July . . .

[Like his late mother, Roosevelt enjoyed knowing royalty, and during the war years he delighted in being the protector of exiled European rulers; an astonishing amount of his time was taken up with sorting out their personal problems.]

∾ *May 31st Sunday.* Very hot yesterday & today. The "Visiting Fireman" is [Soviet Foreign Minister Vyacheslav] Molotov & F. got him to smile & be "quite human"! I knew he would if anyone could . . .

∾ *June 13th.* The P. called up last evening . . . He said he was distracted with all the visitors! One royalty after the other: kings, queens, princesses, Molotov!! He was very funny. He has this coming week quiet, between them all, & will come to H.P. for three days, with only Harry Hopkins & Miss Tully. He said the King of Greece is *awfully nice,* & he will try to get him up here for a visit. His sinus & the [Washington] heat, very troublesome. [Roosevelt suffered from chronic sinus trouble, which worsened when he was under stress. His doctor treated him with special sprays every evening, but they seem only to have made things worse.]

∾ *June 15th.* "The plans of mice & men"! The P. called up last night to say everything is changed — Jimmy & his wife [Jimmy's second wife was Romelle Schneider, the nurse who had cared for him while he recuperated at the Mayo Clinic in 1938] arriving from the West today — Several unexpected things have turned up, so that he won't have a free moment for work. So I am to go down later, perhaps about June 30th —

He said the King of Greece will come to H.P. next week — wants an American wife — The P. told him about his godchild [Margaret "Roly"] Hambley who is not yet 18 — The King is "only 51"! Roly & I are to be taken for a drive with him!!

∾ *June 18th.* A Very Big day! The Pres. came to the Library about 11.30 A.M. . . . "Mr. Weinstein" arriving tonight, i.e. Winston Churchill! Reports about W.C. kept coming in during the day — The last being that he had arrived in Washington too late to fly to Hyde Park before dark. The Poughkeepsie airport is not lighted. Will come early tomorrow & will be met at Hyde Park station by F.D.R., about 9.30.

[In the end, he did fly from Washington the next morning. FDR met him at the

New Hackensack airport, after what Churchill recalled as "one of the toughest bump landings I have ever experienced." Churchill had come because he feared the President had been too sanguine with Molotov about the imminence of an Allied cross-Channel invasion to relieve the pressure on Russia.]

We sorted a large batch of prints, pictures, etc. Then to the Attic, where, with Mr. Shipman & Nixon [Dr. Edgar B. Nixon was assistant director of the Franklin D. Roosevelt Library], a lot of crates & boxes from the N.Y. house were opened. Mrs. R. to take what she wants — We laid them out on top of a row of unopened boxes. The Pres. was cheerful & funny as usual. He called Roly the Scrapbasket, & threw all waste paper toward her. Mr. Shipman continued in his role of "Junk Collector"!

The Pres. asked Roly & me to lunch. I called up Miss Tully: "The P. says there will be four for lunch."

"There are already eight." So it goes!

. . . Off we go. Mrs. R. was sitting knitting on the front porch. With her were Diana Hopkins & a little friend, their governess . . . & Miss Thompson, & Miss Tully & Mr. Hopkins. We all went in to lunch. F.D.R. was in very good form, & full of mischief. He showed Roly, who sat on his left, how well he could eat peas with his knife! Mrs. R. didn't quite approve & explained to the little girls that the Pres. was joking! . . .

Roly & I went right off to the Library right after lunch & to work. Roly is sorting presidential mail for Mr. Nixon & sits on the floor in James Whitehead's room. When we went up to the attic in the morning I opened the door & there she was. She got up, glasses on nose, a lock of hair over her face. The P. greeted her with open arms & kissed her, lock, glasses & all! He *is* so sweet — & she does appreciate it. He took out of one of the boxes, a green leather jewelry box marked "S.D.R." & gave it to Roly.

"Just what she needs."

[Rollie Hambley, now Mrs. J. Morton Hendrick, remembers that, purely because she was Daisy's niece, FDR treated her as one of the family. Among his many kindnesses: when he learned she was interested in collecting autographs, he said he'd get some for her from his most eminent visitors. Daisy bought her a handsome album, and for several months the President secured for her the signatures of many celebrated visitors — statesmen, politicians, royalty — and Shirley Temple.]

◦ *June 19th Friday*. Today, an extraordinary experience of sitting at lunch with Winston Churchill & Franklin Roosevelt.

I walked over to the house about one o'clock, & as the President drove up with W.C. by his side in his little blue car, I waited by Fala's pen until the P. should be carried in. When I reached the hall, Robert [McGauhey, the Roosevelts' British butler] was asking Charlie [Fredericks, Secret Service man] how many there would be for lunch. No one else in sight.

I stood looking out through the front door. In a minute or two a pair of grey legs appeared on the top step, followed by Mr. Churchill, short & round, his eyes very blue. Seeing a strange woman, he stopped on the lower stair landing & examined a painting. I started to gaze at something, too — it may have been the trees!

He turned & came down the last two steps — he smiled — I smiled. We shook hands — I introduced myself — We wandered down the hall to the Library. He has never been here before — was interested in everything — We wandered back to the hall — Harry Hopkins appeared. Then Com. [Charles R.] Thomson [Churchill's police bodyguard] and John Martin [the Prime Minister's secretary]. We all wandered to the enclosed porch. Lunch was announced, & we all stood up for the P.M. to go through the door first. He stopped for me; so I went through! The P. was waiting at the door of the dining-room, Miss Tully with him . . .

It was a fascinating lunch. One could only watch these two men talking. They were both in fine form, rested & playing on & with each other . . . Both like Molotov; both think he understands English, though they conversed only through interpreters. W.C. thinks Molotov was persuaded that F.D.R. & W.C. are sincere in wishing to bring a better world out of the present chaos — F.D.R. said he was warned that he would find Molotov "frozen." He *was* frozen, until after dinner, when F.D.R. says he said something humorous & Molotov smiled! After that he was "quite human." I would call that a real victory for F.D.R.!

Mr. Churchill said he *almost* got to the point of saying to Molotov: "I wish I understood Russian as well as you understand English." But *not quite*.

There seemed to be real friendship & understanding between F.D.R. & Churchill. F.D.R.'s manner was easy and intimate — His face humorous, or very serious, according to the subject of conversation, and entirely *natural*. Not a trace of having to guard his words or expressions, just the opposite of his manner at a press conference, when he is an actor on a stage — and a player on an instrument, at the same time.

After lunch, we all dispersed. The last word I heard Mr. C. say, was to arrange to telephone his wife.

The Pres. called me over to him & asked me to "speak to George" about tea at [Top] Cottage tomorrow! I went over to do so, at 4.30, after the Pres. & Churchill had left for tea with Laura Delano. I told George I didn't quite know what to tell him, but to have tea, some sandwiches, & some cake. George suggested he send a bottle of scotch & some ice in case Mr. C. might like some. He evidently takes it quite regularly.

[Daisy did not attend the "tea" at Laura Delano's home south of Rhinebeck, but it is worth describing. The President's showy cousin shared with him an enthusiasm for cloying drinks and took special pride in a Tom Collins that called for several varieties of rum. When Churchill, whose strict fidelity to Scotch even Daisy had come to understand, arrived, Miss Delano asked whether he would like one of her specialties. He would not, he said: Scotch, please. Laura Delano did not like to be turned down, even by the Prime Minister of England, and so, as he and the President settled themselves in chairs on her terrace, she continued to concoct one of her specialties, then carried it to him. Absorbed in conversation, Churchill took the glass and gulped at it without looking. Disbelief clouded his face. He glared at his hostess, then spat out her drink onto the flagstones.

Laura Delano never really liked Churchill after that, she said.]

☞ *June 21st Monday.* . . . At 4, we drove over to the cottage. George soon came with supplies for tea. He brought out a card table & put iced tea, sandwiches & some cookies on it. On another little table he had scotch & soda.

The P. soon came with [his special representative in London] Averell Harriman & his wife, rather pretty & nice, though lacking in personality. Averell H. himself is quite attractive and good-looking. He sat on the front seat. Mr. Churchill, Mrs. H. & Harry Hopkins on the back seat. When he came in on his wheel chair, the P. asked me to pour tea. Sugar, lemon, mint, ice & tea! I got confused & when I changed the order, I forgot either the sugar, or the lemon, or the mint, or a spoon, at the end! Don't think anyone noticed but Miss Tully, who I wished was doing it instead of me! When everyone was served, I moved my chair over near F.D.R. I had made him some egg sandwiches with mustard greens — He loved them & ate nothing else.

Conversation was a little slow. Everyone sits around waiting for the P. & Mr. C. to speak — It must be quite a strain on them both —

The P. said I could take some pictures. I took several, & hope they will turn out. The P.M. turned right around in his chair & smiled for me!

These two men face a horrible problem: of deciding where the United Nations should attack — the different heads of the army and navies disagree about it, and these two have the terrible responsibility of making a decision. Both seemed a little tired and absent-minded though this might not have been noticed by anyone who doesn't know the P. as well as I do.

[Just before coming to tea, Churchill had expressed his concern to Roosevelt that the Germans were making alarming progress toward the manufacture of an atomic bomb just when their bombing of Britain was making British research on atomic weaponry virtually impossible. FDR reassured him that the United States would assume that responsibility. Two months later, the Manhattan Project got under way.]

Harry Hopkins & the P.M. get on very well. Roly thinks they are closer than the P. & the P.M. Perhaps she's right. I haven't seen enough of them to know. Harry Hopkins is not impressed by important people — Royalty, etc. — but strikes me as too anxious to show he isn't! He is almost familiar with the Cr. Princess Martha. That's the difference between him & the P., who doesn't have to show anyone he is not impressed by greatness of any kind. He is one of them. This morning, Mr. [Christian] Bie [caretaker of Top Cottage] spoke of that: how simple Great People are — not afraid to be "themselves," etc. It was a memorable occasion.

[Rollie Hambley was still a teenager, but her observations were shrewd beyond her years. After Daisy had arranged for her and a young British friend, Anne Curzon-Howe, to dine with the President and Winston Churchill at the White House the previous January, she wrote up her impressions.

                                                            January 14, 1942
    Dear Deedle [a family name for Daisy],
        . . . We got to the White House at 7:15 very out of
    breath . . . Before 7:30 came round Mr. and Mrs. Louis
    Adamic [the author of *The Native's Return*, who later got
    a whole book out of this evening, *Dinner at the White
    House*] and a very good friend of the President and Mrs.
    Roosevelt called James Milton.
        . . . We met Mrs. R. in the hall and she introduced us

to the Pres. He was so nice and kissed me in the same
way he does when only the family is around! Of course the
whole assemblage, including Mrs. R., looked on I suppose
wondering who I was. After a short while (during which
we had cocktails) the P.M.'s Naval attaché, Commander
Thomson, came in looking very exhausted and stood in a
corner. Five minutes after that, the Prime Minister and his
secretary, John Martin, came in and were introduced to
everyone. I was introduced as "Rollie, the Godchild," and
Anne as "Miss Curzon-Howe, a fellow compatriot."

The Prime Minister is about 5′7″ and quite fat about
the waist . . . He has a very pink face, whitish-red thin hair,
and very piercing pale blue eyes. He looks just like his
pictures and his nose has a very strange shape — it looks
as if it were chiseled. He doesn't have nearly as much social
charm and personality as the President, but he is very quiet
and asks leading questions.

. . . I was next to the President and could also look
across the table into W.C.'s blue eyes. James Milton, the
friend of Mrs. R., was next to me and talked incessantly
about Peru. He couldn't talk of anything else and if I tried
to switch to another country he would always revert back
again. Mrs. Roosevelt talked a good deal, as the Adamics
and Miss [Malvina] Thompson were friends of hers.

The P.M. talked to the Pres. a good deal about South
America. He is not a conversationalist for formal dinners.
He is much more apt to ask very deep, thought-provoking
questions. He has a habit of asking a question and then
when the person is nicely involved in a long oratory, the
P.M. will suddenly turn away and join in another conversation just as if he were listening to both and thought the
other more interesting. He has a very keen mind much
more so than the Pres. but of course he has not all that
wonderful charm and personality. It is as if his round che-
rubic face had an entirely different mind behind it. When
he smiles he looks just like a little boy with dimples but you
can't help remembering the kind of man he is underneath.
He has a very dry humor and is a typical Englishman in his
manners. He has a very poor voice. One can hardly understand him it is so indistinct and stammering, but he uses the
most wonderful language imaginable. He speaks very often

in similes and metaphors, comparing the Germans to hawks, and [German Foreign Minister Joachim] Von Ribbentrop to a clown.

To show an example of his dry humor — he was looking very gloomily down at his plate but with a twinkly eye, and said how perfectly dreadful the man was to bomb all the beautiful scotch whiskey and cigar warehouses. He said he didn't know what would happen to a country when its supplies of whiskey and cigars ran out.

He and the Pres. also [told] a very gruesome tale of the P.M.'s box of cigars which had been sent from Cuba and which was filled with worms. At that point I let out an awful groan and refused to eat any more food, but he seemed to delight in my illness and went into more & more detail of how they crept through each cigar . . .

When dinner was over (we had very rare roast beef and Yorkshire pudding!) Mrs. Roosevelt rose and said that she was going to Constitution Hall to hear [conductor Arturo] Toscanini. Thinking that it was an appropriate time I backed away to say goodbye to everyone, but the Pres. took me by the hand and said, "Stay here, we're going to finish our coffee." So — there we were left with the P.M., Commander Thomson, and Sec. James Martin. The Pres said that he knew it was a mean trick but that ever since I had seen Sir Ronald Lindsay . . . I had been determined to marry a Scotsman. He asked Churchill if he wouldn't find me a nice Scotch laird. It turned out that James Martin was Scotch but not a laird.

The Pres. told them about my autograph book and he asked me to call Miss Tully and tell her to ask the P.M. to sign my book. The conversation went on in a very amusing way concerning cigars, the 30 points, German religion, Von Ribbentrop, Carol of Rumania, Zog of Albania, whiskey, college reunions, and growing old. The P.M. said that a woman was as old as she looked; a man was as old as he felt; and a boy was as old as he was treated.

He also looked very sadly at me and said "You know I must be the oldest man ever to have been in the White House." The Pres. said there had been someone 95 there, so he cheered up. The Pres. said he had received a very good picture of W.C. from Vancouver except that his face was too round and his hair too red and there was too much of it.

CENSOR THIS — *Je n'aime pas Madame R.* The Pres & W.C. could get on better! . . .

Loads of Love
Rollie]

[On June 21 Churchill and Roosevelt returned together to Washington, where they learned the Nazis had crushed the South African garrison at Tobruk and British armor at El Gazala and were advancing toward Egypt. Sometime that week, FDR called Daisy just to talk, and she jotted down on a separate piece of paper a little of what the President said. Someone had evidently told Daisy that, despite the Allied setbacks, victory was certain.]

F. said not necessarily — that he told Sir John Dill that the trouble with the British is that they think they can beat the Germans if they have an equal number of men, tanks etc. F. says that is not so — The Germans are better trained, better generaled — "You can never *discipline* an Englishman or an American as you can a German" —

I asked where the blame lies for the present situation in Egypt. He said partly Churchill, mostly the bad generals — F. was depressed over the situation. If Egypt is taken, it means Arabia, Syria, Afghanistan, etc., i.e. the Japs & Germans control everything across from the Atlantic to the Pacific — that means all the oil wells, etc. of those regions — a bleak prospect for the United Nations.

[The White House]

July 5th Sunday — 9.50 A.M. I'm sitting up in bed, writing on a folded newspaper. A large G.E. fan, on the mantelpiece, is blowing a soft breeze at me, gently ruffling the pink silk blanket cover, and the corners of the Washington *Star* & parts of the N.Y. *Times* which are now being used as my desk. I'm in the Northwest corner, with two large windows — It's a little room, tucked away behind the Lincoln room . . .

I am trying to realize that I am actually *staying* here, in the White House! The President "commanded" me down here for a week, to work on his [state] senatorial papers. We left Hyde Park Friday night, travelling from Highland on the West Shore & B.&O. lines. Harry Hopkins, his fiancée, Louise Macy [the former Paris editor of *Harper's Bazaar*], & I, in the Pres's car. Secs. in other cars . . .

Mrs. R. was so nice & took Mrs. Macy to the Blue Room. Then she brought me to this room, telling me I had better stay here through the week. The room is occupied by her friend, Miss [Lorena] Hickok, who is away all this week. So here I am!

Last night there were 3 separate dinners in the W.H. Mrs. R. told the P. she was having a dinner of women: "You won't want to come to that, we are to discuss . . ."

Elliott & his wife had some friends for dinner & a movie. "Do you want to dine with them?"

"No, give me a tray in my study." Mr. Hopkins & Mrs. Macy were going out, so I had a tray with the P. & we got started on the 1910 Political papers . . .

[W]ent off to the Hambleys' for lunch. At 2 P.M. the P. drove up to the house & Betty & I got in with him. Roly went into the next car with Capt. McCrae & Harry Hopkins. Mrs. Macy had to leave for N.Y. so was not in the party. The procession moved out into the country, to what the papers are calling Shangri-La, "a cottage in the country"!

No one is supposed to know, in order to give the President some privacy, and also for safety. But I am sure alien spies can find it out without the slightest trouble. [This was to be FDR's first visit to his brand-new Maryland hideaway, a former demonstration recreational site built by the Civilian Conservation Corps in the heart of Catoctin National Forest, seventy-five miles from Washington. It would later be renamed Camp David by Dwight Eisenhower in honor of his grandson.]

It is very well done: The P's "cottage" consists of a living room, an enclosed porch, a bath & room for the P. 3 other rooms & a bath for those who go with him. Way off, through a vista, you can see the plain of [Frederick, Maryland].

The Filipino crew of the "Potomac" were "on board" with a marvelous meal. The P. was cheerful & delighted & rested, after his week in Hyde Park. H.H. & I took a walk to the swimming pool, with Fala. Betty & Capt. McCrae went another way — Roly put on her spectacles & read a book on the porch. The P. read *Jane's Fighting Ships!*

Marines, Secret Service in every direction. All have their little houses in the trees, & it comes over one that all are there for *one* purpose: to guard the person of F.D.R.!

All the way home, F.D.R. is funny & relaxed. Teases me and has a wonderful time seeing me act my part of prim spinster!

∾ *July 6th Monday* — Just finished my breakfast of coffee, toast, marmalade, a fried egg & bacon & some cherries. At night a little plate of fruit is put by your bedside — I found the special one for the P. was put in here by mistake so I have *specially* nice fruit. I know it is his, for there's a little slip of paper tucked into the napkin, marked "The President."

. . . Mrs. R. came & said she was leaving but I must stay right here & be sure to call on the usher for anything I need. "If you don't seem to have a meal coming to you, don't just sit & starve!" I promised I would not!

∾ *July 9 — Thursday.* . . . I was working on the papers when the P. called me in to his study, to tell me that he was "going to have an awful day." That Sec. [of War Henry L.] Stimson [a Republican] is "practically endorsing" Henry Cabot Lodge Jr. [running for re-election to the Senate as a Republican from Massachusetts] . . . "I am going over to my office & will spend the day blowing up various people . . ."

[Rhinebeck]

∾ *July 27th.* I was up to my elbows in soap-suds, washing handkerchiefs which have been accumulating, [when] Mama called (in the usual Suckley fashion which has to reach from downstairs to the top of the house & around corners & down the hall to the bathroom) that the White House was on the telephone for me! The President wants me down there for a few days' work & wondered which would be most convenient for me — next week, or the week after . . .

He had spent a restful Sunday at Shangri-La, with the Frank Walkers [former treasurer and national chairman of the Democratic Party, now postmaster general] as guests — I asked whether he hadn't had anyone else. He laughed & said no, knowing that I meant the Crown Princess: It amuses him to be teased about her.

He said he felt a little better about "things." He feels they are not as bad underneath as they look. Though he couldn't mention it on the phone, I think he referred to Harry Hopkins's trip to England this past week — a secret trip which I haven't seen mentioned in the papers — The P. told me about it on his last visit to H.P. — the different generals, etc. Just had to agree on a united policy about the conduct of the war —

[Hopkins had flown to London to begin working out the details of Operation Gymnast (later, Torch), the proposed American landing in North Africa meant to draw Nazi troops away from the Russian front and ease the pressure on the British in the Middle East. General Marshall and Secretary Stimson had opposed it in favor of a cross-Channel invasion the following year. Roosevelt overruled them, in part because he believed American morale would suffer if United States forces were not soon seen to be striking back.]

[Hyde Park]

〜 *July 30th.* . . . At 4.30 the P. took me for a little drive through the woods to the top cottage for a little rest. We had glasses of ice-water & talked (he did!) . . . He told me about Harry Hopkins's trip to England last week; about ⅔ was accomplished by it — a pretty good proportion perhaps — Also about H.H.'s wedding in the White House on Thursday. All very simple and quiet, though the P. said he had to "dress up" in his white suit — white shoes — etc!

He said he is not as despondent about the war as he was, some time ago.

[Washington]

〜 *Thursday 6th.* . . . [Queen Wilhelmina of the Netherlands] addressed Congress at 12.15 — & from there went to the "Potomac," with the P. & Mrs. awaiting her for the trip to Mt. Vernon —

I went to work, after carefully drawing the screen across my north hall so that I would not be seen when the party returned — At about 5 I heard sounds of the party coming home, but continued with my work. Suddenly a black face looked at me from around the screen, disappeared. "Yessir, she's here" — then the P.'s voice: "Come to tea, Margaret!" I found the P. in the Hall, with Mr. [Howell G.] Crim [a White House usher] & the coloured man. I protested that I was dusty & in a mussed dusty dress —

He insisted!

I begged for 5 minutes to go & change & wash —

No — The Queen would be there only for 5 minutes — I must come as I was — Well, I could wash my hands — right there, in his bathroom!

You can't do much when F.D.R. makes up his mind, specially if a Queen & Mrs. R. are having tea on the other side of a nearby screen!

So, I washed my hands & found the P. waiting for me: he knew I would feel shy about coming in by myself in that messy outfit!

The Queen is very sweet & gentle & friendly in her manner — She has *good* manners — for she doesn't make you feel awkward — She steps forward herself and shakes hands, every time she sees you . . .

∾ *Friday 7th August.* . . . At just about 4.15, the P. calls from the hall: "Margaret, come out & say goodbye!"

The Queen — Lady in Waiting — [her secretary] Mr. Von Taets, & an officer whom I haven't seen or met, stand around the P. The Queen comes toward me hand outstretched: "I have signed in your book." I murmur, "How kind . . . that is wonderful," etc. realizing that the P. has asked her to sign in "my godchild's book," & she thinks *I* am the godchild! There is no use explaining — off they go down the hall to the elevator & the P. escorts them to the station . . .

[Hyde Park]

∾ *Aug. 19th.* The P. came over for a short time in the morning — then went home to receive former Empress Zita of Austria and her daughter the Archduchess Adelaide, who is 28, has a Ph.D. from Louvain, & is a professor in Fordham University! After lunch the P. brought them over to the Library & asked me to take them around! I don't think anyone recognized them.

The Empress is slender and still pretty, with a gay responsive laugh — not at all the Tragic Queen she was last year . . . They were enthusiastic about the Library & everything in it, and very intelligent in their comments. The President was wheeled outside to see them off in their taxi which they hired at the [Poughkeepsie] station.

Then he asked me to go with him to . . . [visit] the [Archibald] Rogers Place [Crumwold, the massive stone château a half-mile north of Springwood, in which Daisy had first glimpsed FDR in 1910]. The P. has heavy worries about the world just now, & when in repose, his face is over serious & drawn. His moments of relaxation are few.

After we left the Rogers, he drove south, & the S.S. car which was in front naturally thought he would go out the main road. Instead, he turned to the right. The S.S. started across the field to get in front of him again. He put on the gas, & there was a regular small-boy race, between the Pres. on the drive & the S.S. car on the stubbly field. The Pres. lost all his worries for about two minutes & was driving at full speed & having a fine laugh. All the S.S. enjoying it just as much as he. It is quite wonderful to see how they love him & seem to enjoy guarding him.

We went to the Top Cottage, and took in a pile of books on trees & birds, etc. We sat on the porch & talked for a while in the quiet cool evening sunlight. He talked of his boyhood & schooldays — a thing he rarely does — He said he was unhappy in school, for his bringing-up, with his parents, travelling, etc. made him old for his age, and he found the other boys so young and immature and ignorant that he supposed he showed his opinion of them, & they in turn didn't like him.

Then, when he went to Harvard, he found that the college was run by a small handful of mostly Groton men, of whom he was one. This group chose the officers of the incoming class. F.D.R. saw no reason why the Freshmen should not choose their own officers; so he organized the class & they did elect their own. That was the time they called him a "Traitor to his class." Perhaps it was the beginning of his political career. One sentence of his specially struck me, when he described how a group including himself got together to organize the Freshmen . . . "Two boys *who were born politicians & I, who was not* . . ."

[Either Daisy misreported this tale or FDR misrepresented it himself. Roosevelt showed absolutely no sign of wishing to rebel against his class at Harvard — he lived and ate and associated almost entirely with fellow graduates of Groton and other exclusive preparatory schools — though he bitterly resented being turned down by his father's club, the Porcellian, and was further disappointed when he ran fourth in a field of five for class marshal in his last year. After he had left Harvard he did attempt to organize what he called the "western" members of his class — by which he meant those living west of Massachusetts — in order to have a larger say in reunion planning. In that, too, he was defeated.]

He talked at length also about his conversation with the Empress Zita, & his idea of how to deal with the Austrian situation after the war. In general, his idea is that all those little countries shall be "managed" for a year or two by neutral commissions of perhaps 3 men each, who will feed the babies, and in general put the countries back into some semblance of normality. Then have bona fide plebiscites, so that the people can decide what form of govt. they want. This applies to Archduke Otto also. The P. said the Empress was sympathetic and interested in the idea . . .

[Hyde Park]

✑ *Sept 4*. Raining. The P. arrived about 9 A.M. Telephoned me at about 11.30. Won't be able to get over [to the Library] until late afternoon, as he is working on his Labor Day Speech, and has 4 typists from the W.H. for that purpose. He asked how we liked yesterday's speech to the Youth Congress in Wash. Said he is proud of his adaptation of the phrase "fiddles while Rome burns"! Put it in at the last moment!

[On September 3, FDR had addressed the International Student Assembly at Washington and said, in part, "There is still . . . a handful of men and women, in the United States and elsewhere, who mock and sneer at the four freedoms and the Atlantic Charter . . . They play petty politics in a world crisis. They fiddle with many sour notes while civilization burns."]

He told me to come over for lunch. I said perhaps he was too busy. "I MUST EAT!" says he! So I'm going! . . .

✑ *Sept. 5th*. . . . [After five] we started off, with the usual cavalcade, for our house [Wilderstein] . . .
We put the P. on the sofa, facing the only remaining view of the river. [Trees now obscured the rest because the Suckleys hadn't the money to keep them cut.] He was delightful & cheerful. Told Mama of how St. James' Church Vestry chose Mr. [Frank R.] Wilson as their rector. "The best they have ever had." He thinks it much better to let the "Village" do it, as they know what kind of a person will be congenial. Mama still thinks the "River" should decide!

[By the "River" Daisy's mother meant members of the wealthy families who had traditionally held land along the Hudson; the "Village" consisted of others in the community who had served them a generation earlier.

The country was being transformed by the war effort, and in September, FDR invited Daisy, Laura Delano, and Harry Hooker to come along on an inspection tour of defense plants and military installations. It would be a top-secret two-week train trip — across the continent to Washington State, then down the Pacific Coast and back through the Southwest and South to Washington. Mrs. Roosevelt was to be aboard at the outset and again at the end.

Daisy recorded her impressions of the journey in pencil in a stenographer's pad.]

[The White House]

↬ *Sept. 17.* Thursday — Harry Hooker, Laura Delano and I assembled at the W.H. in time for cocktails at 7.10 P.M. Harry & I had already taken baths (supposed to last for the whole trip!) Laura chose a "quiet bath" in preference to dinner.

After dinner, the P. picked out some boxes of his 1920 campaign papers for me to work on and then went for a bath. Harry & I waited in his study. He came back saying he would never take another, for he felt hotter than ever. He looked tired but keyed up and rather excited over getting away on this trip. He acknowledged that the situation in the Solomon Islands was bad [the fighting was still fierce on Guadalcanal more than a month after U.S. Marines landed there], & he was afraid, that morning, that something might happen to keep him from going.

However, at a quarter to 10 we started for the train. The P., Mrs. [Roosevelt] and Laura and Fala in the first car, Miss Thompson, Capt. McCrae, Harry Hooker and I in the second. Miss Tully & Mrs. Brady [are] also with the trip.

We got on the train at Silver Spring, [Maryland, and] got under way at exactly 10.15 P.M. &, though I can't quite believe it, even yet, here I am — on board — to tour the country with the P. of the U.S.!

We sat up in the observation car until after 11, with orange juice. Fala much the center of attraction. Donald Nelson [head of the War Production Board] had come on board, so he & the P. discussed munition plants, the new airplanes, etc.

Finally, Mrs. R. made the move and took Harry, "Tommy" [Malvina Thompson] & me to our staterooms in Car #3. I have [stateroom] B.

Laura is in the *President's car.*

↬ *Sept 18th Friday* — My usual night — wide awake — Hope for better behavior tonight.

At 10.30 [in Detroit], we all assembled for our first inspection. The Chrysler [Tank Arsenal] . . . Gov. Murray Van Waggoner and Mr. [K.T.] Keller [president of Chrysler] & the President [rode in his car]. Laura & I, Adm. McIntire & Steve Early went *in the next car.* Tully, D. Brady & H. Hooker in the third.

It was an extraordinary experience for a person who had never had it before. The train had been backed into the factory and the workmen knew of the visit only because of the extra guards, SS, etc, They clapped & waved, broad smiles on their faces. We drove right through the factory, between machines at work. At first parts of machines, gradually assembling, until at the end there were the finished tanks —

. . . The majority of workmen are of Italian & Polish descent but born here, &, I should judge, larger physically than their parents, also regular Americans. At the end a boy with a yard-long Polish name plowed [his tank] through water & mud straight up to the President's car, stopped and pushed his head through the hole with a smile. People standing around looked rather alarmed as the tank plowed forward, but the P. had a good laugh. It was a monster performing his tricks & lacked only the final bowing of the front legs, like the elephant in the circus! 30 tanks a day —

We got on the train again & went the 20 miles to Dearborn, to the new Ford airplane factory [at Willow Run] — In March, trees were growing where now stands a huge building, a mile & a half long, which is going to turn out different types of airplanes — Gov. Van Waggoner went on the train with us . . . He & the P. talked of factories, politics, roads, etc. He told that when [Henry] Ford built this new building he came to the city line, & because of taxes did not wish the building to cross into the next county, so he built an L off to the side [instead]. Mr. Ford was much surprised when the P. said to him, when they reached the end of the building, "And so this is the City Line!"

. . . Mr. Ford, 80, extraordinarily well preserved, erect, slight, and his son Edsel, met the train — Same arrangement of seats in cars — We drove to the building & were met by cheers and clapping. All work was suspended. Word had gone out 3 hrs before & the way was lined with the workers. A great many girls. They had happy satisfied faces, most of them.

. . . At dinner, Mrs. R. teased the P. about his affectionate manner to Mr. Ford, patting him on the knee etc. He evidently made headway with him for Ford was ready to go along with anything the P. said!

☞ *September, 19th, Saturday.* I felt rather sick all day yesterday as the result of 2 very hot days of preparation & no sleep. So Dr. McIntire gave me a yellow capsule, & I returned to my room right after dinner . . . & slept until about 4 [A.M.]; when we were arriving at the Great Lakes Naval Training station [outside Chicago]. Sailors & marines stood silent guard on the tops of buildings & about every hundred feet on the ground in the light of . . . flood lamps. We shifted back and forth on sidings & finally stopped —

. . . At 9.30 we all met in the P.s car, got off & into waiting cars . . . The station is . . . not quite finished yet, 68,000 men. We saw [the men] doing their various daily duties — a company doing setting-up exercises, a couple of blocks further a group of negroes raking a yard & singing in unison, two or three companies singing as they march, another jumping over obstacles & in & out of trenches. etc. etc. We drove about 35 miles around the station before returning to the train. A group of nurses in white uniforms saluting just as well as the men.

Before we started in the train again, Mrs. R. left with Miss Thompson for Washington. We continued the 55 miles to Milwaukee [and] a made-over factory, making turbines mainly. Impressive for the expert, but to the ignorant just a lot of heavy rather rusty-looking iron castings!

[After] Mrs. R. & Miss Thompson left . . . I was "ordered" to move from Car 3 to the P.'s car, into Mrs. R's room. It's much nicer, as I don't have to go through the diner, & the S.S. car.

[The Secret Service men] occupy a whole car, with a sitting room, right next to the P.'s car. Some of them [are] always on duty. When the P. is not in the observation room or when we stop anywhere, two stand on the back platform . . .

At each inspection point, the Gov. of the State & the head of the plant join the P. to take him around. No Congressmen, so that there is no politics involved . . .

Special soldier guards wherever we go. It's difficult to realize I am part of it, instead of standing on the curb to watch it go by!

∾ *Sunday Sept. 20th.* Going through North Dakota — approaching Bismarck, the capital — flat & wide & lonely; wheat & grass & scattered cows & sheep. Bismarck has a sky-scraper! You see nothing else as you approach from the East accept a clustering little town of low houses, but there is a Main St. & some stone 4-story buildings.

We went right through to Mandan a few miles beyond, where we stopped 15 minutes & I ran Fala up & down a cool, green park next to the station. Every one in the station was speaking about the Special Train. A little girl bent over Fala & looked at his license tag. Her mother said "What is his name?"

"I don't know," she said, & suddenly stood up and looked at me with startled eyes! The tag reads: "Fala, The White House, Washington, D.C." Her mother will put two & two together!

At that moment "All aboard" took us on again, & off we are, through the "Bad Lands" . . .

Clocks back an hour. Noon, by (this timing?), & I am writing on my knee. F.D.R. is reading *They Were Expendable* [a best seller by W. L. White about the fighting in the Philippines]. Harry Hooker half lies on the sofa reading a magazine article by [Allan] Nevins about F.D.R. Fala stretched [out] in the hall. The back door just about a foot open.

On & on, on a one-track line. Perfectly straight for a stretch & then an unreasonable curve, & straight again. A lonely homestead every two miles. A few with a few trees — rarely a human being in sight, but once in a while a woman standing in her doorway, one hand on a hip — looking at an unscheduled train.

. . . We had dinner at 7, and dispersed about 9.30. The P. did stamps & talked . . . Laura, Harry & I with him & Capt. McCrae & Mrs. Brady came for dinner. The P. is relaxed & cheerful. He gets a dispatch or talks to Washington once or twice a day, & so far there has been no specially bad news. We pray things will get better, not worse, but I think he is prepared for a good deal of "worse" mixed with the "better" before we are through with all this horrible fighting.

✧ *Monday Sept. 21st.* . . . 4.15 P.M. All day coming down through the beautiful valley of the Clark River, which flows into the Columbia. At Athol [Idaho], the 4 Boettigers came on board & we came by train to the naval training station on Pend Oreille Lake, a most beautiful site, a safe distance from the Pacific. The way the camp is being developed is a miracle, almost as though Aladdin's Lamp were in use. Laura, Harry & I were driven in car 2 by a young Lt. who had only been here four days but knows a lot of details already. They are paying some of the laborers $15 a day, counting overtime. After 6 days in operation they already have some 5 or 6 thousand men & their uniforms & equipment ready, etc. etc.

The whole thing is an extraordinary achievement, but the P. is "furious" because they have cut down all the trees, instead of leaving them between the buildings. Off again about 4.30.

F.D.R. is so happy to have his family around him & they adore him so, that I am keeping out of the way! expect to go to bed right after dinner with the *Readers Digest* . . .

✧ *Tuesday Sept. 22.* 7 P.M. At the Boettigers, on Mercer Island, Seattle. It has been a tremendous day — everything just about on time. At Fort Lewis, Fala was photographed in front of an official car with the white star on the door — there was quite an interesting review of trucks, ski troops, etc. The setting is lovely with Mt. Rainier in the distance & the beautiful Douglas fir on the surrounding hills. When it is not misty, as it was today, the P. drove in an open car as usual, the commanding officers with him.

The drive to Bremerton [Navy Yard] was about 30 miles, the road guarded all the way, on both sides, by soldiers at attention. Very few people recognized the P., though once in awhile a group of squealing girls showed they had seen him! The precautions are very heavy particularly on the West Coast, because of the many Japs. Two S.S. men stand on the running boards of the P.'s car all the way & also on the S.S. car so that it is difficult to see the P. if you don't know exactly where he sits . . .

The country is dry & dusty looking, but the rolling hills & the trees are beautiful. The mist is natural to the climate, which is damp and rarely very cold. The sail on the Ferry from Bremerton to Seattle very beautiful. A slight mistiness. A mine sweeper was dragging its net on our left . . .

Seattle is impressive as you approach. Blimps hang suspended over her . . . [At the] Boeing Aviation Plant . . . the workers evidently knew nothing of the P.s coming & looked up vaguely from their work as we drove between the machines. It seemed incredibly crowded, though in perfect order. When we came out, the word had spread & workers were running to get a view of the P., clapping & smiling. We see many women in these plants, & they tell us more & more are being taken in. Here, they were even welding, with masks on. All in trousers, of course. In this plant they look rather "tough." In most of the others they were more feminine, hair well groomed, smiling & happy-looking.

From here we drove by a back way around Seattle to Mercers' Island, the Boettigers' place — John says it is ten minutes from his office. The house is low and rambling: an old farmhouse with additions — very homelike & attractive. At the back a lawn slopes down to Lake Washington . . . A patrol boat slipped silently back and forth all the evening, & the place was guarded by soldiers all around —

The Boettigers' two dogs & Fala & Sawdust [Laura Delano's Irish setter] had a marvelous time rough-housing . . . It was a terribly nice evening, very natural and homelike. Sistie is very pretty and sweet and sensible. Buzzie a sweet boy. Little Johnny awfully cunning. F.D.R. very peaceful and happy. Said it's such a peaceful place. He should spend a week or two there for a real rest.

⌒· *Sept. 23rd.* 4.20 P.M. The Aluminum Co. [of America, at Vancouver] was most interesting in an entirely different way from everything else we have seen. Long sheds filled with . . . electrolytic cell furnaces are burning 24 hours a day & 7 days a week — No stop is possible. Only a handful of men, about 10 to a shed. We saw the electric furnaces & the pouring out of a huge vat of the molten aluminum, making "pigs" of about 15 lbs. each. They cool very quickly & lose the rosy color the minute they start cooling.

. . . We got back on the train & went slowly to the [Henry J.] Kaiser Shipyards [at Portland] — They have 10,000-ton merchant vessels under construction & one was ready for launching. [She was the U.S.S. *Teal*, whose keel had been laid just ten days earlier, setting a new ship-building record.] The work men were all lined up . . . A wooden ramp was built in the shape of a horse-shoe, the middle facing the bow of the ship.

Three cars, including the Pres.'s, drove up on the ramp — The rest of us went to the platform & climbed up — the P. was exactly opposite, a little higher than we. Anna Boettiger was given a "bouquet" of Defense Stamps tied with red white & blue ribbon. The ceremony began with a prayer by a priest . . . At the end of the prayer, the voice on the amplifiers spoke directly to Anna, who stood waiting, the bottle of champagne in her hands. He dramatically proclaimed "The first rivet is out . . . The second rivet is out . . . The eighth rivet is out!" Crash went the bottle, showering Anna to the skin, & down the ways went the Ship — It is a most moving scene, specially now, when you realize that that ship may be sunk by a submarine on her very first trip out.

Returning to our train we drove around the shops where they are making the various parts & assembling them as far as possible. Large portions of the ships were loaded on huge trucks with rubber tires ready to be taken to the "ways." This is Mr. Kaiser's "secret" for getting a ship built in 14 days!! The P. likes both Mr. K. & his son Edgar who was there with him, said Mr. K. is a "dynamo."

We got back on board our train & started south in the Willamette Valley. [Then] Fala & I went out on the platform for the beautiful winding ride up the Cascades. Dust or no dust I wouldn't miss it for anything. Laura and Sawdust joined me & we stayed there until it was getting dark . . . Up through a beautiful gorge, a macadam road below winding along with the Willamette River. Dr. McIntire was thrilled. He used to fish that stream when there was only a trail. His parents trekked to Oregon in 1847 & 1852; [now] he is the P.'s doctor!

. . . [At dinner] we sit at the table for at least 1 and ½ hours —

the conversation very gay, teasing & amusing, & everything possible was discussed — I listen most of the time. Laura gets teased by him constantly. He is getting a real holiday, in spite of the messages from Washington & the officials at the points of inspection.

The Douglas fir is magnificent. Laura & I kept interrupting the P. to look at a particularly beautiful vista, or a particularly lovely group of trees . . .

~ *Sept. 24, 1942.* 1.45 P.M. back from Mare Island Navy Yard [north of Oakland] — Submarines, chasers, transports, all under repair or construction. One sub had nine Jap. flags painted on her side with a sketch . . . of a sinking ship — representing what she had done. The crew looked very young —

The P. drove up to see the sailors wounded at Pearl Harbor, in the hospital.

Stardust . . . had swallowed a piece of red white and blue ribbon, & proceeded to get rid of it on our way back — All's well however!

. . . Much enthusiasm for F.D.R. along the road — the people out here are noticeably healthy and happy. A good many Chinese workers among the whites.

We crossed several bridges. The hill country is bare & burnt yellow . . . A new development is the MOTEL, headquarters for trailers & cars!

. . . The Oakland [Navy Supply] Depot was most interesting as another example of the work of a few months. Tremendous stone houses full of supplies for the forces & more huge buildings going up.

. . . All the afternoon down the flat valley, [with] mountains East and West of us. Orchards of prunes, peaches etc. etc. Hardly a weed — The hills all burned a pale gold — I had a good nap, & could hear the P. talking . . .

At dinner the P. refused to be sensible and was very funny, & talked complete nonsense & tried to make Sawdust be quiet. After a futile struggle, Sawdust finally gave up & collapsed his long bones. Fala looked disconsolate. So Anna picked him up.

~ [*September 25*] 10.15 A.M. . . . We got off the train a little after nine. Inspected the Douglas Aircraft Plant [at Los Angeles]. The blue lighting has a horrible effect on the looks of the workers. Skin looks green, brown hair looks purple, they seemed apathetic. I would if I had to work in such light. Just driving through hurt my eyes . . .

1.30 [on the way from San Juan de Capistrano to Camp Pendleton] Laura, the dogs, Harry and I together as usual — Sawdust gets sick every few hours & we have a dramatic interlude in our car, as we drive along a road [lined] thickly with special guards at attention: Laura holds the door open with her left hand, holds Sawdust by the neck with his head through the door. What happens to his body is immaterial — I slip my fingers through her belt & brace my feet, so that she & Sawdust won't go headlong out of the car, dragging Fala and me after them. The driver looks firmly ahead to his duty, fortunately. Harry sits calmly, & tactfully keeps his eyes to the front.

The drive . . . is perfectly beautiful. The Pacific, calm, sunny & a little misty, on our right, dried-up hills on the left. Our procession had about 10 cars, mostly Army — [olive drab] & driven by soldiers — At the head a motor cycle — Then a couple of S.S. cars, then the P.'s car with two motor cycles, then more S.S. cars, then generals & the rest of us. We drove to Camp Pendleton, visited the old Rancho Santa Margarita, which is to be used for officers & distinguished guests, then [because they were behind schedule] we drove a steady 50 mph to San Diego . . . & visited the Naval Training Station . . . [with an aviation school] & the Marine Base all concentrated in one area — a good target for the enemy!

We continue — Laura, the President, Harry, & I.

↘ *September, 26.* . . . The sun rose over sagebrush country, absolutely flat with outcroppings of mountains & hills, prickly pear . . . [and] cactus with strange arms. So far, we have passed only one irrigated area with a lot of cattle grazing on nothing & drinking in water holes . . . It is very hot outside, lovely inside with the cooling system. We are in the valley of the Gila River, but I don't see any water. (Gila Station is dry & dirty. A family of pale-haired children swing like monkeys on a rope from a tree. In an enclosed porch the fat mother in a white gown & the father in very little were relaxing on a couch. Most of the people look Mexican with their straight black hair & copper skins. So far, no cowboys in sight) —

. . . As we went through El Paso, a man jumped on the train at one street & off at the next — the S.S. on the back platform promptly telephoned forward —

[The train slowed on the outskirts of Uvalde, Texas, for a courtesy call on Roosevelt's former vice president, John Nance Garner, who had hoped to succeed to the presidency in 1940 and was thought to harbor considerable resentment against FDR.] The P. wondered if there would be crowds at the station! We stopped — two small boys advanced & were interviewed by 4 heavy S.S. men! Laura & I sat with the P. waiting, the 2 dogs on leashes — In a minute or two, along came Mr. Garner, alone, walking down the side of the train from the station, up the steps & into the observation room — Hale & hearty greetings on both sides. Garner patting the P. on the head, in fact rumpling his hair! The meeting was for 6 minutes, very nice altogether, & Garner got up, shook hands all round, said, "God bless you, Boss," and went briskly back to his little ancient car, and drove off by himself towards Uvalde village . . .

∾ *September 28.* Sitting up in bed for breakfast [at a siding outside Fort Worth], I was facing a country road which crosses the track right behind our car. The procession of autos stretching around the curve, I can count 17 closed cars . . . [and in] front of them 3 open cars for the P. and the S.S. Also the jeep for the photographers . . . Soldiers with MP bands on their arms stand on guard in all directions, guns on their shoulders, in high grass.

[To] Dutch Branch Ranch [home of the Elliott Roosevelts], a lovely low one-story house, designed by Elliott & [his wife] Ruth [Googins Roosevelt]. The ranch has about 1,500 acres. We drove around to see the Arab horses & the white face cattle in the field. Laura says they have built everything — roads, fences (50 miles) . . . The children ride around on their ponies.

Amon Carter [a Texas oilman] sent his usual present of a hat [like the one FDR wore last year] of grey ermine & beaver. He told the P. it cost him $175.00. He is famous because he has acquired enormous financial power. He talks continually in terms of $$. Very few like him, but when he is crossed by anyone, he turns around and breaks that person. He dresses very well. He has given a park, a hospital, etc, to the city — has, in a word, put Fort Worth on the map.

The P. says there is great rivalry between Ft. Worth & Dallas. The people of Ft. Worth travel to NY & have a veneer of N.Y.

The people of Dallas are perhaps more well-bred . . .

∾ *Sept 29th.* . . . We backed into the [Andrew J.] Higgins yard [at New Orleans] a little early, & while waiting I saw Mr. Higgins talking to our 3 press representatives. He is the same type as Kaiser, a genius at getting things done, constantly inventing new gadgets. His trouble is that he is too blunt & fights with everyone, so that the maritime commission hates him & won't play ball with him — *But,* he turns out the goods! This building we visited is comparatively small, every inch filled with small boats in various stages of construction. Some torpedo boats & landing boats. They are using a plywood of pressed wood with a gummy glue of Mr. Higgins' own invention. It can hold anything, oil or water etc. The P. says this is one of his present problems — to get the right people to let Higgins go ahead . . .

↝ *Wed. Sept. 30.* Camp Jackson [Columbia, South Carolina] is another large infantry training ground — A beautiful situation on high rolling land, with a view for miles in every direction. The soldiers were all drawn up along our route for miles — Others marched before the P. and disappeared over the hill, raising a mist of dust, their guns and helmets showing against the sky. During the review the P. sat in the car — the rest of us piled out & stood on a reviewing stand — Fala watched for about 10 minutes, then turned his back & looked elsewhere . . .

After returning to the train, we had a good hour to wait, so Laura & I started off for a walk & let the dogs run free for a while. The S.S. watched us go with anxious eyes but I reassured them & we got back shortly . . . During our walks I usually speak to the guarding soldiers & make them release from their wooden attitudes — they all know about Fala . . . & are thrilled to see him. In a small way he represents the P. to them —

It is our last evening on board. But the P. said the trip had worked so well with us four that he will take us on another! No complexes — no quarrels — etc.! We all get along peacefully, & of course we all just think of him, to make it nice for him. The P. said several times . . . this was the most restful & satisfactory [trip] he had ever taken. A great compliment to us for not having controversial talk, etc. Laura thought it remarkable that there had not been a single "sharp word."

So I think he has had a real mental rest, & is now ready to go back & "talk turkey" to a good many people — He can talk from what he has seen with his own eyes.

The story is to break tomorrow A.M. in detail. [The President's wartime travels were reported only after they were safely over.]

↝ *Sunday, Nov. 8, 1942. A historic day, last night.* At Shangri-La — The P. came to Hyde Park a week ago Friday & showed the movie of our trip out west in September to the whole staff at the Library —

It was very interesting as a whole — more so than we expected, as so much of it showed the P. in a car talking to different governors, generals, industrialists, etc. However the pictures showed quite a lot of background: tanks, airplanes, launching the ship in the Kaiser plant, the troops marching by at Camp Jackson, the family at Fort Worth. etc., etc. The "staff" were delighted & seemed to appreciate the fact that the P. arranged for them to see it . . .

They also showed an English film, "Next of Kin," for the President's approval — I have heard since that "they" decided it is too realistic & harrowing to show to the Public. I don't agree . . .

Wednesday night. I came down to Washington on the P's train, arriving 9 A.M. Thursday the 5th . . .

For weeks, the P. has had something exciting up his sleeve — Only a handful knew about it, though everything, down to the very date, has been planned since July. He spoke of an egg that was about to be laid — probably over the weekend.

[On] Friday, the P. asked Roly and Poppy [Roly's sister, Catherine Rutsen Hambley] & me to come to Shangri-La for the week-end, but [warned that we] might have to return Saturday afternoon if the hen laid an egg!

The P., Poppy & Fala and I drove out at 4 P.M. Harry Hopkins & G.G.T. in another car. Roly & Louise H. were both working Saturday morning, so couldn't get off til Sat. P.M. Poppy was put in the S.W. double room, Harry in the S.E., I in the single room. Quite cold — large fires in all fireplaces —

There was a general feeling of excitement. Telephone calls now & then, but the P. keeps conversation light — teases everyone.

After dinner . . . [w]e sat around for a while and then went to bed early — All night, there were flashing lights in the woods about the house. After putting out my lights, I looked out. The woods are lighted all around — A guard stood immobile 20 ft. from the house — Every few minutes a soldier came around the corner, gun on his shoulder, walked on to the north, silently —

Saturday morning I lighted my fire about 7 A.M. — Isaac had had a box with paper & kindling put outside my door — Then I got back into bed — At eight, a silent whispering Filipino brought my breakfast in . . . One can hear every sound from one room to the other. The porches on the doors and the doors themselves creak & snap & groan!

After reading the paper I got up & after a while took Fala for a walk — As usual stopped to talk to the guards — they are usually Southern, very polite & evidently delighted to talk — they must get tired of seeing nothing but men, & even a 50-year-old is nice to talk to. The guard at the gate told me they had had an "incident" which explained the lights and extra soldiers during the night.

When I got back to Shangri-La I found the P. sitting in the enclosed porch. He told me that one of the guards last night had challenged [what he said were] a dozen or so men with guns, in the dark. The dozen men refused to stop or answer, so he reported to headquarters. All available soldiers & S.S. were called out, beat the woods, etc. Much excitement! It turned out that two boys were looking for skunks, & being "natives" & independent, saw no reason for answering the challenge! All's well!

Saturday . . . I was amused at cocktail time when Louise began to tell me I *should* take a cocktail to please the P!! I just laughed & said F.D.R. had far more important things to worry about than whether I do or don't drink cocktails. F.D.R. was much amused when I told him about it — specially at the idea of Louise telling *me* how to treat him!! . . .

My impression is that Harry has already established the definite idea [that] *his first duty is F.D.R.* Throughout the week-end, Harry was in & out of F.D.R.'s room from breakfast time on. Louise stayed in her room all Sunday morning . . .

There was a feeling of suspense through dinner, though the Pres. as always was joking & teasing . . . I took a flash photo at dinner, but got Isaac to snap it so that I could be in it.

About 8.30, we left the dining table after a delicious dinner of which the main course was *musk-ox* — (Elliott Roosevelt was sent on a detail to find air bases for the U.S. in the north. As he was flying over the 5,000 ft deep ice-cap of Greenland he saw a black mass on the ice. He flew lower, to see that the black mass was moving. He flew down to perhaps 400 ft & found the black mass was a herd of musk-ox, frightened at the airplane & running at the most amazing speed. The plane slowed to the least speed they could go, without coming down. This was around 60 mph. & the musk-ox *almost* kept up with them. They estimated the number to be somewhere between 15–20 thousand! They brought back photographs to prove it. This was a scientific discovery, as the musk-ox is supposed to be practically extinct.) It was like the most tender beef but with a tiny difference in taste which can not be called "gaminess."

As we were getting settled in chairs & on the sofa with the P. he suddenly said that at nine "something will break on the radio." Of course Harry Hopkins knew about it, probably Miss Tully did, & young [Commander R. W.] Berry knew, as he works in the "Map Room" under Capt. McCrae.

The portable radio was brought in, as the huge expensive one doesn't work well (quite usual!) & at nine we got the news of the landing of our troops on North Africa! Morocco, Algiers & Tunisia — Until quite late we all sat around the P. [leaving] the radio on, he getting word of dispatches by telephone from the White House. It was terribly exciting.

By now what happened is History, & in the papers — But it *was* thrilling. And for the P. it was a tremendous climax, for he had been planning it, arranging it, for months . . . [It was thrilling for the country, too; American troops were striking back at last.]

After lunch we started back to Washington, Roly Hambley & I driving with the P. He paid us the great compliment of going to sleep for about a half-hour. I had to wake him as we approached the city: It wouldn't look well for the P. of the U.S. to be seen driving through the streets with his eyes closed & his head nodding!

⌒ *Tuesday Nov. 10th* [En route] back from Washington to Rhinebeck. The Nat. Archives have no funds to send us rambling so my expenses on these trips are to be paid out of the [White House] travelling fund. [FDR himself checked over Daisy's expense accounts, urging her to do her "homework" again if he found she had added wrong.]

⌒ *Nov. 26th Thanksgiving Day*. We went to our Union Thanksgiving Service (in the Baptist Church, this year) at 10 A.M., [then] rushed home, & arrived just in time to turn on the radio for the Service in the White House. The thought that seems to have been paramount in everyone's mind was how wonderful it was that the head of a nation should be leading a religious service for the whole country — Alan Frost's wife called me up afterwards, very much affected by it — Everyone felt the same thing. Imagine Hitler doing such a thing! The P. read his own Thanksgiving Proclamation with great seriousness & earnestness.

⌒ *Nov. 27th*. Walter Tittle arrived at the Library about 10.30. [Daisy had shown several of the artist's etchings to FDR, who had agreed to sit for him. Later, Tittle wrote a book about his experiences with FDR, *Roosevelt as an Artist Saw Him*]. His sketches of the P. are good. We discussed them quite frankly — I said *just* what I thought. He said my criticisms were a tremendous help — The P. came about 11.20, and to my great relief, *liked* the sketches. He sat quietly at his desk until one. Mr. Tittle sat on the Chew Chair & drew & talked. [This Chippendale chair, once owned by Chief Justice Samuel Chew of the Provincial

Court of Pennsylvania, had been left to Daisy by her older cousin Miss Elizabeth Lynch, and she, in turn, had presented it to the President for his new office in the library. As FDR liked to tell every guest about to sit in it, Justice Chew's friend George Washington had been there first.]

. . . He was entirely alone at the house, except for Diana Hopkins & her little friend Susan, so he asked me to go to lunch with him. We took a picnic basket & went to the cottage & had: scrambled eggs, cold turkey, mixed vegetable salad, toast (tended & buttered by F.D.R.). [It was a matter of great pride to FDR that things were arranged at Top Cottage so that he could personally serve his guests without help. A toaster, bread, and butter were set up within easy reach on a card table before the fire, and he buttered each piece of toast with a flourish.]

Our conversation was momentous. To begin with, he plans a trip to Khartoum to confer with Churchill and Stalin. Khartoum is the nearest point to the three & all three would fly, of course — The thought of F. taking that trip frightens me, but then, I would have been afraid for him on the Western trip if I hadn't gone, too! I know I shall do some good old fashioned praying while he's gone!

The reason [for] the trip is that there is a growing demand for a definite statement about our intentions after the war — F. feels he must get a definite agreement with Churchill, Stalin & Chiang Kai-shek.

He thinks Stalin will understand his plan better than Churchill. In general it consists of an international police force run by the four countries — All nations to disarm completely, so that no nation will have the chance to start out to conquer any other — Self determination to be worked out for colonies over a period of years, in the way it was done for the Philippines. I wondered how the Empire owners will take to it — Queen Wilhelmina, for instance! F. said he gave her a hint about it! Perhaps she didn't realize what he really meant . . .

Prof. Nelson Brown came, to go over the tree Plantation with F. We got into F.'s little open car, Fala keeping my chest warm from the winter winds by standing up on my lap & leaning his body against me, for warmth, the while leaning his shoulder & head outside of the window. Mr. Plog & Prof. Brown sat in the back — We drove all around the plantations, Prof. Brown & F. discussing the condition of the trees, plans for planting 30,000 more next spring, etc.

When we returned to the house, Mr. Plog vanished — Prof. Brown went off in his car & F. & I transferred into the big car & were driven by Monty to Laura Delano's house. She met us at the door, looking well . . . We had a lovely time at "tea" with a crackling fire & Tom Collinses. Polly is so sweet with him & he is devoted to her. Three dogs lay around on various sofas & chairs. F. was happy & full of stories. He told us he is planning another Inspection trip next April. Polly, Harry [Hooker] & I to go again. It's too good to be true, that I should go on a second trip of this kind!

F. drove me home from Polly's. He confessed on the way that he felt "ivre" [drunk] — Polly must have made his [Tom Collins] very strong. Mine had *nothing* in it, and was very good! . . .

ᨄ *Nov. 30th.* Monday — Looking back over the weekend, I have a definite feeling of cheerfulness & hopefulness. F. is already planning for the peace. He said that he believed the Germans are beginning to break up, & "cannot last indefinitely under present conditions." [The British Eighth Army, victorious at El Alamein, had driven the Nazis out of Egypt. Allied forces had secured Algeria and Morocco and were driving on Tunisia. The Russians had broken the German siege of Stalingrad and were on the counteroffensive.]

Of course, I think of the difficulties: The people who won't cooperate, the selfish people who want something for themselves out of it all, the people who still think in terms of Empires, etc. F. thinks of it as an inevitable development of human relations, and sees the difficulties far more clearly than I, but sees over & around and beyond them. He knows he will have to work out the peace; and that will take years. May God spare him to do it. One sees no one else who could do it, at the present moment . . .

ᨄ *Dec. 15th 1942* — P.M. On my way to Wash. for 3 days work in the North Hall . . . Two young men, a white & a Filipino, sat across the aisle, hand-cuffed together. The Filipino had a sensitive refined face. A drunk, cheerful & good-natured, presented a ticket for Harrisburg. It took two conductors to finally get him off the train at Baltimore & him back to Philadelphia!

Later — I was met at the gate by Monty in an army uniform & another chauffeur who took my bag and led me to the side entrance of the station, which the P. uses! I got into the P.'s car, & off we drove. Monty said that if I had not come on that train, the P. would have come to meet the next one! I was tempted to go back & be met again!

[The White House]

ᨄ *December, 17th.* . . . Mrs. R. is here: result: much activity — Some people in the blue bedroom are telephoning their friends. The lady is having the friends come to the W.H. to see her — the husband is going out, but says "it is a nice hotel." F.D.R. said yesterday it *is* a hotel & half the time he has no idea who is staying here . . .

∿ *Dec. 18th.* . . . Went into P.s study for cocktails. Mrs. R. very nice and very busy — About 10 she went off to her train to somewhere, while the P. took the McCraes & Tully & me to his train for Hyde Park — Great excitement over the new [presidential] car. [*The Ferdinand Magellan,* especially built by the Pullman Company and the Association of American Railroads, was armor-plated on all four sides. It weighed twice as much as an ordinary Pullman and included four bedrooms with toilets, a bathroom, a dining section and galley, and an observation room at the rear.] . . . Decoration is a grey-blue & tan — Very nice. Fala tried all the chairs & decided he liked the one with the arms upholstered —

∿ *Dec. 19th.* Arrived H.P. about 9. Had breakfast & then I went over to the Library — The P. came over about 11.30 & went around with some "experts," appraising various things for income tax purposes — Very cold . . . [FDR] then drove me home in his closed car —

[Wilderstein]

∿ *Dec. 20th.* My 51st Birthday! Xmas [Renée Chrisment, a close friend of Daisy's and a frequent guest at Wilderstein] made me a huge chocolate layer cake. It came in very well, for the P. brought the [John] McCraes to tea. It was bitterly cold, way below zero, & I tried to get the P. to keep his coat on when they carry him in & out of the house — But to no avail . . . He'll get his death of cold one of these days, but what can one do!

The library looked very nice & was comfortably warm, with a big fire roaring all day — The P. sat on the sofa. He brought me for my birthday the framed coloured print of the Salisbury portrait [of himself], a lovely picture. [Frank O. Salisbury was an English portrait artist.] I have hung it in Kathy's room, the only empty space.

Entre nous, I love best the photograph of it which Salisbury gave to Mrs. James R. & which Mrs. R wrote on & which F.D.R. gave me after Mrs. R.'s death.

The party went off very well. Mama told F.D.R. that I am very old-fashioned; Arthur discuss[ed] the Riviera — The P., as always, is the one focus of everyone's eyes & thoughts . . .

1943

The Luckiest
Person Alive

[The White House]

᭗ *Jan. 6th Wednesday.* . . . Basil O'Connor & his Mrs. arrived for the night — They & the Hopkinses, F.D.R. & I for dinner — As there were six we dined in Mrs. R.'s West Hall — The P. faces the windows. I sat opposite him (very proud!) with the little old lady brass bell at my right hand. I always have to be told to ring it by F.D.R.!

It was a peaceful congenial party for F. as they don't have to be "entertained." They talked old times a good deal . . .

[On Thursday, January 7, Daisy watched from the House Gallery as FDR delivered his State of the Union Address to Congress. In it, he looked forward to a postwar world in which the young people now fighting the war would want not only "the opportunity for employment," but also "assurance against the evils of all economic hazards — assurance that will extend from the cradle to the grave. And this great Government can and must provide this assurance."]

᭗ *Jan. 7th Thursday.* . . . Below us, flanked by two middle-aged Congressmen, was Clare Boothe Luce [the playwright and a Republican congresswoman from Connecticut] looking serious & intent throughout. The P.'s speech was well received on both sides of the house, though it was rather noticeable that the Republicans didn't clap much (hardly at all!) at the part about future security against want — F. was serious and deliberate, only 2 or 3 times making a point with a smile. He looked well and, from the comments, did not show how tired he is . . .

After lunch, the P. went up in the elevator & the rest of the guests said goodbye & dispersed. I saw the P. for a few moments on the 2nd floor . . . He inquired almost like a small boy: "Did you think that speech was all right? Did you like it?"

I reassured him!!! . . .

⌒ *Jan. 8th Friday.* Returned to the White House for dinner & work afterwards — We only got through about half of the piles — The rest will have to wait 'til my next trip. I think F. has mixed feelings about this trip [to Casablanca]. He is somewhat excited about it — The adventure of it — seeing all he will see, etc. On the other hand it is a long trip, with definite risks — But one *can't* and *mustn't* think of that — He is going because he feels he must go; to plan for the future, to really *see* the situation in N. Africa — He will see [General Henri] Giraud [Roosevelt's candidate to command the French forces in Africa], [General Dwight D.] Eisenhower [commander of U.S. Army forces in the European theater] — etc. W. Churchill first & foremost, of course. He asked Stalin to meet them but Stalin answered that he could not possibly leave Russia now — One can understand that.

⌒ *Jan. 9th Saturday.* . . . . About a quarter of 11 the P. appeared & handed Fala over to me, harness, muzzle and leash for the trip. I wished him all the best luck on this secret trip. He is leaving as if to go north to Hyde Park. At a certain siding, the train will be picked up by the regular engine & start south for Miami — He goes with all one's prayers —

I went to the station [to go home to Rhinebeck], checked Fala & stood near the train gate, the crowds getting thicker & thicker, at least half of them in the service. At last we were allowed through — A guard said the baggage car was at the far end — It seemed a mile, with Fala on one hand — my heavy bag on the other. No baggage car on *that* end — They said it was at the first end — We dragged back to where we started & inquired. "No, lady, there is no baggage car on this train, you can't take a dog on board, you'll have to wait for the next train, at 1."

We checked the bag, & Fala & I walked around & around & around, hunting for grass plots — Fala hunting for smells. A company of M.P. boys passed us & some of them called out "Fala!" not at all knowing it was Fala himself, but just because the pup has caught the popular imagination. Fala & I smiled unconcernedly —

When we went to the one o'clock train, the baggage car man said they were not supposed to take on anything for N.Y. I protested violently & he silently took poor Fala with the stiff muzzle on his nose. I left him looking very miserable, found the other half of the baggage car was for passengers, got settled in the second seat, went in to see if Fala was still alive, found the conductor, got permission to take Fala in the seat with me — He may have been in the baggage car 15 minutes all told! Much relief on both our parts — He slept on the floor most of the way — twice he sat up & looked out of the window — He is really a most satisfactory pup —

I didn't mention above that F. asked me to take him for the duration of his trip as Arthur [Prettyman, the President's valet] is with him, & George will be having a vacation, and there is no one else to look after him. Mrs. R. said she would be there off & on but thought it an excellent idea for Fala to get 2 or 3 weeks of exercise.

When we spoke of it first, I remarked that I could leave Fala at Wilderstein in the dog pen — "Oh don't," said F. "he hates to be left behind — take him to the Library with you every day, & walk him during lunch."

⤳ *Jan. 10th Sunday.* F.D.R. well on his way —

⤳ *Jan. 11th Monday* — On to Hyde Park. I left Fala outside for a while in the middle of the morning but he was cold, so I brought him in. He spoke to everyone in the Library and then lay down quietly in "my" office — At 12.30 I took my sandwiches, walked down the road into the woods, eating as I went. We were gone 40 minutes, Fala never stopping for one second — flying up rocky cliffs like a mountain goat, plunging into ravines, then trotting quietly right in front of me. He was very good; always looking around to see where I was — We went up the steep incline to the South lawn of the Big House. A huge M.P. stood guard — quite interested . . .

I said to the M.P.: "If you ever see Fala wandering around alone I wish you would let me know at the Library."

M.P. looking questioningly around: "Yes, I will, where is . . . ? Is — er — is he a very old 'fellow'?"

I, to M.P.: "No, he's only three, here he is."

M.P.: "Oh! I thought you meant an old man."

We both laughed —

The rest of the afternoon, Fala slept and woke & got his stomach rubbed a few times —

F. must be flying toward S. America now — or is he spending the night in Trinidad? I don't understand why I am not more worried about him. It may be because I saw how well they guard him, on the Sept. trip. The rest is in the hands of God . . .

[FDR to Daisy]

Jan. 10, 43

Sunday
on train

Just going to bed, as we have to get up at 4:30 A.M.! You know
how I "hate to get up in the morning" — I've had to keep the shades
drawn all day — I had the rear one up — but found myself waving
to an engineer & I fear he recognized me —

It is still quite cold though we are halfway down Florida —
Yesterday seems *so* far away —

Monday Jan 11th

We got on the plane [a Pan-American Clipper] at 5 A.M. but
didn't get off till six — Hardly anyone saw us transfer — The crew
of the plane did not know who was coming till we actually got on
board — & then they had a fit.

The sun came up at about 7:30 & I have never seen a more lovely
sunrise — just your kind. We were up about a mile — above a level
of small pure white clouds so we couldn't even see the Bahamas on
our left — but soon we saw Cuba on the right & then Haiti — I
asked the Captain to fly two miles to the right & we passed over the
"Citadelle" of the Emperor Christophe — which I had not seen since
1917 —

Then over N.E. Haiti & the W. part of the Dominican Republic
— Then out over the Caribbean — high up — I felt the altitude at 8
or 9,000 feet — and so did Harry & Ad. [William D.] Leahy — The
cumulus white clouds were amazingly beautiful but every once in a
while we could not go over them & had to go through one — that
meant some hard bumps for a minute or two —

At last — 5 P.M. — we saw the N.E. Coast of Venezuela & then
the Islands of the Dragon's Mouth with Trinidad on the left — The
skipper made a beautiful soft landing & Ad. [Jesse] Oldendorf [com-
mander of U.S. forces in the Caribbean] came out & took us ashore
to the U.S. Naval Base — one of "my" eight which we got for the 50
destroyers in 1940. It is not yet finished but is operating smoothly.

With it came a grapefruit plantation & a hotel on the N. Coast
& thither we went for the night. Gen. Pratt came to dinner — he is
in command of the Army base about 30 miles away. Ad. Leahy felt
quite ill — he had flu ten days ago — Ross McI[ntire] is worried as
he is 68 & his temp. is over 100 (degrees) — We will decide in the A.M.

Jan. 12

Tues. Up at 4 A.M. This is not civilized. Leahy seemed no better & we had to leave him behind — He hated to stay but was a good soldier & will go to the Naval Hospital & get good care — I hope he won't get pneumonia — I shall miss him as he is such an old friend & a wise counselor —

We left the water at 5:30, crossed the Island & first saw land again at 7:30 or 8 — British Guiana, then Dutch, then French G. — but we were very high & went way up over hundreds of miles of nothing but forest & swamp — Most of the time we were over the clouds — a thrill at first but I am bored to death with them —

A good lunch, then a nap, then the mouth of the Amazon below us. I have no desire to show you this part of the world. But if we are exiled by post-war isolationists we may have to try our luck in So. America —

At 3 we landed at Belem — we were taught to call it Para — went ashore at our flying base & sat comfortably at the officers quarters with Ad. Jonas Ingram, Gen. Walsh & Maj. Arnold.

Then at 5:30 back on the plane which had taken a full load of gas — & now we're off for Africa — A long hop — 2,400 miles.

Jan. 13

Wed. A good long night's sleep — only 2 or 3 times the bumps were bad. I got up at 8 & found we had had squalls & head winds — but we have enough gas to get in at 12 which is 4 P.M. in Bathurst.

Later — We arrived safely — both planes — & Capt. McCowan met us & we toured the harbor of this awful, pestiferous hole & then came on board U.S.S. *Memphis,* where I've had a good supper & am about to go to bed — Tomorrow at six we leave for a 1,200 mile hop in an Army plane for that well known spot "Somewhere in North Africa."

I don't know just where. But don't worry — All is well & I'm being carefully taken in charge by all & sundry. And I'm getting a wonderful mind rest. It's funny about geography — Washington seems the other side of the world but not Another Place — That is way off & also very close to —

I don't know when this will be taken back & you *may* not get another before I telephone! Lots of love — Bless you

Casablanca
Thursday Night
Jan. 14

An amazing day! As you know we got in to Bathurst [the Gambia] yesterday P.M. — & we all went to bed early on the *Memphis*, & got up in the dark this A.M. — went ashore at 7 A.M. a drive through the tiny town to the airport 22 miles out. A paved but very bumpy road, through crowds of semi-dressed natives — thatched huts — great poverty and emaciation — On the whole I am glad the U.S. is not a great Colonial power —

Through a wood — and then an incredible up-to-date U.S. airport — only 3 or 400 U.S. troops & mechanics but every day more & more of our planes are going through on the way to the front. We got off at 8:45 in a C54 transport plane — the runway was a steel mesh net 6,000 feet long. [Brigadier General] C. R. Smith — great friend of Elliott — used to be head of the big air line to Calif. via So. route — Now in charge of the air ferry.

We flew north along the Coast & in an hour came over Dakar & got a good look at it — Then over St. Louis, a very old French port —

Then inland over the desert — Never saw it before — worse than our Western Desert — Not flat at all & not as light as I had thought — more a brown yellow with lots of rocks and wind erosion. Five hours of this at an elevation of 6,000 feet. Then ahead a great chain of mountains — snowy top — The Atlas run from the Coast in Southern Morocco East & North & then East again till they lose themselves in Tunis — We flew over a pass 10,000 ft. & I tried a few whiffs of oxygen — North of the Mts. we suddenly descended over the first oasis of Marrakesh — a great city going back to the Berbers even before the Arabs came — We may go there if Casablanca is bombed.

At last at 4 P.M. Casablanca & the ocean came in sight — I was landed at a field 22 miles from town & driven under heavy guard & in a car with soaped windows to this delightful villa belonging to a Mme. Bessan whose army husband is a prisoner in France — She & her child were ejected as were the other cottage owners & sent to the hotel in town.

W.S.C. came in from next door, & we have a staff dinner here for twelve — Who do you suppose was at the airport? Elliott — looking very fit & mighty proud of his D.F.C. [Elliott Roosevelt had recently been awarded the Distinguished Flying Cross for carrying out a series of dangerous low-level intelligence-gathering flights.]

Wed. Jan. 20

I have not added to this for six days because of the Winston hours. [Churchill insisted upon talking — and drinking — into the wee hours of the morning; trying to keep up with him taxed Roosevelt's strength.]

I sleep to 9 A.M. — then morning conferences — then a luncheon — then a nap for an hour, then more talk — & a dinner at 8 which lasts to an average of 2 A.M.

F. Jr. gave me a complete surprise by turning up the day after I got here — The U.S.S. *Mayrant* waiting to take an empty convoy back. He had no idea I was here. That was Friday last & he did not leave till Tues. A.M.

We are getting on very well with our staff conferences. W.S.C. agreed the first night to try to bring Giraud [who expected to be proclaimed leader of the Free French forces in Africa] & [General Charles] De Gaulle [who loathed Giraud and from his headquarters in London demanded recognition as leader of all Free French forces everywhere] together — I got Giraud from Algiers on Sunday morning but De Gaulle refused Churchill's invitation to come from London. He has declined a second invitation — says he will not be "duressed" by W.S.C. & especially by the American President — Today I asked W.S.C. who paid De Gaulle's salary — W.S.C. beamed — good idea — no come — no pay!

Thurs. 21

De Gaulle will come! Tomorrow! I went "up the line" this A.M. beyond Rabat . . . reviewed about 30,000 Am. Troops, saw Ft. Media & the Am. Cemetery — a very stirring day for me & a complete surprise to the Troops.

I forgot to mention that Mon. night we had 5 WAACS to dine — Awfully nice girls but very military & efficient!

Saturday 23

Finished the Staff conferences — all agreed — De Gaulle a headache — said yesterday he was Jeanne d'Arc & today that he is Georges Clemençeau!

Sunday 24

At Marrakesh — We got De Gaulle & Giraud to shake hands & be photographed — They agree to continue conversations — Then W.S.C. & I drove here from Casablanca — 140 miles — Troops all the way to this fantastic villa built by Moses Taylor in 1927 — Marvellous view of the snow capped Atlas.

Mon. 25
U.S.S. *Memphis* — Left Marrakesh at 6 A.M. & got here at 5 — like coming home.

Tues. 26
A bit of bronchial trouble & a slight temperature — but I went out in a big launch for 2 hours with Lord Swinton, the Brit. Resident Minister for W. Africa. I am not impressed by what I have seen of the Colonial Gov. of Gambia but I think S. is a good man to supervise all these colonies.

[FDR continued on to Brazil, then Trinidad.]

Sat. 30
Left Trinidad at 6 A.M. got to Miami at 4 P.M. Birthday party 8,000 ft. up over Haiti — I drank CPs health.

[Hyde Park]

༅ *Jan. 30th Saturday.* Same sort of days — doing our best in some heavy snow, on icy roads, etc. F.D.R. not back for his birthday —

༅ *Jan 31st, Sunday evening.* Radio announces that F.D.R. is back in the White House — Sighs of relief!

[At Casablanca, the Allied leaders had made a series of important decisions about the war: they would invade Sicily in 1943, put off the cross-Channel assault for a year, and accept only unconditional surrender from Hitler.]

༅ *Feb. 1st.* F.D.R. called me up at the Library, about 9.30 A.M.
"How is Fala?"
Will let me know if I am to take Fala down or if he will be coming up over the week-end. Said he was tired after the trip. I know he isn't getting any rest now — with several of his family there & probably a huge accumulation of work. I told him we all thought he *should not* take the risks of such a trip.

"Well — not for some time anyway."

Which means nothing! It was good to hear his voice, safe at home.

◦ *Feb. 7th Sunday.* . . . I got to the Library about 11 yesterday A.M. after waiting in the village for the sand truck to go down the icy roads — It was impossible driving before that. F.D.R. had arrived early & left a message for me to call him. He came over a little later — I *was* glad to see him & told him we had all been worried to death for three weeks, & *he should not do it!*

He said he didn't like flying a bit, & after the novelty of flying over clouds, came to dislike them. All his party have been feeling miserable since they got back — He just hasn't let himself give in until he got here — Then, he "let go" & feels exhausted. Would sleep late, Sunday, Monday, & Tuesday mornings. However, he spent most of the day working in the attic of the Library — sorting out "horrors" [ugly gifts] to be destroyed, or melted down for the war, etc.

He looks well. Fala was shy, but delighted to see him. F. picked him up & hugged him — When F.D.R. was showing the Watsons around in the afternoon, I went off to my office & wondered if Fala would come. He looked at me but trotted after the P. I was very glad . . .

[The White House]

◦ *Feb. 14th.* Last evening, there were, at dinner: Admiral & Mrs. [Richard] Byrd [aviation pioneer and old friend of the President], Mr. & Mrs. Shad Polier, she [Justine Polier], the daughter of Rabbi [Stephen] Wise; Harry Hooker & I, and, of course, the P. & Mrs. R. We had dinner downstairs — The P. looked very tired, but did his usual part of "Exhibit A," as he calls it, by entertaining the party — Everyone hanging on his words.

At nine, he said he had to go to work & left the guests, calling to me to go with him. He got on the sofa in his study and said he was exhausted — He looked it. He said: "I'm either Exhibit A, or left completely alone."

It made me feel terrible — I've never heard a word of complaint from him, but it seemed to slip out, unintentionally, & spoke volumes. Mrs. Watson said at lunch, on Friday, that "he is the loneliest man in the world." I know what she means. He has no real "home-life" in which to relax, & "recoup" his strength & his peace of mind. If he wasn't such a wonderful character, he would sink under it. But many have said that, referring more to his public life, & without perhaps realizing the side I am speaking of here —

. . . Later . . . I went in to the P.'s study [and] we launched into a discussion of "class consciousness." Very interesting. He thinks there is much less of it than I do. For example, he had met with his Church Vestry at H.P., most of them from the village — He thinks they look on him as the same as themselves. I am quite certain they do not, from my knowledge of Rhinebeck village people, who feel very definitely the difference between "River" and "Village." It *is* vanishing, but has not yet disappeared, and may not do so until all the big places & old families are no more — The P. is such a dominating personality, that he probably sets the whole tone of his vestry meeting, & is conscious only of the spirit of cooperation which he himself infuses into it . . .

✎ *Feb. 16th.* Mme. Chiang [wife of Generalissimo Chiang Kai-shek] has been staying at the house since Friday or Saturday. I can't find out which, as she was expected last Wednesday & evidently enjoys changing her mind and her plans —

Mr. Nixon came at 11 A.M. on Sunday, on request & waited until 2.30. This morning, Robert [McGauhey, the Springwood butler] called me up. Miss Tully had called him last night from Washington to arrange for Mme. Chiang to be shown around the Library by me. Robt. said he would let me know just as soon as Mme. Chiang made up her mind. About two, Robt. called up again, with a laugh in his voice: Mme. Chiang would see me at 3, 4, 5, 6, or 7. I explained to Robt. that I have to take two people home at 5.15 & that we have no extra gas for me to come back — Robt. said he would change the appointment, & call me back —

At about 3 P.M. Robert called again: Mr. [L. H.] Kung, Mme. Chiang's nephew, said that Mme. Chiang would see me at 6. I explained again, about my passengers & the gasoline. Robt. offered to change the appt. About 3.15, Robt. called again: Mme. Chiang will see me at 5!!

It's now 4.30, & I am wondering just how long Mme. Chiang will keep me waiting when I get to the house. There *is* an awkwardness about the whole situation, as she doesn't know *why* she has to see *me,* when she has already seen the Library — I'll try to explain!

Later at home. I had the nicest time . . . Mme. was lying on the bed, in a shell pink bed jacket, a lovely Chinese coverlet over her —

My very first impression from the doorway was that she looked old, & tired. As I came near, she was pretty, round cheeked & very charming & smiling. I did a little apologizing & explaining, which doesn't seem to have been needed — She could not have been nicer — said she was sorry I wasn't here over the week-end as we could have taken walks together — invited me to visit them in China! It's something to get as far as being asked — though I am never apt to be able to accept. We talked of the country, the snow, the homelike feeling in the house — she feels the presence of Mrs. James Roosevelt in every room. [Madame Chiang had earlier visited Hyde Park, and the President's mother had been her hostess.] She went to the cemetery & felt it there, too —

I wondered if she has a sense of humor, and *think* she has, but with reservations. She impresses me as having had nervous prostration as a result of the 5 yrs. of war in China. It is a wonder that she is as well as she is. I started to leave at 5.15, but she said, "Oh no — I must have tea."

At that moment Miss Burden brought in a little tray for me & a bedtable for Mme. So I naturally stayed — for another fifteen minutes — We got on very well, on local simple subjects — I wonder if we would get on if she became "intense" on some subject. She would just think me very dull, I suppose!

↷ *Feb. 27th.* . . . At the W.H. I was taken to Miss Hickok's room & changed my dress & washed up, just in time for the P. to send for me. The Dr. was with him, just finishing treating his sinus. The Dr. turned him over to me, as nurse:

"Use the spray in ten minutes."

"Give two aspirin & soda at 8.30."

It is the P.'s 4th day in bed, & he still feels somewhat miserable though his fever has gone. Last Tuesday, without any warning, he felt ill at about noon. He lay on his study sofa & slept 'til 4.30, when he found he had a temp. of 102. The Dr. found it was a toxic poisoning, but they can't ascribe it to anything they know of. [Every presidential illness, no matter how slight, alarmed Daisy. The President's secretary, William Hassett, dismissed this one as just a "stomach upset."]

On Wednesday they gave him 4 doses of a sulpha drug — from which he will have to recover —

I stayed for supper with him in his room; a nice little supper: corn soup, creamed chicken & peas, stewed rhubarb, coffee. He had a bed tray, I a tray on a separate little table, like seeing Mme. Chiang last week! I seem to be seeing "The Great" very informally! The P. doesn't look well, but is improving. We started cutting out & making a "Dymaion" World map. I was sent home early —

When I gave him his aspirin he suddenly said: "Do you know that I have never had anyone just sit around and take care of me like this before." He meant that, outside of trained nurses, which men hate to have hanging around, he is just given his medicine or takes it himself. Everyone else has been too busy to sit with him, doing nothing.

ॐ *Monday March 1st 5.40 p.m.* The P. is better — got up about noon & I believe worked with Tully & had various conversations. Called me in a little before three. He had gone back on his bed for a little nap. At four he got up & into his study where I went & talked to him until "Martha" was announced as being in The West Hall — He put on the lovely new watch & chain & jade (translucent) pendant given to him by Mme. Chiang, to show to Martha & Olaf . . .

Later — a very nice tea — Martha sat on the sofa with F.D.R. —

Mrs. R. poured tea & had 5 friends — One, a Mrs. [Eliot D.] Pratt [Trude Pratt, who would eventually become Joseph Lash's wife] is German & questionable, according to the S.S., but, with Joe Lash, who comes under the same category, is constantly here —

The party divided naturally into two — The talking was easy & relaxed — F. looked pretty well, though still a little peaked.

ॐ *Wednesday, March 3rd.* . . . F. looking rather better, after a good night — He had a lunch conference & was very tired afterwards . . . We had an [air-raid] alert, which I watched from the . . . window — When the 3rd signal sounded everything stopped on the streets — all but a few stray individuals vanished, supposedly in the shelters — Soldiers in their helmets, & with guns pointing, lay stretched behind trees on the lawn, facing away from the W.H.

I told F. about it & took him to the study window just in time to see the last soldier getting up, as the alert was over. He hadn't seen it before, & was much interested — then he went off to bed again —

ॐ *March 4, 1943.* [The tenth anniversary of FDR's first inauguration] . . . The Hopkinses for dinner. F. ate well, & looked a little better afterwards. Louise tries very hard to be entertaining & sweet to him. She is very nice, and thoughtful, & is making Harry & Diana very happy — but she isn't interesting enough or amusing enough to warrant all that talking she does to F, and he can't help looking a little

Five of the six Suckley children coasting down a Swiss hillside during the winter of 1898: Robert, six-year-old Margaret (Daisy), Arthur, Katherine, and Elizabeth. The family would not return permanently to the United States for another ten years.

First encounter. After vacationing again in Switzerland in 1922 (opposite), Daisy, then twenty, returned to Dutchess County and there accepted an invitation from Sara Delano Roosevelt to come to tea at Springwood, the Roosevelt home at Hyde Park. There she met forty-year-old Franklin Roosevelt (above), newly ravaged by infantile paralysis and starved for companionship.

"Did you know," Daisy asked FDR in September 1935, "that Excelsior [right] is a magic bird? He is." Using FDR's carved wooden gift as a sort of mental surrogate, she imagined herself traveling with him that month to the dedication of Boulder Dam (opposite) and aboard ship in the Pacific and, over the years, to Teheran and Cairo and Yalta as well.

EXCELSIOR!

Daisy often carried a Kodak, and Roosevelt sometimes turned it on her. He made the portrait on the opposite page at one of their favorite picnic spots, Sunset Ridge on Silver Mountain near Pine Plains, on August 8, 1940. The other two pictures were taken in the Oval Study of the White House, to which he and Daisy often retired after dinner. At left, she pretends to be fascinated by an old Roosevelt family account book, and below, she sits a little self-consciously on a lion skin that had been a gift to FDR from Emperor Haile Selassie of Ethiopia. The occasion was her fiftieth birthday, December 20, 1941.

FDR was a willing subject for Daisy's camera too, whether gazing fondly into her lens on the porch at Top Cottage (opposite) or sprawled out after dinner at the White House, his feet on a specially made rest, within easy reach of the basket of papers needing signatures that followed him wherever he went.

These pictures demonstrate as no words can the implicit trust Roosevelt placed in Daisy Suckley: her two photographs of him in the wheelchair in which he spent much of his waking life are the only such images known to exist anywhere. Five-year-old Ruthie Bie (left) was the granddaughter of Christian Bie, the caretaker at Top Cottage; at right, FDR waits on the Springwood porch to start a yacht trip down the Hudson in the summer of 1937. Secret Service men dragged the car cushion out of the President's Ford (above) so that he could be part of a 1940 picnic on Sunset Ridge.

FDR posed for this pair of gag pictures in his study at the Roosevelt Library. Above, he pretends to dictate to Daisy's teenage niece Margaret (Rollie) Hambley, who plays the "good" secretary; below, with Fala occupying his desk, he murmurs to the "bad" secretary, saucily perched on the arm of his chair.

FDR listens from the back platform of his special railroad car, the *Ferdinand Magellan,* as an army band serenades him at Fort Riley, Kansas, on April 25, 1943. Henry Hooker, Daisy, and Laura Delano stand in the doorway. This second trip aboard the President's train, a tour of military installations, was one of the high points of Daisy's life.

April 1945, the last week at Warm Springs. FDR goes through his mail in the living room of his cottage, and Daisy, with Fala and Laura Delano's Irish setter, Sister, poses on the porch in the warm Georgia sun.

Daisy Suckley in her nineties at Wilderstein. Shortly after she died in
1991, her papers were found beneath her bed in the third-floor bedroom
in the tower at left.

tired at making the extra effort. I notice this change in him as the months go by. I at least know enough to *keep quiet!!* . . .

[Hyde Park]

☙ *March 9th Tuesday.* . . . I gave [the President] some sound advice on resting & taking care of himself, which he will ignore, but he may do a little of it, for he says he feels like a rag, & is much annoyed at himself. Once, he said, he supposed it was "old age." In a sense, of course, it is that, for as the years go by, he is slowly losing some of his capacity to get over things — and he will have to take care of himself if he is going to be well. I hate to see him looking even a little tired. There is a pinched look in his face, and his hand sometimes shakes. He went back to Wash. on the night train.

☙ *March 15th.* . . . The papers are very thrilling these last few days, with all the talk of what is to be done after the war. It gives one the hope that something can be done which will be constructive and perhaps prevent a recurrence of the present war. It will need a tremendous amount of educating of millions of people, specially in Germany, Italy, & Japan, for their whole education for years has been leading up to the present. It is all the more fascinating to me, because F.D.R. has been planning & talking about it for months — and years — I pray he succeeds, & gets the backing of other nations & of his own country. I wish he could get out of the W.H. and perhaps head the new international organization! I doubt if there is anyone else in this country ready to do it, and *able* to do it.

☙ *March 16th.* I wrote F. last week about the Fala movie, so he called me up this evening about it. He wants to see it next Monday, the 22nd, in the White House. I am seeing it in New York this Friday evening. [FDR had granted Daisy permission to help an MGM film crew make a short film at Hyde Park based on her book on Fala.]

F. said he is having a very interesting week. [British Foreign Secretary] Anthony Eden is awfully nice, and "conversations" [about plans for postwar Europe] are very "satisfactory." He doesn't want Congress to start a fight at this time, on what we shall do after the war, but the subject is put before the world, & the world is beginning to think about it. He is feeling better, will work on his "basket" this evening & go to bed about 10.30. Tomorrow, he hopes to go out for a ½ hr. drive, perhaps to Arlington & back — just to get a little fresh air. I suggested he might go the other direction, meaning to the Norwegians at Bethesda! He laughed — He rather likes being teased about Martha. She *is* attractive. Much charm — tall, slender, & a good figure . . .

[New York]

❦ *Friday, Mar 19th*. . . . [I] took a taxi to some place on 48th & B'way where they have pre-view studios. Mr. [Herbert] Morgan [in charge of short subjects for] Metro Goldwyn [Mayer] met us. We saw the movie [*Fala, the President's Dog*] twice through & liked it very much. The only trouble is that it hasn't enough of the President — But we have to be thankful they could get the one scene where he gives Fala his supper! Mr. Morgan explained some "secret" details: a squirrel was brought in a cage & let out at the proper moment so that Fala could chase him to a tree on the W.H. lawn; a piece of bacon was put under the bottom of the scrapbook which Diana [Hopkins] & Fala are looking at with such interest; a piece of bacon was buried with the bone Fala dug up in the lawn; a substitute for Fala had to be put in for the kitchen scene, as the photographers were not allowed to take the kitchen in the W.H. This was also true of the telephone girl scene. The substitute dog had shorter hair than Fala, so they glued extra hair on him. The P.'s room & the breakfast tray were all faked, but very well, for I asked Mr. Morgan if the bed wasn't really the President's . . .

I think they could have done the fish scene better if they had followed the story more nearly — Also they should have put in the part where Fala wakes up the sailors by licking their feet — That is very funny . . . On the whole it is a very amusing little "short" & should be popular in the newsreel . . .

❦ *Monday the 22nd*. This evening, F.D.R. called up from Wash. They had just seen the Fala movie — He said he loved it all . . .

❦ *March 24th*. Mr. Morgan called me to report about his visit to the White House to show the film. He had a thrilling time, sat next to the President and thought him a very wonderful person — full of charm & so pleasant and cheerful — He will vote for him for a 4th term!! Mr. Morgan said one could judge of what the President is, by the atmosphere he creates around him, from Fala's happy cheerful disposition, on up the ladder — He couldn't get over the way Fala sat & watched the whole thing through. He will try to get Laura Delano to attend the "première" at the Press Club and, in a little ceremony, accept the film for the F.D.R. Library — they wanted me to do it, but I promptly declined! I told Mr. Morgan I had quite enough publicity with my name on the screen, already . . .

[Hyde Park]

~ *April 2nd.* F.D.R. arrived this morning . . . He looks better than on his last trip — He has had a very busy week — Anthony Eden staying in the W.H. the last 3 days before going on to Canada. The P. says A.E. is the nicest type of Englishman, very clever. He thinks he sees the future as F.D.R. sees it, but is not sure that he has the strength to go against the conservatives in England. Winston Churchill of course, would not ever "see" much beyond the British Empire. A.E. told the P. that the P. will have to run for a 4th term — "We need you in the peace conference."

F.D.R. told him he could help more if he were not President . . .

We went to the Cottage, made tea & toast in front of the fire, & talked. The P. was relaxed & peaceful, & talked mostly about his hopes for future peace. He has it all worked out in his mind already — The problem is to get the selfishness out of the conference. He thinks this country will be powerful enough to *force* the others — *if necessary*. After all, we haven't gone into this war to have the whole thing start up again. He told again of his conversation with the Sultan of Morocco, on digging oil in Morocco, & keeping it there *for the Moroccans:* "The first time, Mr. President, any foreigner has ever given us advice for *our* benefit" . . .

~ *April 3rd.* . . . If F.'s plans work out, he would like to be chairman of the peace organization, whatever his title would be. He wants to do it *"simply,"* not at Geneva in a huge building, etc.: Have meetings yearly in different countries . . . The org. itself might be run with a comparatively small staff, half the year in an island, like Horta in the Azores — the "Chairman," "Sec.-Gen," or what have you, would have a staff of two assistants, men who know the situation inside out & from beginning to end: Hopkins & Winant. Then the secretaries, Tully & two stenographers. He would have a house, not very large — There would be another for the secretarial staff — A small group of houses would probably be built to house staff of other nations. There will have to be a good airfield.

It's all very exciting, & perhaps it will happen — if the P. keeps his health & strength — He counts on the Germans "cracking" by about next July — he can then definitely state he will not run for a 4th term . . .

[The President was about to undertake another inspection tour of western and southern military installations, then meet President Ávila Camacho of Mexico at Monterrey. Once again, Daisy and Laura Delano were invited along.]

↝ *Tue. Apr. 13* — Shopping for a white hat to wear in Monterrey. Roly took me around the shops until I finally found a nice big hat for $5.00 which F.D.R. approved when I showed it to him on the train, later! I was thankful, as he calls most of my hats "peanuts," and I must do credit to him before the President of Mexico!

I went to the W.H. at a ¼ to 11, upstairs, to Polly's room, the blue room, Fala was hovering around the door, much interested in "Sister" [Laura Delano's Irish setter]. Sister is dignified, with her 9 years, but is friendly.

. . . At a quarter to two we were told to gather downstairs. Polly & Sister took a walk on the W.H. lawn, Fala tore around after Sister. Finally, the P. & Mrs. came down. He got into his car, we said goodbye to her & got into different cars & off we went to the train, inside the mint building, & off, on schedule, at about 2 P.M. For the moment, Polly & I are the ladies of the party. Leighton McCarthy [the American ambassador to Canada] & [Basil] Doc O'Connor go to Warm Springs, both being trustees. Harry Hooker, Capt. [later Rear Admiral] Wilson Brown [Captain McCrae's successor as naval aide and a former commander of a carrier task force], Adm. McIntire are the others.

The P. went to his [stateroom] & slept for about 3 hrs. He looks very tired. Polly & I unpacked. Sat around with maps etc. At 6.30 the party for dinner assembled & had cocktails. At seven we went in to dinner . . . Then back to "deck" where we had an easy nice evening. F.D.R. talking about everything, but *not* politics. All the men seemed to agree to bring up only light topics. Jokes about fishing trips they had been on together, etc.

F.D.R. marked my map for me. Doc O'Connor teased him. Polly & I scribbling at the schedule of the trip — Sister & Fala settling down one minute, up & moving the next — Fala, a little black shadow after Sister, & sometimes getting a warning growl from her if he bores her too much — To bed about 10 P.M.

I am in Mrs. R.'s stateroom, [so] I shall have to move out when she comes on board at Fort Worth. Polly in the same she was in before, Adm. McIntire in the 4th. This new car is bright & cheerful & clean looking. The "deck" a *so* much better size.

Old [Henry A.] Lucas in attendance. He told me his wife said to him: "I hope you have as nice people as on the last trip," a direct compliment from Lucas his'self!

⌇ *Wednesday Apr. 14.* As usual, a poor night . . . I looked out about 6.30. We were still in S.C., flat country, just beginning to grow — that clean "spring" orderliness — larches freshly green — little patches of gardens just showing their green lines. The poor little huts of the darkies with no cellars — Soldiers on guard at all crossings. The train moves at a moderate steady pace, none of the racing of so many through trains. (On the trip last Sept. on one occasion, the train was going faster than usual, lurching & bumping. F. sent word forward to slow down . . .)

⌇ *Thursday April 15th 8.25 a.m.* . . . [At the Marine training base at Parris Island] they had several thousand on the parade ground for F. to inspect. He spoke a few words to them, into a microphone, though he announced the day before "no speeches." They just poke the mike at him & he has to say something — He always says the right thing. Col. Smith said his coming that way has a tremendous effect on the morale of the marines.

The rest of the day we rolled through the same sort of country . . . the season advancing as we came South . . .

At dinner were us four, F.D.R. & Polly, Harry & I, and Mr. O'Connor and Mr. McCarthy — All are congenial with F — friends of long standing. O'C. is quite a wit, & very amusing with F., teasing him in a pessimistic almost sour way at times. Polly & I say little, but she is very quick, & attractive, and thoughtful. I find myself more & more fond of her — She's very genuine. F. loves having her around — she is sweet & affectionate with him. She gives the impression of being worldly wise, but often blushes, if teased — She is sensitive & very fine . . .

⌇ *Friday April 16th 8.20 a.m.* Maxwell Field [near Montgomery, Alabama] was fascinating . . . We stopped at the landing field, where 100 planes started off into the air, circled out of sight & returned, passing over the field again, in formation, flying low.

Lots of little children squealed, "Fala," so Fala did the rounds, wagging his whole body. He seems to know he must be kind & polite to everyone — It's just part of his exalted position!

We next moved on to a reviewing ground where 4,000 young aviators, standing in groups of 800, sang the air corps song. F. "spoke a few words" into the microphone to them. I always feel it is too bad, on these occasions, that they have to stand at attention, & can't respond in some way — As we drive by, we can see their eyes travelling from right to left & back, the rest immovable.

Near where our train stood, was an exercise field, where 4,000 boys in blue trousers with a white stripe down the side, & white shirts, were: boxing, moving dumbbells, running obstacle races, doing calisthenics of different kinds, archery, medicine ball, shadow boxing, jiujitsu, etc. They told us that in the first 4 weeks of training they gain 7 lbs, lose 2 inches around the waist, put on 2 inches on the chest, as a general average — these boys are learning what it is to be physically fit. It is bound to do something for them in life. I should think it would make them want universal training for their own children — *without* the thought of aggression.

. . . At three we had arrived at Ft. Benning, outside of Columbus Ga. [and] saw a "problem," a battle, in which they use real ammunition. Once in a while someone gets hurt if he doesn't heed the signals and signs, as, for instance, where land mines are laid. Capt. S. told us we were the only women who had been allowed to see this for the last six months. It was beautifully put on & one can see its great value in training, but Polly & I had the same thought that it is a sad commentary on civilization that all the energies of man have to be, for the moment, concentrated on the destruction of man, and the training of men must be for personal aggression. We saw tanks in the battle, & a man who seemed to have been hurt. We don't know if he was or not, for Capt. S. told us they fake that too, and that the men with stretchers don't know whether it is a real case or not. Further on we saw classes in hand to hand fighting — the sort of thing they have in the Pacific Jungles, with the Japs — It's all horrible when you stop to analyze it, but it's a fight for survival . . .

It was a beautiful day, but, for this season, very chilly, the wind blew, & we travelled through the area in a cloud of dust. F. in an open car . . . 40 miles to Warm Springs. We came by a back road to the little White House, F.'s cottage, a sweet one-story house, on a point, so that nothing but a sky-scraper could possibly be built in sight of its south exposure.

. . . Polly & I walked the dogs down the hill to Georgia Hall [the main building] for supper . . . [There were] 100 patients in all . . . the great majority in wheel chairs. F. stood up with his braces, holding on to his chair & made a serious, soft-voiced little speech, then was wheeled to the door of the dining room where he stayed to shake hands with each patient that filed through. It was an experience for them all. I took Fala in by the main entrance & he did the rounds — all of them thrilled to see him & touch him. It is just a *little* like touching the President! Back to the train which moved down the track from the W.S. Station for the night . . .

◦ *Saturday April 17th 8.35 a.m.* Breakfast [aboard the parked train] just finished. Comfortable on my bed, with a sheet hung across the window so I can see & not be seen. We stand alongside a long corrugated tin shed. Army cars are parked, numbered, for our cavalcade.

Yesterday [was] a perfect day for F.D.R. at Warm Springs. He was very happy, surrounded by old friends who love him. I was delighted to see the place, having heard so much about it. We left the train about 10 A.M. F. drove the little car he has had for years down here. Mr. Botts, the registrar, also a victim of infantile, uses it when F. is not here.

[Fred Botts, a skeletal polio survivor, arrived at Warm Springs on the same train that brought FDR for his first visit, in the autumn of 1924. Roosevelt had come in a private compartment. Botts had been barred from riding in the Pullman because there was no place for his wheelchair and so he had ridden in the mail car, inside a sort of wooden cage fashioned by his brother so that he wouldn't be too badly battered by the movement of the train.]

On the back [of the car] is a beautiful *special* license plate: deep red background, & "F.D.R.–1, The President." Harry sat in front, Polly, the dogs & I in the back. F. drove us around showing us cottages he has had a hand in building (his mother's, his first & second, etc) telling us about different stages in the building up of the Foundation. It is certainly a monument to him, his imagination and his faith & his love for his fellow sufferers, and it is very lovely. Peaceful and beautiful. The houses homelike and attractive, mainly white, among trees.

We went to the big pool & swam for perhaps a half hour. The water is exhilarating & I really enjoyed the experience, though neither Polly nor I wanted to go in! F. sat in the sun afterwards, while we dressed. I had Roly Hambley's discarded bathing suit of two years ago

— very pretty, but much too large. It would have fallen off if Roly hadn't lent me a gold safety pin to fasten together the very low back!

F. was visibly expanding and blossoming, all day — From the pool, we went up to his cottage, sat on the porch in the sun. Nothing in sight but the trees, the sunlight, the sky & a distant view . . .

From there to the Knob for a picnic lunch prepared on the train & served by the train stewards: fish chowder, sandwiches, deviled eggs on toothpicks, cold drinks. F. showed us the extent of the Foundation property, which now included his farm. We saw his tree plantations, and a forest on what used to be a cotton field — the view is magnificent, in 3 directions. F. asked Cornelia Dewey [a young polio patient living in Warm Springs] to sit next to him. She was in seventh heaven! All the doctors & their wives, the Manager & Mrs. [Louis Haughey], etc. etc. all took turns. Fala had a marvelous time wandering.

We stayed there, getting sunburned, until about 3 — went back to the cottage, via the "fernery road" which had just been scraped, very fortunately, for even so it is about as rough as three cars can manage to get through. We crossed one rickety wooden bridge which F. warned might & probably would collapse under us! It didn't. We also drove around the camp where the soldiers are put up who guard him. A dozen or so were lying around on the grass, jumped up & stood at attention, but smiled & relaxed when F. smiled at them as he drove his little car around them. I hate to see them standing like wooden images — I suppose it makes one think of Hitler & his mechanized human beings abroad . . .

[B]efore the P. arrives in Warm Springs, a S.S. detail pulls all the beds apart in the cottage, pokes needles through the pillows & mattresses, goes into every nook & cranny with flashlights. All the time we were there, a large canvas hose was attached to the hydrant. A fire among the dead leaves & the trees would be serious. The country is very dry, the roads dusty. Mrs. [C. E.] Irwin [wife of the chief surgeon] remarked that they once suggested surfacing the roads to avoid the dust. The P. answered that "we want to keep things simple." So no more is said about it. That place *is* F.D.R. — His absence, the cause of whatever real difficulties there are . . .

I myself had quite an insight into the problems of Warm Springs from Mr. Haughey. There are two schools of thought about the place: the medical & the human — Dr. Irwin represents the first. The P. represents the second — the Medical cares nothing about patients of more than a few months — The P. *and* the old patients care about continuing to help them — There isn't enough money in their care for the doctors — F. is quite upset about the situation & wishes he could give the time to it himself —

⁓ *Saturday, the 17th — after Ft. Oglethorpe.* . . . The cars that carried us around [at Fort Oglethorpe] for the inspection were driven by WAACS, very neat & set-up, most of them with hair curling under their military képis. They drilled very well, passing in review before the P. . . . I was particularly impressed with the swinging stride of those girls — so different from the usual highheeled trip of most women — Adm. Wilson Brown remarked afterwards that the training was going to do much for our future generation of Americans, if only from the point of view of health & physique.

⁓ *Sunday April 18th at Camp Joseph T. Robinson, Ark. near N. Little Rock, Ark.* Polly & I remarked yesterday that we two women are the only women in this country to see these camps in this way — as the Commander-in-Chief sees them — except, of course, that we are in second place, & talked to Captains, colonels & lieutenants, while he talks to the State Governors and the Generals. We do appreciate it, & are very conscious of the privilege, but F. makes it all seem so natural that we have to keep saying to ourselves: "Do you realize that this is *you*, doing this . . ."

Camp Gruber, Okla. About 12,500 men paraded before F. without their guns, etc. One of the generals told us it would have taken over 2 hrs. if they had paraded with their motorized equipment . . . Last May, there was nothing here but farms — Now it is a huge camp with a parade ground 3 miles long! . . . The grass on the parade ground was planted only 3 weeks ago . . .

When Polly & the dogs & I got back to the train, we took them walking down the tracks . . . [Troops] were standing at ease, waiting for F. to come back. They all knew about Fala, had seen him on the screen last week — recognize him from his generally black mop-like appearance! All wanted to pat him, & talk to him. At one point, a soldier picked him up & sat him on a wall. Some thirty crowded around for a touch of him. One boy held up a hair of Fala's & asked how much they would give for it. I suggested to the boy who held him that he charge a quarter a pat! He took it up at once, & there was much joking & laughing . . . Polly saw the mob surrounding Fala &

me & was *mildly* alarmed — but the minute I said I thought I'd have to take Fala back to the train, the "mob" fell back & dissolved. All those boys will write home about it.

A workman was doing something to the back of the private car. He saw Fala & asked if he could pet him. Fala wagged his tail as usual. The man said: "Well, this is quite a day for me; I work on the President's car, & now I am petting the President's dog!"

The P. & all the men came back about 7.45; all enthusiastic about their supper. The P. told them at supper that in the W.H. he never had such good beef stew, carrots, macaroni, home baked bread, butter, & coffee! Poor Mrs. [Henrietta] Nesbitt, the W.H. housekeeper! [Mrs. Nesbitt was a Hyde Park caterer whom Eleanor Roosevelt had hired to manage the White House kitchens. FDR disliked her and detested her pallid cooking, but was unable to get rid of her. She was evidently as imperious as she was inept; when the President sent her a memorandum detailing his dislike of broccoli, she ordered the chefs to serve it to him, anyway. "It's good for him," she said. "He *should* like it."]

~ *April 19th Monday* — *Tulsa, Okla.* Inspection of Douglas Aircraft plant at 10 A.M. 4-motored bombers assembled with parts sent from Willow Run Ford plant — [Henry] Ford has delayed them by not being able to "convert" [from automobiles to airplanes] as quickly as he planned & promised — However a bomber comes out, finished, every 16 days. They also manufacture small dive bombers under the same 4,000 ft. roof . . .

At Ft. Worth, 7.30 P.M. Mrs. R., Ruth, Chanler & Tony [Elliott, Jr.] got on board, [Ruth Googins Roosevelt, Elliott's second wife, and their two children], also Sumner Welles & Ambassador [Francisco Castilia] Najera (Mexico). We stayed up until 10 listening to them talk about the future peace — *Very* interesting — the perpetrators of the war, like Hitler, Himmler, etc. shall be court martialed in their own countries & "liquidated," not sent to some distant island to turn into heroes and martyrs, with the danger of their trying to come back — Argentina, the only S. American country not collaborating, is receiving "silent treatment," and is much annoyed! The Irish Free State are to be treated the same way, & told that if they won't cooperate now they can't expect to have any say *after* the war.

~ *Friday April 20th 9 a.m.* I am in a large stateroom in "the other car," Adm. McIntire & I having moved to make room for Mrs. R.,

Ruth & the children. I am thoroughly spoiled by travelling in the private car, & find all sorts of faults with this: It rides roughly, there is no closet, there are no drawers, the color is gloomy, etc. etc.!! However I've had an excellent breakfast of quail (left from supper last evening) ordered by F.D.R., coffee and grapefruit. The coloured porter wants a big tip & is too obviously attentive. Old Lucas in the P.'s car looks gloomy but is devoted & faithful & means it. I'll be glad to get back there on Thursday [when Mrs. Roosevelt was to leave the train].

Apr. 21st Wednesday, 8.30 a.m. . . . Yesterday was an "unforgettable" day. It became very warm and sunny as we approached *Monterrey* . . .

The Pres. of Mexico's train stood on a siding as we came in . . . The rear end of our train, with the ramp, stood on a crossing. On each side of the road was a flagpole, with two men waiting for the signal to pull up the American & Mexican flags. After a few minutes of waiting the P.s & their parties came out & started down the ramp. Clapping from the crowds.

At a signal a band started playing, up went both flags — The 2 national anthems were played when the P.s were standing near their open car —

People threw pink confetti & roses as the P.s drove by — We got some too — Little children rushed into the street to pick up the roses after they had fulfilled their duty of being thrown — The people give the impression of being happy & simple & childlike. Their greeting was spontaneous and natural — Many made the V for Victory sign — specially the school children — We V-ed back at them . . . some of them waved little American flags — there were a few red heads & a few fair heads, the women seem lighter coloured than the men. The very large majority have dark skins, black hair, straight or curly — the beautiful white & straight teeth are so general, that I kept thinking they must be false! They said it comes from the corn & lime they eat . . .

We drove to the Governors Palace, a beautiful building of Spanish architecture with two inner courts — The P.s drove into the first court. We were ushered on through the second onto the terrace facing the square with the statue of Juarez and the mountains beyond — A platform with a railing had been built for the P.s . . .

Then the mechanized troops came by, on foot & on wheels. A company of Cavalry had beautiful black horses. When the infantry do "eyes left" before the P.s, they make a double salute by stamping their feet twice, a sort of *one* "goose step." The troops are a deep coppery brown, strange features, showing the mixture of Indian & Spanish. They seemed, most of them, wiry & rather short — the officers inclined to solidity & corpulence! Their uniforms adequate but badly fitting — Bands & drummers moved by with them, & between their playing, a string orchestra in sombreros, played across the street —

When the review was over, the P.s returned to their car — we went in search of ours . . . The troops lined along the road were awfully young: in some places were boys — they seemed very vague as to what they were supposed to do. One would be standing stiffly at attention, his gun held straight in front of him; the next kept an apparently permanent salute with a frozen face while a third would be very much "at ease," with eyes anywhere but straight ahead. At one point an officer was walking from one end to another of a line standing at attention, with his hand pushing each gun down & evidently telling the soldier he could relax! . . .

We finally arrived at what seemed to be a reviewing stand; the field full of boys & girls, with white shorts & long dark trousers, the girls white waists with short sleeves, & black skirts. The P.s were in the stand already — Mr. [Guy] Spaman came along, looking distracted as most of the S.S. men do on these occasions. He thought us lost! We went to the stand & enjoyed very much the exhibition given by the school children, of their calisthenics.

While it was going on, Polly was working with characteristic Delano-Roosevelt energy, getting the other women organized to go "shopping" between this part of the program, and the dinner! She was very successful, for by the time we got back into our car . . . it had been arranged that Mrs. R., Mme. Camacho, the ladies with her, Mrs. Messersmith, Ruth, Polly, "Tommy," etc. would all go straight to Sanborns [Department Store] . . .

Mrs. R. & Mme. C. drove off with a police escort — we were supposed to follow but our driver thought better of it, promptly went off into another direction & drove 80 miles an hour through narrow streets heading toward the mountains, tooting his horn constantly weaving in & out, to right or left of other cars; I decided he was probably kidnapping us for ransom. The only ray of comfort was that we seemed to be racing car No 7, for we would pass it only to be passed by it a few moments later: if we *were* being kidnapped, car No 7 was, too — *or* we *might* all be on our way to Sanborns. This happened to be true, for our driver suddenly skidded around a narrow corner & there was Sanborns — Our driver all smiles — we decided perhaps he wasn't so dumb after all.

We went into the store, and about 10 minutes later Mrs. R. & her party appeared! Polly went straight to the silver department. I wandered around trying to find something I wanted, within my purse. I got some linen-topped shoes for Poppy [Daisy's niece] & Gabrielle [Leake, a neighbor of the Suckleys], and a riding crop for Roly — also a miniature bull fight for F.D.R. Had them wrapped & asked what I owed. I was told that Mme. Camacho had given orders that no one should pay for anything! A gracious gesture but very embarrassing. I went up to Mme. C. & tried to thank her . . . F.D.R. said later not to worry — it would all come out of the Mexican Govt.!

. . . [At dinner] the P.s talked through a young interpreter who stood directly behind their chairs, & mopped his brow from either heat or nervousness . . .

At nine o'clock Pres. C made his broadcast in a dull monotonous chant, followed by our Pres. in his usual face-to-face manner.

I had a lovely time with Adm. Brown on my left & the Amb. to Brazil on my right. The latter told me that all South Americans have complete faith in F.D.R., that he has changed the entire relationship between the U.S. & the other countries. The only worry they have is whether his successor in the W.H. will want to, & be able to, keep up the policy of the "good neighbor" . . .

Back on board [the train] F soon appeared feeling happy & elated over a completely successful day, planned by him as a gesture of good will by the big U.S. to a smaller neighbor. The P. of the U.S., as usual, went more than half way, with his hand held out in friendship . . .

∾ *April 21*. . . . [T]he P. of Mexico & Mrs. C. came on board our train and rode with us out to a siding near the main line . . . The Camachos said goodbye & got on their train. We started and when we came to our side of the Y we stopped, then came the Mexican train and passed by — F.D.R. stood on the platform & waved to the Mexicans standing on their back platform —

F. is so completely perfect in a thousand little ways. He remains always the gentleman at heart. I am entirely certain that Pres. Camacho *loves* him after these hours together, just as everyone *loves* him who knows him. Miss Thompson remarked that Mike Reilly was exhausted with his work of doing all he could to protect the Pres. & that he would be relieved when this particular episode was over — She said not only his *mind* will be relieved, but his *heart*.

[Fort Worth]

∾ *April 22nd Thursday.* . . . It was a lovely restful day for F. [at Elliott's ranch]. He was completely relaxed & happy — Did some work, signed some papers, talked calmly about many things, played a little with the grandchildren.

. . . The day passed peacefully, reading, taking a bath (a great event after 10 days of washing piece-meal & balancing on one foot while the other is up in the basin!) About 6 P.M. we took a little drive around the place, looking at the cows and calves & Arabian colts. Ruth has a fine looking cowboy called Carleton. Big & straight & handsome. His greeting with F. was straightforward & simple & friendly —

At 5 P.M. Mrs. R. & Tommy left to take the plane to Phoenix & the West Coast. F. says Tommy is the wonder of the age. She works steadily 18 hrs. a day, flying with Mrs. R., arranging accommodations, typing, etc. etc. He said she saves Mrs. R. from many unscrupulous people who get around Mrs. R. through sympathy.

[Tommy's opinion of Daisy and Laura Delano was less charitable. Perhaps echoing the views of her employer, she found Miss Delano "imperious" and Daisy altogether too worshipful of FDR, who, she reported to a friend after the trip had ended, "had two meals every day with them and only once or twice had any others on the train at meals." And she was not amused by all the fuss they made about their dogs: "She [Laura Delano] had to get off at every stop, find a grass spot and wait for the biological functions, which she then discussed in detail with anyone who would listen. One night she was off the train and the secret service did not realize it until the train had started. They threw her on and threw the dog after her and were much annoyed."]

∾ *Saturday April 24.* [Colorado Springs] . . . The track winds back and forth around the mountain side, giving beautiful views down into valleys & across plains. It is poor pasture land, with pinon pine, the only trees . . . F. said there is so much lime rock that if one could find some way of getting rain there, it is probable that the soil could yield good crops. He thinks there must be some sort of tree that would grow. Then, the forests, by precipitating rain, would change the whole picture.

All along the line, at crossings, bridges, cuts, etc. a pair of soldiers stood guard. Many had pup tents set up. Many had little fires burning. As Polly & I stood on the back platform, some waved as their "at attention" ceased with our passing . . .

Arrived in Camp Carson at 3 A.M. where we now are. When I looked out of my window at 7.30 I saw two soldiers stiffly at attention, facing toward the right. I looked to see what was there & saw Fala, with Arthur [Prettyman] trailing him. Arthur has the figure of a S. American diplomat. Though very black, his features are refined & rather Jewish. He is a little portly, & walks with great dignity. The bunch of fur which is Fala wriggles & waddles in front of him.

Later . . . At Denver we drove from Fitzsimmons Hosp. to Lowry Field, Remington Rand Ordnance Plant, & back to the Hosp. where we entrained. The impression I have is of vastness, and a miracle of quick construction, and a view of the result of the "melting pot" in this country. 50% men & women at Remington, cheerful, well-fed human beings, who, with all their lack of culture, are the backbone of the country, & probably the finest "mass" of population in the world. The women were dressed in pale blue 1- piece overalls (much like Mr. Churchill's air-raid zipper suit), and red bandannas tied tightly about their heads . . . People were collected all along the route full of spontaneous enthusiasm. Women & girls jumping, waving, laughing & cheering. The men grinning broadly & waving.

. . . [Later we] settled down to a quiet evening, just the four of us. It was warm, so we opened the rear door — Fala stayed on the platform until a rain & lightning storm overtook us & it was dark —

On & on through western Colorado & Kansas. The RR grade goes up & down with the surface of the country — Drab little towns, treeless. But cheerful healthy people. At many places, they stood in rows & waved with evident excitement, when F. would smile at them. After dinner F. got out his stamps; the rest of us read. F. complained of a headache, so Polly & I both took his temperature — (none!) Polly gave him some soda & he went to bed with an aspirin. I hope he'll be all right in the morning. It is probably from the glare on the long drive, & having to wave & smile all the way — He had to give up going into the hospital wards, there was no time.

᨞ *April 25th Easter Day.* [Fort Riley, Kansas] . . . Detrained at 10.30 & motored around to the amphitheatre for Easter Services. There were some 15,000 troops seated there. The service was disappointing . . . To begin with, they had an elevated stage, at the back of which was an altar covered with white cloth & with 7 branch candlesticks & a cross, in brass — The altar was ignored during the service which was definitely evangelical. On the right sat the clergy, three of them without distinction; on the left sat a choir of 28 officers. They sang pretty well, but they were "performing" to an audience, rather than worshipping God . . .

The one point of beauty was a solo by Private Carl Anderson, a negro with a beautiful voice, who used to be a preacher — He sang with a depth of feeling which was very moving & seemed to express the religious fervor of the negro race — The simple gesture of his hands while he sang came from his heart.

At least four microphones stood about the stage, & were moved from the piano to the preacher, & from the singers to the reader. It would have been more satisfactory if they had had no altar at all, & had treated it quite simply as an outdoor *meeting*. Pa Watson was barely hiding his ribaldry, and Tully, a Catholic, was whispering to Dorothy Brady . . . When the service was over, F. walked to the entrance of the improvised canvas-covered passage, turned & waved. Later in the day, a nice young N.Y. soldier told me they were all terribly disappointed that he had not spoken a few words to them.

. . . After lunch we returned to the train, F. slept for an hour in his chair while Polly & I took the dogs walking. Fala spoke to the M.P.s — young men from all over the country — All smiling nice boys, intelligent & good mannered. They all *love* F.D.R. Wonder how he does all he does. One boy said he knew of only one other person who approaches him in *charm* & that is Queen Elizabeth, whom he saw passing through N.Y.C. Several thanked me for bringing Fala around.

A little later, about 5.30 P.M. F. came out on the back platform and sat on a chair, Fala sat next to him on another . . .

The band came & stood to the left, the color guard facing F. It was a beautiful sight. A stiff breeze throwing out the colors in the sun. They then gave a series of old tunes, like "Caisson" & . . . Pershing's old song, etc. Then, the officers came over to say goodbye; Polly & I rushed the dogs out to grass, to be called back with "the train is leaving"! We got on board, the band played "Should old acquaintance be forgot," the train started imperceptibly, everyone stiffly saluting the commander-in-chief — It was a beautiful sight and the kind of thing that brings a lump in your throat, specially when the commander in chief is a man like F. & crippled besides — Our driver told us he had not the slightest idea that F. couldn't walk, that his brother officers also had never thought of it. F. is all the more an inspiration to them —

We could see the "colours" getting smaller & smaller until we rounded a bend.

[The trip ended at Washington on April 28th. In May, Churchill came again to Washington for the Trident Conference, at which he and FDR agreed that the cross-Channel invasion of France — called Operation Round-Up, then Operation Overlord — would take place on or about May 1, 1944.]

June 9th. [Rhinebeck] F. called me up last night from Washington — Wants me to go there to work after his next visit, about June 22nd. My puppy is the problem. [Daisy now had her own Scottie, a female named Button.] He says to bring her along & put her in Fala's pen, at the W.H. I think I'll probably leave her at home to the tender mercies of the entire family — F. said he will be taking another trip in about two months. I know he means to meet Stalin somewhere. He feels it will do a great deal of good toward mutual understanding & working out a better system for after the war — Churchill spoke to F. about the election next year — told him: "I simply can't go on without you" — in other words, F *has* to continue being Pres. as long as this war continues . . .

June 22nd Tuesday. [Hyde Park] It always seems to be the *end* of things! Now, it's the last day of an exciting week-end which began last Friday. In the Library, carpenters & workmen were banging hammers, pulling things apart, putting up a stage, and lights & fixtures. In the P.'s room you couldn't hear a thing.

. . . After dinner, Mrs. R's chauffeur took me home in the P.'s car. I feel rather guilty having the extra gasoline used for me, but it is "in the service of the King" & justified for that reason.

Mrs. R. seemed really tired, but she never seems exhausted — which is a different thing. Or, perhaps she never gives in to feelings of exhaustion, like the rest of us! . . .

June 22. . . . Mrs. R. asked me for lunch at the Val-Kill Cottage. F.D.R. drove me over in his little blue car. We sat on the lawn, all trying to keep under the shadow of a small tree. An iron, glass-top table with different town chairs. F.D.R. & Mme. Chiang sat on one side, Mrs. R. stayed in the house for a while, arranging the serving of the food. Miss Thompson, Mr. Earl Miller [a New York State policeman, and close friend of Mrs. Roosevelt] . . . flitted in & out with plates . . . Mrs. R. finally settled down with us. Someone brought a tea tray which I served to the Chinese ladies.

Mme. Chiang in good form, all smiles, held the Miller baby on her lap for a while . . . I feel she is always acting — F.D.R. does too — You never get beneath the charming manner . . .

We left a little after 3, the P. dropping me off at the Library, to close my desk . . . I walked over to the big house & into his study, where I found him talking to Mr. Plog about numerous matters, including the statue of the praying girl, which stands at the moment on the porch outside his study door. It is to be put somewhere on the north side of the building, where *he can't* see it. *We* will, however!

[Ralph Stackpole, the sculptor responsible for the kneeling bronze FDR had seen in 1915, a copy of which he had hoped to obtain for Top Cottage, was understandably honored by the request, but the original had long since been stolen, and, in any case, he had radically altered his style over the intervening decades. And so, instead of trying to re-create the statue FDR had admired, he presented him with a new proto-cubist one, accurately described by the President's correspondence secretary, William Hassett, as "a huge hunk of a female in domestic travertine, big breasts, mammoth in all of her proportions — no curves, no grace, no delicacy . . . modernist in every aspect." Stackpole was sure the President would love it; it was inspired, he said, in part "by the great building of your administration, especially Boulder Dam." It weighed two tons.

FDR did not love it, was so appalled by it, in fact, that when it arrived he asked his staff to put it somewhere on the grounds where he would be certain never to see it again. It is still there, masked by evergreens, at the farthest edge of the parking lot.

A small model of the original did eventually make its way to FDR and was given a place of honor on the Top Cottage mantelpiece.]

✧ *July 6th.* At 10.15 [P.M.] the P. got into the big car — I got in with Button on my lap . . . Button full of curiosity and pep, slipping off my silk knees, looking around, licking the P.'s chin — At the station, we went right on board & I put Button on her own "quilt" . . . on my bed, & tied her — Lucas brought three large paper hat bags which covered the whole floor of my stateroom. As usual, large glasses of orange juice were brought — the P., Sam [Rosenman], Lydig [Hoyt, a Groton classmate and Dutchess County neighbor of the President's] & I talked for a little while & then the P. said he was going to bed —

Lydig said he didn't think a woman could be un-chaperoned until she's 66 — and that this trip, with me, alone with 3 men, "will get out"! I think 3 men ought to be able to chaperone us all!

~ *July 7th.* [The White House] . . . At 8.30, the P. appeared on his little chair & we all piled into the car — I do so enjoy being with men of this kind; all three, intelligent, and *nice,* and sweet & simple in their manners & outlook.

At the White House . . . everyone is much interested in the new pup — specially when the P. introduces her as "Fala's fiancée"!

I asked Lizzie, the older coloured maid, to roll up the bathroom rugs and the little one in the bathroom hall, "just to be on the safe side" with the puppy — She not only took the rugs away, but covered the floor with newspapers! She's probably had experience with other puppies! [Lizzie — Elizabeth McDuffie — was the wife of Irvin McDuffie, for many years FDR's valet. A formidable woman in her own right, she sometimes spoke on the President's behalf to black audiences.]

[Mrs.] Wilma [Hughes], a younger maid, came around & took some of my dresses to press — She is the nicest girl, very responsive and loves the dogs, so we have a bond —

I am in the Blue Room. I have covers on two chairs, and a large piece of chintz for Button to lie on my bed, while I eat breakfast. With a radio & a telephone next to the bed, I am very luxurious. An air cooler in the window draws the fresh air in from outside, but it seems very close & warm. The hall has much more circulation, with any number of fans going all day.

About 11.30 A.M. I went out & took Fala & Button for a walk . . . Round & round they go — after squirrels and birds — never getting dangerously near anything, but just as excited in spite of the fact that they never catch anything. Fala knows every inch of the 4(?) acres which comprise the W.H. grounds & which the P. calls the "back yard."

. . . The two little hills in the "Park" have each a machine gun, with two soldiers. They sit there, in silence, and immovable. An "emplacement" of brown boards has been built, covered with vines. The effect is that of an old wall — At the gates & around the lower end are booths, with soldiers, and regular W.H. guards. All are having a stupid time, with nothing happening (thank goodness!).

. . . The large round pool is empty, but a gardener informed me that it is filled for special occasions, & the jets turned on — Iris surrounds the pool some three feet deep — A sign of the war is that there are weeds among the iris plants and the lawn is not kept very closely cropped, except near the W.H. However — it doesn't show unless you are right on it. I sat on the edge of the pool for perhaps a half hour, while Fala & Button "hunted" [for grasshoppers] among the iris . . .

Soon we are told that the P. is on his way over from the Executive Offices [for tea] . . . We all go down (4.30 P.M.), meet the P. on the main floor, & trail him out to the front porch where General Giraud, General Marshall, [and] Admiral Leahy [are waiting].

. . . [T]he general is tall & fine looking — a real *gentleman* of the old school. The P. says he does not know how to deal with De Gaulle, who is out for himself, & wants to be the next ruler of France — in whatever capacity may be expedient when the time comes. As usual, the rest of us listen most of the time. Gen. Giraud is charming, talks easily. The P. talks easily in French to him; even tells him a joke in French. Adm. L. & I decide the P. *should not* take airplane trips like the Casablanca trip — But how to stop him?

The P., in the most natural manner, dismisses the party by moving in his chair as though he were getting up, and saying "I know you all have to dress for dinner . . ." Everyone bows & smiles — The General kisses my hand, because he thinks I am "Madame."

July 8th — Late in the P.M. I took the dogs for another walk — We sat for a time in the garden off the East Wing — It is restful there — a little concrete pool, now empty, is in the middle of the lawn, a carved stone bench at each end . . . Fala stretched out on the grass, his legs straight out behind him. Button wandered — stopping for a short rest once in a while. Both red tongues hanging out. I sat on a stone bench & looked around. This is a new view of the W.H. . . . It comes over me so often, that there is so much of beauty to enjoy in this lovely W.H. and everyone is too busy to enjoy it. Right after this, I was walking back toward the pen & stopped to speak to a guard — "Miss Suckley, you have brought life to this place"! He then told me that for days on end, not a soul goes down the lawn or under the trees, except the gardeners and the changing guards.

. . . The 2 Hopkinses, Ruth & I were with F.D.R. for dinner — Louise led the conversation with the subject of the breeding of dogs, and the birth of illegitimate children at the hospital where she works. This was followed by the question of how much clothing one wears when taking a sun-bath on the roof, where one may be beautifully seen from some club or other nearby — This paragraph is catty, but it is part of "History" that Louise Hopkins lives in the W.H. She is pretty, and I think has all good intentions, but she's "not very bright" as the P. put it one day, and her conversation is never illuminating, at least what I have heard of it. She *does* make Harry & Diana, happy, however . . . and that is her principal job.

After dinner I went out & got my Button. She lay quietly asleep near the fireplace while the P. & I worked. The P. was tired — the day had been a heavy one, and his sinus bothered him . . . After about an hour of work, I suggested he go to bed — He wouldn't do that, so I refused to work any more, got out Kipling's "Plain Tales from the Hills," & he read 2 or 3 little stories out loud, yawning constantly, & at around 10.45 decided to go to bed . . .

᳀ *July 9th.* . . . 10.12 P.M. . . . The P. is having a state dinner (stag) for Gen. Giraud . . . [He] told me the dinner would last until around a quarter to eleven, so I was not worrying about being in the hall when he should come up, possibly with General Giraud. Just two minutes ago, half way down a side seam on my new nightgown, the elevator door suddenly opened — I heard the P.'s voice — I grabbed my diary, my pen, my workbox, & my nightgown — started to flee!

The P. stopped me, laughing, half way down the hall already, & followed by the General. My thimble flew to the right, my spool to the left. The General laughed & we shook hands — the P. spoke over his shoulder as he was wheeled into his study: "The General & I are going to have a heart to heart talk — We have landed in Sicily! The word has just come!" . . .

᳀ *Saturday, July 10th, 11 p.m. en route to Shangri-La.* Mr. & Mrs. James [F.] Byrnes [Byrnes, a former congressman, senator, and Supreme Court justice, was the director of the Office of War Mobilization and one of FDR's closest counselors], the dogs, the P. & I all got into the car . . . The Byrneses are real people, and *so* nice. Every moment of the trip was agreeable and restful and amusing for the P. One thinks of everything in connection with him, and of people also, whether they will be a help or a hindrance to him. Miss Tully & Harry Hopkins came in another car — Louise came out later, after returning from her hospital work. [She was a volunteer nurse's aide at Columbia Hospital.]

. . . After dinner we went to the Mess Hall for a movie . . . We all sat on the front row, and Button watched most of the movie & got very much excited when men were charging each other & shooting each other on the screen & expressed herself, as usual. The P., on my right, thought it very funny. Louise, on my left, whispered that I really *ought* to control Button & discipline her before it is too late!!

We sat around after coming back from the movie, to get news about the *invasion of Sicily* — During dinner, we had tried also, but static is very bad and reception not good up on this hill, even when the weather is clear — Louise was bored and impatient — and showed it. The Byrneses are delightful — Just as nice as they can be.

❧ *Tuesday, July 13th 2 p.m.* [The White House] . . . The P. is awaiting a word from Stalin as to when they can meet — I hate to have the P. take the risk, but he feels it is essential for the future — If it occurs now, it will be in Alaska; if it occurs late in the Fall, it will be North Africa, or Stalin may not feel able to leave Russia now — I hope so, as the risk of the trip is very great —

❧ *July 14th Wednesday.* . . . The news from Sicily is pretty good. Thank Heaven.

July 15 — Thursday — Still very hot and sultry, unless you can find a breeze. When I saw the P. around 11, for a few minutes, he spoke of a "disagreeable day" before him, for he has to, somehow, settle the quarrel between [Henry A.] Wallace [then vice president of the United States and director of the Board of Economic Warfare] & Jesse Jones [secretary of Commerce and director of the Reconstruction Finance Corporation] — He said he was going to strip them of their controversial powers & give those powers to Leo T. Crowley. [Wallace and Jones were quarreling over authority. Each believed the other's agency undercut his own. FDR resolved things with characteristic indirection, appointing Crowley to head the altogether new Office of Economic Warfare, which rendered Wallace's agency virtually powerless.]

Another problem he has is [Secretary of State] Cordell Hull's feelings! Mr. Hull is somehow jealous of Sumner Welles, who is a very useful man. Every time Mr. Welles has a talk with the P., Mr. Hull imagines they talk about all sorts of things besides the subject Mr. Hull knows about.

. . . Button & I went to the swimming pool — My bathing suit had vanished, but was recovered on the 3rd floor, "being pressed," the P. said — The P. came from his office about a quarter before six, Fala quite happy again. Button collapsed on the floor of the shower in the ladies dressing room, Fala on that of the P.'s. It was so cunning to see them emerging, when we called them from the pool, one from each door, leisurely & tails waving with their bodies rather than wagging!

The swimming is good for [the P.]; gives him a little exercise, stretching the body & leg muscles — It's an awful pity he has not someone of his family here with him. Someone with whom to "do nothing" . . .

⌐ *July 19th Mon.* [Hyde Park] . . . Later in the P.M. the P. came to the library & worked 'til about 4.45. He has to return tomorrow P.M. to make an answer to the Pope re the bombing of Rome. He looked preoccupied & a little worried. [Allied bombs had flattened the railroad marshaling yards of the city, killing fourteen hundred and bringing a protest from Pius XII.]

He also has on his mind his possible meeting with Stalin in Alaska — Stalin has set no date & has not committed himself. The P. said W.S.C. wanted to go to the meeting, but F.D.R. won't let him. He wants to talk, man to man, with Stalin, & try to establish a constructive relationship. He says that the meeting may result in a complete stalemate, or that Stalin may refuse to work along with the United Nations, or, as he hopes, that Stalin will be willing to work *with* the U.N. How much F.D.R. has on his shoulders! It is always more & more, with the passing months, instead of less & less, as he deserves as he gets older . . .

[On July 25, Mussolini resigned and was placed under arrest, leaving King Victor Emmanuel as supreme commander of the Italian forces and Marshal Pietro Badoglio as premier. Three days later, FDR told the nation "the first crack in the Axis has come." He also called Daisy.]

⌐ *July 28th Wednesday.* [Rhinebeck] The P. called me up from Wash. in the midst of the complications and excitements of the Italian situation. Present plans will bring him here, for the day, Saturday morning. If he can spare the time he will leave that night for a fishing trip in Lake Huron . . . at a place without a name, on a siding which used to serve a lumber camp . . .

Otherwise, he will simply stay here until Sunday night & return to Wash. The Stalin meeting is "on," some time after Aug. 10th. I just hate to have him take these trips by air — It is much too dangerous — But he feels he has to, so he has to — His feelings are mixed about them, he told me — He doesn't *want* to go, but he has to put every possible effort into going because he thinks it will help in planning the future of the world — So — all we can do is to wish him Godspeed and pray that all will go well . . .

∽ *Aug. 2nd.* The "Praying Girl" was moved this A.M. from the porch at the big house to the spot [north] of the Library, where it will eventually be hidden by growing spruces! 14 people collected to see it placed: the entire Library staff, including me & all the work-men on the place; about 6 of them actually did the moving & shifting into place. The comments were very amusing, from one suggestion that it would sink of its own weight if *not* put on a pedestal, to all sorts of suggestions as to methods of hiding her! The P.'s last words were that we should put her out of *his* sight, before he returns!

∽ *Aug. 3rd.* Yesterday, Bert Andrews of the *Herald Tribune,* called me up from Washington . . . Mrs. [Ogden] Reid told him that Drew Pearson had spoken about Button & Fala on the radio and had written about Fala's possible progeny. Mr. Andrews was to go to the W.H. to verify the story and write it up — Result: Article headed by picture of Fala, on first page of second section of *Tribune!* My first experience with the press! After this I shall either be "out" or "off the record." But the article was amusingly written —

∽ *Aug. 9th Monday* — The P. has just returned from his fresh-water fishing trip — On the telephone, he said it was a real success — the place [on the north shore of Lake Huron], much like the Maine Coast — rocky, wooded, 100s of islands, cool on the whole, very nice — He says he'll take me there, *perhaps,* next year!

They fished every afternoon, sometimes until 8.30 in the evening.

He will arrive here on Thursday morning, also Mr. & Mrs. Churchill & their daughter Mary, from "somewhere" else . . .

∽ *Aug. 14th.* Mr. Churchill & Mary came last evening. The P. asked me to lunch with them at Mrs. R.'s cottage, today, and "to take care of Mary Churchill" who is a Lt. in [the Auxiliary Territorial Service] and "they say she is a nice little thing." The P. told me to have the Churchill pictures hung together in the central section: F.D.R. & W.S.C. painting in the middle with the Atlantic Charter etc., the drawing of W.S.C. by his teacher on the left panel, the painting [by] W.S.C. of Marrakesh on the r. panel. [Churchill had presented Roosevelt with a painting of a sunset view they'd enjoyed together after the Casablanca conference.]

Later. Malvina Thompson called me up & asked me for lunch — so I am doubly asked — it is always more "comfortable" to have an invitation from Mrs. R. to *her* cottage, rather than have the P. just appear with me (as he used to do when Mrs. James R. was alive).

Still later. Another "memorable" day — But how casually I take it! The P. came to the door of his room, driving his own car, W.S.C. on the seat next to him. In the back were Commander Thomson and Mr. [John] Martin — Fala had appeared & I held on to him, so he & I got in the back, and off we went through the woods, to the Val-Kill swimming pool — Mr. & Mrs. Gray [David Gray, a one-time play-wright, was now minister to Ireland and was married to Maude Livingston Hall, the youngest of Eleanor Roosevelt's maternal aunts] and some girls were already in the water —

Mrs. R. was just coming out. Mr. Churchill & the P. & I sat on green iron chairs, to watch. The others went off to get into their bathing suits. One girl turned out to be Mary Churchill, very pretty, somewhat plump, a beautiful swimmer and an attractive, intelligent, straight-forward personality.

Another child was [Eleanor's brother] Hall Roosevelt's youngest daughter [Eleanor], with two little girl friends. She has a definite Theodore Roosevelt look. The P. & the P.M. talked rather casually, and after perhaps a half hour we all got into the car again and drove around to the picnic ground back of the cottage. Mrs. R. had a couple of card tables set up; a broiler on wheels, for the hot dogs, and all supplies laid out for a large picnic lunch. She put me at a table with the P., the P.M., and Mrs. Gray.

Harry Hopkins looked sick — white, blue around the eyes, with red spots on his cheek bones — Adm. Brown was there, too. It was all nice, and informal — largely "self-service," though I did seem to get waited on by various people. First a fish chowder, the Fairhaven, old [Delano] family receipt; then hot dogs & corn pudding, followed by tomato salad and raw fruit for dessert —

Fala rushed down to the edge of the pond & spent the whole time we were there after a muskrat, half in & half out of the water! He *did* get a pat & a piece of sausage from Mr. Churchill first! Mrs. R. tended the hot dogs & the children handed them around.

Mr. C. ate 1 & ½ and had a special little ice-pail for his scotch. He is a strange looking little man. Fat & round, his clothes bunched up on him. Practically no hair on his head, he wore a huge 10-gallon hat. He talks as though he had terrible adenoids — sometimes says very little, then talks quite a lot — His humorous twinkle is infectious. Mary & he are evidently very close; now & then they would joke together . . .

~ *Aug. 15th.* . . . About 11.30, the P. came to the L. with the P.M., Com. Thomson & Mr. Martin, and Mary . . . Mrs. R. came, & told Mary & me to go with her in her car, as the P. couldn't take all of us — I flew to my desk for my purse, Mary flew to the house for hers — I jumped into Mrs. R.'s car & we drove around the back way to the house. There, I asked to sit in front so my hair wouldn't blow to pieces . . .

Mrs. R. took us through the woods — She drives *very* carefully, toots the horn on curves, smiles at all policemen & guards as we go past them — Miss T. & I got out at the pool — Mrs. R. & Mary drove on around to her cottage. Roly was there in a white bathing suit of Mrs. R., her skin so brown from L.I. that she could easily pass for a quadroon! Miss [Nancy] Cook, in a blue bathing suit, was lying on a chaise-longue. She is getting old, looks vaguely unhappy. Not so, Miss [Marion] Dickerman, who looks contented & well. They both thought I was Katherine Grant [the daughter of the President's uncle Frederic Delano]!

[Nancy Cook and Marion Dickerman had been close friends of Eleanor Roosevelt and were still co-owners with her of Val-Kill. They considered themselves close to the President, as well. That they were still unclear as to just who Daisy was is evidence of how secretive FDR could be and of how wide was the gulf between the intimate worlds of the two Roosevelts.]

. . . Mrs. R. came & made a dive & a splash or two. The P.M. decided to go in, too. In a pair of shorts, he looked exactly like a kewpie. He made a good dive in, soon came out, wrapped a large wool blanket around himself & sat down to talk to F.D.R.

. . . I took away the impression that Churchill *adores* the P., loves him, as a man, looks up to him, defers to him, leans on him. He is older than the P., but the P. is the bigger person, and Churchill recognizes it. I saw in Churchill, too, an amount of real greatness I did not suspect before. Speaking of South Africa, Ch. said General [and Prime Minister Jan] Smuts is one of the really *great* men of the world — "a prophet — a seer" — his very words — He wants to get him to London, for his "mind on post war Europe" . . .

The P. was relaxed and seemingly cheerful in the midst of the deepest problems. Mrs. R. is taking a flying trip of 6 weeks to the South Pacific. The P. wants me to go to Wash. & help take care of Mrs. Churchill when the three come down about the 26th . . .

[Roosevelt and Churchill traveled to Canada for what came to be known as the Quebec Conference, at which the two leaders again confirmed their intention to mount a cross-Channel invasion the following spring, and agreed as well to exclude the Soviets from their joint atomic research.]

☞ *Aug. 26th.* The P. came from Ottawa, looking well, but tired. He said he would try to get rested before Churchill comes to Wash. next Wednesday — Mary C. is coming also, and will fly to Ft. Oglethorpe, to see the WAACs. I am to return to Wash. with the P. on Sunday night & work all next week & return here with him the following Thursday or Friday — My only objection is that I hate to leave Button behind, and I don't want to take her to the W.H. at this time. It would complicate matters with Fala.

The Quebec Conference was a success but Russia is a worry — the P. said a message had come from Stalin which was "rude — stupidly rude." [Stalin, in cabling his vehement objection to waiting another eleven months for Overlord, accused his allies of having failed to consult him. The Soviet Union, he said, "does not find it possible to associate itself with such a decision." Churchill proposed an immediate meeting of the Big Three; FDR suggested that he and Stalin meet alone, then denied to Churchill that he'd done so. Stalin again said he could not leave the Soviet Union, still fighting for its life against the Nazis.]

Churchill wanted to send back an answer — even ruder! F.D.R. persuaded him to wait until he comes to Wash. next week — The P. believes he can do more by consistent politeness, but they fear Stalin may be building up a case — The Allies not opening a second front, etc. — and make a separate peace with Germany — It is what I have feared right along, from Stalin's "excuses" for not meeting F.D.R. etc. It is the first time the P. has expressed such a fear, to me; probably as a matter of policy . . .

☞ *Saturday, August 28th.* . . . The P. came to the Library about 4 — chose 4 chairs & 4 tables for his cottage. We took them up there & the S.S. moved them, & beds & mattresses to the 2nd floor bedrooms just made by Mr. Bie. [Top Cottage had originally had just two bedrooms, both on the ground floor. In 1943 more small bedrooms were added upstairs, evidently for children and grandchildren who wished to come and stay there.]

— The P. was very cheerful & seemed relaxed. He also [ordered] trimmed the bushes along the walk to the cottage because, the day before, they showered him with rain drops. By this time he decided we would have a picnic supper, sent for some eggs & bread & butter — He toasted the bread on the electric toaster, sitting by the fire on the sofa . . .

The P. talked about a good many phases of the present situation in the world . . . [H]e had great hopes that Anthony Eden would be a progressive and helpful in the post-war world, [but] after seeing A.E. in Canada, he feels he is no more progressive than W.S.C. and that he will be "difficult to get on with." It is a disappointment . . .

◦ *Monday Aug. 30th.* [The White House] . . . Old Lucas has gone [from the President's train] — he was caught pocketing tips left with him for other men. I'm sorry for the poor old thing, but, for years, he has been getting old & deaf, and inefficient, and certainly the P.'s train car should have the best porter available. The new porter, Fred, seems excellent, and *very* nice & cheerful. *He* has now reached the highest point in his career! . . .

Ruth, Elliott, the P. & I had dinner in the P.'s study — the nicest evening. The more I see of the "children" the better I like them. It is wonderful how they turn to "Pa" with all their problems. He never treats them like "children" and they all love him. Elliott seems to be very close to "Pa," & "Pa" to him. Elliott & Ruth are completely "one" . . .

◦ *Tuesday, Aug. 31st.* Breakfast in bed, the newspaper, at work in the North Hall at 10. Saw the P. for a minute before he went to his office . . . moved from the yellow room to Miss LeHand's little suite on the third floor —

It is very nice & comfortable, but I miss not seeing trees, and from the bed I can't even see a window! I keep a fan going all day, on the floor of the living room. It keeps a steady draft through the bedroom, into the bathroom, & up through a ventilator in the bathroom ceiling. The walls are covered with photos of the P., Mrs. R., and people around the P. Many books, first editions, & books by the P. on the shelves — I wish I had time to read them!

. . . Mr. [Churchill] didn't feel well; he had a cold. He is difficult in conversation when he doesn't want to talk, perfectly delightful and very witty when he wants to be. He makes no effort just to "talk" with the person next to him, but is very responsive *if* interested! Mrs.

C. & Mary are delightful & make anyone feel comfortable — Better manners!

. . . The P. looked rather tired, with dark rings under his eyes . . . Louise Hopkins looked pale & thin. She told me afterward, that Harry is really very ill. The Dr. prescribes 3 months of complete rest — Harry argues: "All those boys at the front are fighting & getting hurt & dying. I have a job to do here, & I'm going to do it." A new light for me in which to see H.H. — and, what is more, through the lips of Louise. [Hopkins was indeed very ill, unable to assimilate food. He had been hospitalized for exhaustion after the Quebec Conference and had dragged himself out of bed to be with FDR for these talks with Churchill.]

After dinner, we all trailed the P. to the basement hall in the east annex. A regular movie outfit had been set up. We saw a dumb [comedy] called "He Dood it," about a "pants presser" . . . The P.M. was wandering during most of it & came back for the "spirited ending"! He has brought two more of his books for the P. in the pink binding. These complete the set of his writings, in 1st editions which he has had specially done. The movie was over at 11.50 & the P. dismissed us very easily, by saying he had to go over dispatches with the P.M. . . .

☞ *Thursday, Sept. 2nd.* . . . I find myself falling into the role of temporary manager for Mrs. Churchill. After several telephone calls between our rooms, including one with the P. in which he "orders" me to his study at 10.30 to plan for Mrs. C., he finally comes out of his room at 11. I hand him present plans: Today: Mrs. C & Mary & Ruth & I in a car to Lincoln & Jefferson memorials . . .

At the Lincoln we climbed the steps — The C.s felt about it as everyone does — It is impressive, and "very moving," as Mary C. said . . .

All were *less* impressed with the Jefferson. Mrs. C. & I were bothered with the dirty water which two dirty mops were flopping around the floor. We decided a hose would be much better, and that we don't care for the statue — It lacks personality . . .

At dinner: The P., Mrs. C., Archbishop [Francis] Spellman [of New York], Mr. Martin, GGT, Averell Harriman, Mr. Arthur Bowes-Lyon, brother of the Queen, the P.M. & I. I sat opposite the P. with the P.M. on my right & Mr. B-L on my left. The latter is pale. He asked whether "people like us, who have been underfed & nervous," will become normal again after the war. As the P. puts it, almost everyone

is "shell-shocked," in one way or another. You notice it in their manners — they are "distrait," they can not "throw it off" & be social
and charming & amusing in the old sense. This is one noticeable way
in which the P. is so outstanding — He is completely normal mentally
& spiritually, although he has, in a way, more responsibility than
anyone —

Speaking of Mr. Hull the other day, he said Mr. H. was so upset
over being criticized in the papers during the past year; also the differences over Sumner Welles, etc. Finally, the P. just reminded him that
for the past 10 yrs. the P. himself has been attacked constantly & has
been able to survive it & still smile, whereas Mr. Hull received *no*
word of criticism for the first nine yrs. & can't stand it! This kind of
thing is more wearing on F.D.R. than the *real big* problems of the war
& the future peace — The "little foxes" that gnaw at the roots of the
vine —

After dinner, we went down to a movie called "Mr. Lucky" —
another [comedy]. Amusing in spots — dull mostly — I think the hour
or two of such a performance allows the P. to think, & to *not* have to
talk to his guests . . . It ended about 11.30 & we all scattered — P. &
the P.M. into the map room. Great things beginning to happen in the
Mediterranean.

⌁ *Sept. 3rd . . . a.m.* The British have started the invasion of Italy —
It so happens that I was with the P. at Shangri-La when the invasion
of N. Africa took place — Then I was here when the Sicilian campaign
started, & I am here now, for this new move. The first was of course
the most dramatic, because the least expected . . .

Mrs. Churchill came out of her room about noon & asked to be
taken around the grounds — She is so nice — We seem to get on —
As usual with anyone who thinks about it at all, she asked where I
live, what I am doing etc. I give all details at once, about my house,
my work at the Library & down here — so they don't have to wonder
any more. The Sec., Miss Hamlin, kept coming to me for one thing or
another: Dr. McIntire's name, a piece of sealing wax for the P.M., what
arrangements are made for Williamsburg tomorrow, etc., etc. Even
Mr. Searles asked a question or two.

The P. said Ruth & I were to lunch with him & the P.M. at 1 —
It was a delightful quiet party . . . The P.M. was *very* amusing, his pink
face twinkling at his own stories of how he got away with supplies of
whiskey during a month trip among the Redwoods, in Prohibition days!

5.30 p.m. . . . . We drove [with the Churchills] to Mt. Vernon in the rain . . . Ruth went in with Mrs. C. & Mary — I stayed in the car with the P. It didn't seem polite to leave him waiting, alone, and, of course I love to be with him, anyway! There are few enough opportunities. Some 20 people were coming up to see the house; they were kept waiting at the door until the Churchill visit was over. They had their own show, with the P. sitting there! I had to go & hurry up the party, as the P. had to get back — He was amusing all the way back, telling funny stories —

When we reached the W.H., poor Mr. Searles was having a fit — He hasn't been having things too easy during this visit, for he hasn't been told when & what is happening & has a hard time finding out! Ruth & I usually "don't know"! I think the P. has been so rushed with the P.M. on top of all his routine business, that he sometimes forgets to give orders — Today, for instance, he evidently thought everything was arranged for Mrs. C. & Mary to visit Williamsburg tomorrow — Mr. Searles knew nothing about it — and a plane & two escorts have to be produced etc., etc! [Mr. Searles then] asked if *I* had invited Justice & Mrs. Byrnes for dinner tonight!

Mrs. R. should be here to attend to all this sort of thing — The P. shouldn't have to — and it *has* to be done . . .

✑ *Sept. 4th* Saturday. . . . . 2.30 P.M. Ruth & I had lunch with the P. in his study — He said he was so sleepy his brain wouldn't work, and he would take a nap at 3, after working with GGT. Just at this moment, in breezed the P.M., full of all sorts of things, on his way to the Press Club lunch — He will be back at 3.30 to work on so-&-so with the P.! So vanishes the nap!

✑ *Sunday the 5th.* . . . . At lunch . . . as Ruth was out, I sat opposite the P. with the P.M. on my right. Mrs. [Ogden] Reid on his right, never stopped talking one minute, except to get the answers to her questions. She was trying to get him to promise to speak at the [*Herald Tribune* Literary] Forum in Oct. As far as I could tell he didn't commit himself.

After lunch the P. led us into the Red Room, gathered the two attorneys-general for 15 or 20 minutes. Mrs. Reid, having monopolized the P.M. through lunch, asked if she could speak to him for 5 minutes — Out on the terrace they went, & stayed until the [other guests] had left & the P. sent Mrs. C. out to rescue the P.M.! After everyone had shaken hands I introduced myself as the owner of Fala's fiancée! And reminded her that Arthur used to write financial articles for the Paris *Herald* — She *said* she remembered, but I don't believe she did! The P. said "she's the most persistent woman" —

∾ *September 6, Monday.* [En route to Rhinebeck] . . . If you want to see love & tragedy, go to the Grand Central Station. In the [newsreel theater] were two young couples — The boys' arms protectively around the girls' shoulders, the girls trying to hide their tears in the dark, but wiping their eyes & once in a while letting out a muffled sob.

Up on the Vanderbilt Ave. ramp, an attractive, tall, distinguished girl, with dark eyes, stood with her bags, waiting for someone. He was a navy officer — For a few minutes they stayed, hands locked, talking, with serious faces — Then they kissed & she started down the stairs, a red cap carrying her bags — He started toward the street, turned, came back, leaned on the parapet. The girl was walking across the station, wiping her eyes — head very erect — Three times, she turned & looked — he waved, leaning over the parapet — she disappeared through the gate & he turned & went out. I was almost in tears myself! . . .

I'm dying of heat, now entering the Highlands — everything sticky & hot. Another thrilling week is over, & I try to coordinate my impressions — At the informal "family" meals, both the P. & the P.M. were "themselves," and intensely interesting — the P. full of charm, always tactful, even when he has to be "painfully" truthful & perhaps harsh. He is harsh, but with a smile which tells you you are wrong, but there is no ill feeling toward you because of the wrong — It's more that you are mistaken — in all probability because you don't know the facts. I've never known a person who so consistently tries not to hurt people . . .

The P.M. on the contrary snaps out his disapproval. They say he fights with everyone, jumps all over them. One person alone he doesn't jump on, & that is the P.! The P. laughs about it: he says that if the P.M. ever *did* jump on him, he would just laugh at him! As I have said before, the P.M. *loves* F.D.R. Mrs. C. told me that, too, out of a clear sky —

The P.M. recognizes in the P. a man with a greater soul & a broader outlook than his own — It is very evident to a person who has had such wonderful opportunities to see them as I have. I consider W.S.C. a "great man," also, but he has not yet achieved the spiritual freedom of F.D.R. . . . They get along beautifully, and understand each other. The P. is all for the Democratic ideal because he loves it &

believes in it. The P.M. is working for it because he thinks it is inevitable . . .

˷ *Monday, Sept. 13th.* [Hyde Park] Another interesting week-end — At the library, we were hectic over the Nat. Archives exhibit, to get it ready for the P. to take down on his train Sunday night.

The P. came on *Friday* morning, in the midst of it all — I got him a seat cushion off one of the big blue chairs & ensconced him on the floor in front of a cupboard — He worked there for and hour & a half while I flew around getting things done, my desk piled high, two "trucks" & a table-full of things waiting to be taken care of —

I went to the house for lunch with him. Sam Rosenman was there, Mrs. [Anna] Rosenberg [a specialist in labor and personnel relations, regional director of the War Manpower Commission, and unofficial liaison with labor leaders], D. Brady & a typist. After lunch the P. told the others to go ahead with *their* work on his speech & he came back to the Library for a while.

Mrs. R. is very bright, nice looking, and seems very nice, but she has a certain over-anxiousness to talk & "be seen" which is probably from her being Jewish. One can hardly blame them for being self-conscious, with all the talk & feeling about them and against them. The P. says Mrs. Rosenberg helps him with the *labor* parts of his speeches & is *very* good.

On *Saturday* there was fresh excitement, for the Empress Zita with her two daughters, Charlotte & Elizabeth, came from New Hampshire by car for lunch. They are delightful people — very aristocratic. I find I *do* like well-bred people; they don't make you uncomfortable!

[L]ater, the P. came over for an hour of sorting. He said, "en passant," that he had had a good frank talk with the Empress, who had thanked him for it. He told her that it might reasonably happen that Otto would be called to the *Hungarian* Throne, with Adm. [Nicholas] Horthy quite naturally stepping out of the Regency: but that in the case of Austria, it is quite different & they will probably want a plebiscite. The P. says (*not* to the Empress) that Otto unfortunately "has no sense" and has already gotten in wrong by trying to organize an Austrian army in this country —

Sunday had another thrill in store for me, a dinner "en famille" with the Churchill party . . . Mrs. C. came in . . . looking very well, with her attractive smile, her arm in a sling with a cracked bone from tripping & falling. She had on a figured blue silk dress & her grey wool coat over her shoulders —

Mary appeared looking very blooming & a little plump — she has a lovely smile. I gave her the *True Story of Fala* signed by the author, and by the P. on the frontispiece picture of himself & Fala. She has had a wonderful time on this trip.

John Martin, Com. Thomson, . . . Brendan Bracken, all collected, and Mrs. J. R. Roosevelt. Finally the P. & the P.M. We had cocktails & sherry by the fireplace. A fire felt good as there was a first very definite chill of autumn. After a while, we followed the P. in to dinner — a delightful, cheerful dinner. The P.M. remarked on how well the P. looked — we all agreed that it was extraordinary — It seems as though the trials & difficulties of the office of President, in these days, act as a stimulant to the P. They may take the place of the exercise which he can't have like other people.

. . . I liked [Major] General [Sir Hastings] Ismay [secretary of the Imperial Defense Council]. He & John Martin & Mrs. C. & Mary all have normal manners — With all her charm of manner, Mrs. C. is very English & reserved — Mary shows more of her American blood in a more "easy" manner — The others haven't *bad* manners, they just *haven't any!* Lord Moran [the Prime Minister's physician] belongs with the mannered group — It is amazing, on thinking it over, that not one of that entire group of people has the really charming good manners of the old school, like the P. & Mrs. James R. who was past master of the art of making others happy!

Mrs. F.D.R. does it too, "from the heart," if she happens to notice you . . .

We sat at the table until about 10 P.M., then the P. led us to the Library for another 15 minutes. He is host & hostess & housekeeper all in one — it is really amazing with what ease — At 10.20 the whole party started to move — Sitting on his wheelchair, with all the Churchill party standing around, he sent for Jennings, and, in two minutes, arranged for the visit, next week-end, of John [Roosevelt] & Anne [Clark Roosevelt] with two children & a nurse, and 6 Norwegians with a maid.

Then, as I was starting to say goodbye all around, he told me to "come along" with them & see the C.s off! He drove his little car, Mrs. C. by him in the front, the P.M. & Mary & I (squashed between them) in the back — It was a beautiful moonlit night. We drove down through the woods to the railroad siding, where the Churchill special stood waiting. It was a thing to see & remember.

The P.M. at the last moment leaned into the P.'s car — "God Bless You," he said. I heard the P. saying, "I'll be over with you, next spring . . ." All got on board. Mary stood on the platform, waving a last goodbye — I stood to one side, so that the P. could be seen.

"Goodbye, Mr. President," called Mary.

And then, to my surprise, "Goodbye, Miss Suckley, and thank you so much."

Off the train went, heading north around the rocky headland —

[The White House]

◦ *Tuesday, Sept. 14th.* . . . [Today the President] is getting relaxed after the P.M.'s visit, which means late hours, etc., & was quiet & getting sleepier & sleepier as we ate! After we finished I suggested he lie on the sofa & sleep for a half hour, but he wouldn't do that — He said if he did, he would feel exhausted for the rest of the day. He did close his eyes for a few minutes, after yawning several times, & was fast asleep, sitting in his chair, before he knew what was happening to him. I didn't move for fear of waking him & I was prepared to put my finger on my lips if anyone should appear — No one did, however.

From my chair at the left end of the desk, I could see the formal garden. A spray was throwing tiny sparkles on the roses and green grass — little white clouds floated gently over the White House —

Suddenly, the P. opened his eyes & sat up straight in his chair, with a laugh! "I feel much better," he said. He slept almost ten minutes, though he thought it was only one! It helped, however, & he started to work again, at once, with D.B. [Dorothy Brady], on his basket. It was then 2.30. I returned to my North Hall work.

. . . Louise passed the hall, about 7 P.M. Harry Hopkins is really very ill, but he has returned from the hospital. He has only half a stomach & should never touch liquor, but he hasn't the sense to resist it. Besides that, he has been kept alive by having regular blood transfusions for the past months — perhaps a year or two — and it may be that the body cannot indefinitely absorb outside blood —

If anything happens to him, it will be a definite loss to the P. In the first place, they are real friends, & the P. is very fond of him. In the second place, he is very useful to the P. — The other day, the P. was telling someone that when a group of men are arguing and haggling over the details of some problem, and perhaps talking at cross purposes, Harry will be sitting quietly saying nothing, taking it all in, and then, in one sentence, he will put his finger on the point of the argument, and clarify the whole thing —

Ruth & Elliott, the P. & I, had dinner in the P.'s study — Elliott was telling the P. about his difficulties in persuading Gen. [Hap] Arnold about this new reconnaissance plane which he wants to have made by a man called [Howard] Hughes — It goes faster than any other, a necessity for reconnaissance, as they are unarmed & rely on speed alone — Elliott says he has accomplished what he came for, & has the approval of Gen. Arnold, etc. but Gen. A. has given him no help whatsoever & has rather grudgingly allowed the thing to go through. Elliott is an example of a great many men in his position. He has been on "duty" for 3 years, is sick of it all, longs to get home and has only one present thought: to get the war over — Anything which retards that goal is distracting — I could feel how he felt —

"Little" Ruth was feeling it in a very personal way, and suddenly turned to me, smiling, with tears in her eyes. "He's a nice boy, isn't he, Margaret — I'm so happy to have him here —" I almost cried myself — so much was being said and felt, which was not put into words — [In fact, Ruth and Elliott were already discussing divorce.]

Another thing Elliott said, which is important, is that a story is going the rounds that the reason this Hughes plane [the D-2] is to be made is only because of pressure by the President, because his son, Elliott, is trying to get it done — This is completely untrue — Elliott was ordered home from North Africa to "sell" the plane to Gen. Arnold — [He did sell it; Arnold ordered $43 million worth of D-2s from Howard Hughes.]

᪣ *Wednesday September 15th.* . . . At 7 [P.M.] the P. came out of his room, as usual preceded by Fala, who rushes around in great excitement at the prospect of his supper — The P. was very tired & "keyed up." He said he had had a dreadful day and had hoped for a quiet evening. Instead, Commander & Mrs. Walker (he commands F. Jr's boat) came for cocktails at 7.15 and remained until 8, when the P. said, "Well, I shall have to be getting along."

Elliott & Ruth, Harry & Louise were at dinner. We ate in the West Hall. Elliott & Ruth both expressed themselves on White House food, called it a National Scandal — tasteless, without variety — no red meat — etc., etc! To me — it is luxurious & delicious and full of variety, compared to our simple cooking at home! Mrs. Nesbitt, the housekeeper, is the "goat," as usual. It is true that she hasn't the background or experience or initiative to run a "White House," but Mrs. R. insists on keeping her — In relation to the P., *my* criticism of the food he has is that it is much too rich for his good.

We finished dinner at 9.15 — The Elliotts & Hopkinses said goodnight — The P. went to his corner of the sofa in the study, to go through a box or two with me. As soon as the door was closed he relaxed completely, yawned & yawned. He said it was the greatest possible rest to be able to just be as he felt & not have to talk & be the host. It's a great compliment to me, but I don't see why he can't do the same thing with the Hopkinses & Elliott & Ruth. It has apparently become a habit *not* to relax, but to force himself to keep up the outward appearance of energy & force — It must be very exhausting!

He rang for Arthur about 10.30 & went off to his room, smiling through satisfactory yawns!

~ *Thursday, Sept. 16th.* The battle of Salerno is still raging, but the reports sound a little more encouraging for the Allies.

~ *Tuesday, Sept. 21st.* [Hyde Park] . . . The 7 Norwegians came on Saturday evening. The Cr. Princess quite exhausted, after the illness & death of her children's nurse . . .

Today, [she], Mme. Ostgaard & Mr. Weddell were sent in the P.'s car to the nurse's funeral on L.I. The P. is in charge of the children. At lunch today, Harald sat on my left. He picks at his food, & evidently eats almost nothing, for he took only a portion of hamburger, a piece of Melba toast with butter, & a glass of milk — No vegetables & no dessert, though the latter was a delicious plate with fresh peaches & whipped cream. Very few people can get whipped cream these days, unless they have cows. Eating with the P. is always a luxury for that reason: Cream, butter, eggs, vegetables, chicken, all off the place!

Ragnhild & Astrid are nice well behaved little girls. Ragnhild, the elder, is a head shorter than Astrid. They seem strong & healthy, but the P. says they are "teary" & nervous. I suppose the result of their parents being 1st cousins. Harald has his mother's features & her charm. There is something pathetic about him — One wonders what his future will be . . .

~ *Wednesday, Sept 22nd.* . . . About 3.30 P.M. the P. came over with the Grand Duchess of Luxembourg, René, prince de Bourbon, Margarethe [and the] Cr. Princess of Norway — He sent for me & introduced me as "My cousin, Miss Suckley," as he always does. The Grand Duchess is tall & slender & aristocratic, essentially well-bred, with lovely manners. I think she is pretty, with quite a lot of color. Margarethe is handsome & dark-haired, with a deep voice. René is plain, with black hair & mustache, not much of a personality;

but all have the friendliest manners. I *do* like good breeding & polite manners!

. . . The P. seemed rather quiet and a little pre-occupied — perhaps tired. He is having trouble with Cordell Hull & Sumner Welles who hate each other & want "to kill each other," to put it mildly! Why can't they forget their personal animosities & try to help the world, by helping the P.? . . . [On September 26, FDR would finally announce his acceptance of Welles's resignation, written more than a month earlier.]

The Crown Princess has become so much easier of manner & so much more approachable, since living in this country, though strangers still call her "snippy." She is very shy, I think, & so, at times, rather stiff. With the P. she seems to be entirely natural, & very sweet and solicitous of him. He is devoted to her, and gets much pleasure out of knowing her and being able to be such a help to her . . .

╰◦ *Wednesday* — *Sept 29th '43.* [The White House] . . . In N.Y. I did some necessary shopping, passed a mirror in Stern's & was horrified at the shabbiness of my hat! 5 minutes in the ground floor hat department, put a $7.50 tricorn on my head — It fits, will stay on in a wind, & *I* think is not too unbecoming! The best will come, however, when the P. sees it! He threatens to take me to the Princess de Bourbon's shop & get me a *large* hat — (which requires a hand to hold it on!). He & Mama don't like my hats —

The trip from N.Y. to Wash. on the 2.30 was hot, dirty & uncomfortable. A nice looking young marine on his way to New River N.C. sat next to me. He fell asleep, and all but drooped over onto my shoulder — I debated whether to let him sleep or whether to wake him — He had a cold, however, which roused him before he actually rested on my shoulder . . .

At the Wash. station, I looked in vain for a W.H. chauffeur; decided the P. had forgotten I was coming . . . I found a taxi & told the man "the White House," & got in. He then proceeded to get other passengers: two more young marines, & two women. One woman was half drunk & gave him some "back talk" — She was soon dropped off, then the two marines. The last passenger was a very nice-looking woman from Colorado. She said the great ambition of a western visitor to Washington is to get as close as possible to the W.H. The chauffeur asked if I thought he would be allowed to drive up to the door — I thought he would, if I knew the SS at the gate. I did, & in we drove, much to the joy of the lady from Colorado!

At the W.H. everyone was very solicitous about my arriving in a taxi. "The boy" had just telephoned that I hadn't come on that train, & received orders to wait until the next .

Mr. Searles took me up to the blue room, informing me that the Cr. Princess, the princess of Bourbon, Adm. Leahy & Major Hammond would be at dinner — I hurried to get at least clean *looking* & went in to the study, where the party were having cocktails. Fala wiggling about as usual, hopeful of a scrap of something. I find I kiss the P. now, when arriving & leaving. So many others do it that it seems strange not to, in view of the fact that I am always introduced as a cousin. We Suckleys are not much on kissing, but it is quite easy to lean over & offer a cheek to the P. & leave an airy kiss behind!

I then shook hands down the line, ignoring precedence: Hammond, Leahy, Martha, Margarethe. The two women looked very "distinguée." Martha in a pink dinner gown with a shirt waist collar & long tight sleeves, & a very closely fitted slinky skirt. Margarethe in a lovely long-sleeved black dress . . . She is a Danish princess, sister of Prince Axel, F.D.R.'s old friend. Her husband is the brother of the Empress Zita. She & Martha are doubly related. (I am using their first names purely for brevity. Not in the spirit of some people who have never even seen F.D.R. and speak of him as "Frankie"!)

Martha becomes more attractive as one sees more of her. I can see why F.D.R. likes her so much. She is gentle & sympathetic, has a sense of humor & is very responsive. He teases her all the time & she is very teasable & reacts with laughing & blushing.

At dinner, I sat opposite the P. with Adm. Leahy on my right & Major Hammond on my left. The princesses on each side of the P. It was very nice — everyone could put in a word, & the P was "himself" — No one to act up to!

After dinner, we went downstairs for a movie, something about looking for a cook. The newsreels showed the battle of Salerno — soldiers landing, airplanes swooping around, guns, explosions — Modern warfare, in a word . . .

Mrs. R. got back from her trip to the S.W. Pacific last Friday, but has left here already — I don't know where to!

It is fortunate that the P. has his mother's social talent. He manages a dinner party, seating & all, just as easily as the most experienced hostess, & with less self-consciousness than most.

The problem of Mr. Hull & Sumner Welles seems to be settled — Mr. Welles is out for good, as the Senate would not confirm him if the P. were to give him an appointment. This is because on a certain occasion, years ago, when drunk, he behaved "in a manner unbecoming a gentleman."

[William C.] Bullitt [former ambassador to the Soviet Union and to France] who wanted his position in the State Dept. dug up the story, told it to "Cissy" [Eleanor Medill] Patterson [owner and publisher of the Washington *Times-Herald*] . . .

[On September 17, 1940, aboard a special train carrying mourners back to Washington from the Alabama funeral of Speaker of the House William Bankhead, Sumner Welles, reeling from too many whiskeys, had propositioned several black porters whom he summoned to his special compartment. All of them turned him down and one lodged a formal complaint with the Southern Railway Company.

Welles was an old friend of Roosevelt's, had attended Groton, been a page at his wedding, was a married man. FDR had been instrumental in pushing his career, despite rumors about his drinking and his private sexual habits.

William Bullitt loathed Welles and may well, as Daisy suggests, have wanted his job. In any case, in 1941 he told Roosevelt of the railroad incident and was asked to forget about it. It would never happen again, Roosevelt assured him; he'd assigned a bodyguard to see to that. Bullitt, who believed Welles "a criminal" because of his homosexuality, vowed never to accept another State Department post until Welles was dismissed. When it seemed that newspapers were about to print the story, in August of 1943, FDR reluctantly asked Welles for his resignation.

Bullitt indignantly denied in writing that he had ever told Mrs. Patterson of Welles's indiscretion, but FDR refused ever to speak to him again. "He was raving after Bullitt left his office," Dorothy Brady remembered, "raving!" He was sure Saint Peter would let Welles into heaven despite his drinking, he told a visitor; but Bullitt, who had "destroyed a fellow human being, would be sent to Hell."]

The P. told me the whole story, which is unsavory. The only excuse is that Sumner Welles was drunk, & didn't know what he was doing, and was completely unconscious of any of it when sober again. It is the kind of thing to ruin his career, however. That demon Drink again — *Why* can't men ever learn? The P. never wants to speak to Bullitt again . . .

At seven, the Hopkinses & I gathered around the P. for cocktails. Louise has given up trying to reform me, and is quieter & very sweet. The conversation was led by the P. and was interesting, Harry being an intelligent person, when not indulging in dumb talk about drinking & vulgar jokes about women. I wish I could take moving-pictures of people when they are acting like civilized human beings &, in contrast, when they act like idiots under the influence of alcohol! It would be an eye-opener to them . . .

∽ *Sept. 30th Thursday.* . . . At 9.45, I called up the P. to remind him about telling the Dr. about a pain in his side. He sounded very cheerful — said the pain had moved & the Dr. had left! . . . So much for that. He will go on a diet! (But will he?!) . . .

When I reached the W.H. [this evening] the red-coated band in the front hall were playing a lively tune. I went in through the usher's office & started to look through the dining room door at the dinner just as F.D.R. came out, looking very well & handsome in a white suit. I backed into the hall by the elevator & watched from there — Immediately behind his chair walked three Arabs in long black robes over white, matching turbans on their heads — I couldn't see their faces very well as they turned in to the red room . . . I got an impression of very dark skin & black eyes — they walk in a slow dignified swing — their robes swaying with them. I wonder if all the others would have the same gait in the same costume. I doubt it; we are always in a hurry; to get nowhere! — & we walk badly.

. . . [Later] the P. told me about the dinner, the speeches, etc. It evidently went off well & Crown Prince Faisal [of Saudi Arabia] made a nice speech, in which he stressed the wisdom of all nations trying to be real friends, for the benefit of the nations as a whole, etc.

The P. gave them the same advice about their oil as he gave to the Sultan of Morocco — to use [the money it earned] to irrigate their deserts . . . He is educating them by degrees — It will be interesting to see how many will learn & will be able to benefit from what they learn.

∽ *Oct. 1st, Friday.* . . . [J]oined the P. for tea in his study — He had as guests Otto of Austria & his sister, the Archduchess Adelaide, the "professor" at Fordham University in New York. Harry & Louise were invited too.

. . . It was interesting to meet Otto. His mother & sisters I have described elsewhere — they concentrate on him as the great object of their lives — to restore him to his place on the throne. Otto is rather small, with "pretty" features — a great handicap — he should have been a girl. He has a very nice face, agreeable manners, is responsive & has humor, but he doesn't impress one as being a very *strong* man.

The P. has urged him to get into our army — his answer is that "they" — his followers — "won't let him." He lives in Wash. in an apartment which serves as a headquarters for those who hope to put him back on the throne — the P. says he does nothing but intrigue for the future — His brothers & sisters all are working at something or other. The P. thinks the 3rd brother is the best of the boys —

The P. said he had said the same thing to Peter of Yugoslavia & George of Greece. "Go into the Army; go to the front with the soldiers; if you do get killed, it's just too bad, but you will have done the right thing." They would have gained a lot in the eyes of their subjects, too, which would help them later, if they survived the war.

[Shangri-La]

〰️ *Monday, Oct. 4th.* A beautiful fall day . . . The P. had an awful nightmare last night. I woke out of a sound sleep, to hear him calling for help in blood curdling sounds! When he appeared at 10 A.M. he told us he thought a man was coming in "through the transom" & was going to kill him, & then sat down on the edge of his bed. It all happened in a minute, I suppose, & quiet settled down again on the night. Judge [Fred M.] Vinson [director of Economic Stabilization] heard it too, but recognized it for what it was — Mrs. Vinson said *he* has had the most awful ones, too, so she's quite used to them. He didn't look any the worse for it this morning & we all had a good laugh about it. I wondered why the SS didn't rush in, but he says they are quite accustomed to his nightmares!

[The White House]

〰️ *Tuesday, October 5th.* . . . At 5, Betty Hambley, "Martha" & Mme. Ostgaard & I collected downstairs in the radio room, & waited for the P. GGT & Mrs. Eben arrived, very much in their best clothes. Mary Eben has very good taste & dresses very well. She was thrilled at being invited — she said she didn't often see the P., even at a distance. Martha had a new black winter suit & very smart hat. The P. took Martha, Betty & Fala with him. Tully, Ostgaard, Eben & I in the next car.

We drove into the basement delivery entrance of the Nat. Archives, & a long procession of SS., Archives officials, ourselves, etc. went up in the elevators & through the halls to the Rotunda, to see the F.D.R. L[ibrary] exhibit. The P. was much pleased with it. His only criticism was a lack of material in the big case. GGT didn't like the choice of [letters from] Prominent Persons. I explained that, of the small number we have at Hyde Park, some letters couldn't be used for political reasons, others because they are too personal, etc.

. . . Back to the W.H. for tea & "scotch & soda," Martha, Betty, Mrs. Ostgaard & I indulging in tea — At 6.30, the P. dismissed the party, went to have his sinus treated. The Hopkinses came for dinner. [Harry Hopkins had stopped living at the White House after three and a half years and moved with his wife and daughter to a house in Georgetown. The President was now more dependent than ever on Daisy for company in the evenings.]

Afterwards, the P. said he didn't feel like working, so I got my tapestry & Kipling's "Brushwood Boy" & he read aloud. It was just too nice & all too short.

At 9.20 Martha called him up: she was frightened to death at having to broadcast. The P. laughed at her & I know made her feel better. We listened in — she spoke very clearly and didn't sound frightened at all — Her voice is harsh on the radio, strangely enough, for it isn't at all so, in conversation. Right after the broadcast, the P. called her up to tell her it was all right.

What a friend he is, to so many people. One never ceases to wonder. I think the secret of his enjoyment of life is that he understands life & people so well that he can't be disillusioned, and so never becomes cynical. He loves the good, hates the mean & evil, tolerates weakness. This is my last evening of *this* trip — It always seems to be the "last evening." The visits pass so quickly!

Wednesday Oct. 6th. A bad day for the P. He had one thing after another all day, including a delegation of Jewish rabbis & dedicating an airfield . . . [The delegation of nearly four hundred Orthodox rabbis, organized by the Emergency Conference to Save the Jewish People of Europe, had come to Washington to present a petition to the President, calling on him to create an agency to rescue what remained of European Jewry and to press all nations to open their doors to Jewish immigration. Roosevelt refused to see them, pleading the pressure of other business. He had recently given orders that all such matters were to be addressed to the State Department and apparently did not wish to risk the wrath of other Jewish groups opposed to the Emergency Conference. Marvin McIntyre received the petition on his behalf.]

[Hyde Park]

ᴥ *Friday Oct. 8th.* . . . I went over for lunch. Mrs. R. was sitting under the portico with . . . a friend of a soldier she knows in the Pacific. Princess Juliana [of the Netherlands] was out among the trees with her 3 babies. There were just the five of us for lunch. Mrs. R. spoke of her trip to the Pacific. She is getting 500-odd letters a day from parents of boys she saw out there who have written home about her visit. She feels it was very worthwhile — that she did real good by going.

 . . . [In the afternoon] we all piled into the car & drove at 50 miles an hour to Cruger's Island [actually a peninsula jutting out into the Hudson, about twenty miles north of Springwood]. We went a little way along the track, then parked facing the swamp, & watched the 1000s of birds collecting there for the night. In the daytime they scatter all over the country, to feed — they stay here until some time in Nov. depending on the weather. The P. is awfully interested, birds being one of his many hobbies. Mrs. R. was frankly *not* specially interested . . .

ᴥ *Monday Oct. 11th* — The P. came to the Library about 10.30, with Gen. [Walter Bedell] Smith [Gen. Eisenhower's chief of staff] . . . He suddenly announced to us both that we were lunching with him "at the cottage." He wasn't sure which cottage! We went first to the house . . . then drove to Mrs. R.'s cottage. No one around, so we went up to the Hill Cottage, where we found Mrs. R. & Harry Hooker walking up and down, unable to get in —

 There were just the seven of us, and we listeners had the most interesting time. We set two card tables in front of the fire: It worked very well — all but the coffee! I poured for everyone except the P. who wanted it at the end of the meal, and Ethel [Franklin Jr.'s wife] & me, & [then] discovered there was but just enough in the thermos for the P. So I took it out to the pantry, so no one would drink it. Ethel & I exchanged whispered explanations — Finally, when we had finished the cold chicken & ham & tomato salad, the P asked for his coffee — I went out, heated it up, brought it back, and poured it & put the cup at the P.'s right.

 He & the Gen. were immersed in conversation. The P. said "Won't you have some coffee, General?"

 "Yes sir thank you" — and drank the P.'s coffee!! Ethel & I exchanged looks & were furious — Not only did we not have coffee, but the P. didn't — and the General had two cups —

After lunch, Mrs. R. moved over to the fire bench, between the P. & the General; & the three talked about the front, the Italians, the Germans, Italy, our officers & forces — Of the Italian King, the Gen. said that he didn't agree with some people who say he is a moron. He is getting old, but during the morning hours, he is alert & intelligent, has a real "political sense."

Of the Italian campaign he said we had put over the most tremendous bluff in attacking with five divisions, when the Germans have [more]. Of Gen. [Bernard Law] Montgomery, he said the General will argue & disagree & do a lot of talking when the Generals are sitting around a table planning; but the minute Gen. Eisenhower says what is to be done, Gen. Montgomery goes ahead & obeys orders — Gen. [Harold] Alexander does just the opposite: He will agree in conference, & is then just as apt to think up something different to do later. It must be very bad, where concerted action is expected — [Daisy seems to have got this backward: Alexander was predictable, Montgomery more likely to strike out on his own.]

Gen. Eisenhower has a male & female scottie at his headquarters, & a lot of puppies!

. . . Mrs. R. asked the General how well the negroes "take it." He said they collapse more easily and haven't the *staying* qualities of the whites. Otherwise, they are doing well.

∽ *Monday Oct. 18th.* [Rhinebeck] . . . The P. called me up from Wash. tonight. He had been to Shangri-La over the weekend & enjoyed it, though it was cold — He said he fell asleep twice while trying to write a message to Congress. He just is *too* tired, *too* often. I can't help worrying about him . . .

∽ *Wednesday, Oct 20.* . . . Yesterday morning at the Library, the P. called me up — "I thought you might read in the paper that I am sick and I had better tell you, first." He evidently has grippe for he said he ached all over, and had fever up to 104 and ¹/₄. He must catch these things from visitors, when he is over-tired — but he told me once that he always caught every thing in sight, all his life — I hope the rest in bed will do him good, and that there is nothing serious — It is so thoughtful of him to call up — I hope he'll let me know how he is, tonight —

Later. The P. called up — His fever is almost down to normal, his head still heavy, but he sounded cheerful . . . He will come to H.P. on Thursday night, return to Wash. the following Tuesday night, and leave for the long trip, some 10 days later —

⌁ *Oct 29th.* We expected the P. here this morning but he called up last night to say he would arrive Saturday, instead — He said "things" are "in a mess"; the coal strike, I suppose. I can't ask questions over the phone. He says he "expects" to go on the Long Trip, "thinks" it will go through, but it is not entirely certain, yet. I suppose a lot depends on Mr. Hull's success. I can't help feeling that F.D.R. should have seen Stalin *first,* and worked on him as man to man.

[FDR and Churchill were planning to meet with Stalin at last, probably in Teheran. But first, Secretary of State Hull was assigned the task of going to Moscow to get the Soviet premier to join with the President, Churchill, and Chiang Kai-shek in pledging to establish "a general international organization, based on the principle of the sovereign equality of all peace-loving states." Stalin signed on October 30.]

The P. is not entirely well yet, still aches somewhat & feels tired — He was on the sofa in his study, sorting magazines. I begged him to go to bed early — a useless begging, as he goes when he feels like it!

⌁ *Oct. 30th Sat.* . . . . The flu has left him rather miserable, and very tired, but he can't give in to it. At about 12.30 he was dropping with sleep & let me take him to the big chair by the fireplace, & put his feet on the 2-step stool. I went out to get ready for lunch, and he fell sound asleep —

He is preparing for the Long Trip — Hopes he won't have to go to Teheran, which is full of disease, and involves a flight over the mountains of up to 15,000 ft. He dreads both things for himself & his whole party, specially Harry Hopkins, but "it will break his heart if I don't take him with me." The P. thinks Stalin *may* be suffering from a sort of inferiority complex, whether for himself or for his country, because he is being so very difficult about this meeting with F.D.R. and is insisting on F.D.R. going most of the way. F.D.R. feels the meeting is of paramount importance and he must make it happen, regardless of the cost to himself —

Of the English, he said that W.S.C. sees the future as he does, but that the others in England do *not* — Anthony Eden, he thinks, is the Dictator type. He wouldn't trust him. It is he who is backing De Gaulle, and if the Allies should land in France, both Anthony Eden & De Gaulle would at once establish a dictatorship . . .

How strange it would be if F.D.R. & Stalin were to have to enforce their democratic ideas on England! But stranger things have happened before!

It is very disappointing that Anthony Eden is turning out to be nothing but a reactionary — So many have pinned such faith on him — F.D.R. *did* say: "I have met him only once — I must see him again" . . . perhaps he could do something with him, if he had the chance to try . . .

The P. *beginning* to relax — He *should* have another full week.

$\backsim$ *Nov. 3rd.* The Republicans made a good showing in the [off-year] Elections. Mr. [Neil] Smith [an electrician at the Roosevelt Library] says it was largely because 6 out of 10 housewives are tired of complaints by their husbands about jelly sandwiches for lunch, with the only answer that they "haven't the points"! Steve [evidently another Library employee] tells me *his* mother always manages to give him ham sandwiches, and meat for supper every night — They are a household of 5 working adults, so it can be done!

The P., talking of politics & elections in general, said that he remembers Woodrow Wilson telling him that the public is willing to be "liberal" about a third of the time, gets tired of new things and reverts to conservatism the other two thirds of the time. The P. said that *if* the war is over next year, it will be impossible to elect a liberal president. He wants to get out of domestic problems & help to carry on international ones — I pray & pray that he may be able to.

. . . The P. and GGT arrived for tea at Wilderstein at 5.05, just five minutes after I got there. The library had bulbs in the sockets, the fire was burning brightly and Geraldine [Ryan, a Suckley houseguest] had brought in furniture whose seats were *not* fallen through the bottom! It was all very nice & cozy —

. . . About 6.15, the P. said he must go — I told Charlie Fredericks & he & Monty came in & carried him out. General kissing goodbye all around, and I went off with them . . . [A] little after 10 we got into the car & went to the train.

$\backsim$ *Nov. 4th.* [The White House] . . . Charlie Fredericks' daughter is very ill in the hospital . . .

At 4.30 the P. took me out to Pook's Hill, to see the Cr. Princess. Mme. Ostgaard & I are on good terms — she is no longer so formal; but the P. thinks [her] rather dull, because when the Princess is in the room Mme. O never speaks a word! It is part of her training in the presence of royalty — *I* think she is very intelligent, & terribly nice, & has a sense of humor.

The Cr. Prs. wanted to speak to the P. alone, & took him off to the Library at a quarter to six, the exact moment he said he must leave . . . Without the P. & the Cr. Prs., Mme. O. & Mr. Weddel [P. A. Wedel Jarlsburg] became natural, & talked! We had more tea & cakes! They both feel they will be home for Christmas 1944 — I hope they are right, but really haven't an opinion about it. The P. thinks there is a 50–50 chance.

At 6.30, the P. emerged & we drove back to Washington. The secret talk was about the Cr. Prs' fears for the future of the royal family in Norway — Perhaps I shouldn't write down even that much! The P. thinks her fears are groundless because King Haakon is much beloved by his people — However, the P. is going to get a report about it from the State Dept., whether they have reports that would indicate anything like the Cr. Prs' fears . . .

❧ *Nov. 5th* Friday. . . . The P. was very tired after his long day — He was keyed up and couldn't relax. He has started taking coffee for breakfast again, as, on the Long Trip, there won't be anything else to drink. It is obviously not good for him; it shows in his hands which become nervous & a little shaky — He is a little worried about swelling in his ankles which comes when he is tired. [Lieutenant Commander George] Fox [the President's physical therapist], rubs them before dinner, and he puts an electric vibrator on them at bedtime. It helps the circulation. He should have a slow massage all over his feet & legs — at least 20 minutes a day on each — I think!

He is still hoping that Stalin will meet him at Basra, but, if he won't, F.D.R. is prepared to fly over the mountains to Teheran, though he doesn't tell Stalin that — I am giving him a heat pad for that trip, in case of need —

[Shangri-La]

❧ *Nov. 6th Saturday.* . . . Charlie Fredericks' daughter died last night, in spite of Sulpha drugs, followed by penicillin. He is *such* a kind, sweet person it is very sad. We see these SS men as individuals, knowing nothing of their family life, until something like this happens . . .

Later — I came out to the porch at about 6, after getting into my perpetual short tea & evening dress . . . Found F.D.R. sitting by himself reading dispatches — Stalin definitely won't go beyond Teheran to meet him, so the P. will have to make that extra high flight. Stalin's point is that as commander of the Russian forces, he cannot be away from Moscow beyond a certain number of hours — It is a good point, but I think there is more to it than that — It has to do with his "strategy" toward the outside world — Russia is now so big, and so strong, that she can impose her will, & must be treated *at least* as an equal — This is such a change from, shall we say, ten years ago, that Stalin may be self conscious about it, & so, may be too anxious to prove his point — As I have written before, the P. suggested that Stalin may be suffering from an inferiority complex — Perhaps that covers it.

All we can do is to hope & pray that all will be well with the P & his party — He will be gone about 28 days — they will be 28 dreadfully long days for those at home . . .

~ *Nov. 8 Monday.* [The White House] I am now putting a quarter on my breakfast tray. It takes care of the different butlers who bring it up, and makes them all happy! At Shangri-La, I give Isaac $2.00 for one night, $3.00 for a two-night week-end. He is the head of the "crew" of five or six. All the funny little Filipinos are silent & smiling — wonderful servants, though their English is almost un-understandable. I leave $5.00 on my bureau for the maids. Wilma tells me she really does most of the work. I told her I hoped she would divide with others, according to how much each does.

This was the P.'s worst day. He had 22 appointments — Then saw the Cr. Pr. at 5 about her "worry." He will see Amb. Winant & ask him to suggest to King Haakon [in exile in England] to change the Norwegian Minister to this country — He doesn't want to put it in writing, for it isn't a definite enough thing, but the P. himself has found [the minister] unsatisfactory and with the Cr. Pr.'s fears added, it seems a good time to make a change. I was just closing up my work in the North Hall, saw the Cr. Prs. in the P.'s study; moving around from chair to chair, rather nervously — She waved at me, so I went in, shook hands, and we stood talking, near the study door, until the P. came in — I backed out & vanished —

At a little before 7, Mr. Searles called me up — "Oh, you're in,

Miss Suckley, we didn't know whether you were in or out — you will be the President's only guest at dinner — will you have some sherry?"

I went into the hall & sat under the lamp, doing my tapestry — the P. came up from having his nose treated, called out "I'll be with you in a moment" —

Mrs. R. came from her room in a white evening gown & gold brocade wrap. With a cheerful "Hello" she went into the P.'s room: "Darling, can I come in to say goodnight?" A few minutes later she emerged & went down in the elevator —

I went into the P.'s study just as he came in from his room; Fala wriggling & sneezing with his usual excitement at the prospect of supper — We had sherry & a cocktail, then, for dinner, ptarmigan from Iceland. They were overcooked, but delicious. I ate nothing else & worked to my heart's content over the carcass! As soon as we had finished, GGT came in & did today's mail with the P. When she had left, I pulled down the map of Africa, & that of the Bible lands, & the P. showed me his itinerary of course, as far as "time" goes, subject to weather conditions, etc.

> About 4 days in Cairo, *facing* the Sphinx from his window! From Cairo to Basra by air, from Ahwaz to Teheran by royal train. The only danger will come from possible bandits through the mountains! They will take 800 American soldiers with them, and a pilot engine & a rear guard engine — A real adventure! The P. is all excited over it! I am glad he won't have that 15,000 foot flight.

We then got to work & were still poring over documents & letters when Mrs. R. opened the door at about 11 & said — "It's getting late, Franklin — time for bed!" In fact, they still had a lot of "business" to talk about, & midnight is the one time when they do not get interrupted —

⌁ *Nov. 10 Wednesday.* 9.50 A.M. How lucky I am to be allowed to stay here, in the W.H., almost up to the last minute of F.D.R.'s departure! The Roosevelts do everything in such a simple natural way, that one feels that whatever happens *is* simple & natural! But it certainly is not in the simple & natural course of the life of a Suckley to be seeing, at first hand, the very core & hub of world history — It is fantastic — But here I am!

. . . Mrs. R. & the Hopkinses were at dinner, Susie [evidently a dog belonging to the Hopkinses] much in evidence, begging for food, & finally acting as a footstool for everyone, under the table — At dinner, Mrs. R. brought up the subject of the American fliers who came down in Arabia, & were mutilated & left to die in the desert. She insisted that we should bomb all Arabia, to stop such things. The P. said it was an impossible thing to do, in the first place, as the tribes are nomadic, & hide in secret places etc. Also, Arabia is a huge desert etc. Besides, it would be acting like the Japanese, to go & bomb a lot of people, who don't know any better & have no education etc. I put in one word, to the effect that we have lynching in this country still, but we don't go & bomb the town where the lynching occurs — Harry Hopkins joined Mrs. R. — but their point seemed to me so completely illogical that I restrained myself, & kept silent! Louise likewise — the argument continued quite heatedly until it was interrupted by a telephone call from Anna Boettiger — in Seattle . . .

ᐫᐤ *Nov. 12 Friday.* [Rhinebeck] Fala slept quite peacefully on the armchair in my room . . . I want to keep him out of sight until the papers announce where his master is — Just to stop unnecessary speculation . . .

ᐫᐤ *Nov. 15 Monday.* Cold & clear — rain in the P.M. When I got home, I found a note from the P. written supposedly after he got on board, if Arthur the valet did as I suggested — It is postmarked Wash. the 13th. U.J. [Stalin, whom Roosevelt had nicknamed Uncle Joe] is to meet him — All is in the hands of God . . . [The note is missing.]

ᐫᐤ *Nov. 18th Thursday.* The Berlin radio said yesterday that important things are about to happen in Cairo, as they are doing over a large hotel near the Pyramids!

ᐫᐤ *Nov. 19th Friday.* . . . A note from GGT today saying she will send me any news that may come, and enclosing an "Atlantic Charter" issued by the Govt. Printing Office. The strange thing about it is that there is no original "Atlantic Charter"! It was written up on the ocean, typewritten, & sent to Washington & London by code & so never actually signed by F.D.R. & Churchill.

F.D.R. is supposed to be landing at Oran tomorrow, the 20th. Today I sent off my 2nd letter to go by pouch on the 21st or 22nd.

GGT certainly has a most responsible and exacting position — I think she appreciates it . . .

꙳ *November 21st.* Last night, the radio quoted a broadcast from London to the effect that an announcement will be made shortly from Washington, about the conference between Roosevelt, Churchill & Stalin. This was reported again this A.M. on the radio, but I found nothing in the paper —

F.D.R.L.

Tuesday, Nov. 23 '43

Dear Franklin —

I'll mail this, this P.M. so it can go in the pouch of the 25th. I hope the pouch doesn't get off a day early —

The speculations as to where you are, are most intriguing! The *"news"* on the radio, which I hear at 6.30 A.M. & 12.30 P.M., does not mention your being away at all — But all the commentators, all day, are giving their opinions, and are convinced that you are somewhere out of the country — Every evening, Geraldine [Ryan] "knows" definitely where you are! Three days ago, it was Alaska. Last evening it was Iran — *Most* of the bets are on Cairo, as that city is full of royalties. Poor things, all pinning their hopes on M.F. — one can't help being awfully sorry for them —

I told you I wondered if Fala would learn from Button to come up on my bed — He has been sleeping on the chair — Two nights ago, he suddenly decided he was missing something by being so off-ish, and suddenly, just as Button was jumping onto the bed from one side, he jumped up from the other — They met facing each other — gave each other a surprised look & turned their backs to each other & settled down in two round balls & went to sleep . . . [See opposite page.]

Three pages about our dogs while the world is in a turmoil! We hear that Jimmy is in the new Japanese offensive, & there is a report that Elliott has had to parachute somewhere — I know how you feel about those fine boys of yours, and pray for them & their parents & families — All goes as usual here, in calm & peaceful surroundings.

Today, it is snowing, but not cold — I am arranging the Roosevelt Family papers for microfilming, & wishing I could have *as my assistant* a certain F.D.R. who knows so much more than I do — I could get so much more done in a much shorter time.

gave each other one look and faced in opposite directions + went to sleep —
View from the head of the bed:

Button   m's   Fala
             + at

If they both stay, I wonder how I shall sleep —

Nov. 22 wonder

Fala stayed in the bed until around 2 a.m. I remember hearing the clock strike — and then went back to his chair where he remained curled in a compact ball until I took them out at 2.45. The mornings are cold + stimulating, but a little dark, as the dawn is just beginning to appear at that hour.

Fala has learned to use the dog house! Another lesson — It is a good thing, as he might become rheumatic as he gets older, sitting on the bare ground in every kind of weather — there was no meat, so I gave the dogs Jayness with vects: both were sick.

I hope you are writing very fully and constantly in that notebook — The Sphinx should help you by his very silence!

All the thoughts and wishes & love from your U.S.A. are with you, as well as of

Yours, always,
Margaret

*   *   *

[Hyde Park]

Nov. 25th

Dear Franklin —

It is a beautiful Thanksgiving day, and oh, I *do* realize the many many things for which I am thankful. I think I've told you of them often, for I am the luckiest person alive in so *many* ways —

My desk is littered with the Corr. of James (1) R. [the President's great grandfather] & the Hunts, father & sons; in the midst of it I suddenly realized that I must get this last letter off to you today, to be sure it goes in the pouch of the 28th.

There has been nothing further about Elliott, so he must be safe. I am so glad —

. . . The cat isn't out yet — openly — I wish it were, for I would hear some news. As it is, I am quite sure that Mr. Schickelgruber [Hitler's supposed real name] knows all about it whereas we innocent & harmless people are told nothing!

Do try to get up to H.P. once before you come for Christmas — You will have been away too long *any*way!

How furious you must be about the Patton affair. [While visiting a military hospital earlier in the year, General George Patton, Jr., encountered two apparently unharmed patients who he believed were malingering. He slapped one of them and had to be pulled off by orderlies. In fact, the man was suffering from severe battle fatigue. Reporters got wind of the incident, and for a time Patton's future was in jeopardy. Eisenhower let him off with a reprimand, an act that some columnists chose to criticize again just as Eisenhower was about to be appointed commander of Overlord.]

How small, to make an issue of it, now — You would think there was enough war news without a thing like that. The reaction everywhere is one of annoyance at Drew Pearson [a columnist] or whoever else brought it out first . . .

I can't wait to hear everything: bandits, etc.! And the main big object of the trip —

Hoping to get a letter soon,
with my love,
Always,
Margaret

Nov. 27th Saturday. Last evening, Fala vanished into the dark, & paid no attention to my strident "Fala-Fala-Fala" for 15 minutes! I wasn't really worried — but much annoyed, & he appeared quite cheerfully from beyond the tennis court, covered with burrs . . .

Later, on the radio, a report from London that "it is reported that Mr. Churchill & Mr. Stalin are in conference somewhere. Anthony Eden is with Mr. Churchill." No one else???

Nov. 30th Tuesday. . . . . On the lunch hour news on the radio, it was announced that London has reported that Roosevelt, Stalin, Churchill & Chiang *are* conferring in *Cairo!*

9.30 p.m. Same report, leaving out Chiang — another report said they are at Teheran, Iran. This sounds right. F.D.R. should be back in Cairo tomorrow or the next day —

Fala got burrs on his hind quarters & has pulled out the fur with the burrs in a place which *needs* fur more than any other! I am hoping it will grow back before he sees his master — At this moment the two pups are on my bed, near the pillow, their backs touching . . .

Nov. 30, in the evening. Mama fast asleep in the green armchair, almost inside the fireplace. Robin opposite her, holding forth on some subject or other, *at* Geraldine & Eva [Ryan, sisters, friends, and frequent house guests of the Suckleys'] . . .

On the 7.30 news, we heard that a definite announcement came out of Lisbon that Roosevelt, Churchill & Chiang *have been* conferring in Cairo *in the greatest secrecy.* That some of their conferences took place *in a tent near the pyramids.* That Roosevelt & Churchill *are on their way to Teheran, Iran,* for a conference with Stalin. Reuter's have put it out also.

I found a note from GGT. How nice of her to send me the news — my last letter to F.D.R. went in the Sunday pouch, as I thought it would.

◌ *Dec. 1st* [Wednesday]. . . . The P. should be starting home perhaps Sunday, the 5th. It is amusing that Mme. Chiang went too. (Knowing Mme. Chiang!!) It will be fun to hear the P. on the subject!

◌ *Dec. 2nd Thursday.* The days are passing, *slowly,* when you are waiting for a safe return of F.D.R.! Fast, in every other way — I shall hate to turn over Fala to his master, & I think Fala will be lonely & will miss the home life — Button will miss him very much, without doubt . . .

◌ *Dec. 3rd Friday.* Nothing new about F.D.R.'s whereabouts this morning early . . . I suspect he is back in Cairo, incognito. "On verra!" One can never be "in the know" with F.D.R., unless one is actually with him.

◌ *Dec. 4th Saturday* — Moscow came out with the "scoop" that the meeting with Stalin has taken place. The press of both England & the U.S. are rightly furious . . .

◌ *Dec. 6 Monday* — Nothing special about F.D.R. except that the pres. of Turkey [Ismet Inonu, whom both Roosevelt and Churchill tried and failed to talk into entering the war against the Axis] has been in Cairo with him & Churchill, and today, at 1 P.M., an official announcement will be made.

1–1.15 A broadcast: Roosevelt, Churchill *& Stalin agree!* I'm quite sure this would never have come about in just this way if Churchill had been allowed to send the "rude answer" he wanted to, to Stalin! Was it last summer — from Quebec?

9.30 p.m. F.D.R.'s "soft answer" can move mountains — and *does* — It will be fascinating to hear his description of the whole trip — tonight, on the radio they described the 4 days at Teheran . . . I *hope* F.D.R. is keeping the diary, but fear he is too busy making people understand each other. He expected only *1* day at Teheran, so it must have been a great success for them to have lengthened it out — He *should* be on his way home by now.

A note came today, written on the 20th. [This note does not survive.]

How nice for him to see Elliott and F. Jr. & John Boettiger [now in the army and stationed in North Africa] — He is so proud of the way those boys are doing their jobs — Elliott at the head of the whole reconnaissance air force of the U.S.–Brit.–So. Africa & N. Zealand command — 5,000 men & 250 planes — F. writes that he is in a "secret villa" and every commentator has described it!

⌒ *Dec. 11th Saturday.* Last night on the radio, it was announced that P. visited Malta on Wednesday, the 8th, and that his plane flew over Tunis "on his way home." I don't know when the last happened — *I wish he would get home!*

⌒ *Dec. 11th. . . . 12.45 p.m.* The radio just announced that the P. spent 48 hours with Gen. Eisenhower in a villa called the White House, overlooking the ruins of ancient Carthage . . . I hope this means he did *not* go to Italy. It would be *too* dangerous, even for a "calculated risk."

⌒ *Dec. 15, Wednesday.* When I got home I found a short note from the P. written after [he was] at Malta & Sicily, on a 12 hr. plane trip — and *on his way home,* which is the important thing! [This note, too, has disappeared.]

He says the trip was *almost completely satisfactory, specially the Russians.* How happy he must be about it. I imagine the not *entirely* satisfactory part was Turkey, but we'll see.

⌒ *Dec. 16th Thursday. . . . 8.30 p.m.* The 6.30 radio announced that Steve Early announced that the P. is safely in the U.S. Thank God for that —

⌒ *Dec. 17 — Friday. . . .* At 12, I was just picking up my thermos to go down to lunch when the telephone rang. Mrs. [Elizabeth M.] Dean in an excited voice: "Miss Suckley, Washington calling!!"

Click, click, as I answer & connections are made. Miss Tully, in *her* type of concise quick speech, a decided tone of "elevation": "Miss Suckley, the President!!"

"Oh, Miss Tully," say I, & then the P.'s normal voice. It *is* good to hear him, safe & sound, back in the W.H. He had a really wonderful trip — did *not* stop at the Azores — wasn't in a plane anyway — came by warship, the radio said later, from Dakar.

Will be up here next Thursday or Friday until the following Tuesday, may want me to go back with him. (I haven't yet disposed of the things he brought up the last time!!) Misses his puppy *very* much — I'll bring Fala down next Friday.

Later. A commentator told of the P.'s visit to Teheran — A supposed German plot to "get" him & Churchill and Stalin, & how Stalin begged him to stay in the Russian embassy to avoid trips through the town —

❧ *Dec. 20th Monday.* My birthday, 52 yrs. old — "going on" old age! Mama didn't remember. I wonder if anyone will!

I went to bed at 8.30 last night, with Christmas cards to sign & address. A warm stove and a comfortable bed. At 11 I took the pups around the circle for their final walk & then lights out & asleep — I don't think I moved all night until 5 A.M. as I was in exactly the same position I remember last: on my left side — the pups don't move either. Once in a while they stand up & twist around in the opposite directions before curling into a ball — Button near my feet, Fala on the chair.

Later. When I got home I found the family had remembered! So we had a candle on a cake, and some nice presents, & the dogs each got a piece of cake.

At 9 P.M. Western Union called up that they had a telegram which is "not to be phoned"! They will mail it. Mystery, as I've never received one like that before — the girl laughed a little & said she didn't think it very important: it could wait until tomorrow . . . [It turned out to be a birthday greeting from FDR.]

❧ *Dec. 22nd Wednesday.* . . . Tonight, at a quarter to seven, the P. called up, as he said: "Two days late for your birthday." He will come over to the Library on Friday morning, as soon as he can. I will take Fala down then —

❧ *Dec. 23rd Thursday.* The day before the day before Christmas! Anna came in with her children, also John's little Haven & Douglas. The last two have evidently struck up a friendship, for they move "as one" & smile continually at each other in the sweetest way — they started to rough-house in the P.'s room amongst the decorations on the floor, so we were thankful when they departed, urged by a new idea, followed by the faithful S.S. who shadows them . . .

❧ *Dec. 24th Friday.* All ready — and a beautiful day, but cold — 4° below zero at 8 A.M. 20 above at 2 P.M.

Fala quite impatient — wanted to go right over to the house — but I kept him so I could hand him over personally to his master —

the P. came over at 10.30 in a sweater & grey suit. He . . . took Fala in his arms — Fala wagged violently, then looked away, much embarrassed . . . [T]he P. sat at his desk talking about the trip, opening [gifts] & the diary I am starting him on. I *hope* he'll *sometimes* write in something! [If Roosevelt did begin a new diary, it has not survived.]

[The White House]

᠙ *Dec. 27th Monday*. On Friday afternoon the P. came back to the Library at 2.30, in preparation for the broadcast at three. The room was a mess, with microphones on his desk, Klieg lights facing him from every direction. The dozen or so telephones of the broadcasting systems, two more cameras, and wires all over the floor! Mary Morgan & her youngest boy [Mary Newbold Morgan, a childhood friend and next-door neighbor of the President, and her son, Thomas], Mr. & Mrs. Henry Morgenthau, Mrs. Pratt, Harry Hooker, F. Jr. & Ethel, John & Anne, Anna Boettiger & Sistie & Buzzie, all crowded into the S.W. corner of the room. Mrs. R. sat on the floor behind the P.'s desk, & Anna & Mrs. Pratt moved over by her. The speech was wonderful — the P. giving lots of interesting figures & details, & not mincing words about our intentions to prevent a recurrence of the present "banditry," if it can be done. It *can* be done, if Tom Dick & Harry want it enough to back up the leaders . . .

[Roosevelt reported to the American people on the Cairo and Teheran conferences, warned that there was still plenty of fighting ahead, and assured his listeners that he "got along fine" with Stalin.]

Sunday passed peacefully, all of us rather tired with our preparations! It sleeted toward evening, so that the P. told me to let him know if the roads were too icy, & he would send an S.S. car with chains. However, it fortunately did not turn cold, & [William] Nichols & his wife came for me at 7.30 & took me down to the F.D.R.L. for the 2nd M.P. party. I got my bag & coats etc. into the P.'s closet & then joined the Nicholses & Nixons. There must have been almost 280 soldiers & their girls & wives. All went in line to shake hands with the P. & Mrs. R. . . . . Then we sang carols with much enthusiasm, & then the P. told about his trip again. He said afterward that he didn't do it as well as the first time, but it seemed to everyone to be good enough! After that a man . . . did remarkable feats of memory, & then the P. said goodbye — It was about 10 P.M. & I slipped around the back, to his room, got my things on, & we drove to the Highland station.

[Aboard the train] Mr. Hassett [the President's correspondence secretary] & Miss "Hacky" [Louise Hachmeister, chief switchboard operator at the White House] joined us for orange juice & delicious canapés & then we went to bed.

I have been feeling a cold coming along, & am only thankful it came after I left home — All day, I have taken soda & water in large quantities . . . The P. came from his office for lunch of corn soup, scrambled eggs & stringbeans — nothing else. At two he said he was awfully tired, & went to his room for a nap . . .

At lunch the P. said he has decided to take over the railroads to prevent a nation wide tie-up. It will be announced tonight. He spoke of the Union leaders as "rotten" — Most people agree with him, & it might be an awfully good thing to jail them for fomenting strikes against the government . . .

It is now 5.30 — A setting sun shines in through open Venetian blinds. I sit at the card table near the P.'s sofa, in his study — It is a deserted house, but for the servants & the striking clocks. Lincoln, once in a while, makes a sound — in some corner of the room. [Daisy believed that the creaks and groans of the White House were caused literally by the shade of Abraham Lincoln making its rounds.]

This room looks like a man's workroom without the touch of a woman to straighten things out & put them a little to the right or a little to the left! The P. evidently wants it that way! A large chest on a stand holds cigarettes & cigars from Havana. The P. took several boxes with him on the trip & gave half to Churchill & half to [Stalin] . . .

The P. & I had pigs feet for supper, very delicious & very rich. We spent what was to me a very interesting evening, looking over about a dozen books. I haven't done so much actual "reading" for months! and the P. said it was his first evening of relaxation in two months. As a coincidence or as a result of mind-reading, he said he wished I would do something about the room. So I shall get to work & pull furniture around!

∾ *Dec. 28th Tuesday*. I'm feeling rather wobbly on my feet, & still cough, but don't believe it will amount to much —

. . . I took an orange for my lunch; moved the furniture around in the P.'s study, so that it looks more like a lived-in room than a workroom. The P. decided he likes it when he saw it after dinner.

We spent the evening on a pile of books, as last evening. The P. is feeling a *little* miserably — it is probably a touch of flu for both of us . . .

ᴥ *Dec. 29th Wednesday.* Feeling much better. Admiral McIntire came in, found me quite cheerful, found my room freezing, & departed. At 10, Mr. Fox came in with presidential orders to take my temperature & pulse. Found temp. normal, & "a good strong pulse" though a little fast, 88. "We can't do any business with you!" says he —

The P. gave me the diary he took down on the trip — It is short & "guarded," but wonderful to have, considering the fact that he usually doesn't keep any diary! [This diary has also disappeared.]

Today, the house fills up: Mrs. R. arrives around noon, Anna Boettiger & her three children, toward evening.

It has been peaceful and calm these two days & quite a rest for the P. who hasn't had a moment for two months. Yesterday morning, with Steven Early, he planned the "allegory" of his press conference, in his study, while I sat listening. He had it all in his mind, told Mr. E. about it in about two minutes. Mr. E. thought it would fit in beautifully with the list of New Deal accomplishments . . .

[The allegory FDR and Early cooked up in advance, was delivered in this form:

> Two years ago, on the seventh of December, [the patient] was in a pretty bad smashup — broke his hip, broke his leg in two or three places, broke a wrist and an arm, and some ribs; and they didn't think he would live for a while. And then he began to "come to"; and he has been in charge of a partner of the old doctor. Old Doctor New Deal didn't know "nothing" about legs and arms. He knew a great deal about internal medicine, but nothing about surgery. So he got his partner, who was an orthopedic surgeon, Dr. Win-the-War, to take care of this fellow . . . And the result is that the patient is back on his feet. He has given up his crutches. He isn't wholly well yet, and he won't be until he wins the war.
>
> And I think that is almost as simple, that little allegory, as learning again how to spell "cat."]

ᴥ *Dec. 30 Thursday.* I haven't been off this floor since I arrived on Monday! Still hacking! Mrs. R., Anna & 5 grandchildren arrived after lunch — the P. was kept in bed, so I spent most of the day working in his room, after having lunch with him. He told Mrs. R. he wanted me to have dinner with him as "I hate to eat alone," so the two trays were brought in . . .

Mrs. R. & Anna were in dinner dresses & went to see the Army show afterwards with Mrs. Pratt &, I think, an aide or two. Sistie & Buzzie came in to say goodnight — attractive natural children — Fala was induced to get up on the P.'s bed for a cracker. He has evidently a complex about it, as he seemed really afraid when I tried to push him further up toward the P. A few tidbits will get him over it however — in time.

The P. says he has a present for me for every day!! Monday, Persian prayer-rug. Tuesday, little painted piece of ivory, from Iran — Wednesday, "elephant bell" from Iran — Thursday?!

Buzzie & I sat reading in the P.'s study — Anna was having dinner with him in his bedroom. Soon she came out, said she had had a wonderful evening, being able to talk to him alone, but she thought he had fever. I went in & found him a little hectic & flushed. He felt "at loose ends." At 9.30 we took his temperature which we found was 100 ¾. Gave him two aspirins & soda & a teaspoon of the cough medicine. I called up the Dr. who said we had to expect the increased temp. for the next 48 hrs. as part of the flu The P. must *not* catch cold during the night; he would probably be in a perspiration & should have dry clothes.

I asked him if he would ring for Caesar during the night —

No, says he — But I think he will if he thinks he needs to. He is really very sensible. We laughed at his obstinacy, etc. . . .

ﾟ *Dec. 31st Friday* — I worked all the morning in the North Hall. Saw the P. for a moment as he was finishing his breakfast. His door was open, and Fala wandering around, hoping for a bite. He will now jump up onto the P.'s bed — but is still a little uncertain as to whether it is right, & jumps down again in a minute or two!

The P. feeling definitely better, & with no temp. It is a definite attack of flu, or grippe, as the paper reports it. I am glad I have the same thing at the same time, as it is a good reason for my not mixing with the rest of the family & having my meals with the P.!

ﾟ *Jan. 1 1944 Washington.* . . . Thinking back over the week, I have been, again, among the "privileged few." The P. & I, both of us coughing & sneezing, & feeling like "boiled owls"!

. . . Anna & her children, [Jimmy's] two babies, Kate & Sara, have made the W.H. sound gay & youthful. Baby voices and Percy's (dachshund) excited bark came down through the ventilators from the 3rd floor —

Mrs. R. busy as usual, but not too busy to take half a dozen children to the National Gallery one afternoon — Buzzie spent quite a lot of time reading in the P.'s study, or in his room. He is 13, wants to go into the Navy. Is a nice, bright, upright boy, with the quick Roosevelt smile. He & Sistie call the P. "Papa" (in French!).

Jimmy's Sara, though not pretty, & wearing glasses, draws attention by her sweet personality. Anna spoke of her several times; what an unusually *nice* child she is — quite unspoiled. Jimmy must miss his little girls — one wonders how far a new childless wife can make up for the loss of one's children.

Last night, at 11.30, the dinner party came up from a movie in the basement to the P.'s study — He came from his room, in a white bathrobe, & sat on the end of the upright sofa to the right of the fireplace —

They lighted the fire. 3 butlers brought in a large bowl with egg-nog — besides a few bottles of something or other (the usual necessaries for cocktails) with glasses, & sat them on a little table back of the big sofa — Plain cakes were also served, & little tables placed around, as for tea. In the party were: Bishop Atwood (he likes important people, & why not?), 4 Morgenthaus, Anna, Buzzie & Sistie, Kate, Miss Thompson & Mrs. Pratt.

Mrs. R. looked a combination of matronly & regal, in a voluminous black silk with a black lace scarf. She looked pale & tired, but has a lovely expression — With her & Anna I kept seeing in their faces the constant thought of their men overseas — What a pall hangs over them all —

Anna is exuberant & very youthful & full of fun — Quite a wonderful person, much like her mother. She dresses very well & very attractively — All her clothes & Sistie's are good-looking & "different." Her father loves having her around — She is still a good deal of a tomboy — Somehow we mentioned Indians sitting crosslegged [and] Buddhas sitting "in contemplation." Down squats Anna on the floor, Buddha fashion!

We turned on the radio to get Midnight. Just before, "they" sang Old Lang Syne. We waited, cups of eggnog in hand — The P. said quietly: "Our first toast will be the U.S. of A."

Mr. Morgenthau made the next: "The President of the U.S., God bless him."

Then followed Mrs. R. & "Our boys overseas."

There was a certain solemnity — each one had his own thoughts — A little conversation, a few stories & at 12.30 we all dispersed — I forgot to mention that right after the toasts we all wished each other Happy New Year — It was all cheerful & pleasant, but without "abandon" — According to the papers this A.M. there was plenty of "abandon" in the restaurants!

I said goodbye to Mrs. R. in the hall, & went in to see the P. His head is still stuffed but that is expected, & he is "all right."

Another year has rolled around — Here's to 1944.

1944

The Whole World Needs Him

[Rhinebeck]

 Jan 6th. . . . I am "enjoying ill health," for a change! Got back from N.Y. on Sunday evening, went to the F.D.R.L. Monday & Tuesday. Tuesday, I couldn't eat any lunch & felt "miserably" all the afternoon, so I told Mr. Nixon . . . that I *might* stay home. It concentrated in my tonsils, which have been red & swollen . . .

Tuesday evening the P. called me up — Is running the expected course of the flu & was sitting at his desk in his study, for the first time since he went to bed last week. He made cocktails for 16 in a party of Anna's & was running back to bed before they came up from dinner. It's such a comfort to hear his voice & know just how he is.

 Jan 19th. . . . At about 7, the P. called up — Is coming up Friday night. Still feels up & down. Had a Press Conference yesterday, also a headache — feels better today . . . I asked him if he was worried about all the rumors, etc. about Russia & [separate] peace talks [with Germany] etc. He said he didn't know what it was all about, but thinks it is just a "flash in the pan."

 Jan. 22nd Saturday. . . . At ten, the P. called up, sounding very cheerful — would be over at 11. Dan put bird seed in the feeding-stations, everyone rushed around, getting things ready — Steve hammered away, opening up the crates in the attic. I gathered things on the P.'s desk to ask him about — I was in his room when he drove up, his navy cape around his shoulders. I went out into the warm sunshine to greet him. He looks better than I expected, but says he still gets tired very easily . . .

 Jan. 25, 1944. . . . The [Walter] Tittles came at eleven . . . I am disappointed in two of the [dry-points of the] President. There is a "hardness" about their execution, & a stiffness about the P.'s personality, which he definitely has not. *He* says he likes it. (I suspect because he wants to be through with just another artist!) Mr. Tittle took some photos of the P. to work from, he gets so little chance to draw from him, & is determined to get a really *good* picture. He told the P. he hoped they wouldn't both die of old age before it is finished!

The P. . . . looked & felt tired. He puts in so much of himself when talking to people — & every minute with the Ts he was concentrated & alert, talking of art, of places in Europe, etc. He enjoys it, but he uses himself up . . .

~ *January 26th Wednesday.* . . . At lunch, Jimmy talked about the young, uneducated boys who are learning that you kill or get killed, etc., etc., and may prove to be a real menace if, at the end of the war, they are suddenly given a bonus, and let loose on the country — He thinks they should be kept in the army, or in C.C.C. camps or something like that, until jobs are found for them, or unless they are put back to school — He says many are almost illiterate —

[The White House]

~ *Jan. 30th Sunday.* . . . On Thursday afternoon, he took GGT, D. Brady & me to Top Cottage to hang pictures. Mr. Plain & Steve took over a stepladder, wire, hooks, etc. Pictures were hung in all the first floor rooms & the Chinese porcelain screen fastened to the wall. That little house is a little museum in itself. The P. is going to have everything in it catalogued.

Friday, the P. & I went up again to see how it all was; then he drove me home, & came in to tea . . . Button leaped on the P. with much enthusiasm, licked his face & used all her charm on him! Mama declaimed on the horrors of Mormons & Mohammedans (plural wives!) The P. was his usual sweet & interesting self . . . As usual, I had to miss most of the visit, while I packed my bag — Arthur saw us off at about 6.30 . . .

~ [*Saturday*]. . . . At the W.H. I was handed a little envelope with a card showing where I would sit at the P.'s dinner, by Mr. Claunch . . . The Cr. P. & Princess of Norway stood with Steve Early — Olaf had "grown" since I saw him last year. His face has more character, & more sweetness, too, perhaps my imagination.

Martha looked very regal in a full dress of grey & silver, & some beautiful jewelry. She is very sweet & cordial. The rest of the guests came in, one by one. We were then ushered down the hall to the red room, where the P. sat behind a table with cocktails. Mrs. R. greeted us as we came in. They had whiskey sours, the first cocktail I have ever really liked! I drank it all, with the usual effect of *no* effect!

I talked to Louise Hopkins for a while. Harry has been in the hospital about a month & doesn't assimilate anything — I know he has all sorts of things wrong with him, but I've seen him trying to feed up on regular food & drinking cocktails, etc. when he should be on gruel & baby foods — I am going to write to Louise about it.

We went in to dinner, behind the P. in his little wheel chair — One almost forgets that it is *not* normal to have to be wheeled in a chair. He doesn't let you think of it, and you just see his cheerful, fine face, so full of character. There were of course many more men than women; originally there were only the members of the Cuff-links [the informal club made up of those closest to FDR during his unsuccessful 1920 run for the vice presidency], and the wives are not invited — so it was all the more an honor to be invited. We had sherry & champagne — I made the one glass do for about a dozen & a half toasts.

I wish I could describe the dinner adequately — it was a *quiet* dinner, with everyone thinking of the P. He had a headache, he told me after, but he is so accustomed to playing his part on all occasions that he carried on the conversation as usual, described some scenes of his trip abroad, told some stories about it, such as Stalin & he teasing Churchill.

After dinner, some toasts were made, to the P. & Mrs. R., to the children who were absent, to the secretaries who work with the P., etc. Olaf made a very nice little speech, a little awkwardly, moving his plate, his glass, looking down half the time, but awfully nice. It was a little speech of appreciation for what the P. has meant to "the Norwegians" as a friend & counselor to them since they first came to this country . . . in 1939 . . .

The P. made a little speech, hoping they would be able to be in their own home for next Xmas, so they could start rebuilding — He said he hoped the Norwegians would have a birthday party over there someday, and, in their names, he asked all of us to attend. (The Norwegians didn't back up the invitation!!)

Mrs. R. looks pale & tired. She talked quietly to Sec. Morgenthau most of the time. At 10 she started on her rounds of the Birthday balls — Anna & John took the Norwegians upstairs, the P. went off with his poker players, & the rest of us dispersed.

This morning, Roly & I went to St. John's Church, & heard a

wonderful sermon by Leslie Glenn ("wonderful" because I agreed with every word of it). The gist of it was that — "Yes, we *must* punish the Japs for their inhuman treatment of war prisoners," *but* we must go further than that; we must give them a higher ideal of life in order to prevent a recurrence of the evil, in the future. We have given them the products of the machine age but no principles of the proper use of these products, & now we find ourselves forced to use these same products to destroy them or perish ourselves. I, personally, think the Germans far more *wicked* in their treatment of those they have conquered, because they have the background of a Christian civilization. The background of the Japanese civilization is ruthlessness and cruelty to any form of weakness — They treat their own soldiers that way . . .

◦ *Jan. 31st Monday.* . . . At about 12, Arthur called me in to the P. He said that Mrs. R. & all the children were in his room a while ago. Mrs. R. said, "I am having a large women's lunch today — what are you children doing for lunch?"
"Nothing."
"All right, I'll send you trays."
No mention of the P.
The P. then started to "cry."
"What's the matter, Pa?"
"Can't *I* have any lunch?"
Roars of laughter from everyone, and offers of a tray for him too.
"As a matter of fact," says the P., "I am going to ask Miss Suckley to lunch with me in my office." More laughter —
They are a wonderful, vital family, good, but not *too* good — Blessed with a sense of humor which *can* apply to themselves as well as to others — It is a pity they have had trouble in so many of the children's marriages. I wonder if it comes from a super-abundance of vitality, with the lack of strong principles which seem to be necessary to a human being, and seem to be strangely lacking in our modern society. We think too much of the individual's immediate personal happiness & forget the larger picture . . .

◦ *Tuesday Feb. 1st.* . . . At 11.30 the P. called me — He looks fine but said "It's a hellofaday — everything is going wrong — Jimmy Byrnes wants to resign, because I don't take him enough into my confidence — another prima donna." Then he laughed.
He has to be patting them on the back all the time — I would

want to throw them all out! (But then, *I* wouldn't be able to fill their places) . . .

Later. . . . After being transferred "on paper," from the yellow room to the third floor, I find I am back in the yellow room. As soon as the P. & the Boettigers came up from dinner at about 8.30, I was sent for, into the P.'s study. There was some joking about the P.'s having his wen [sebaceous cyst] removed [from the back of his neck] at the Naval Hospital tomorrow — who should go with him — whether he should go afterwards for a drink at the Norwegians — etc.

Then the Boettigers said goodnight, & the P. tackled a pile of dispatches etc.

The Boettigers are a lovely family — Happy & bright & intelligent — a real tonic. It would be wonderful if they could stay here permanently.

[Anna and the children did stay permanently. She had not meant to remain more than a few weeks, but her father did not wish her to leave and in the end she agreed to stay on for the duration, serving as his hostess whenever her mother was away. "With no preliminary talks or discussion," she recalled, "I found myself trying to take over little chores that I felt would relieve Father of some of the pressure under which he was constantly working." From then on, Daisy would have a strong ally in seeing to FDR's well-being.]

ᐁ *Feb. 2nd Wednesday.* . . . Anna & I are going out to the Hospital with him, & he will return straight to the W.H. after the operation. They are going to keep the wound open so that it can drain & heal from the inside out — I think it will be more of an operation than they imply, but I hope not. Four doctors are to be there — even a *wen,* if on a P. of the U.S., is an important matter! One comfort is that it won't cost the P. anything, since he is C. in C. I'll write what actually *did* happen tonight! I think the P. is more worried than he lets on — It is not an agreeable prospect in any case.

Later. Everything went off beautifully. At 2 o'clock, Anna & I waited in the Diplomatic Reception room. The P. came, we got into the car, drove past Fala in his pen, looking very dejected at not being taken along, out to the Naval Hospital at Bethesda. Every window had faces peering through the panes. We trailed the P. up to Harry Hopkins' room; Anna & I shook hands with him & left the P. for a short visit with him. He looks very badly, but has put on, & kept, two pounds, so he now weighs 128. The P. told the doctors they should put him on the old-fashioned *remedy that works, gruel!* One doctor said: "That's an interesting idea, I never thought of it." All this, in the elevator as we went to the operating floor.

At the door of the operating unit, Dr. McIntire told us we could go in if we wanted to. I think we both felt they didn't *really* want us, so we remained outside. It took altogether about 50 minutes, & when the P. came out, he looked quite cheerful & normal, & had nothing but a local bandage on the back of his head — You couldn't see it, except from the back — The wen came out like a bantam's egg — There were no complications of any kind & Dr. McIntire said it was a perfect performance in every way — The P., from all accounts, instructed the doctors as they worked, & I am sure kept up a steady conversation throughout! Anna & I decided we should have gone in — We "missed something" —

There were nine at dinner. F. jr & John [Boettiger, now back from North Africa and assigned to the War Department] got into a discussion about the strategy of the war — It was a typical family discussion, F. jr. talking louder & louder & rather fast, John B. talking just as vehemently but slowly, & more deliberately — they seemed to think they disagreed, but I think they were talking at cross purposes & really agreed! Everyone else listened. The P. came into it once in a while, but even Mrs. R. said almost nothing!

F. jr. made an interesting statement, in connection with a possible fourth term; that, to a man, from the highest to the lowest, every individual in the armed forces would consider the P. was a "quitter" if he did *not* run again this year, that not one of them ever mentions [General Douglas] MacArthur [who had left Bataan before it fell to the Japanese in the spring of 1942] if he can help it, because they consider *him* a "quitter" for escaping the Japs under the cloak of a presidential order — It shows that the finer things in a man's character are the things that really count when he is judged. All sorts of superficial faults are overlooked.

(The P. looks rather wan & has an "uncomfortable" head. They closed up the incision with eight stitches & the first dressing won't be until Sunday.) After dinner, the P., Ethel, F. jr. & I went upstairs — all the rest, down, for a movie. F. jr. went right off to bed — Ethel & I talked to the P. for a while — Ethel then went off to bed & the P. & I did a little work. He didn't feel up to much, but doesn't seem to like the long night, when he fears he won't be able to sleep —

✧ *Feb. 3rd Thurs.* A somewhat hectic day, with Mrs. R. leaving in the morning — (Ethel & F. jr. at 7 A.M.) All four Boettigers, on different trains: Sistie & Buzzie back to school on the west coast, Anna & John for a 2-week holiday in Charleston, S.C. Little Johnny stays behind in care of McDuffie & the entire household.

Anne & I are left with the P. . . . He is "coming along all right," but feels tired. It will take a few days to get back to normal — Of course, the cut hurts somewhat, too, and the flu still hangs on.

↝ *Feb. 4th Friday.* A very active day for the P. Now, at 6.15 P.M. he has not yet returned from the Exec. Offices — He slept well last night, felt cheerful this morning . . . Had a cabinet meeting, a press conference. He will probably be awfully tired tonight. He wants me to stay until Tuesday, to finish up a batch of papers . . .

Later. Anne went out for dinner, so the P. & I had ours in his study. He didn't appear until after seven, having had a very heavy day. He said he told his press conference about the wen because he didn't want huge headlines: "The President Under the Knife . . ." It appears that someone at the hospital telephoned the press that he had spent an hour in the hospital and had come out with a dressing on his head. Three reporters called up Steve Early in the middle of the night to find out about it.

↝ *Feb. 5th Saturday.* . . . Went in to see the P. before he went over to his office — the wound on his head *itches*. I told him it is a *good* sign — it is healing. He said I was very unsympathetic . . .

↝ *Feb. 6th Sunday.* . . . He & Anne [John's wife] & I had a quiet evening . . . I had a surprising conversation with the P. I told him I had an idea, but hesitated to even mention it, it was so impossible, but why couldn't he run for President, with Gov. [Harold] Stassen [the youthful — and Republican — chief executive of Minnesota] as Vice Pres. Then, when the P. felt he was no longer necessary, he could resign, & a really good man would take his place —

The P. said he already suggested that but the "party" men wouldn't consider it.

↝ *February 7th Monday.* . . . I hate to leave here; it is so nice & peaceful for working & so nice & exciting to see the P. every evening! Besides, I think he needs to have someone to count on, in the evening. He gets lonely when left alone. It is so different when one can walk about, get things for oneself, *do* something etc. Anne is a peaceful soul, & intelligent, too, but she is out, half the time . . .

Mrs. R. arrived from New York at 7.30 in a blue tweed suit. Mr. & Mrs. Jim [James R.] Carey [president of the International Electric Workers Union] came for dinner. She has black hair & eyes and is one of the prettiest young women I have ever seen — a lovely expression too. He was secretary to the C.I.O. & is now on a board, or something of the kind. I think of John L. Lewis [president of the United Mine Workers of America and the CIO] as representing the C.I.O.; big & blustering. Mr. Carey is rather small, very quiet of manner & voice. He & his wife both speak good English too, which rather surprised me —

The P. said he had them in to get their ideas, and to give them, too, an idea. This idea was that of a wage *by the year,* so that a family may live in decency, & know where it stands — As against a possible high wage by the hour, & not enough hours of work — the conversation was way over my head — about "cartels" & "trade unions," etc.

Mrs. R. read some extracts of letters written to her. She gets so many. People evidently think it is incumbent on them to tell her what's wrong with herself & with the President — It was a peaceful dinner, interesting conversation without arguments —

∽ *Feb. 8th Tuesday,* 9.50 P.M. . . . The P. still has a headache — I feel it must come from being constantly tired — never getting *really* rested, specially since having the flu.

I said he should either take a rest or a short drive, every afternoon. He said he hated to drive alone. I said he should ask Mrs. R. He laughed: "I would have to make an appointment a week ahead!" Perhaps he will take Anna . . . How little one can do for him. And now the possibility of a fourth term looms in the near future . . .

[Rhinebeck]

∽ *Feb. 11th Friday.* . . . The P. just called up. Has had a heavy week & still has a constant headache — The bandage is off his head & Admiral McIntire brushed the hair over it & pronounced it "beautiful!" Tomorrow, the P. has to drive to the Lincoln Memorial in an open car — and again in the P.M. to the Navy Yard where he has to broadcast from the car — I told him he should not have that scar uncovered in such cold weather.

"I'll wear a scarf."

"Will that cover it?"

"No."

"You could wear an ear muff on it."

"Yes, & have the other ear muff over my forehead."

What a blessing, that he can laugh & be foolish. He couldn't get through otherwise.

∾ *Feb. 13th Sunday.* The P. called me up in the evening — evidently none the worse for his open air trips yesterday. Harry Hopkins's son died on a hospital ship after fighting with the Marines in the Pacific. [Pfc. Stephen Peter Hopkins, the son of Harry Hopkins and his first wife, was fatally wounded by a sniper while digging a foxhole on the island of Kwajalein.]

I have a letter from [a] Miss [Grace] Gassette [a French healer who peddled special boxes of "salts" that, she claimed, could cure almost anything] about "Mr. F." She cured many cases of paralysis of 20 years standing, in France, where the doctors would work with her, & even consult her. I feel she could do a lot for F.D.R. if he will only agree to try it. What a thing it would be for the Warm Springs Foundation, & every other hospital.

∾ *Feb. 19th Saturday.* . . . I wrote Miss Gassette about him ("Mr. F") last week, & sent on some of her recommendations. He said on the phone that he will take the "basic salts," but would probably forget about them after the first day!

∾ *Feb. 22. Tuesday,* & Washington's birthday. . . . The P. called up last night to say he expects to be here, as planned, tomorrow morning. He is bothered over these *vetoes* he has to send to Congress, another one today, on the tax measure — He says this one would give many special privileges etc. . . . [FDR vetoed the revenue bill, which provided only a fifth of the increase he'd called for, on the grounds that it provided tax relief "not for the needy but for the greedy." Both houses of Congress were angered by his tone. The Senate majority leader, Alben Barkley of Kentucky, who had hoped to become FDR's running mate in 1944, ended any chance of that by denouncing the veto, resigning his post, then being re-elected to it unanimously.

Then, for the first time in history, the Congress overrode the veto of a revenue bill. FDR's once-powerful grip on Congress had slipped dangerously.]

[Hyde Park]

⁓ *Feb. 23. Wednesday.* Warm & like Spring. But our road to the police corner was so slippery that I had two *bad* skids & several smaller ones, and I *barely* got up the Sand Hill — (no sand on it!). The M.P.s had their white cartridge belts on — a sure sign of the P.'s presence.

He arrived at 9 o'clock, & came over to the Library at about 11.30. The back of the head is almost healed up, & won't show at all, when the scab is off & the hair has grown. He looks well, but is tired as usual . . . All sorts of things happened in connection with the veto of the tax measure . . . I told him that looking at the political game in Washington, even into the White House, I can see F.D.R. surrounded by a ring of children who all want his constant attention & get mad if he sees more of one than the other, when they *should* be acting like *men* and helping him. Most of them are primadonnas. *He* is supposed to be always calm & collected & agreeable, no matter what every one else does —

⁓ *Feb. 24th Thursday.* . . . After tea we took some books to the Top Cottage [and] stayed there for a while, talking, the setting sun streaming in through the wide door onto the porch. The living-room looks so attractive — The P.'s things getting gradually arranged as he likes them best.

The P. is tired, as I have said before. He acknowledges it, & wants to get out of his gruelling job, but there is too much demand for him to stay in, not only from this country, but also from all the United Nations — If one could look into the future!

⁓ *Feb. 25th Friday.* . . . He came for me & Fala at 3.15 & drove down into the woods next to the Rogers place, stopping several times to look at different stands of trees. The roads are terribly muddy, a regular April thaw, & we almost slipped off into the woods down near the dock crossing! A half dozen SS pushed the car forward & back into the rut — It was quite exciting & the P. felt very hot when it was over. The three escorting cars prudently stayed behind & the P. [teased] them, saying they were a bunch of cowards . . .

The P. said to me, yesterday, that this flare-up in Congress by Barkley might easily have an effect on the election & might make a condition which would cause him to refuse to run, if there were a split in the party — Senator Barkley has written a too-sweet letter to the

President! [Roosevelt and Barkley had exchanged public letters, declaring their admiration for each other even as they differed over the tax bill.]

[The White House]

•◦• *March 2nd Thursday.* . . . When I came in after my lunch, the big dining room was full of ladies at small tables. I asked Maze [Maisie Washington, a White House maid] what was going on. "Just Mrs. Roosevelt entertaining a few friends, Miss Suckley." There were 60 at lunch . . .

The P. had had a tooth out, at 5.15, & felt rather miserable [at dinner]. I sat next to Mrs. [Frederick H.] Osborne [born Margaret Schiefflin and married to Brigadier General Osborne of Garrison, New York, head of the USO] who is awfully nice & regular "Hudson River." We talked the first half of the meal, until she turned to the P. After that I talked about the coloured problem in our public schools with Anna, on my right . . .

The P. felt feverish & generally miserable & lay on the sofa. Anna & I put pillows behind him & a light cover over him. Then we took his temperature: 100½. Called the doctor, who said to give him 2 aspirins & soda — that it was just a reaction from the tooth pulling.

The P. wanted to be read to. I got out Kipling's "The Butterfly that Stamped" & read to him in my singsong way, which is guaranteed to put anyone to sleep — I thought he *was* asleep, but he would invariably laugh at the funny parts — We all decided he should go to bed. Caesar came & wheeled him off to his room. A half hour later, Anna & I were called in, to find him cheerful & much better, & the fever down to 100 & presumably on its way back to normal — It was 10.30 by then & we left him . . .

•◦• *March 3 Friday.* . . . At 20 to 8, [Harry Hooker], Mrs. Kermit R. [widow of Theodore Roosevelt's troubled second son and a frequent guest at the White House despite the enmity between the two branches of the Roosevelt family], Dr. & Mrs. [Endicott] Peabody [founder and rector of Groton School and a powerful influence on his former pupil] & I joined the P. and Mrs. R. in the P.'s study, for cocktails (and Fala's supper) — Then we guests were ushered downstairs & into the Blue Room where we were announced to the Cabinet & their wives, who stood in a circle around the room in the order prescribed by the august master "Protocol."

. . . It was a very nice, informal dinner of about 40. It really *was* informal, with everyone knowing everyone else and under no strain.

The P. said a few words about the long association of some of the Cabinet members & proposed a toast to those no longer "with us." V.P. Wallace then said a few words ending with a toast to *another* Cabinet dinner, *next year*. I drank it, but didn't wish it for the P.

Mrs. R. then stood up & explained that we were going downstairs for a "double-feature" program. First, 4 army musicians giving an example of the kind of entertainment they give the soldiers in the hospitals. There was classical music on the violin & piano, singing by [convalescent soldiers from Walter Reed Hospital] and then a vulgar comic!

The second part of the program was a war movie, showing landings on beaches, etc. Harrowing, but, I suppose, necessary, so that people may know what we are doing, & why we are doing it.

After the movie, the Peabodys, & the rest of us houseguests were asked to the P.'s study for ginger ale, etc. I like Mrs. Kermit so much. She has great charm & sweetness, & is retiring & shy, so we get along very well, upholding each other in the background of this public life to which I certainly don't belong!

Old Dr. Peabody is a *lovely* person. You feel his spirituality. He calls the P. "my boy," and I noticed a look of real & deep happiness in the P.'s face, when talking to him, which he rarely has. It is a look which shows a state of mind completely devoid of anything but affection & trust & respect & a mutual understanding.

March 4 — Saturday. Not much work this morning! At 10.15, we assembled in the East Room for the annual service. Four clergy, including Dr. Peabody . . . His strong *young* voice is remarkable in such an old man . . .

After the service, Mrs. R. & "Tommy" started off on their journey through the Caribbean, by plane. The P., Harry, & Anna went to the airport to see her off — [Mrs. Roosevelt] loves travelling by air which is a blessing — Tommy feels ill most of the time, poor thing, but is gradually getting broken in to it. She ought to be, by this time!

Anna said her mother was worried by the letters she gets criticizing her for taking these trips. She is doing it for the P., however, & her only worry is whether the criticisms will reflect on him. Where it concerns something she is doing because she thinks it right, she doesn't mind the criticism. I think she is a very *great* person, and that her greatness springs in a large measure from the depth of her love for him.

As far as I can see, she is lacking in only one thing, & that is the ability to *relax & "play" with him.* I have probably written this down before; but it seems so to me, more & more . . .

❧ *March 6 Monday.* Harry Hooker went off at 9.30. One thinks of him as an "old thing," though he is about the P.'s age. He has a fatherly attitude, & always kisses me on the forehead, coming & going, which amuses me when I think about it, as I rarely kiss even the P. unless he has been away a long time. So *many* people kiss the P. that I subconsciously feel it means more *not* to kiss him!

. . . I had lunch at the "Trois Mousquetaires" with Frances Watson [wife of the President's military aide and appointment secretary]. I like her *so* much. She is amusing and kind and independent and a cultivated "lady." She & I discussed the President from start to finish. I told her about my attempts to have him take minerals & in general let Miss Gassette advise him. I am preparing the Gassette letters to be shown to Dr. McIntire in the hope of enlisting him in the crusade. I can see that the P., as long as he is the P., cannot take all sorts of medicines & advice from me or anyone else, without letting his doctor know about it, for his doctor is responsible for his health —

I brought F.W. back to the W.H. with me & we moved the furniture in the blue room. The sofa used to be against the wall, with no light near it. We put it to the right of the fireplace, with its head backed up to the desk so that the desk lamp can be used when one lies on the sofa — It works beautifully. The wing chair & small upholstered chair stand against the left wall with a round table between them, with books and roses on it. It is a great improvement. I asked Anna to come & look at it — She approved —

F.W. & I bought a jar of pure honey & a small supply of Bicarbonate of Potassium as a beginning for F.D.R.'s cure of sinus . . .

❧ *March 7 Tuesday.* . . . We had another quiet evening, beginning with a swim by the P. He walked in the water about 20 ft., & swam a little. Anna went in, too. He is calm & happy & cheerful with her here. She thinks about doing things that are good for him, and she doesn't irritate him. She has tact & humor . . .

He has started taking the lemon & potassium before breakfast! I know it will do him good —

❧ *March 8 Wednesday.* . . . Another quiet evening of work & yawns on the part of F.D.R. I don't know that I have ever seen him so consistently cheerful & peaceful as this week — I give all credit to Anna — for it is all in spite of political bickerings and this horrible war —

❧ *March 9th Thursday.* . . . At two I suggested he sleep for 10 minutes in his chair. In about one minute he was sound asleep, sitting in his chair, his head a little forward, his elbows on the arms of the chair, his hands clasped together. I hardly dared breathe, for fear of waking him! I could hear people talking: GGT dictating to DB., [Secret Service men] in the hall, voices in Gen. Watson's room. They must have wondered at the sudden complete silence in the P.'s office!

At exactly 2.10 he opened his eyes & looked up smiling & rested — I put on my coat & left through the door to the hall — Charlie Fredericks, a coloured butler, & S.S. all waiting for the P.'s bell. They are all the nicest men & so polite & smiling. I go down the hall greeting each in turn. I feel an obligation to do so, because they told the P. long ago that they liked Miss Suckley because she was polite to them & spoke to them, whereas most other people don't seem to see them. Back to work, with the realization that I wouldn't see the P. again until tomorrow morning, a horrid thought! . . .

❧ *March 10th Friday.* At lunch yesterday, I asked one of my rare questions on the political situation — The P. said that without any question, if [the election] were tomorrow he would be beaten — by almost any Republican.

. . . Anna came in to the P.'s study, where we had a long talk about her childhood, her children, and her father. She is a wonderful person; sympathetic, understanding, very intelligent, and full of fun. We discussed all angles of this year's election and F.D.R.'s part in it. She said that the family make a point of never mentioning the subject; that he himself cannot possibly say anything, though he has to do a lot of thinking about it, for if the Dem. Nat. Convention decide to nominate him, he must know what he will say & do — The "prophecies" all say he will retire *somewhat* from public affairs this year, because of poor health — whatever *that* may be worth!

❧ *March 20 Monday.* . . . Raining in Washington, on top of some snow. Found the P. in bed again, with a slight fever coming & going. He needs a complete rest, and a complete cleaning out of his whole system, *I* think! He eats too much, & too rich, food. He eats the *wrong* food, to begin with . . .

Afterward, Anna & John came in for a while & said goodnight, at about 9. He then got ready for the night, which means massage, etc. Then sent for me & I took his temperature (99), gave him some tablets prescribed by the Doctor, read to him (in my singsong voice) "The Elephant Child" by Kipling, until he began to relax, & then put out the light & left him.

[That evening, Daisy began a long letter to Anna, who had left town for a few days with her husband. It was now clear to her — and to Daisy — that something was seriously wrong with her father. He had not bounced back from the illness he'd suffered in December, was losing weight, could not seem to shake his weariness. She first confided her concerns to her mother, who dismissed them outright: she simply wasn't "interested in physiology," Anna remembered; illness could always be conquered by will and determination; her husband was merely tired and anxious about Elliott's turbulent private life.

When she got back to the White House, Anna planned to see Admiral McIntire and insist that her father be thoroughly examined, that other physicians be consulted if necessary. Daisy was delighted — and determined that the potions provided by her friend Mlle. Gassette be part of a new regimen.]

Dear Anna —

You are *very* much missed, as you probably don't need to be told! We spent a quiet evening after you left, your "Pa" doing stamps and sneezing and blowing. I spoke of massage, and did a little on his shoulders and spine, and he said several times that he *loved* it & could feel it right through him & that it made him feel much better — I said he should he have it every day — He said he hadn't the time — I said it took *far more* time getting sick all the time, & feeling miserable.

He couldn't deny that, so possibly that argument could be eliminated. If someone already in the house could do it, there wouldn't be the feeling that a masseuse was standing around waiting, etc! That sort of rubbing on the back requires only two fairly strong palms, and if done for 15–30 minutes stirs up the whole circulation. I've done a certain amount of this sort of thing off and on, as a nurse's aide in the last war in the New York Debarkation Hospital, and since then on various aunts & friends, and I know it helps . . .

It occurs to me that if the doctor would agree to the taking of the minerals, no better time could be found than when he is on the fishing trip. The preliminary clearing out of the sinus cavities, when the symptoms are less severe (as they are when he's away from Washington), would be easier and more effective. Arthur [Prettyman] or Caesar could be told to put the glass of water with the salts at the

President's side, at breakfast time, & just remind him to empty the glass by the time he gets up — .

. . . The *diet* is terribly important. A wrong diet is continually putting "mucus" (poison) into the system. The minerals will start to eliminate the poison but there is a lot of *old* poison to be removed besides all the new which gets put in every day . . .

∾ *Thursday March 23rd.* . . . 6 P.M. — The P. has just gone down for his nose treatment. He has felt miserable all day, with a bad headache, though he *looks* better than yesterday — He got up about 4.30, sat in the study & insisted on going through some boxes — He had already worked for an hour with GGT. He finds it very hard to relax, unless he just falls asleep, sometimes, sitting bolt upright. His head is congested & he has aches & pains. I am convinced it is a sort of general acid poisoning. I am also convinced that Miss G[assette] could put her finger on the trouble in a moment or two —

[Letter from Daisy to Anna continues]

Your father has had a very miserable day, with a constant head-ache from 10 o'clock until about 6.30. In spite of it he actually looks better than yesterday. This evening he has felt much better & I have just left him. He fears he will have a hard time breathing with his nose & his throat both stopped up. The doctor says the tests show he has uric acid. I don't know what the treatment is for that. If you would care to find out just what they have discerned from the tests, and will write me, I will write for Miss G's recommendations. I would write as for an entirely different person . . .

∾ *Friday, March 24.* . . . I found the P. back in bed — but he soon got up again & went down for his nose treatment. He had a slight fever again & he worries about it, but neither he nor the Dr. seems to know how to get down to the first principle. *I* would get on oranges, lemons & grapefruit & *nothing* else for several days, until the fever, the congestion & the headaches had all vanished, then start eating again, but *not* the usual diet . . .

[Letter from Daisy to Anna continues]

The P. is really better today, though tired. I got these two little bottles of Ferrum Phos. & Mag. Phos for *pain & congestion* to be used instead of aspirin. I am thinking that if they could be put up into capsules according to Miss G's formula, they would be easier for the P. to take.

IF, IF, IF, the Doctor . . .!! Forgive this talk-talk-talk — but anything to help your "Pa." Quite apart from relatives & friends, the whole world needs him.

I wish you & John were coming to Hyde Park, too . . .

〜 *March 25th, Saturday, Hyde Park.* Lovely mild weather just made for the P. Mrs. [Lucy Mercer] Rutherfurd is coming up to see him from New York tomorrow, and he hopes to show her around the place, the Library, his cottage etc., so he took things easy — had a good nap before lunch, & after lunch sat in a deck chair in the sun.

He was furious at himself — "I've never done such a thing in my life before — Robert Louis Stevenson in the last stages of consumption . . ." and so on! But he sat there, reading the London *Daily News.* I left him with GGT sitting with him . . .

[Roosevelt's contacts with Lucy Mercer Rutherfurd over the years are difficult to trace. They corresponded from time to time during FDR's first years as President, and when her young nephew died of leukemia he quietly saw to it that the boy was buried in Arlington National Cemetery, where his mother wanted him to lie. He also made it possible for Mrs. Rutherfurd to attend all four of his inaugurations, staying out of Mrs. Roosevelt's sight. She seems first to have visited FDR at the White House in August of 1941 — under a pseudonym, "Mrs. Paul Johnson" — shortly after the first of the series of strokes that incapacitated her elderly husband, Winthrop Rutherfurd, and she returned to the White House several times after that, always when Mrs. Roosevelt was out of town. The women at the White House switchboard and the President's secretaries had standing orders to put her through to FDR right away, and he often spoke to her in French so that no one in the office would understand.

The visit on March 26 was her first to Hyde Park, however, and Daisy's diary is the only known record of it. Her husband had died, after years of illness, just six days earlier, at the age of eighty-two. She was just fifty-two and distressed that FDR, whom she had never stopped loving, seemed to be slipping away, too.

She visited Washington fairly often thereafter, her niece Lucy Mercer Marbury Blundon remembered, staying a night or two at a time with her older sister, Violetta Marbury, at 2238 Q Street. Whenever she came, Mrs. Blundon recalled, two White House cars would pull up quietly out front and wait, motors running, while a Secret Service man came to her mother's door and asked for her aunt. Mrs. Rutherfurd would then hurry out and get into the back seat of the President's car, and the two would go off for a quiet drive through Rock Creek Park. It happened often enough, said Mrs. Blundon, that she came to think very little about the President's visits, even though she had been told never to tell anyone about them.]

☙ *March 26th Sunday* 9.30 P.M. The P. called up to report on his day. He had Mrs. Rutherfurd for lunch, showed her the Library, then to the cottage & she didn't get away until about 6.30. At 7 o'clock dinner, the P. felt fever coming on & went to bed — It was up over 100 but George Fox had come up & dosed him & he thought it was going down already — His voice sounded very "stuffed up."

He has decided to go back to Wash. in the morning. They will be experimenting on him again, at the Naval Hospital — Medicines, treatments, X-rays etc. & they do nothing about the diet or fundamentals. Anna is going to do something, however. [In fact, Anna had already done something. She had finally confronted Admiral McIntire, insisting that her father be given a thorough checkup. McIntire was annoyed at what he considered her interference, but reluctantly agreed.]

☙ *March 27th Monday.* I went over to the house at 9, to say good-bye to the P. His fever was down & he had cereal & milk for breakfast, and orange juice. He left at 25 minutes of 11. He is prepared to go to the hospital tomorrow & be X-rayed etc. I pray they do the right thing by him.

[At Bethesda Naval Hospital, the young chief of cardiology, Lieutenant Commander Howard G. Bruenn, examined the President and was horrified by what he found. FDR was suffering from congestive heart failure. His heart was dangerously enlarged, he was short of breath, and he exhibited dangerous hypertension for which there was then no specific medication. Bruenn urged a strict diet, digitalization to strengthen the heart, and a sharply curtailed schedule.

When Bruenn reported his findings to McIntire the following day, the admiral scoffed at him: "The President can't take time off to go to bed. You can't simply say to him, 'Do this or do that.' This is the President of the United States!" Bruenn persisted, demanding that a team of consultants be called in.]

☙ *March 28th Tuesday.* The P. called up to report on the Doctor's examinations of the morning. He said they took X-rays & all sorts of tests, found nothing drastically wrong, but one sinus clogged up. But they are going to put him on a strict diet, a good beginning. I begged him to get back on his lemon juice in hot water before breakfast. He said he might. The Dr. said last week that he has uric acid.

[That same day, at Bethesda Hospital, Ensign E. E. Ozburn also completed his analysis of the thirteen bottles of Mlle. Gassette's homeopathic powders. All of them were harmless, he reported, but also medically worthless, containing only trace amounts of minerals.

On March 31, three senior physicians — Dr. John Harper, Dr. Bruenn's commanding officer at Bethesda, Dr. Frank Lahey of Boston, and Dr. James Paullin of Atlanta — examined the President at Dr. Bruenn's request. After much debate — "My diagnosis was a bombshell," Bruenn remembered. "We were in the middle of a war" — they backed his findings. There was then no specific drug to lower blood pressure, but they called for low doses of digitalis, a low-calorie diet, dining alone rather than with wearying guests, ten rather than twenty cigarettes a day, and only a drink and a half at cocktail time.

FDR agreed to follow all their recommendations. Dr. Bruenn was forbidden by McIntire to volunteer any information to the President about his condition, and Roosevelt never asked for any. Had he done so, Bruenn said nearly fifty years later, he would have told him the truth, but if anyone at the time had ever asked him whether Roosevelt should run for a fourth term, he believed he would have reluctantly said yes, because, "for better or worse, the war was being run by just three men and it was not over yet." But no one asked him that, either.

Whether McIntire ever confided to FDR how ill he really was remains a mystery, though it seems clear from several of his subsequent conversations with Daisy that he was aware there was trouble with his heart.]

⌀ *April 2nd Sunday*. I've been worried about the P. all this week, with no news. Anna wrote me on Thursday, just before starting for Seattle & her children's Easter vacation. She is worried about him, but feels the doctors are on the right track. The P. is on a strict diet which bores him intensely — good eating is one of the few pleasures he has in his arduous life, & he now has to give that up.

Last evening, I got "desperate" & called up the W.H. at 7.45. I figured that he might be having supper in bed & could talk on the telephone, or, if "up," and sitting at table with guests, he would send word that he "would call later."

When the W.H. operator said, "The President will call you back,

Miss Suckley," I could just *see* Mr. Searles or Mr. Claunch handing him a slip of white paper with "Miss Suckley on the phone" — the P. glancing at it & saying, "I'll call later"!

So it happened — but he had eight people there until 10.30, when he thought it was too late to telephone me; I'd be in bed —

Today, still hearing nothing, I called Polly [Laura] Delano & suggested she call him up & then let me know the result. She, too, felt the doctors are definitely going to "do something" about it, after having a fine talk with the P. himself.

A half hour later he called me up. Said he felt about "the same," is on a diet — had just had scrambled eggs & rice & milk, for supper — "not so bad." The head dietician at the Naval Hospital is arranging about his food & will probably decide on menus for his entire trip south. He *expects* to get off on Tuesday, but may wait another 24 hrs. for the bronchial tubes to clear up.

He said he really had pneumonia. I can't understand how the Dr. can let him do the things he does — like last Sunday, for instance, spending the afternoon in his open car & in the cottage which was chilly. That is where a member of the family *should be with him* all the time, to watch over him . . .

❧ *April 4th Tuesday.* . . . The P. called up around a quarter to 12. They won't let him go on his trip until they have had a consultation with two doctors from Boston and [Atlanta]. They can't come until later this week — I'm worried, for there must be something definitely wrong. [Doctors Lahey and Paullin were scheduled to return to examine the President again and reassess his dosage of digitalis.]

The P. sounds as though he were depressed & worried, too, though he *said* he was merely "bored" with the whole thing. The dietician evidently is not prepossessing! He wants to get rid of her, thinks he can do better himself, & is seriously thinking of having a gun brought to him, so he can simply shoot all the disagreeable people who keep coming back all the time!! He is on a "calorie" diet, which I have never understood, for the word means "heat," and most of our illnesses have nothing whatever to do with "heat" and energy — However — !

He has 3 fruit juices for breakfast, beside his eggs, etc. I suggested he ask if he couldn't take them separately at two hour intervals — All that liquid in his stomach & then eggs on top of it doesn't sound sensible.

He gets up at about noon, goes to his desk in the study for lunch, works with GGT, goes back to bed at 6. He feels so *tired*, all the time. That is not strange, considering that he has walking pneumonia.

❧ *April 6th*. The P. called up last night. He sounds depressed & bored, says he has "sleeping-sickness of some sort." He sleeps 10 hours at night, with interruptions, and after lunch he sleeps another 1½ hrs. Gets "up" around noon, goes back to bed about 6 P.M. but apparently has people in his room most of the evening.

I am avidly reading the *Modern Home Physician*, edited by Victor Robinson! It is full of intensely interesting information, given from a broad unbiased standpoint. Of course, different [doctors] disagree, but this book usually gives both general opinions, and is expressed in simple terms so that one understands what is meant.

The P. expects to leave on Saturday for Bernard Baruch's place near Charleston S.C. to be there two weeks. [A Wall Street speculator and informal economic adviser to several presidents, Baruch had offered the comfort and privacy of Hobcaw, his vast South Carolina plantation, to help restore the President's health.]

I happened to mention sometime back that Grace Dudley [an old friend of Daisy's and the granddaughter of President Charles W. Eliot of Harvard] is at Delray, Fla. & I hoped to visit her someday! He remembered this, & suggested on the phone that I could take some annual leave at this time, visit Grace, join him at the Baruchs' so that I might see the beautiful place, and return to Washington on his train. I am "thinking about it" very seriously, in spite of train travel difficulties etc. It may be the only chance I will ever have to go to Florida!

❧ *April 8th Saturday*. . . . The P. called up at 9 P.M. to say goodbye. He was more cheerful, & full of confidence. He said he had had *good day* all around. The Drs. have found his "charts" improved, his general condition better, they want him to stay 3–4 weeks at [Bernard Baruch's] to *rest*.

[The physicians found the President's enlarged heart had shrunk in size, thanks to the digitalis; his coughing had stopped, and he was sleeping much better than he had been. His blood pressure had also fallen a little, probably, Bruenn recalled, because Admiral McIntire had finally stopped treating the President's sinuses nightly with a spray that contained adrenaline and so had elevated it.]

So my plans are now in abeyance, until he lets me know definitely what *he* is doing. Besides: no word yet, from Grace.

I am more worried than I let anyone know, about him, for there *must* be something definitely wrong, or they wouldn't have these consultations. He had that very bad trouble two years ago, with the white corpuscles. I pray it isn't a bad type of disease.

[The "very bad trouble" was a bout with bleeding hemorrhoids in May of 1941 that had been treated with sulfa drugs and iron rather than surgery and left Roosevelt so anemic for a time that he required two transfusions. The memory of it would haunt Daisy over the next twelve months, though she had the details wrong: it was Roosevelt's hemoglobin count, not his white blood count, that had then fallen dangerously low.]

∾ *April 14th Friday*. Everything happens at once! A long telegram from "Fox" [a code name for someone in the White House travel office] via the Security Bldg., telling me what trains to take & all plans, dates, etc. for my trip to Delray Beach, & then back to Wash. via a day spent at "somewhere" near North Charleston which, being interpreted, means that F.D.R. is having all arrangements for a berth, from point to point, made for me through the White House, and the "somewhere" is Bernard Baruch's place. The fly in the ointment is that he expects to spend an extra week down there, so that I would not be able to come back on his train, & that would mean that much extra expense which I *should* not afford, though I might be able to squeeze it out & leave my bank account with near-zero!

With all this in mind I went over to the Security Blg. & got Mr. [Edward] Fauver [Office of Telegraph, Telephones, and Travel] on the phone. He sent a telegram asking if I can postpone my trip until the following week. This was 12 noon. At 4 P.M. he called up with the answer just received: "Any day will do except the 27th & 28th when I may have visitors from the Antipodes." This *probably* means that Churchill is to be there. I am intrigued to know!

∾ *April 15th Saturday*. . . . Mr. Fauver called up this morning. He has the accommodation on the "East Coast Champion," Atlantic Coast Line, leaving Wash. at 7.40 P.M. April 24th, and arriving the following day, at Delray, at 5.22 P.M. He asked about return accommodations, but I said I couldn't tell him the dates. Instructions would come to him "from the other end." We agreed it is difficult to make definite arrangements when one can't even talk freely & clearly on the phone! (I am writing the P. re all this.)

He is mailing the tickets, registered, to me, at Rhinebeck.

~ *April 22nd Saturday.* . . . At about 4.15, Mr. Fauver called me up with a message from the P. — a telegram or teletype from Charleston to the W.H. As well as I can remember, it said: "Plans for Florida fine. I will write to you there. I am definitely better." No signature. I feel much relieved . . . [Daisy made her way to Delray and waited for word from FDR.]

~ *April 27 Thursday.* . . . When we came back to the house, a message on a piece of paper under a stone by the front door for me, directed me to call operator 3, Delray Beach — *Important!* So back into town we drove, found the telephone office closed, so went into Mrs. Cromer's boarding house. No one in sight, but the telephone is near the front door & Grace knows Mrs. Cromer. It took ½ hour to get a free circuit through.

Mr. [Guy] Spaman [Secret Service agent] talked in a most casual friendly manner: "How are you Miss Suckley . . . the boss wanted me to ask if you got there safely & if everything is all right . . . the boss suggests that it would be nice if you could come here for a couple of days before he returns to Washington and go back on the train with him . . . He is feeling much better . . ."

So — I am taking the 9.11 next Wednesday night, arriving N. Charleston 9.30 the next morning & will spend two days at Bernard Baruch's house! It is unbelievable again — quiet, say nothing, Daisy Suckley!

~ *May 1st Monday.* . . . About 9 P.M. a car drove up to give me a message that I am to call up the No. 3 operator again! in the morning!

~ *May 2nd Tuesday.* . . . On the radio yesterday, we heard that Mrs. F.D.R. told her press conference in the morning that she had seen the P. last week, that he looked very well, but that he might be staying away for another week "to complete his cure." We wondered how that would affect my plans — until the message came last night —

I'll now get dressed & we will drive in to Delray Beach & put through the call — for *new* plans! I had almost hoped I would be asked to stay on at the Baruchs' for extra days until the P. returns back to Wash.! But that would be expecting too much!

Later — the call went right through — Mr. Spaman wanted to know if I had my ticket & reservation etc. — That I am expected Thursday morning at N. Charleston — The "boss" evidently hearing the radio reports wanted me to know that this part of *my* plans are *not* changed! What next? . . .

∽ *May 4th Thursday.* . . . My berth was comfortable, but I hardly slept at all — The train seemed to run on a rough track and to stop with violence — However, I got through the night, got out my picnic breakfast of a raw tomato & some sandwiches — I ate the first, of delicious "green cheese" & half the second, of some salty little fish. *Much* too heavy for breakfast & I felt sick all day as a result.

The train was $1\frac{1}{2}$ hrs. late at N. Charleston. On the platform were George Fox, Dewey Long [in charge of White House travel arrangements] & an SS called [Steve] Lloyd, I think — I know all three & felt quite important! We got into the small SS car & drove the 60 miles to Mr. Baruch's place, most of the way on the straight uninteresting highway which goes down to Florida.

At Georgetown S.C. we turned off onto a local road for a few miles, then through a gate, guarded by marines, into the Baruch plantation, then five miles on a sandy road to the "park" gate. This part of the place around the house is completely enclosed by . . . wire & gives Fala a perfect place to wander at will. We drove up to a very attractive brick house, modern & fireproof, but in plantation style with the high 2 story pillars over the porch. It seemed almost natural to come into the place, for all the President's people, whom I know so well, were around — The S.S., the Admirals, Pa Watson, etc. — even the Potomac mess crew of Filipinos. The only strange faces were Mr. Baruch himself, and his daughter, & Dr. Bruenn of the Naval Hospital.

I was taken through the phalanx into the living-room, to the P. I am *so* glad to see him, but, under his tan, he looks thin & drawn & not a bit well. He is on a strict diet, feels good-for-nothing, has just had some sort of an "attack" which seems to be in the upper part of the abdomen. He says they don't know what is the matter with him — I wonder if perhaps they don't want to tell him — [When he returned to Washington, it was found that he had developed gallstones.]

He gave me the two bits of letters he wrote but didn't get around to signing or finishing or sending.

[FDR to Daisy, unsent, incomplete, and written in an alarmingly shaky hand]

Tuesday —
A lovely place — plantation for a King — big house about 8 miles from the station — Bernie, Ross [McIntire], Pa, Bill, Leahy, & I — and my mess men from the Potomac — We are up the river about 10 miles from the sea — lovely trees — a modern fire-proof house —

I am really feeling "no good" — don't want to do anything & want to sleep all the time.

I love your letter — keep sending —

Tuesday [sic]
I'm too sorry about Maude [Stoutenburgh] Elliot — She was really a grand person & I wish her husband had been, too! Remind me to tell you about the "Pines" [probably a Stoutenburgh property in Hyde Park].

I forgot to tell you that Dr. Bruin [sic] came down, too — He is one of the best heart men — Tho' my own is definitely better — does queer things still —

I wish so you were here.

[Daisy's diary continues]

. . . Mr. Baruch is a tall slender, grey haired, attractive man, in his 70s, an awfully kind — sympathetic manner. (Also a certain *reputation* for fondness for the ladies!) His daughter, Belle, tall & dressed in riding habits, is strong & healthy, lives down here all the year, is planting peanuts this P.M., runs the plantation & is gradually taking over pieces of the land from her father. She is a little awkward in manner, from shyness, but very nice.

. . . I spent a couple of hours lying down & getting my things out, then put on my best brown & white silk dress, & joined the P. on the porch until just before dinner — It was lovely sitting there in the half shade of the big trees with the grey moss and the river beyond, bright & calm in the sunlight —

The dear P. — always so thoughtful for others — I hate to see him tired, & having to make a constant effort at conversation. At dinner, Pa Watson was at once the talker, the clown & goat — Everyone teasing him about the Belgian baroness . . . whom the P. calls the Spy — about the hair tonic that puts hair on bald heads — about the medicine against sea-sickness, etc.

Everyone conspires to keep the atmosphere light, for the P. I feel, however, that it is as much of an effort for him to keep up this sort of talk as to discuss what really is interesting & vital to him. We sat at the table for two hours, then, into the living-room. The P. talked to the doctor, Adm. Leahy & me for a little while, then went off to bed — I went upstairs to my room, with the good excuse of not having slept on the train — The others settled down to gin-rummy — I heard them all going to bed at 10.30. One couldn't imagine a more quiet orderly household.

A *wonderful* bed!

↭ *May 5th Friday.* . . . Downstairs at 10, I went in to say good morning to the P. He had had a good night & looked better & had his papers all over the bed, to read before getting dressed. I tried sitting on the porch but the mosquitoes were a bother, so I retired to a corner of the living-room & wrote . . . letters to go by air in the P.M. to be mailed from Wash. The others in the household came & went, we talked a little & then I'd go back to my writing.

Dr. Bruenn came along & I talked about the P. He relieved me by saying the P.'s blood is all right — I had feared the trouble he had two years ago — From a later talk with the P. the trouble is evidently with the heart — the diastole & systole are not working properly in unison — but there is definite improvement. [It seems clear from this and the above unfinished note to Daisy that someone, probably McIntire, had told Roosevelt at least something of his condition.]

Mr. Baruch's little trained nurse [companion, and social secretary], Miss [Blanche] Higgins, seems to be an awfully nice little person. She walked about the place with me showing me the playhouse, the stables, the garage, the guest houses, the coloured quarters, etc. It is lovely under very beautiful live-oaks, the sun shining through the grey moss . . . Fala and Patsy the spaniel joined us half way 'round. After a while the P. came out onto the porch, then Lt. [William G.] Rigdon [traveling secretary and stenographer] appeared with a few papers to be signed. At one we all went in to lunch, the P. eating a mouthful of something — It looked like minced chicken on toast.

After lunch Mr. Baruch & Dr. Bruenn left by plane for Wash. (with the mail pouch). I had a good talk with the P. about himself — He said he discovered that the doctors had not agreed together about what to tell him, so that he found out that they were not telling *him* the *whole* truth & that he was evidently more sick than they said! It is foolish of them to attempt to put anything over on *him!*

From 3.15 to 4 he took a nap, then we all got into the open SS car . . . the P. in front next to Monty [Snyder], Adm. Leahy & I in the back. Pa Watson & Adm. McIntire in another SS car, & off we went for a beautiful drive to the beach on the other side of the peninsula. The long-leaf pine are beautiful — very tall & straight — 16,000 acres of them on this one plantation. When we came to the mounted coast guard headquarters, we transferred into four jeeps and paraded along the sand a mile or two, a beautiful sea on our left, sand dunes on our right.

Monty saw a crab vanish into a hole, so we stopped & the entire party including the SS watched Monty digging & digging until the poor frightened animal was finally dug out and examined, its eyes popping up like two little periscopes — He scurried back as soon as released. We turned around & drove back to where we came on the beach & sat on the sand for a half hour behind a glass screen made by the coast guard for the P. They had a comfortable cushioned chair for him, but I like the sand best! It was perfect sitting there, the late afternoon sun behind us, a fresh breeze "blowing the cobwebs out of our brains" . . .

~ *May 9th Tuesday*. . . . Belle Baruch talked steadily to the President mainly about her life abroad with her horses — She & her father are evidently very close; she refers to him constantly —

It is interesting to get a view of him [Baruch] in this setting — He is, I might say, *notorious* for his succession of affairs with women. On the other hand, he is the soul of kindness and generosity, is constantly helping people, supplies a nurse & a clinic for the negroes on his plantation; there are a church & school he supports also; he hates his daughter to put on any make up — wants her to dress in attractive feminine clothes, behave in the most exemplary way, etc.

I often think of Roly Hambley's remark that she finds that among the typists & stenographers she works with, the ones who are kind, & generous, & loyal, & help you out of a tight place, usually turn out to be some important man's mistress! One doesn't quite know how to answer. I suppose the truth is that so many "good" people are also narrow & without understanding & charity toward others — It would be a good thing if the two types could learn from each other what is good in each . . .

We returned to the main house for the P.'s rest, had early supper at 6.30 & boarded the train [back to Washington] about 7.30, on a quiet road crossing near Georgetown. People stood at corners to wave

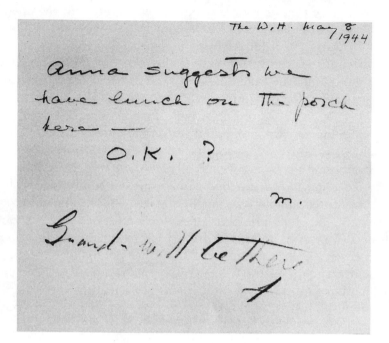

The W.H. May 8/1944

Anna suggests we
have lunch on the porch
here —

O.K. ?

m.

Lunch will be there

to the P. — The little elevator on the rear platform very slowly &
deliberately lifted the P. up to the platform level, Charlie Fredericks
on it, too. They say they will "step it up."

Fala started up an aluminum set of steps, after me, slipped &
tumbled down, to be picked up & handed on board by Mike Reilly
— We started right off . . .

[The White House]

Sunday & Monday passed very quickly. Everyone wanted to greet the
P., see how he looked & felt. Anna & I held long talks about his
"routine," & how difficult it is going to be to keep him to it — On
Monday we had — or she had — the brilliant thought of suggesting
lunch on the porch — [See note above.]

    . . . [A]t one o'clock, Anna & I were ready for lunch —

    . . . [I]t wasn't until almost 1.30 that he came out into the hall
saying: "The trouble is that Margaret didn't allow any time for me to
dress, on the schedule."

"Well," I said, "you were supposed to dress when your last appointment left you at one."

"Between one & one?" says he.

We had a nice cool lunch on the porch — The lawn looking "as green as green" — The P. looked across at the Jefferson Memorial & decided to give instructions for trimming the trees back, in the vista.

. . . [A]round 6, found the P. still being massaged. Chairs were on the grass in the rose garden being arranged by Anna . . . The P. finally came out after 6.30, the sun just about to set behind the State Dept. He was there long enough to see how nice it was and how private, and to say he would try to do it every afternoon . . .

[Rhinebeck]

⌁ *May 11th Thursday.* The P. called up from Wash. Is feeling "all right" — has "kept the rules" pretty well — goes with Anna to Shangri-La this P.M. to return to the W.H. Sunday night — Hopes to arrive here at H.P. next Thursday morning, in time to see his dogwood in bloom at the Hill-top cottage . . .

⌁ *May 16th Tuesday.* . . . When I was at the W.H. last week, I asked the P. if he thought Stalin might perhaps come to see him nearer home the next time.

The P. said: "I think he may."

I asked on what he based the thought & he answered about in the following words: "When I first got to Teheran, Stalin came to call on me. Of course I did not get up when he came into the room. We shook hands, & he sat down, and I caught him looking curiously at my legs and ankles. Later, I entertained him at dinner, and was sitting at the table when he & the others came in. When Stalin was seated, on my right, he turned to the interpreter & said: 'Tell the President that I now understand what it has meant for him to make the effort to come on such a long journey — Tell him that the next time I will go to him.'"

The P. then said it would probably mean going to Alaska, or at least some point nearer the U.S. than the other side of the world! I suggested that Stalin might easily fly over the North Pole, straight to Washington, or to some point in Canada, & he agreed that was a possibility.

Stalin evidently had no idea that the P. couldn't walk.

F.D.R. can, if *anyone* can, bring to the surface any fineness & softness there may be in one who has chosen to call himself "Steel" . . .

❧ *May 18th Thursday.* . . . The P. called up last evening . . . He leaves Wash. tonight & plans, while here, to get his work done in the morning, so he can be free the rest of the day. I must try to get him out in the sunlight during the afternoon — Perhaps I can get him to work on his porch at Top Cottage —

❧ *May 19th Friday.* . . . About 11.30 A.M. the P. came, suggested we go to the Top Cottage, instead of his coming into the Library, to see the dogwood. We put a couple of chairs in the sun, north of the porch, & just talked, quietly, about the view, the dogwood, a little about the coming invasion in Europe. Next week is the time, the exact date depending on wind & weather & tide. If possible he hopes to stay 'til Wednesday night.

[Actually, the date of D-Day was not yet firm. In discussions with Stalin at Teheran, Roosevelt and Churchill had committed themselves to landing on or about May 1. Shortages and complications in the planning process pushed the date back to early June. Initially, June 5 was settled on, but when meteorologists warned of extremely foul weather on that date, General Eisenhower was forced to put it off until the sixth. Meanwhile, the Allied air forces were well along with plans to pound German coastal defenses and inland lines of communication so as to seal off the invasion areas — without giving them away. It is proof of FDR's extraordinary trust in Daisy's circumspection that he felt free to confide these momentous secrets to her.]

Wants me to go down with him — spend the next week-end at Shangri-La — depending, again, on the invasion. How that event hangs over us — has been hanging over us, for months, and here it is, almost at hand.

The P. seems pretty well, but not right yet — His schedule, up here, is good: Work with GGT from about 10 A.M. to 11.30 or 12. Come to the Library, or drive. Lunch at 1. Sleep until 3.30 — Drive, or sit in the sun, or whatever may come into his head, until dinner. To bed, early — Mrs. R. is here with him. They will go to the cottage this P.M. The sun will be shining in on the porch . . .

GGT is staying at the Nelson House [Poughkeepsie's best hotel, home to the press and some of the presidential staff whenever FDR was at Hyde Park] so that the P. can be *really* quiet & not tempted to even think of work.

᭯ *May 20th Saturday.* The P. was busy working with GGT until 12.15, so I walked over to the house, for lunch with him & Mrs. R. I love the P.'s "diet" — in fact I like it much better than the regular, more complicated meals!

. . . Mrs. R. is *so* fine, and so interesting. These are the first two days they have been alone together, for years. After lunch she went off to her cottage, the P. went upstairs for his rest & I retired to the Library. At 3.30 the P. came over & thought he would just sit in the car & have me bring out papers for him to go over — The day was *perfect.*

However, just before he came, Alice Dows [friend of FDR and one of Daisy's cousins] arrived with two Canadian boys: a Merchant Marine & an R.A.F. She asked if she could "just give him a hug" — I said I thought *two* hugs would be all right. So, when he arrived, I brought her through the P.'s room and out to the car. She told him about the two "boys" & he promptly suggested having them brought in. So I gathered them in from the main exhibition room, for a unique experience in their lives. They *will* have something to tell about their vacation on the Hudson!

᭯ *May 22 Monday.* Cloudy — but the P. has had three perfect days . . .

[He] looks worried and tired, and his color is not good — But he makes an effort to be natural & talks along & jokes — Little Fala stayed nearby & got a tidbit which he didn't seem to want at all.

After lunch, the 65th Street house rugs were unfolded in the hall, 3 of them picked out for Hilltop, most of them very good orientals, to be put in storage in the Library. The P. says Mrs. R. is wanting to clear everything out & he's afraid she'll be getting rid of things they will want later, when the children settle into homes of their own!

At about 2, the P. went off into the big library to take his rest on "Mama's sofa." I returned to the Library.

. . . At 5 we went to Hilltop with some books & pictures and I made some tea & he toasted some of the Mickleham bread — He loves it, and "the Missus" is ordering it for him.

I asked him if he had decided on a vice-president.

He said: "I haven't even decided if I will run myself."

"What is going to decide you? For you are practically nominated already."

"What will decide me, will be the way I feel in a couple of months.

If I know I am not going to be able to carry on for another four years, it wouldn't be fair to the American people to run for another term."

"But who else is there?"

"I *have* a candidate — but don't breathe it to a soul — there is a man, not a politician, who, I think, I could persuade the country to elect. There would be such a gasp when his name was suggested, that I believe he would have a good chance if he were 'sold' to the country in the right way!"

I did gasp a little when he mentioned the name of Henry J. Kaiser [the Pacific Coast shipbuilder whose skill at turning out Liberty ships for the Navy had so impressed the President — and Daisy — back in 1942]. As the P. says, it was a sudden thought on his part, but the more he thinks about it, the more he sees in it. Henry J. Kaiser has proved himself a genius in production. The P. thinks he can learn where he is ignorant & without experience, such as politics, dealing with Congress, International affairs, etc.

I asked *how* he would get on with the Churchills, Stalins, etc.

The P. said: "He's more like them than I am."

I said: "But your strength lies in the fact that those men *look up* to you. Just another man like themselves, will bring the whole International problem down a peg, to the usual materialism."

The P. didn't answer that. A little later he said he thought Mr. Kaiser would ask his teaching & guidance in dealing with other nations. Perhaps he is right — he usually is, and perhaps Mr. Kaiser is just the sort of dynamic person the country needs at the present time, *if* the P. does not feel up to going on with the job . . . [Roosevelt's enthusiasm for Henry Kaiser dimmed quickly when Sam Rosenman found evidence that he had once advocated a sales tax.]

∾ *May 23rd Tuesday.* Raining all day off & on — The P. came over to the L about 12.30 & worked in his room until 1.15. We went over quite a pile of things, the P. sitting on the yellow covered sofa, his feet on the new stand made down in the shop — They are now making a second one, hinged, which will be easier to carry around — He finds it so comfortable, that he will probably take it everywhere with him . . .

I suggested the new Persian rug from the Shah of Persia for his room at the Library & while he was resting, we all got to work at it . . . It took 10 yrs. to make this rug, & it is supposed to be worth $20,000. There are 50 knots to the square inch. It feels like velvet, has every possible colour & harmonizes with everything — It is really beautiful & perfect for this particular room . . .

↷ *May 24 — Wednesday*. . . . Went to Dr. Sheldon [a Poughkeepsie veterinarian] to see how the Fala–Button combination is working out — Both very anxious to come with me but Button was very flirtatious & after seeming to tell me she was glad to see me but was having a *lovely* time, she started her "pursuit" of Fala. Dr. S. says that evidently Fala has never mated & at his age, they often seem to not quite know what is expected of them. He said that Button was going to show him, if anyone could — We agreed that if the mating does not occur tomorrow he will do it artificially — this is evidently quite a usual thing & has no ill effects anywhere. The P. had no objection, & he *does* want Fala to have some descendants —

. . . A lot has been done these five days, in a quiet way, sorting rugs, deciding on changes & improvements etc. etc. in the main house. Mrs. R. would like to make more changes but I think the P. wants to keep things as his mother had them, as far as possible . . .

[The White House]

↷ *May 25th Thursday*. . . . The P. received Gen. Watson, Sam Rosenman, Mr. Hassett & had a good time holding forth to them for an hour. At about 11 he sent for me: "I've had a good conference & accomplished a lot: I did most of the talking." And then he laughed his hearty laugh, that comes from his head & heart . . .

The P. is to have his test at the Naval Hospital tomorrow A.M. for the gall-bladder, so after lunch Anna & I plied him with dye pills at 5-minute intervals, our three watches apparently working on different speeds, to judge by the arguments as to when the five-minute periods came along! . . .

At about 7.10 we all assembled in the P.'s room: Boettigers, Belle [Mrs. Kermit Roosevelt] & I — As Belle said later, that is the hour when the P. seems to relax. He casts off his heavy responsibilities, talks nonsense, teases etc. as he mixes cocktails. It sometimes stretches over to ¾ of an hour, but it does him good just because he does relax at that time. At dinner he talks easily, too, but sometimes more serious subjects come up, specially when Mrs. R. is here, and then he gets tense & concentrated again. Last night he again had to go through the dye process, and put on an act for our benefits . . . The P. was having a good time being natural & not having to consider every word — At 10 he finally went to bed — so did the Boettigers. Belle & I sat in the hall talking about him for a half-hour before we went to bed —

During dinner he told us a remarkable story about how Theodore

Roosevelt happened to become a Republican. [TR] told the then head of Tammany Hall that he wanted to run for the Assembly. That gentleman told him he, T.R., was the sort of young man they wanted — that he must join the party & *in a year or two* Tammany would nominate him . . . T.R. wanted action NOW, so he went to the Republican organization, ran in a Democratic district *and got himself elected!* [FDR loved to tell this tale, for which there is not a shred of evidence.]

Another remarkable story of the same sort, in which Senator [Henry Cabot] Lodge of Mass. wrote [Herbert Hoover] a half-dozen letters to prevent his leaving the *Republican* party, was told F.D.R. by [Mrs. Augustus Gardner], who read him Senator Lodge's letters. After she died the letters were not found. It is supposed she destroyed them — a great pity.

[Daisy has garbled this story, another of FDR's favorites and just as implausible as the one about TR's becoming a Republican. In 1919, Roosevelt claimed, he and his friend Franklin K. Lane, the secretary of the Interior, had together persuaded Hoover to run for President as a Democrat, when Henry Cabot Lodge and the Republican boss Boies Penrose talked him into joining the GOP instead. FDR and Lane did urge Hoover to become a Democrat, but Penrose and Lodge were, as Hoover himself said, always his bitter enemies and would not have welcomed him into their party. The missing letters — supposedly read aloud to FDR by Mrs. Gardner, Lodge's daughter-in-law — appear to have been a bit of embroidery stitched together for this telling.]

◦· *May 26th Friday.* All schedules are upset today — A little after 10 the P. went off to the Naval Hospital for his gall-bladder test. I hope the dyes are working properly! Before leaving he planned for the weekend [at Shangri-La] that the Watsons are invited for the 3–4 days "so that Margaret will be properly chaperoned"! Anna & John will be there Saturday night & Sunday but John has to be at work Monday morning again. In the midst of this household, where everyone is so busy thinking about *important* things, it does seem absurd to have to waste even a moment on whether "Margaret is properly chaperoned"! But of course one does have to think about it, even though Margaret is 52½ and shouldn't have to be chaperoned at all —

. . . The President had a very strenuous day — at the hospital, & then trying to get caught up during the afternoon, besides having a press conference.

He looked very tired at dinner, which we had on the porch — Belle, he & I. It showed after dinner by his talking rather excitedly — I don't suppose anyone outside would have noticed it, but I have seen so much of him that I can hear it in the tone of his voice, when he is pushing himself.

He told us about getting "ship-wrecked" at the age of three, when sailing for the U.S. with his father & mother. When only a day out from Liverpool, they ran into a terrific storm. Three times, the 6,000-ton boat was submerged but finally came up to the surface. Six men were washed overboard. The donkey engine broke loose, crashed into the navigating room, broke the captain's leg. The young officer who then had to take command, proceeded to continue on the voyage. The passengers, under the leadership of Mr. R., signed a petition that the ship return the one day back to Liverpool. The officer refused as H.M.'s mail must go through. Mr. R. argued that the lives of the passengers were more important than H.M.'s mail . . . Finally the officers turned the ship with great skill, & got it back to Liverpool in 36 hours — Then, the young officer & the Captain were both about to be dismissed from H.M. Navy, the Capt. for getting his leg broken, & for allowing the ocean to disable the ship, the young officer, for turning back with his majesty's mail. Mr. Roosevelt, however, first threatened to take up the matter with the British Gov't. [and w]hen that failed, he threatened to make an International incident of it. The result was that the Capt. was promoted, & the young officer was given a boat of his own command — ! This is an example of the background of F.D.R. Justice & fairness, in spite of red tape.

[The *Germania,* bound for New York from England, did indeed founder on Easter morning in 1883, though only one person was washed overboard, not six; and the elder Roosevelts did maintain their customary stoicism in the face of adversity. Sara Delano Roosevelt wrapped her fur coat around her frightened son as water streamed into their cabin, saying, "Poor little boy. If he must go down, he's going down warm." But the business about James Roosevelt's leadership of a revolt by the passengers is almost surely another invention.]

[Shangri-La]

ᐁ *May 28th Sunday.* . . . Back at camp, the Sunday papers were displayed & the rest of the household all on deck — the P. sat on the terrace so the rest of us did, too . . . At four, the P., Frances & I got into the back seat of the little open car — Fala in front, between

Monty & Charlie Fredericks — The Boettigers, Pa Watson & GGT in another car — We toured the battlefield of Antietam . . . The P. wasn't usually recognized until he had passed a given point, for no one expects to see him crowded in a small open car with two hatless, wild-haired women! The three large following cars, however, give it away, & there's usually a following shout, "There's the President!"

We didn't get back until after seven, had dinner at once . . . There's always lots of conversation when there are 2 or more Roosevelts present. They all are bursting with thoughts about almost every subject & can be profoundly serious or highly frivolous at a moment's notice! I have to confess that I find a good deal of *the frivolous* conversation sometimes entirely too *broad* for my taste! But I can see how, in the case of the P., that sort of talk is really a rest & a reaction from the tremendous weight of responsibility on his shoulders.

They get a certain amount of amusement out of me when I just don't "get" some joke! . . .

✧ *May 30th Tuesday.* . . . Caesar is sick, so Isaac the Filipino is being valet to the P. in his place. The mess crew are splendid servants. They hardly seem to be human beings. I try to imagine them out of their role as a mess crew, but have never seen the slightest side-tracking from their role. And yet, they probably have families, a social life, homes — The P. says they were wonderful on the trip to Teheran — would produce large dinners under the most difficult circumstances . . .

[The White House]

✧ *May 31st, Wednesday.* The P. decided, last night, that as he has no special plan for the coming weekend, and the Watsons want him for a visit to Charlottesville, he will go there —

Talking about it, he said he wished they would put him in the main house instead of in the little guest house. It was agreed that I should call up Frances and tactfully suggest it. Writing a note this A.M. seemed to be better so I did this, and sent it to "Pa" [Watson] for him to deliver — It was meant to be a sort of "whispered aside," so that Frances' plans need not be interfered with too much. In *our* family it would have happened as intended — but in *this* household, no.

The General received the note, read it, didn't quite understand it, consulted Anna, who agreed it wasn't clear, came up to me, consulted her father, etc., etc. It became almost an Interstate issue, to be finally settled by the P. himself, who suggested that he & Mrs. R. shall have the two rooms on the main floor! The rest of us will be disposed of elsewhere . . .

✥ *June 2nd Friday.* A.M. I am packed and ready to start right after lunch for Charlottesville. Many family discussions as to who is going, & when — The P. & I go today, "Pa" probably with us, Mrs. R. & the Boettigers tomorrow, A.M.? P.M.? In the meantime, I suppose Frances is trying to plan accommodations — Fala has to be left behind because of the Watson dogs —

The P. told us to be *on time for lunch at 1!* At 1, Anna & I wandered downstairs — no sign of the P., so we wandered over to the P.'s office door — We let Fala out of his pen & in to the P. — The Sec. of the Navy [James V.] Forrestal [who succeeded to his post after the death of Frank Knox] left the P., & we cheerfully went in. "I have another appointment," says the P., very busy at his desk —

We retire to the hot porch. Mrs. R. turns up with two crippled officers who are lunching with her & are to shake the P.'s hand — We all wait, shifting from one foot to the other — very hot. At last, the "appointment" leaves, & 5 of us march in. "I must sign this mail, you girls can blot for me." The P. signs; GGT & Anna "blot." Three is too many, so I retire to the side lines, study the Currier & Ives, finally sit down & wait. Mrs. R. & the two "boys" have left. Finally, it is almost 2, the P., Anna & I, Fala trailing along, go to the magnolia tree [on the South Lawn of the White House, said to have been planted by Andrew Jackson] for lunch.

Mrs. R. comes for a moment to say goodbye — She has decided that she won't go to Charlottesville after all. She has too many things to do before & after — The P. & I start about 3, leaving a sad Fala in Anna's arms. He looks *really pathetic!*

The drive down took us just under three hours, the road excellent & very little traffic . . . Approaching the hill on which stands Monticello, we took a country road winding around the next hill. On the slope of this hill is Kenwood, the Watsons' place — 100 acres, mainly woods — The house is of white brick French, very simple lines, beautifully furnished with mainly old French furniture . . .

Pa & Frances & F.'s niece, Enette Nash, greeted us at the front door. The P. was shown to the first room, overlooking the "sunken garden." I was given the second room. The P. decided to have his rest. Frances took me on a sightseeing tour around the house & outside &

to the P.'s little cottage in which he usually stays — Anna & John are being put in there. It is a charming little place for two people, a large living room, a double bedroom & bath & a little kitchen-pantry. I think the P. loves it, but I think he doesn't like to be off by himself — perhaps because of his illness . . .

↝ *June 4th Sunday.* . . . The P. began to dictate his "taking of Rome" speech, to John [Boettiger. Word had just come that the U.S. Fifth Army had marched into Rome]. They worked steadily on it until 6.30 — cocktail hour. John takes it down long hand — The P. gives him odds & ends of thoughts & John vanishes to work on putting these pieces together, grammatically &, I might add, dramatically —

The P. seems tired, & seemed to have to make an effort — From my observations of these last 2–3 weeks, it looks to me this way: Two or three or four days in Wash., when he is rather keyed up, get him over-tired. He gets away, & for the first 2 or 3 days, it is a question of getting relaxed. The next day or two he is getting rested, & then the whole process is repeated — Just how this is to continue, only time can tell. If he can continue to gain *more* than he loses, he will be all right, otherwise, he will get sick again.

We sat on the porch after dinner under a moonlit mackerel sky — The P. was making a definite effort & I longed to suggest bed to him, but didn't feel it was my place, with Anna there.

. . . It has been an exciting day, with dispatches about the taking of Rome (by special messenger from the Map Room), speech writing & typing . . . I was thrilled to be in the room when the P. dictated & corrected & revised his Rome speech for tomorrow night.

Without any question, *he* writes his speeches — Whoever "helps him" is doing the "mechanical" part, possibly suggesting a helpful phrase, reminding about a small point, etc. The P. is just as ready to *accept* a suggestion that sounds right, as he is to reject it if he doesn't agree with the other person. His clarity of mind is amazing, as is his open-mindedness.

Tonight he talked a lot about Teheran. John & "Pa" said that without the P., the conference would have been a tragic failure. It is what I sensed & have suggested. Stalin loves & trusts the P. The P. is the "solvent," the "Moderator" between Churchill, Stalin, etc. The P. used the word "Moderator" as the possible title for the [head of the] future League of Nations. It would be a good one. The P. would like to be that person if he could. Who can see that far ahead — even he can not.

◇ *June 5th Monday.* . . . The P. is prepared to issue a statement to the Press this P.M. to the effect that De Gaulle has *asked* to come & visit the P. & that the P. *will be glad to receive him* if he comes. (Very different from an invitation from the P. as head of the state, to De Gaulle *who is not a head of a state.*)

. . . We assembled in the P.'s study at seven. Fala had not been taken to the Watsons, so he rushed in, full of excitement at having his master home again. Johnny Boettiger did somersaults on the sofa. Then we went to dinner in the West Hall. The P. & Mrs. R. had a discussion about De Gaulle.

At 8.30 we went down for the P.'s broadcast on the taking of Rome. It lasted about half an hour. Mrs. R. went off with some friends who are in the yellow room. The Boettigers & I stayed down to watch the taking of the newsreels. [The President reread selected passages of his radio addresses for the newsreel cameras.] Then to the P.'s study, for orange juice. The Boettigers went to bed & the P. & I [worked on manuscripts] until 10.30, when Mrs. R. came in with some correspondence.

Now, at 11.05, the radio is describing the taking of Rome — No word yet of the [D-Day] invasion, which the P. says is starting tonight.

◇ *June 6. 12.45 a.m.* On the radio: A report from Germany that "The Invasion has begun." I fell asleep with the radio going, softly. Suddenly woke. It shows that we listen subconsciously —

12.49 a.m. German radio says landing forces are battling at Le Havre, that German warships are fighting Allied landing craft. No Allied confirmation. "They say" it might be an Allied feint.

7.30 a.m. My radio has been on *most* of the night — Just loud enough for me to hear the reports — I seemed to wake up when a report was being given, though I would sleep through music, etc. Between 6 & 7 (I think) Gen. Eisenhower spoke to his troops — He had announced the invasion at 3.32 . . .

I . . . went in to the P.'s room. He had slept well all night, but now, at 9, had the radio on & all the night dispatches. I told him all that I had heard over the radio, & for once, knew the details before he did! It was a novel experience for him. [It was also tactful of him; he'd actually been up most of the night and must have known far more details than she could possibly have heard over the radio.]

He looks pretty well; I think I can truthfully say that he is getting slowly but steadily better — I hope and fear, with millions throughout the country, that he will run for a fourth term. The world needs him.

The [D-Day] prayer, which was written & worked on by Anna & John, at the Watsons', was very fine, & beautifully read by the P. this evening. It is wonderful, in these days, to find the head of this huge nation leading the people in prayer. Imagine Hitler or Stalin doing it! And yet, I wonder if Stalin may not go back to his priest's training and, under the personal influence of F.D.R., regain something of the spiritual which he has cast aside these many years. This may be a fantastic thought, but it is not an impossible one. ·

[Rhinebeck]

❧ *June 18th Sunday.* A Big Day for us! All this past week, there has been much activity on our place — Cutting the lawn, raking & weeding the drive, scratching the paths around the house. This morning, Xmas & I covered the two porch sofas with fresh chintz, Robin scrubbed the whole porch, I moved all the *best* porch furniture out there, & arranged it so that the middle "lane" was free & there were chairs in groups of two, with small tables available, etc., etc. Mama had polished the tea tray yesterday . . .

A 4 P.M. we could see nothing further to do that *could* be done, so we relaxed & waited.

Mama sat in her usual chair behind the tea tray, [in front of] the door into the parlor which is never opened. At 4.40 the sandwiches, cake, cream & lemon were brought out, also the orange juice.

. . . In a while, the P. & his cavalcade appeared on the drive in a cloud of dust. Arthur & I went forward to greet them, Button on the leash — Fala got out first & I let Button off — they dashed out on the lawn & played together — Princess Martha & her cousin, the Princess Margareta de Bourbon, stepped out next, & then the P., carried by Charlie & Monty. Roly had followed Arthur & me, so we all shook hands & I led the way up onto the porch around to Mama & the tea tray.

The P. sat in his usual place in the corner. I then had to make introductions. I introduced the visitors individually to Mama, & then turned and introduced our household to them all, in one sweep. Everything went off very easily and quietly, the girls moved around, and conversation was easy, and no one was left isolated. Little Ragnhild sat on a stool next to her mother; a rather pathetic little figure, as she is plain, and is not responsive, & rarely smiles.

The Crown Princess hasn't much to say, but as the P. talks all the time anyway it didn't make much difference. It is strange, however, that a person in her position, & with so much natural charm, has no *manner!* Even in her own home, apart from pouring the tea & possibly passing a sandwich, she leaves the guests to take care of themselves . . .

The P. looked pretty well — exactly like Mme. Shoumatoff's picture of him, in fact! With his face in the full light, his eyes were blue & I wished we could put a sky behind him, & the navy cape over his shoulders! I didn't get a chance to talk to him, and conversation was pretty general, as the party was stretched out along the porch. But Mama says the P. talked a good deal, & in good spirits. He seemed to me rather quiet, however, without his usual "élan" — but that may have been due to the arrangement of the party — It was too big a party to be concentrated around him, and he seemed to me to be a trifle isolated off in his corner . . .

۰ *June 20, Tuesday.* . . . Xmas [Renée Chrisment] found [FDR] looking much older than last year, but otherwise pretty well. After the tea at our house she said he didn't have his usual energy & vitality & effervescence. I noticed that he sits rather tiredly on his chair, and you can see his heart thumping beneath his shirt. In the few moments I had to talk to him, he said the Texas delegation were making trouble & that if there is a split in the Democratic Convention, he will *not* run. There would be no justification for a *fourth* term if he wasn't about unanimously demanded!

Mr. [Fred] Shipman [director of the Roosevelt Library] found that $9/10$ of the *officers* abroad are against him, & are putting the blame on him for anything that may go wrong over there. The *soldiers,* he thinks, are *for* him, as I have heard from many sources. It is, again, a question of the "minority royalists" & the common "majority."

I pray that the P. does not have to go through a period of illness and disappointment like Mr. [Woodrow] Wilson. Here we are, only a month away from the Dem. Convention & the P. doesn't know if he will run, or not.

[The White House]

۰ *June 22nd Thursday.* In the North Hall again! . . . This morning, the usual routine of arriving, Anna & Johnny at the door, waiting, breakfast on the P.'s desk, on trays, while Adm. Leahy brought the latest dispatches. The first definite news of the battle with the Japanese fleet, between the Philippines & the Marianas, came in the form of one sentence from Adm. [Chester W.] Nimitz [commander of the Pacific Fleet. This was the Battle of the Philippine Sea, in which the Japanese lost three carriers and four hundred warplanes].

John R. is in it, so it is a *personal* worry for the P.

The P. seems definitely better to me, though he says the blood pressure is still acting queerly & against the rules: up in the morning, after a good night, instead of down, as one would expect. The P. has decided to stop cocktails for a time, & take sherry instead. Everyone with high blood pressure I ever heard of has always been deprived of *all* stimulants. It is possible, that because of the constant demands on the P. that the doctors think it best to allow him a "lift" toward evening. He says that without it, his legs get cold . . .

We don't yet know whether Button is having puppies or not, but if she does have them, it will be around Aug. 1st when the P. will be in the Pacific. [He had scheduled an inspection tour of military bases and defense plants that would take him all the way to Hawaii.] We have arranged a code: When I was eight, Mama told me I arrived into the world on a sunbeam through the window — So Button & Fala's offspring will be announced in somewhat this fashion: "Four sunbeams came this A.M. all shining brightly, including the pa & ma." That will mean all is well with "mother & children."

I hope he won't be disappointed! Counting the chickens before we even know whether there are any eggs! Button is full of life & health, however, so everything *should* be all right . . .

The dear P. looks *pretty* well, & is improving steadily, as far as I can see. He is always on the trigger for any possible teasing, & to catch the other fellow who may make a break! As long as he is like that I feel he is getting along!

[Shangri-La]

✧ *June 25th Saturday 8.30.* Yesterday morning, at 11.30, the P., Mr. Justice & Mrs. Jimmy Byrnes, & I started from the W.H., Fala sitting dejectedly on the floor, since Mr. Justice was occupying his seat! In another car was Dorothy Brady . . .

At the entrance to the Naval Hospital at Bethesda, we stopped to pick up Sistie & Buzzie who had had a "check-up." Anna returned to Wash. [state] to come out later with John. Anna looks like an older sister with these children of hers. She is a really remarkable person, much like her mother, but I think with a broader understanding of people as individuals. I think Anna can put herself in the other person's place. She has not, on the other hand, the crusading spirit her mother has —

[After lunch] I sat with the P. reading [aloud from Sara Delano Roosevelt's] childhood diary. He was playing solitaire — The P. suggested teaching [the children] "knock-knock," a card game. I joined them, & won the second time, true to "beginner's luck"! After two rounds, the 3 children put on sweaters & jackets & went out — Sistie poking her curls into a felt hat of D.B.'s put on backward (to keep the rain from the curled ends of her hair!). Sistie is very pretty, & tall, like her mother. Very sweet & attractive, too. Buzzie, whom I have always thought a replica of his father, is becoming more & more like Johnny Roosevelt, his uncle. The R. strain is very strong & appears in every grandchild.

The announcement was in yesterday's paper, of the marriage of Ruth Googins R. [Elliott's second wife] to Elliott's N. African pilot, Col. [Harry Eidson] . . . F.D.R. seems to feel rather bitterly about this divorce & marriage. A "mistake" because of youth and inexperience is understandable, but when it happens a second & third time, it shows an instability. Poor President, it is too bad he has these family worries on top of all the others.

↬ *June 26th Monday. Back at the White House* after two very nice days on the mountain. The Byrneses are sweet people & very restful, except that the Justice *loves* to pass the time talking, & kept the P. most of yesterday afternoon & evening, though the P. first of all tried to play cards, & then tried to read a detective story — Every half hour the P. would take up the book, Mr. Byrnes would stand up, still talking, & a moment later, sit down again! The P. was looking more & more tired, so finally, at 10, Mrs. Byrnes, DB & I decided it should be suggested that he go to bed; I was selected spokesman & he took the hint at once & went to his room . . .

[Byrnes did not do *all* the talking that weekend, for during the course of it, he would later write, FDR offered him the nomination for vice president. Roosevelt had already assured Henry Wallace that were he a delegate to the upcoming convention, Wallace would have his vote. And he would soon allow that he would be happy if either William O. Douglas or Senator Harry S Truman of Missouri ran with him in November.]

↬ *June 27th Tuesday.* . . . The P. was weighed today & has gone down to 174¾ — He wants to go up a lb. or two, to not be *less* than

175, & not more than 180. He feels better thin, however, and walked much more easily in the water than a month ago. His colour is pretty good these days, when he is *not* tired. It is the heart, I suppose, which can go just so long without a rest.

∽ *June 28th Wednesday.* . . . I . . . dressed for tea on the porch. Dr. [L. K.] Kung (who, with his wife, really "rules the dynasty" in China) & the Chinese Ambassador came in . . . The only barrier seems to be language. These people are "congenial," understand our point of view etc. Dr. Kung [a nephew of Mme. Chiang Kai-shek] brought a message from the Generalissimo to the Pres.: Chiang feels, since the meeting in Cairo, that the Pres. is not only his friend, but his elder brother, and begs him to remember this if at any time Chiang may send a message that may sound frank. Chiang will speak what he has in his heart & mind as he would to an older brother.

The more I think of this, the more extraordinary and wonderful it becomes, and the more imperative it is for the P. to continue his work of trying to make a better world —

The P. sent word, confidentially, & by word of mouth, that later this year, he hopes for a meeting of the *four* powers: Churchill, Stalin, Chiang & himself — probably in Scotland, or North England — with a laugh he said: "I think that Stalin, Chiang & I can bring Brother Churchill around." F.D.R. with his honesty, his vision & his charm, welding together completely incompatible & otherwise suspicious elements —

At dinner, there was interesting talk about the Far East. What will be our policy toward Japan after the war? Will the Mikado be allowed to remain? Will he be removed & the country isolated, "quarantined," until it works out a system of government that can live *peacefully* with the rest of the world. The P. said he hasn't made up his mind about it — Not enough is known *yet* about Japan, & the subject as a whole, for anyone to have an intelligent opinion. He said there are *at least* five different possible plans —

In regard to the Far East in general, which means the yellow race, which is far more numerous than the white, it will be to the advantage of the white race to be friends with them & work in cooperation with them, rather than make enemies of them & have them eventually use all the machines of western civilization to overrun & conquer the white race. The P. sees all this, so clearly, & is working incessantly for a sane future world — One wonders if there are enough others to see it, and to prepare for it. We all need to be educated & educated &

educated — I sometimes wonder if the P. couldn't do as much good *out* of office, by speaking and writing — and then, I see how his personality works on these selfish & suspicious people, and I think it is essential for him to stay in office —

One thing I know is that *he* knows best & will do what he feels is right — regardless —

We listened to Dewey's acceptance speech [Thomas E. Dewey, governor of New York, had been nominated for President at the Republican National Convention] — He said little & though his radio voice is excellent, he didn't ring true, & carried no conviction of any spiritual depths — I shall watch him steadily slide down hill from now until Election Day, unless I am completely mistaken! However, as Anna said, one must not minimize his evident strategy, which will include harping on the subject of the *age* of the members of the cabinet, F.D.R.'s health, etc.

ᴥ *June 29th Thursday.* . . . A little episode, last night, should be recorded: Sistie & Buzz went out for dinner with their father [Curtis Dall], who is a Lt. Commander. When they came in at about 9.30, they went right up to John Boettiger, kissed him, hung around him in the most affectionate touching way, to let him know that even though they had been to dinner with their father, John is the person they really love. It was really touching.

[Hyde Park]

ᴥ *July 1st Saturday.* . . . At 4.15 . . . we went to Top Cottage. We sat on the porch working . . . until 6.15. The P. felt tired & listless. He said he would *like* to go to the sofa in the library & go to sleep for a half hour, but he couldn't because the room would be full of people — Mrs. R. bringing some newspaper women to dinner, 11 in all — The P. wondering how he can "escape" afterwards!

ᴥ *July 3rd Monday.* A beautiful day. At 11.30, the 3 rings telling the M.P.s that the P. is going out, rang in the little booth opposite the Library — I was sorting things in the P.'s room. An SS came to the outside door — to get the wheelchair, open the door, etc.

"Oh," I said, brightly, "you're new, aren't you?"

"Oh no, I've been with the Pres. two years". . .

I *am* bright! For the next 45 minutes he & I were in & out up & down the ramp, taking the wheelchair down, covering it so it wouldn't be too hot to sit on, finally, at 12.15, bringing it back into the room, because the P. was due at Val-Kill at 12.15, & obviously would not come in . . . At 12.18 he drove up, Fala between him & Charlie [Fredericks] on the front seat. He couldn't stop, but would bring the P.M. of New Zealand [Peter Fraser] & his wife to the Library at 4, if he could arrange it.

He looked well & was full of mischief, with his usual happy laugh . . .

The New Zealand P.M. is a Labor man, good, solid, middle class people. The P. agreed when I remarked that it is not often that you have a man in the colonies (as with us) who is a *gentleman* — and that that fact is a great asset to F.D.R. Though they might not acknowledge it, they do look up to him all the more, for that reason.

We shifted to Stalin. Stalin told one of the Poles that "the President is my friend, we will always understand each other." I told the P. that his relations with Stalin are one of the great triumphs of his career, and only the future can tell how *much* that relationship is going to count in rebuilding our shattered world — Before they met, there was doubt & suspicion on Stalin's part, & also, probably, on the P.'s. Now, there is the basis for talking, for working things out together — but the P. smiled & said he keeps his fingers crossed!

∽ *July 5th Wednesday.* The P. came over at about noon, looking rather tired. He said he had had a hectic morning, with one thing on top of the other — De Gaulle arriving tomorrow: *one* headache.

He has to tell V.P. Wallace that the Dem. Party do *not* want him: *another* headache. The dear P. hates to hurt people's feelings, but he says the opposition to Wallace has become very strong & active in the last 6 weeks, and something has to be done about it. He is sending two people out to the West Coast to meet Mr. Wallace & break it to him, when he arrives from China.

[No one was actually sent. Instead, on July 12, one day after an awkward lunch with the vice president, during which Wallace did not take the hint, FDR dispatched Robert E. Hannegan, the party chairman, to deliver the bad news. Wallace refused to accept it.]

At about 3.30, the P. came over to the L. It was very hot, & he said he felt "let down." He got into the big blue velvet chair, with a cushion behind him & his feet on the new stool. Until 5.30, he stayed there, relaxed & really resting, though we quietly went through 5 large envelopes of letters. At 5.30, he sent me home in an S.S. car, but said he would stay there and read for a while. It is the first time he has used his room, here in the L., in this way — It is a lovely peaceful quiet place to which he can retire.

He is, *I think,* rather uncertain in his mind about himself: whether he really is strong enough to take on another term — whether he ought to try it, when the future is so difficult — On the other hand, whether it is not his *duty* to carry on, as long as he is able . . . Terrible decisions to have to make . . . for he *has* to make them, himself. Sometimes, he looks fine, other times he looks thin, & pale, and old. If one could only *do* something to help him. The doctors are so *half*-efficient, with all their modern methods — they don't *cure* him of his sinus, etc., they just temporarily ease him until the next attack.

A rather extraordinary thing has happened this spring & summer, since, in fact, I gave Anna Miss Gassette's pills & instructions, to give the doctors: The P. has *not* had to have his sinus treatment even *once,* as far as I can find out!! It is *possible* that Miss G.'s instructions have been a challenge to the doctors, & that, though discrediting them, the doctors have really used them. The P. takes two pills after each meal — One is supposed to contain vitamins. The other, the P. says they don't tell him. *Could* it be a concentrate of minerals?? This may not have anything to do with his improvement, which *may* come from his change of diet & these secret pills — I wish I knew! I am hoping to get Mlle. Gassette & Lenny to see him some time, when things are quiet & Lenny can spend an hour on the P.'s feet. There is no telling what *might* be accomplished. I hope & pray, for Bobbie, & for the P. . . .

["Lenny" was Harry Setaro, a one-time boxer and trainer whom Daisy's mystical French friend Mlle. Gassette believed to be a genuine healer. One of nine sons born to an Italian immigrant and raised in South Philadelphia, he started boxing for pennies at the age of eight, served as a sparring partner for the great Joe Gans, fought for a while under the name Harry Lenny, and then became a manager and trainer. He worked Joe Louis's corner the night Louis won the heavyweight title from Jimmy Braddock. But Lenny also developed an early interest in healing through massage, and Daisy was already hoping that he might be able to help her confused nephew as well as FDR.]

∾ *July 7th Friday.* The P. saw De Gaulle yesterday — will have lunch with him today — The P. said he would call me up about it, some time over the week-end — I can't wait to hear how the Prima Donna be-haves! Whether "she" is Jeanne d'Arc or Clemenceau or both!!

∾ *July 11th Tuesday*. No word from the Pres. . . . but, poor man, how can I expect him to crowd in just one more telephone call. I know so well what his day is, that it is always amazing when he *does* call up!

He announced to his press conference this morning, that he *will* run for the presidency if he is wanted — that settles *that,* at least, & his wondering & pondering is over. I know how mixed his feelings are on the subject, so I can commiserate & congratulate with equal truth-fulness — He evidently feels well enough to carry on —

∾ *July 14 Friday*. . . . The P. called me up the night before last. He confessed to an exhausting week, & that he must keep going for another 24 hrs. His voice sounded tired & he was working on the V.P. problem. That meant talking, discussing, trying to find compromises between disagreeing parties, etc — In a word, thoroughly harassing & wearing . . .

Anna came in & talked about the V.P. problem. Apparently it is still "on the griddle," but the P. is trying to get it *out of* his hands. Anna is a splendid go-between & "contact man," & evidently knows enough not to do the wrong thing . . .

Later. I spent the afternoon clearing up the things in the P.'s room. At four thirty he came over for me & a bunch of books & 2 Chinese shelves, etc. & we drove up to the Hill Top Cottage. He is committed to running for a 4th term, but of course it is nothing new, for he has felt right along that he *must* do it, if he is wanted. He confessed he is harassed by the whole thing — He wants to leave Wash. & the heavy responsibilities and lead a half-way normal private life — but he can't — his letter of July 11th expresses it perfectly — [In it, FDR said that "for myself I do not want to run," but "reluctantly, as a good soldier . . . I will accept and serve in this office, if I am so ordered by the commander in chief of us all — the sovereign people of the United States."]

Wallace & Byrnes both want the V.P. post. One of them will probably get it. The P. says Wallace is much nearer to the P.'s thoughts & view of things but is a poor administrator — Byrnes would be a good executive. *But:* 1. he used to be a Catholic [and hence would alienate Catholic voters because he had become a Protestant], 2. he would lose negro votes [because he was a southerner], 3. he would alienate some of Labor, 4. [left blank by Daisy]. Both are good old friends of the Pres.

Well, by next Friday, that question will have been decided & the P. can relax on the high seas, with no newspapers and no telephones.

July 22nd Saturday. Since last week many things have happened. Neither Wallace nor Byrnes is chosen to run for V.P. [Senator Harry S Truman of Missouri was], the Pres. is nominated for a 4th term. Hitler & Tojo have each lived through a crisis.

[On July 18, Japanese Premier Hideki Tojo was removed from office, and on July 22, Berlin revealed that a group of highly placed German officers had made an unsuccessful attempt on Hitler's life.]

What is happening in Germany is still uncertain, but the signs are hopeful from the Allied point of view.

Last evening, I was pleasantly surprised at getting a telephone call, via the W.H., from the dear Pres. He was "very far away," & wanted to be sure everything is all right before he goes still further. He had made two long "inspection trips" in the last two days, was speaking from his train, and "needed some sleep," but said he was "all right." A last pouch would arrive in two hours that should have my note.

[That week Daisy took her niece Rollie Hambley to see Mlle. Gassette and the mysterious Lenny at his room in the Flanders Hotel, on West 48th Street in Manhattan. Lenny had already seen her troubled nephew Bobbie and pronounced him completely curable, provided he was removed from the institution in which he was now living and put under Lenny's care. The boy's head had been flattened by a physician's forceps at birth, Lenny assured Daisy, which caused "constant pressure" on his brain. His pituitary, too — the "master gland," Lenny called it — had failed, perhaps because it was ill-formed.

Rollie, too, needed treatment, he said, and he massaged her feet for twenty minutes to prove it. Almost fifty years later, Rollie — now Mrs. J. M. Hendrick — remembered only being bored by the treatment. She felt no better coming out than going in, she recalled, but Daisy was dazzled, convinced that Lenny possessed great powers.]

And now to Bobbie again. As I think quietly about it, it becomes more & more of a miracle, an "act of God." Here is Mr. Lenny, a man without education, speaking poor English, an ex-prizefighter, who trains young prizefighters, has taken a real interest in Bobbie, *wants* to make him well, & *believes he can* make him well. Mr. Lenny is training a young fellow of Bobbie's age . . . Evidently this young man, "Steve," . . . is to take charge of Bobbie, get him on some job he can do. In the evening, Bobbie will be with Steve when he "trains," spar with him, learn how to "punch the bag," rub Steve down, use the electric vibrator on him, have Steve do the same to him etc., in other words, work & play *with* another man, and no longer be a sick man, sitting around, doing nothing. Lenny wants to give Bobbie "treatments," three times a week at first, reducing it gradually, as he gets well.

[Daisy was already planning that FDR be given treatments, too.]

☙ *July 25th Tuesday.* A note from F.D.R. written on the 21st just as he was settled in his "new quarters" & about to sail on his Pacific Trip. [This note, too, has disappeared.] God bless him and put new strength and vigor into him. The world needs him *so* much, not to speak of a hundred individuals.

☙ *Aug. 8th Tuesday.* Mrs. R. brought over Dr. Kung . . . He is a short, chubby little man, but very pleasant and with a quick sense of humor.

   . . . After lunch, Mrs. Pratt appeared in the doorway. She had brought [Marian] Anderson [the celebrated African-American contralto whose 1939 concert at the Lincoln Memorial was arranged by Eleanor Roosevelt after the Daughters of the American Revolution refused to let her sing in Constitution Hall], with two coloured & two white friends . . . Mrs. R. sent word for me to take them around. There were visitors to the Library whose eyes wandered toward the black & white combination! I can imagine their comments later.

   I must confess to a funny feeling about it myself, which I recognize as purely prejudice, for the five women could not have been nicer. Well & simply dressed, dignified, intelligent. The funny thing is that I had *no* feeling about Dr. Kung, the Chinese. I suppose the negro Problem is too close to us to be looked at without prejudice.

☙ *Aug. 10th Thursday.* The noon radio announced the 3-day visit of the P. to Hawaii. Fala was not allowed on shore because of a dog quarantine, so the sailors took care of him, and plucked his hair for souvenirs!

The release of this [news] means, I think, that the P. is back in this country — or very near the border! Again, we are thankful for his safety.

∽ *Aug. 12th Saturday*. At 8 P.M., the P. spoke on the radio from his cruiser, in the Bremerton Yards at Seattle. His voice sounded strong, but, being on the look-out for anything "wrong," it seemed to me as though he was tired and that he once or twice got mixed up on his words — this would mean nothing with anyone else, but we expect perfection with the P. & any tiny slip of *any* kind always worries me! I hope I am all wrong and that he is feeling wonderfully rested & benefitted by the trip.

[Daisy's alarm was justified. The Bremerton speech marked the first time in months that FDR had attempted to stand in his braces. They no longer fit because of the weight he'd lost and therefore caused him severe pain. A brisk wind ruffled the pages of his speech, too, making it hard for him to keep his place. And, after he had finished and been helped away from the microphone, he complained to Dr. Bruenn of "one hell of a pain in my chest that lasted half an hour." The President had suffered an attack of acute "substernal oppression," or angina, Bruenn concluded, which shot toward both shoulders simultaneously. "It scared the hell out of us," Bruenn remembered, but it did no damage. It was the only time Roosevelt's heart condition ever gave him any pain, and he evidently told no one else about it.]

∽ *Aug. 21 Monday*. . . . The P. has a good colour, & every one thinks him looking very well. He does, except for a sort of pallor and a strained look about the mouth which you see in sick people. He says he feels pretty well, but *tired,* most of the time. He has to save his strength to appear a few times in public before election — After that, he can do as he pleases. He spoke from the destroyer in Bremerton *standing up* for the first time in a year, & found it pretty exhausting. He says the muscles are "just not there . . ."

∽ *Tuesday, Aug 23*. . . . At 4.30, the P. came over & we took some things to Top Cottage & sat on the porch, talking, for an hour or so. He is *not* going to England — Has decided that as Stalin can't leave Russia now, it would not be *politically* wise for F.D.R. the Head of the State, to take such a trip to visit W.S.C., the Head of the Govt. They will meet in Quebec, as the last time, about Sept 9 or 10.

↩ *Aug. 29th '44 — the White House.* . . . I came down yesterday from N.Y. to Wash. in Mrs. R.'s drawing-room . . . It was my first experience travelling with Mrs. R. She & Miss Thompson sat opposite each other, I sat next to Mrs. R. and a friend of Miss T. sat opposite me.

Mrs. R. was very sleepy & took a 15 minute nap — then she woke up completely, sent for a table, & got to work at her correspondence. She dictated half a doz. letters & her "column" for Labor Day. She dictated with perfect ease, making only a couple of corrections as she went along — Then she took a book, but began to doze off & finally put up the book & just sat back in her seat.

A sailor looked in the door, & asked her what his chances are of being retained in the Navy after the war — She talked to him in a friendly way, shook hands with him & he went off quite cheerful & smiling having talked to her . . .

The Pres. appeared quite late for cocktails and dinner, looking awfully tired. He has lost $2\frac{1}{2}$ lbs since starting on the trip to Hawaii & they are giving him an eggnog at 11 and a large glass of orange juice at 4, plus his regular meals. He was in good spirits at dinner, however, much joking & teasing.

Rosser [Bobbie's paid companion] . . . came in at 12. The problem of Bobbie & Lenny is difficult. The hospital won't let [Bobbie] be treated by a man they don't know about. In any case, they won't allow an outsider — even a doctor — to treat their patients. They are willing to have him take the minerals and he is doing that. Bobbie needs three treatments a week, & Lenny thinks he can make him completely well, but in the meantime, someone has to be with him who will be responsible to the doctors at the hospital . . .

The Pres. . . . sent for me, to report on my conversation with Rosser, and is going to speak to Adm. McIntire tomorrow morning, & see what action can be gotten out of everybody concerned. He says we should approach the problem quite impersonally: "Here is a boy, Bobbie. The doctors have pronounced him in a chronic state which will deteriorate with time. A man turns up who believes he can cure him with a limited number of treatments. Perhaps the man is a quack; perhaps he can't cure him. However, perhaps he *can* cure him. One must try"

— This is where the problem stands at the moment.

[On September 1, 1944, en route from Washington to Hyde Park, the President asked that his train stop for several hours at Allamuchy, New Jersey. There he was met by Lucy Mercer Rutherfurd, whose husband had died the previous month. Some writers have sought to make this meeting seem an assignation; Daisy's detailed account of it proves them wrong.]

➤ *Sept. 1, Friday.* Rutherfurd House, Allamuchy, N.J. Another adventure! I am sitting on a cushion on the grass at the water's edge — Fala is "hunting" for something, or anything, in the muddy grasses — entirely happy & not worrying at all about getting away —

We arrived from Washington at 8.30, were met by Mrs. Rutherfurd & [John] Rutherfurd [one of Lucy's stepsons], at the crossing where the train stopped. She is a *lovely* person, full of charm, and with beauty of character shining in her face; no wonder the Pres. has cherished her friendship all these years —

[Daisy already knew Mrs. Rutherfurd slightly. They had met casually at Aiken, South Carolina, in 1922, not long after Lucy Mercer married Winthrop Rutherfurd, the much-older widower whose children she'd been looking after. "Mrs. R. is young & attractive, about 24, and seems to fit her place as stepmother to the five children wonderfully," Daisy had confided to her journal then.]

She came on the train hatless & stockingless, in a black figured dress, & black gloves — She is tall & good-looking, rather than beautiful or even pretty — Though I remember her as tall & calm & pretty & *sad*, when her daughter was 6 mos. old, at Aiken. She does not look sad now, but how little one knows about the inner life of others. The Pres. with all his intense interest in life & in people, with all his joking & teasing, sometimes, in repose, looks really sad.

Johnnie Rutherfurd is a giant, and seems awfully nice. His wife is small & slender — his twin boys, of seven, just about the best brought up children I have ever seen. I wanted to slip away & write & read, but one child after the other felt impelled to "take care" of me. We found a long string to tie up Fala, as I can't be trailing perpetually after him & he is better off out of doors, anyway. Then we found a bowl in which to give him water . . .

The Pres. is going to look over the whole 1,300 (?) acres — farms, woods, etc. & advise them what to do. It is the usual problem of diminished incomes & how to keep a large place going with fewer servants than one needs — I said I would stay behind & be nurse to Fala! So here I am in a delicious breeze, under a cloudy sky — The water lap-lapping at my feet — It is 11.15.

Later — It has been a lovely day for all of us — I returned to the house & sat with Mrs. [Benjamin R.] Kittredge in her room, talking about Jack Hamlin [of Rhinebeck] (of all people!) and about the excitements that always go with the coming of the President to any place — Mrs. Rutherfurd had a lovely room all ready for the P. to take his rest, even to turning down the best linen sheets — but he wasn't going to miss any of his visit & did not rest until we got back on the train.

There was much discussion as to how the Pres. should be seated at table. The S.S. told Mrs. Rutherfurd that the Pres. should be at the end of the table — he said he wanted to be at his hostess' right. The hostess couldn't decide whether to go against protocol . . . I finally went to the Pres. & he settled it: he sat at Mrs. Rutherfurd's right!

At lunch were: Prince & Princess Alexandre Chimay. She was married to [Rutherfurd Stuyvesant] a brother of Winthrop Rutherfurd, & after his death married this dear old gentleman. We had a good time talking half French half English, good practice for me! They live at "Tranquillity" the old Rutherfurd house a mile or two away — Then there was Johnnie Rutherfurd & his little wife, and Mrs. Guy Rutherfurd [born Georgette Whelan], whose husband is at the front somewhere, and Alice Rutherfurd [Lucy's stepdaughter] and her husband, Arturo Ramos, who is attractive & charming, but doesn't amount to a row of pins, as far as I can find out, he isn't bad, but he just isn't anything — not a too high recommendation.

We had a delicious lunch, with two negro waiters. First, a jelly soup, then squabs & vegetables, salad, and ice cream. Mrs. Rutherfurd had planned for lobsters, but when the Pres. told her he had had lobsters the night before, & would have them again at Val-Kill this evening, she left them out.

We sat around until 3.35 and then dashed off to the train & got started on schedule, I think, at 3.45 — or very nearly. It was a really lovely day, centering around Mrs. Rutherfurd, who becomes more lovely as one thinks about her — The whole thing was out of a book — a complete setting for a novel, with all the characters at that lunch table, if one counts the absent husbands and wives etc.

The house is an English Manor House, built by Winthrop Rutherfurd when he married Alice Morton [Rutherfurd's first wife, the daughter of Levi P. Morton] — The older Rutherfurd place . . . is a mile or two away —

Soon after we started, we had tall glasses of orange juice, and the Pres. told me a few things about the country-side, the different members of the family, their present problems, etc. & then he went off to his stateroom for a nap. I studied my speedwriting. We reached the

Highland station at 6.45. Mrs. R. stood waiting on the platform, and we drove via Dorsey Lane to Val-Kill for supper. Mrs. Pratt was giving the dinner & had a specialty: "appelkuchen."

✧ *Sept. 4th Monday, and Labor Day.* . . . At three, the Pres. came to the Library & said he didn't want to work, but to "play." So I jumped in & we drove to Top Cottage & sat on the porch for a couple of hours, talking if we felt like it — half the time, saying nothing. He says he won't be at all surprised if he is beaten in the election, that everyone is so confident that he will get in *anyway*, that the Democrats are just not bothering to register for voting. I *hope* it won't happen that way — It would be a tragedy for the whole world.

The Pres. was feeling "low" and "logy." He didn't know what was the matter with him . . .

✧ *Sept. 6, Wednesday.* . . . At 4 P.M. the Pres. telephoned from Wash. said he felt miserable — "like a boiled owl" — his voice sounded heavy — he said it was a stomach upset, & he had a tea party & a conference before him, & would then go to bed — I was much worried & called him at 9.30. He was in bed, had had milk toast, & would soon go to sleep — He sounded better & thought he had just eaten something that disagreed . . .

✧ *Sept. 10, Sunday.* A purely social day for a change! . . . When I got to the big house I rang the bell, & Coates showed me out onto the lawn where Gen Watson & the three admirals were sunning themselves & "carrying on." The conversation seemed to center around Pa Watson's wardrobe, which he gets at Brooks Bros., & was most amusing.

In the meantime, the Pres. was still working like a slave in his dark little office. At about 12.30 he came out & sent word for us to come. He was sitting on his wheel chair in the main hall, facing the front door, waiting. His back is not so straight as it was — he is tired, and sitting upright is an effort.

I went up and kissed him — he said he had had four awful days and was really tired. We got into the little blue car — Fala & I on the front seat — Adms. Leahy & McIntire in the back — the others in another car. Off through the woods & up to the Top Cottage, where Mrs. R. [and] Miss Thompson . . . were waiting to get in, with large dishes full of fried chicken, vegetable salad, stuffed eggs, rolls & butter, and apple tarts . . .

When asked how he was feeling, he
said he felt just tired, not up to anything
and that, as on the trip to S.A. in 1936,
he couldn't sign his name properly.
To show that he wrote the two sigs.
above.

It was a very good lunch, but the Pres. was too tired to eat &
"picked at" his plate . . . [See above.]

While we sat there, word came that Mr. Churchill & his party
would arrive at Quebec tomorrow morning — The P. gave orders to
leave from the main house at 4 sharp, for the train — Mrs. R. leapt
to her feet to "do some work" before that time . . .

[At Quebec, Roosevelt accepted Churchill's offer to send the main British fleet
to the Pacific to aid in the defeat of Japan. One evening, the two leaders
watched *Wilson,* a film biography of the President under whom FDR had
served in World War I. It included a poignant portrayal of the ailing Wilson's
decline and death. Afterward, Dr. Bruenn found the President's blood pressure dangerously elevated.]

∾ *Sept. 17th Sunday.* 9 P.M. — 15 mins. ago, the telephone rang, just
as I was about to drop into bed, exhausted after a long "social" day.
(Nothing exhausts me as completely as that sort of a day, where one
is laughing & talking and doing *nothing,* much as one may be enjoying it!)

Well, the call was from the dear Pres. back in Hyde Park from the
Quebec Conference — He said it was a *good* conference; much was
accomplished; he wanted to *sleep* all the time.

"*Le petit bonhomme et sa femme arrive demain matin à dix heures.*"

"*Celui qui etait le Prince de Galles viendra à midi, parler avec le petit bonhomme.*"

"I will come to the Library at that time, if possible." "Anna has come up" — etc. He also said he was "all right," but needs sleep, and asked about Bobbie Hambley.

⌁ *Sept. 11th Monday.* A *big* day! At about 10 A.M. Mrs. R. called me up & asked me for lunch, *with* the P.M. & Mrs. Churchill & the Duke of Windsor! Then she called up again & asked me for tomorrow "to even up my lunch table"!

At 12, the Pres. drove up to his door, coming across the grass from around the S.E. corner of the Library, very much to everyone's surprise. In came: The Pres., the P.M., Mrs. Ch., the Duke of Windsor, Anna & John Boettiger — The Pres. sat at his desk and got "Edward" & the Churchills to sign in the visitors' book . . . We wandered around, showing things off to Mrs. C. who was charming and enthusiastic. I like her very much. I felt she was worried over the Pres. She has certainly had many periods of worry over her P.M. but the P.M. looks *better* to me, because he is not so florid and not so fat as he was. The Pres. on the other hand worries me. He gets so awfully tired, and has no chance to rest. This campaign will wear him still further.

He is to speak at the Teamsters' Union dinner at The Statler, Sat. the 23rd. He said: "I just can't stand up to make that speech."

Harry Hopkins & I said there was no reason why he *should* stand up —

At one we all went over to lunch . . . As usual, informal & nice — Mr. C. makes amusing & sometimes brilliant remarks — His sense of humor is unfailing. Windsor is completely insignificant *looking,* but charming & quick, and I should think a delightful companion. You can't help liking him, & feeling sorry because he is an exile from his home & country — *But,* the fact remains that he was too *small* a man, or *too little of a man* to do the job he was born to. His wife, a completely unscrupulous woman, as is proved by her past life, does, however, seem to keep his devotion & make him happy . . .

⌁ *Sept. 20th Wednesday.* . . . The Pres. & I . . . went to the big library & I got him to lie on the sofa. He didn't actually sleep, but dozed a little, & would open one eye & say something funny in a sleepy voice. *My* role in the Pres.' life seems to be to help him to relax! Others stimulate him. Still others interest him. A very few irritate and bore him, but *very* few.

Adm. Leahy came in toward 7, with a dispatch on the progress of the war. Anna appeared, looking fresh & clean & attractive in a white waist & red skirt. Then came cocktails. The Pres. roused himself & went off to get washed up for dinner. He reappeared at the dining room door, very much "groomed," with his tie & coat on — He also looked less tired, and talked with much of his usual pep at dinner. Conversation was very interesting: on Haiti etc, etc. His visit there in 1917. He told us the story of his reception there & how he had to make his little prepared speech in French three times over before he finally got to the Sec. of State, for whom it was prepared, & explained to him that he would not repeat it for the *4th* time!

. . . The Pres. says he feels there is an excellent chance of his being defeated in the election — that Dewey is making a very good campaign. The Pres. is planning his life after he leaves the W.H. It will be so different, without the many "services" supplied to him by the govt. He will "write" and can make a lot of money that way — Also, his corr. will be tremendous — he feels he won't be able to afford Miss Tully & that *she* would not be happy in Hyde Park, away from her family — More problems! He wants me to perfect my speedwriting. I will at least be able to fit in somewhere, to help him out. "On verra."

◦ *Sept. 25th Monday.* The Pres. made his first campaign speech on Saturday night, at the Statler hotel — It was extremely clever & he never spoke with more "pep" and humor — A few speeches like that and we won't worry about the results of the election on Nov. 7th.

I called him up on Sunday morning, to tell him how fine it was — He was really pleased with the reception it got, and *he* got! They cheered him for 5 minutes & interrupted him 58 times! Right in the campaign again for 6 more weeks!

[He did not stand up to address the Teamsters, but he did deliver one of the most memorable speeches of his career, centered on the Scottie to which he and Daisy were both so devoted:

> The Republican leaders have not been content to make personal attacks upon me — or my wife — or my sons — they now include my little dog, Fala. Unlike the members of my family, Fala resents this. When he learned that the Republican fiction writers had concocted a story that I had left him — at a cost to the taxpayers of two or three or twenty million dollars — his Scotch soul was furious. He

has not been the same dog since. I am accustomed to hearing malicious falsehoods about myself, but I think I have
the right to object to libelous statements about my dog.

Delivered with gusto, the speech brought down the house and invigorated
the Roosevelt campaign.]

The Norwegians are back for their Fall visit, so we won't see much
of him these few days . . . The Cr. Prs. had brought crayfish from New
York [for lunch]. We must have spent at least an hour pulling them
apart & getting out the delicate little pieces that can be eaten! The
Pres. looked preoccupied & awfully tired & drawn. His face is thin
& lined & I worry a lot about him. I don't understand just how he
made that speech Saturday night. He must have done it through sheer
will-power & determination.

 Sept. 27 — Wednesday. The Cr. Princess & I talked about the
Pres. yesterday. I could see that she worries as much about him as I
do. We agree that it would be best for him to win this election, as his
heart is so completely in the desire to create a better world — even if
he cannot get through four more years — It is hard to talk about, &
harder to write about — but I am really frightened at his condition.
He seems to me to be slowly failing; and I think always of the Leukemia — But we all want to keep him *happy* —

[Roosevelt had never had leukemia. Again, it was his hemoglobin count that
had fallen alarmingly low during his struggle with bleeding hemorrhoids in
the spring of 1941, but Daisy had somehow gotten the impression that his
white blood count was low. Alarmed, she had looked up this isolated symp-
tom in a medical encyclopedia, concluded the worst, and confided her fears
to no one; they appear later in the diaries, as well.]

[Rhinebeck]

 Oct. 5th. At 3.15 P.M. the Pres. called me up from Wash. to say
he will be here at H.P. tomorrow — *To Rest!* He sounded a *little*
husky & said he had not been feeling well, & probably would sound
queer on his speech on the radio at 10 P.M.

Later. He sounded a *little* tired on the radio, & coughed exactly
once — Otherwise all right. [His address, intended to bring out the
largest possible Democratic vote, called on all Americans to "devote

the rest of our lives and all our capabilities to the building of a solid, durable structure of world peace."]

[Hyde Park]

᠅ *Oct. 7th — Saturday.* I brought down 12 marrow-bones, took them to the house, introduced myself to Mary-the-cook [Mary Campbell] — whom I have, strangely enough, never met before, explained to her how to cook them, to have four for the Pres. & me, for lunch, and the remaining eight for Sunday, for Mrs. R. and whatever guests may be there. The Pres. reminds me sometimes of "the poor little rich girl," for, as an example, he said rather plaintively: "I never *can* get any marrow bones in the W.H." Mary-the-Cook said she had not cooked any for years! This Mary-the-Cook, by the way, is Mrs. James Roosevelt's Mary, and the Mary who is quite convinced that no one else knows how to cook satisfactorily for the Pres! [FDR shared Mary Campbell's conviction, and she was eventually brought to the White House in the hope that her familiar dishes would enliven his dwindling appetite.]

Word came for me to go to the Pres. at 20 mins of one. Charlie [Moore] & [John H.] Pye [employees of the Roosevelt Library] met me at the front door & both escorted me to the Pres.' room, where he had decided to stay quietly in bed for lunch. A small table and chair stood in the bay window for me, and soon, the two trays were brought in. We had pea soup, marrow-bones on toast, with string beans and baked stuffed potatoes, and melba toast. The bones were a *great* success and the Pres. loved them . . .

Before lunch . . . we discussed how the Pres. wants to change his room, make it larger. He hopes to get this done next spring.

I suggested straightening the fireplace even if it should have to stand out into the room a couple of feet — but he said that would be a "major operation." The Govt. allows only $500 for improvements . . .

The dear Pres. says he is suffering from "sleeping sickness"; I told him it was just plain over-tiredness. The truth is that he never has the chance to get really rested — It worries me very much, as he has no longer the power of "come-back" which he used to have.

᠅ *Oct 9th Monday.* Yesterday I awoke at 3 A.M. feeling very "queer" — I kept on waking up, and feeling "queer," had breakfast, still feeling "queer" — I decided it must be the marrow-bones, and worked myself into a state of worry about the Pres. At 9.45, I rang up Charlie Fredericks, told him how I felt & asked if the Pres. was well.

Charlie laughed at my plight, very unsympathetically, & switched me onto the Pres. who was eating his breakfast & feeling O.K. He was very solicitous — told me to stay in bed etc. I answered that if I did, "the family" would get 3 doctors & 3 nurses for me, and that instead, I was off to Church & a lunch party at [Mrs. Francis] Crowell's [a cousin of Daisy's, living in Rhinebeck]. The Pres. said he would call up this afternoon to find out how I had survived the lunch. At about 4 he called up, in the middle of his afternoon nap. By that time, my entire lunch had left me, and I felt much better! He had had a large lunch party, and had people for dinner too: the Morgenthaus, I think he said.

I write all this down in detail, because it is so amazing that he can keep his wonderful human interest in the people he is fond of, in the midst of all the outside, national & international duties & interests he has — He can worry over a minor indigestion of mine, or a bad headache of the crown princess, or the broken leg of the child of a secretary, at the same time as he is arranging to meet Stalin & Churchill, or to speak at a dinner of the Foreign Policy Ass. in N.Y. on Oct. 21st — It is all part and parcel of that individual: F.D.R.

At 12.30 the 3 S.S. bells rang and the guards & I got on our posts, ready — In about 15 mins. the Pres. appeared in his little blue car; said he would not get out. Mr. Brooks [former superintendent of the Staatsburgh estate of] Ogden Mills [a Republican financier and Treasury secretary under Herbert Hoover] was brought out, & sat in the car talking to the Pres. about the old place, etc., etc. until after one — then I got in, and we drove two hundred feet to where Mr. Plog was working in the garden. Stopped & talked to him about the crack in the greenhouse furnace — Drove on to the house for lunch. Just the two of us ... At 2.30 the Pres. got the idea of taking his nap in the closed porch, which he called the "etymo-logia" [because of the mosquitoes that seemed to congregate there] (much to his mother's disgust!).

Here I am, sitting near him as he sleeps, Fala wanting very much to get out.

Charlie Fredericks went out & told the SS man who was on guard to keep out of sight, so the view down the river is clear & there is nothing to disturb him but the distant sound of an airplane, the twittering of a bird, or the "turning of the worms"! I am going to study my speedwriting.

The Pres. forgot about the sounds that usually wake him out of doors & slept a good hr & a half, with 3 or 4 eye-openings at intervals, which hardly woke him. I think that having someone sitting there quietly, allowed him to relax completely.

When he woke up we got to work at some of his longhand: *The Diary of the Larooco* — He enjoyed reading it over and I got numerous answers as to who had written some sections, who initials meant, etc.

[The *Larooco* was the dilapidated houseboat on which Roosevelt, Missy LeHand, and some of his friends cruised for several winters off the Florida coast after he contracted polio.

That same day, FDR and Daisy went over the script for the second Fala film, to be shot in and around the Library later that month. It called for the dog to come upon servants packing a car with Mrs. Roosevelt's luggage and say, "Well, I guess she's off again." Daisy wrote "omit" in the script, and the scene was never shot. Another scene had Fala passing the Val-Kill cottage and saying, "This place is where the Mrs. does her work — when she's home." It was changed at the President's insistence to "when the Chief can't get home."]

[The White House]

ᖷ *Oct. 12th Thursday*. A beautiful day. Mr. "Bernie" Baruch to lunch with the Pres., Anna & me, on the roof. The conversation was fascinating. Mr. Baruch impresses me with his clear mind, his idealism & his understanding. As he put it to the Pres.: "You have just one object at the present: the war & the following peace." The Pres. agreed, but said it was difficult to concentrate on that double object with everyone insisting on his doing so many other things, such as speeches & appearances in the campaign . . .

The Pres. looked remarkably well at lunch. Mr. Baruch was much impressed with his appearance — I think he will get through this campaign by sheer will & determination — What a relief when it's over!

ᖷ *Oct 13, Friday*. . . . In the little basement kitchen John Pye was cooking a delicious fried chicken birthday-lunch for Mr. [Maurice C.] Latta [the executive clerk]. I was so enthusiastic about the delicious aroma & look of it that Pye promptly wanted to produce a meal for me! By a couple of hours later, Mrs. Eben had planned a lunch with Pa Watson and Sam Rosenman for next Wednesday. I am a little embarrassed about it, as someone must be footing the bill! I suggested to the Pres. that he come, too — but he was afraid he might cramp Mrs. Eben's style — I suppose, too, that it would be treading on someone's toes — favoritism — etc. etc. How *stupid* that there is so much jealousy etc. everywhere you turn — It would be a little change for the

Pres. to lunch, just once, in that kitchen-dining-room, or dining-room-kitchen, whichever it is!!

At lunch in the sun-parlor, Mrs. R. told us that she and Anna were having some people to dinner, and as the Pres. doesn't want to see outsiders, I should have dinner in his study with him. I did not object!

. . . The Pres. was annoyed. He had had an unsatisfactory day — At his press conference, they asked him a lot of stupid questions.

All day he was seeing uninteresting people whom he *had* to see, purely because a campaign is on. As a climax, he had Cardinal Dennis Dougherty [of Philadelphia] for tea, "a purely political chore." From his & Anna's accounts of the Cardinal, he is a completely gross person — Perfectly huge; the Pres. said he *rolled* rather than walked out of the room. Anna said he was dropping his tea down the front of his clothes! It sounds *most* unattractive, but quite in keeping with his behavior at the Library last year, when he forced his way in, after hours, and signed his name in the President's Visitors' book, on the plea that he and "Frank" are intimate friends! Since that day the Visitors' book is kept in the cupboard, except when wanted by the Pres.

The Pres. unburdened himself of some pent-up feelings & ended up with a laugh and the statement that there are just "3 more weeks to next Tuesday," and that after that he will see who he likes and no one he doesn't like — no matter *how* the election goes . . .

∾ *Sunday, Oct. 15.* . . . Anna & I have been discussing his looks — he doesn't eat *much,* and doesn't like the fruits & vegetables he *should* cat — *But,* his *colour,* this week, looks better to me — Though he looks tired & thin, his spirits are good & he seems to be rather energetic.

∾ *Oct 16 Monday.* For the fourth day, the Pres. is not having his full rest. Mrs. R., Anna & I lunched in the sun porch on the roof with him, & when I suggested that he take his nap there, he said "yes" in a vague tone & promptly went off to his office!! At 5, the tea for the Supreme Court. Anna & I pouring tea at separate tables, so as to be sure of cutting the tea down to a half hour, as the Pres. had an appointment for 5.30.

What actually happened was quite usual: Mrs. R., Anna, the dogs & I were in the Red Room at 5.05. Two tea tables were set, the kettles boiling cheerfully . . . I sat at the one near the fireplace, Anna at the other — The Pres. sat on the sofa to the right of the fireplace. As soon as he came in, the justices were ushered in from the Blue Room, where we could see them through open doors. They came in file, around from the main hall. Anna introduced me to them all. I have met most, if not all of them, at W.H. receptions, but not to talk to any of them. I had a lovely time during the *almost* hour that followed, talking to Justices [Felix] Frankfurter, [Frank] Murphy & [Robert H.] Jackson.

Jackson can best be described as an awfully *nice* American.

Murphy is a strange looking red headed man, with eyes that don't seem to match, and very bad teeth. He is quite oblivious to these defects, however, and is considered much of a "ladies' man." We talked about the war & the human spirit, & I found him very interesting, & got along with him very well. But I never seem to find a "ladies' man" at all attractive in that sense — probably because that sort of a man doesn't look at *me* in that way!!

Justice Frankfurter, I found most delightful and congenial — The President has told me that his mind is so brilliant and so quick that it is a definite mental exercise to keep up with him; so I was rather frightened at the prospect of talking to him. However, his manner is so simple and friendly and sympathetic that I had no qualms at all. He evidently has the same quality which the Pres. has of coming down to your level, and never making you feel uncomfortable for being stupid!

. . . After dinner the Pres. looked really exhausted, but we turned on Mr. Ickes in an amusing & typical Ickes political speech, and the Pres. woke right up . . .

◇ *Oct 17th — Tuesday.* . . . When I returned to the W.H. there were all sorts of movements — Mayor LaGuardia was talking to Anna, after lunching with the Pres. — the Pres. was at his office — Mrs. R. was receiving Lord & Lady Gowry [Roosevelt family friends] on their way from Australia to England . . .

[Crown Princess] Martha had come to talk to her husband on the phone, about her operation. The only way she can do this is by having the Pres. call him up and actually address him. She has to talk in English. I seem to remember that a couple of years ago the Pres. got the connection through for the children to talk to the king & to their father. One of the children said something in Norwegian & the connection was cut at once — Such is war time . . .

◇ *Oct. 19 — Thursday.* I lunched with Frances Watson at the Hay-Adams [Hotel] then rushed "home" to the sun roof, as the Pres. told me to & had a fascinating half hour listening to Henry J. Kaiser explaining his plans for reconversion to the Pres. He is an amazing man. A perfect dynamo, but talked quietly, clearly and slowly, in explaining his ideas — I can't attempt to repeat what he said, but two things stand out in my memory: he repeated several times that the Pres. should take credit for the carriers used in this war, and that in Kaiser's discussions with big business men, whenever the others say something or other can't be done, Kaiser says: "We'll attend to that for you" — and the others *have* to go along — Kaiser is an extraordinary man.

At 5.30 there was a tea for 100+ good democrats. The Pres. sat in the Red Room, and greeted them all. Anna acted as hostess, and soon I went into the State dining room & got them started with tea, coffee & sandwiches & cake — Bette Davis was among them . . .

I spent most of the time talking to them, in the role of "one of the President's secretaries." I have fun trying people out, by telling them I work for the Pres. The snobby people put on a condescending expression, and then, when they have definitely shown me that they realize I am "just a secretary," I let them know in a round-about way that the families are neighbors and have been friends for 2 generations. It is amusing to see their rather nonplussed expressions! They are the very few, however, for *most* people, I think, take one on one's own merits.

After dinner, the Pres., looking very tired after a long day; but had Robt. Sherwood [the playwright and a presidential speech writer] and Sam Rosenman in, to work on the speech, also GGT. I sat in the room & wrote the attached:

Writing a speech.

In the Pres. study — The Pres. sits at the end of the sofa. GGT at this end of it. Opposite are Bob Sherwood and Sam Rosenman, deep in the brown leather sofa, each with a sheaf of typewritten sheets in his hand — The Pres. with a cigarette in his left hand — in the familiar holder — reads his copy, pondering deeply — Every once in a while he gives a suggestion for a change, or a new thought to be added —

A ½ doz. questions come up about what politicians are to be picked up, & where — GGT goes to the telephone to let the proper person know — Miss Leith of For. Pol. Ass. calls up GGT with some questions — who outranks who, at the speakers' table?

Back to silence — everyone waits for the Pres. to say

something — Pages turn over, rustling in the quiet — Harry Hopkins comes in — hands in pockets, goes out again. A thought by the Pres: GGT takes it down. Silence again — the Pres. reads on — puts in a word — GGT offers opinions & suggestions, which are sometimes taken — Sherwood & Sam make suggestions but in a quiet way which does not obtrude on the Pres. They are not aggressive, but heard just as well. Why is it that women get a "defensive" manner?

10 o'clock — I slip out, to wash my hair — At 11, with a bath towel around my shoulders to "catch the drip," I peek around the corner: Harry Hopkins is in the big chair I vacated — the President's voice is dictating . . .

11.30 to bed for me — I wonder how long he must keep on into the night — [The address on which FDR and his aides worked so hard so late was to be broadcast nationally from a New York dinner of the Foreign Policy Association. It was a plea for a strong postwar peacemaking role for the United States and was to be the climax of the President's first full day of campaigning, which would include miles of driving in an open car through steady rain, helping to convince voters the President was not as ill as rumors and recent photographs suggested.]

∾ Oct 22 — *Sunday morning*. On the Roosevelt siding at H.P. 8.30 A.M. Yesterday was a wonderful day for me! We left Washington Friday night, arriving at the Brooklyn Army Base, early — The attached schedule gives the program for the morning, except that we were losing time all along the route & were an hour late arriving at the Wash. Square apartment. [The program has not survived. Eleanor Roosevelt had recently bought herself a small apartment at 9 Washington Square; this would be FDR's only visit to it.]

Mrs. Brady & I were put in car 4 with Geo. Fox and Mr. Long. At the last moment, GGT in car 3 seemed to be alone, so Mrs. Brady went in with her, and I had the 2 "young" men alone — On this trip, an innovation was a policeman on the front seat of each car — a very good way of carrying your protection along with you, in case of need — He turned out to be an unusually nice young fellow, refined & with a sense of humor, and intelligent —

It rained & drizzled the entire four hours of the drive & the Pres. sat in the open car all the way. Mrs. R. joined him at Ebbets Field —

The Pres. and others to whom I spoke thought the crowds very "satisfactory" from a political point of view, except at one or two points where they expected more — But considering the weather, which was thoroughly damp, cold, & disagreeable, it seemed to me quite astoundingly good —

Arrived at Wash. Square. The Pres. felt a little chilly & rather weary, so he took a little drink of whiskey & water (I suppose!). We had a light lunch of rice & eggs, spinach, biscuits, soup & applesauce with cream for dessert. Just the Pres. & Mrs. R., Miss Thompson & I.

For the Pres. I called up Prc. Margareta de Bourbon for news about the Cr. Prc. Her operation had been performed — everything entirely normal & without complications — I then called up Hackie, who connected me with the W.H. telegraph room, & I sent a cable to Olaf, dictated by the Pres. — I was glad that everything was right with Martha, for he would otherwise have been worried —

After lunch he went off for a sleep of two hours . . . At 7.07–7.10, we all went down in the elevator, and in a flurry of cars, S.S., and policemen, went in the rain to the underground drive of the Waldorf — The Pres. was taken on his chair up to the "reception" of the Foreign Policy Ass.

. . . It was a fascinating evening, for the F. P. Ass. membership is 80% Republican & the Pres. was quite prepared to have a strong, unresponsive audience & was equally determined to make them responsive! After the first 50 words or so, he had them with him, and it was obvious that, *as a whole,* they were intelligent broadminded people, who can see the other side of a question even though they might not agree with it.

At the next table, Mrs. Eben was weeping with emotion — typically Irish! I leaned over & asked her if she was having a "good time" & she answered through her handkerchief, "Oh, wonderful" . . .

[Hyde Park]

⌁ *Oct 22nd Later.* I went right over to the Library, and spent the rest of the day (Sunday) with Mr. Herbert Morgan and his "crew," on the new movie short: "Fala at Hyde Park." The Pres. came out and drove his little car down the drive, picked up Fala and drove on again, for the final scene in the movie. The day was perfect, with bright sunlight.

At 4.30, the Pres. was alone, with nothing to do, so he drove me home in the big car. Mama was at our front door when we drove up

& spoke to the Pres. a few minutes — and he drove off — He looks tired, but has no real bad effects from Saturday. Thank God. The next two weeks [of campaigning] will be bad —

❧ *Oct 23rd Monday.* All day on the [Fala] movie — In the afternoon they did Arthur Prettyman and Fala at Hilltop cottage & a scene at the Val-Kill pond. A frog conveniently turned up for Fala to try to get at. They tied a string to his leg, & got a perfect picture of him — At 4 P.M. the Pres. picked me up, with some work, & we spent an hour at Top Cottage, surrounded by movie lights & wires for some shots they have not yet taken. We then drove back to the house, & we had tea brought in — also Fala's supper. Mrs. R. returned from making a speech on voting, in, I think, Beacon. An S.S. took me home — exhausted —

❧ *Oct. 24 — Tuesday.* Such perfect luck in the weather — They got a lot done. The Pres. left his hat, coat & little car, for them to use for various connecting "shots" in which the Pres.' face would not show — At 3, I wrapped up the Pres.' coat & sent it off, special delivery, with covering letters to GGT & Charlie Fredericks, so the Pres. will be sure to have it for his next trip. [The short, made in technicolor, was not released until after the President's death.]

❧ *Nov. 3 Friday.* . . . 9.30 P.M. The Pres. has just called me up from the W.H. He broadcast at 9, and I missed it because someone on the radio said he was to speak at 9.30, although the papers correctly listed it at 9. It was stupid of me. [In the address Daisy missed, FDR warned of "whispering campaigns [and] . . . malignant rumors of every origin," and pledged to build a postwar America "better than we have ever known."]

He sounded perfectly fine, full of humor and pep; and he described last Saturday's speech making in Chicago, in the funniest way: He was driven onto a platform in the middle of Soldiers Field, and found himself in the middle of a flood of lights, all turned on him. He couldn't see any of the thousands who were looking at him. After searching in every direction he finally discovered the edge of the audience, at one point, "half a mile away." The wind was blowing and carried his first page away. The mayor caught it, fortunately, and from then on, held two corners of the pages throughout the speech. The Pres. got going, came to a place where applause was indicated, and couldn't imagine why it wasn't forthcoming — He was just about to start on the next paragraph when it came, and he realized that Soldiers Field is such a huge place that it takes an appreciable time for sound to travel —

Fala & I are to lunch with the Pres. & Adm. Leahy, before the movie shot — That will be nice. The Pres. said 3 times: "I miss Fala terribly."

He counts 4 more days until Nov. 7, & then he can do & say what he pleases — *whichever* way the election goes.

Nov. 4 Saturday. Real Indian summer. I hope it is so with the Pres. as he travels to Boston & makes platform appearances on the way —

[Hyde Park]

Nov. 5 Sunday. . . . The Pres. waved from his desk, as I went up to the front door. In the hall, Admiral Leahy was reading a sheaf of papers. He said he gets this sort of thing every day, has to analyze it, pass judgment, and make a recommendation to the Pres. Half the time it is almost a question of "tossing a coin" to decide one way or another —

Arthur came for me & I sent Fala in ahead to his master. When I came in, Fala was in his master's arms and licking his nose — The Pres. was full of pep — "exalté" — as he put it. Two more days & then preparations for his meeting with Churchill & Stalin. He expects to start on that trip [to Yalta, on the Black Sea] about Nov. 22nd. All our prayers will go with him then, as always — Mrs. R. had, for lunch: Admirals Leahy & McIntire, Mrs. Kermit Roosevelt & a bunch of people whom the Pres. had never seen before — 14 in all —

After lunch, Fala & I joined Mr. Morgan & Mr. [Gunther] Fritsch [a cameraman granted special leave from the Signal Corps to film the President's dog] at the stable and spent two hours in rather chilly weather, getting shots of Fala in the sun, which kept vanishing behind clouds. Results rather questionable. The cat brought by Ray Smith scratched everybody and was put back in his cage without being photographed. Fala did his end of it perfectly. When it came to the pail of water being thrown at Fala through the stable door, Fala did the right thing, but the camera didn't "pan" quickly enough to catch him & when he was asked to come across the same place again, he made a large circle around the wet spot!

✑ *Nov. 6th Monday*. Windy & chilly. A half-hour "blizzard" in the morning, which melted before it landed —

. . . At 1, the Pres. was due to leave [for his traditional final campaign swing through nearby towns], but got off at 1.15, with Adm. Leahy and Sec. Morgenthau in the open car with him. He put on a sweater under his suit, & got into the Joe Davies, Russian fur-lined overcoat [a gift from Joseph Davies, his ambassador to Moscow], so he will be all right in spite of the cold — He was in splendid form, cheerful, and full-of-the-devil! The campaign seems to have done him more good than harm, and I am wondering if it is not in line with my theory about what is the matter with him, and that the exercise and fresh air are stimulating his glands.

✑ *Nov. 7 Election Day 1944 & 8th*. F.D.R. for the fourth time, elected Pres. of the U.S. It has become trite to say he is an amazing man with an amazing career — And what more does the future hold for him!

I took Mama, Eva & Geraldine down to Rhinecliff to vote — all four of us voted straight Democratic, then I joined Mr. [William] Nichols at the Dows, where I left my car. [Daisy and William Nichols, who was living in a cottage on the Dows' place, evidently took turns driving each other to work at the library.]

At the Library, we saw the Pres. drive off to do his voting, around noon. Afterwards, he stopped at the Library & came in for 15 minutes before going on home for lunch — Mrs. R. & Anna & Johnnie had gone on ahead —

At 4 P.M. he came for me, & we all piled in to go for tea to the Top Cottage: Anna & John, Admirals McIntire & Leahy, Fala & I. We lighted a welcome fire & spent a couple of hours up there, very peaceful and restful — Then back to the big house where we washed up & gradually collected in the library. Cocktails were brought in at 7.10. There were: The Wilson Browns, the Gen. Watsons, Nancy Cook, Marion Dickerman, Harry Hooker, the Boettigers, the Roosevelts, Mrs. J. R. Roosevelt, & I. Toward 7.30, the Sherwoods, the Rosenmans, Morgenthaus, [Gerald] Morgans, [Alice] Dows, [Mr. and Mrs.] Lytle Hull, Mr. Fred Delano, Laura Delano etc., etc., came in for dinner set at small tables — It was an unusually nice party, with few "odd" elements — After dinner, the Pres. retired to the dining-room table, which was cleared & had three telephones on it, & chairs around, some tabulating sheets were put there and the ticker machine in the next room started — Radios in the "snuggery" and in the library & in the dining room were turned on and kept going all night until Mr. Dewey finally conceded the election. Before he had finished making his statement to the press the Pres. was writing a telegram to him and hurrying it off.

The "tired old man" put one over on Dewey that time (on top of the election!), for Dewey had to explain to the press that he *would* have sent a telegram of congratulation if he had not heard that the Pres. had gone to bed! The night was like the other election nights, with the Pres. & a handful of helpers: Anna, Mrs. Pratt, John, Mr. Hassett, etc. bringing the ticker reports to the Pres., then carrying them out to the other people outside. The Pres., every once in a while, would send for someone to come in & see what was happening — I didn't go in until quite late, and as the others gradually went home, or up to bed, Laura Delano, Harry Hooker & I more or less settled down for the night at the empty end of the table. Adm. Leahy & Basil O'Connor stayed most consistently at the table, listening to the radio & writing down the numbers of votes as they were reported from various states. The Pres. read the ticker reports with hardly a stop, from 9 P.M. to 3.15 A.M., when Mr. Dewey made his statement —

Only one real interruption when the [Hyde Park] torch parade had to be spoken to, from the terrace. It was chilly out there, but F.D.R. only, with cape open, seemed unconscious of it. The rest of us hugged our coats about us —

Throughout the night F.D.R. was always ready to look up with a smile, from his ticker, say something amusing, greet a newcomer or say goodbye to someone — He looked pretty tired toward the end, but was full of "fight"! We all cheered when we heard Ham Fish [the President's congressman and one of his most savage Republican critics] was beaten — The only disappointment was that Clare Boothe Luce got in again . . .

꙳ *Nov. 10, Friday.* . . . Coming down in the train from P'ksie, I sat with a very nice looking woman of my age — Being full of the election, I thought it would be nice to talk about it, *if* she was on the same side of the fence, so I started: "Well, it is nice to have the election over, isn't it."

The lady: "Well, I *suppose* the country will survive" . . . !

I tried again: "It has been such a very *horrid* campaign."

The lady: "I don't feel that at all, for Mr. Dewey has been *so consistently dignified and truthful!!*"

I gave up *that* subject, & veered quickly to the safer subjects of gardens, dogs, etc. . . .

[The White House]

ᔪ *Nov 11 Saturday.* . . . I came to the W.H. at about 8.30, & found the Pres. just settling down after dinner with Mrs. R. & Miss T. He has a stack of complimentary letters & telegrams & read about half of them before going to bed — Mrs. R. went out to make a speech somewhere.

Harry Hooker is in the "Queen's room," very ill, with a thrombosis. The crisis is today; [Alonzo] Fields [White House butler], when he brought my breakfast, said the nurse said he had had a good night. They think he got a chill on the drive to our house on Thursday. If he is getting along all right in 3–4 days, he will go to Walter Reed for some 6 weeks' complete rest.

ᔪ *Nov. 12. Sunday morning.* . . . Harry is being kept quiet in spite of himself, & doesn't know he has a clot. The nurses say he wants to get up — They would have much less trouble if they would *tell* him. The danger won't be over for a month or so, while the clot is being gradually absorbed . . .

Mr. David Lynn, Capitol Architect, and [Congressman Thomas J.] Halsey, Sec. of the [Inaugural] Committee, [came to see the Pres.]. Before they came, the Pres. said he would horrify them by telling them that he wants the inauguration on the W.H. portico, and *no* parade — We sat down for tea, I pouring, & Mr. Lynn leaned over & whispered that he *hoped* the Pres. could be persuaded to have the inauguration on the portico of the W.H.!

I said: "That's interesting! Just wait & see what the Pres. has to say about it"!

They think the committee will agree, without any trouble, specially because [Senator] Harry Byrd [Democrat of Virginia] is always for economy, & the whole thing will cost perhaps $1,500, as against $43,000 in past years — The hotels cannot complain, as they have more than they can do anyway and, as the Pres. says, there are no good troops to parade, only WACS & WAVES . . .

Later. I've had a lovely Sunday, "taking care of" F.D.R. who would have been completely alone if I had not been here — He is definitely relaxing after the past few weeks and is somewhat "let down." However, when anyone is around to talk to, he automatically braces up — At tea yesterday, he was animated and amusing, and looked remarkably well — Mr. Lynn remarked on it to me.

. . . At 4 we went out in the car to the Ickes farm. Their house is charming — full of sunlight — a large central hallway with twin staircases — Mrs. Ickes has hundreds of chickens — The two children are very sweet. The boy of 5 rather too shy — The girl of 3 very friendly and bright, and the image of her father — Mrs. Ickes is charming; very pretty, with beautiful red wavy hair which she wears simply. It always seems strange to see a young attractive woman the wife of an older man — in this case 35 yrs older, I understand. [Ickes had married Jane Dahlman in 1935, not long after the death of his first wife in an automobile accident.]

We had tea, could stay only about 40 minutes, as the Pres. had to get back to have his nose treated. What a bother that nose is, to him. Away from Wash., it doesn't bother him much, but here, he gets "stuffed up"; has to spend about a $\frac{1}{2}$ hr. almost every evening, getting it cleared out!

. . . After dinner, he talked about his ankles, which feel stiff and heavy. I offered to massage them for him. I put in a half hour on the right ankle & foot, until he said it felt almost like a normal foot & leg. I then worked on the right one, which is the most helpless, for 20 minutes, until the Pres. was so sleepy he said he would have to go to bed. I tried to do the kind of manipulating that Lenny does, and strangely enough, I found highly sensitive places in the sole of the foot, just by rubbing with the "ball" of my thumb. Unfortunately my knowledge is *very* slight, and as "a little knowledge is a dangerous thing," I didn't dare do anything but the gentlest kind of rubbing where it hurt — I am so sure that Lenny could help F.D.R. — and so incapable of getting them together —

༄ *Nov. 14 Tuesday.* . . . [W]alked up to 61st Street and up to the 11th floor — The nurse said that the wife of the Swedish minister & Prs. Margarethe were both with the Cr. Prs. so we sat down to wait. On the door was a sign: "Silence." and from inside came peals of laughter! In a few minutes out came the Swedish lady & departed. Mrs. Ostgaard took me in and vanished while I was shaking hands with the Cr. Prs. & her cousin. I must have stayed there an hour, and enjoyed every minute — Martha was very cheerful and laughed like a child over everything and nothing! She looks a *little* thin [after surgery], but very well & bright. They say they are keeping her there because she is still anemic. I imagine they also enjoy having her, with huge bills being paid every week!

Prs. M. gave me a page to read from a letter of a friend in Paris. He describes the atrocities committed by the Germans on women & little children — so horrible that it is hard to believe them — One doesn't *want* to believe them, but one *must,* in order to prevent their happening again. It is so horrible to think of members of a Christian nation doing such things which they know are wrong, as against the Japs who have no such background.

As I got up to go, I remarked that I must go to the Bank to get enough money to buy my ticket back to Wash. In one breath, Prs. M. said the banks were closed, & Martha ordered me to hand her her purse from the closet shelf, & gave me a $10.00 bill! *Me,* borrowing money from the Crown Princess of Norway! . . .

Here I am back at the W.H. waiting to see the Pres. for a moment, to give him Martha's note. He has been working with GGT with the door closed, & now I hear Mrs. R. & Anna talking to him — 11 P.M.

Anna came to my door asking why I was so exclusive — or seclusive. I went in to the Pres.' study, to find Mrs. R. in a lovely bright red dress talking to him. After a while they both left & I sat down and reported on my N.Y. trip. Nothing is yet settled about the Pres.' plans. He wants to put off the European trip until after inauguration, and in that case will go to Warm Springs for 2 weeks, taking Anna & Johnny, & possibly Polly & me.

᎒ *Nov. 15 Wednesday.* . . . Didn't see F.D.R. until about 4.30, when he took me along on his visit to Sec. Hull at the Naval Hospital. [Hull, secretary of State since 1933 and now seventy-three, had entered the hospital suffering from exhaustion.] I sat in the car during the hour he spent with Mr. Hull. The Pres. looks tired today, for he has had a succession of people and no rest, but he still looks *so* much better than a month ago, and has his *old* "fire" back. His humor fortunately never leaves him.

. . . [In the evening] I did some writing & studying & reading in my room, keeping out of sight so as to let the family have some privacy & talk to Elliott, who just landed from Europe. At 10.30 I washed my hair, put it up in combs & was about to get into bed when Anna came in, with an "order" from F.D.R. for me to appear in his study! She got a towel from the bathroom, pinned it about my head, much like a catholic sister, & dragged me in! With my striped blue &

white Japanese kimono and a large bath towel about my shoulders, I was certainly well covered, but it was not *quite* the costume in which to appear before the P. of the U.S.

He got some fun out of it, however, so it's all to the good — The poor man certainly needs all the "fun" anyone can give him.

He received a lengthy cable from Churchill, which sounded like an apology for perhaps doing & saying too much to De Gaulle!! But of that, I am not competent to judge! [The problem with De Gaulle involved his demand for a large increase in the Free French Army, an increase that could be effected only after the war. Churchill and FDR found themselves somewhat at odds over the desirability of restoring France as a major European power: Roosevelt was emphatically against it.]

Nov. 16 Thursday. . . . Everything is settled . . . the Pres. will leave for H.P. Tuesday night, to spend Thanksgiving up there. The following Sunday night Polly & I leave with him, stop over here in Wash. until the evening, & go on to Warm Springs for two weeks. The Pres. needs a rest and a change. He has two huge "baskets"-full to catch up with, besides the daily interviews, daily mail, daily problems — Just now there is a "difference" between two of his most important men. The Pres. says it is his own fault, for when there is something to be done, he tells the person available at that moment — the person [to] whom the problem *should* go, gets annoyed because he doesn't know about it . . .

Nov. 22 Wednesday. . . . The Pres. called me up. He is alone but for the secretaries & asked me to come for lunch & stay on for supper. So I brought over a folder of work, & this diary & my shorthand — and now, at 3.05 P.M., I am sitting at the foot of the sofa, my work in front of me, & the Pres. is fast asleep on the sofa. He is tired and doesn't feel awfully well, with odd aches & pains around the region of his belt, and no appetite. At lunch, we had corn soup, fish & peas, which he ate without relish. Then we had rice pudding with brown sugar and rich cream. *That* got him — and he took two helpings.

He planned to drive up to the cottage, but Geo. Fox dissuaded him, & we are to stay down here, have tea, then go upstairs, & he will get into bed for supper. I am to stay & have a tray with him. I often think he must long to be left alone, but when the rare occasions to be alone come, he wants *someone* with him. Up here, I seem able to fill the bill, of a person whom he doesn't have to speak to but who *is* someone nearby. I suppose he feels that need purely because he cannot get around himself —

We are to leave Saturday night, instead of Sunday, because the S.S. begged for the extra day "to wash their clothes" before they go to Warm Springs! Being interpreted, that must mean that the poor wives need a little more notice — You have to do your laundry at home these days! . . .

☙ *Nov. 23 — Thanksgiving Day.* And we have *so* much to be thankful for in this country. We don't half appreciate it . . .

The day passed quietly. [The Pres.] & Mrs. R. had their lunch alone — a remarkable occurrence! He wants me to go to see Ellie [Roosevelt] & Mrs. [Grace Walton] Clark [the widow of Appleton Clark], tomorrow or the next day. [Miss Roosevelt and Mrs. Clark were the children of the President's late uncle John Roosevelt.] No one pays any attention to them since Mrs. James R. died. Mrs. R. "hasn't the time" to bother about them — a strange inconsistency in a woman whose every thought is to help her fellow man.

The Pres. has lost 10 lbs in the last 2–3 months, and is, I think, rather worried about it. He looked very thin today, & his "aches & pains" worry me, but what *can* I do? Nothing, except perhaps to give him whatever cheerful companionship I can, when he wants & needs it. His mind is wonderfully active and interested in everything, as always . . .

☙ *Nov. 25th Saturday.* . . . The Pres. needs a change very much. This week has been too cold for him to get out, so that it has not done him much good — and he has done a lot of work trying to bring down the top of his "basket."

. . . Monty came for me in the Pres.' car at 8.30. I found the Pres. & Mrs. in the big Library, he playing solitaire, she, reading. At ten we got into the car & drove to the station at Highland, & at 11 the train starts —

Off on another delightful adventure — to [Washington and] Warm Springs this time!

☙ *Sunday, Nov. 26.* . . . I got back to the W.H. in time to join Polly & F.D.R. in the car, to go & see Sec. Hull at the Naval Hospital. He is no better, and has resigned. F.D.R. is to tell the Press tomorrow —

. . . The Pres. was better today — & consequently more cheerful & "himself."

❧ *Nov. 27 Monday.* . . . During the afternoon, we packed [for Warm Springs] — Polly has lots of bags, including her meat-bag for the dog, and we scurried around, finding tags for them all — nice red ones, from a drawer in the Pres.' room! We said goodbye to Harry [Hooker] in "The Queen's room."

It is a sad disappointment to him to miss this trip, and to us also, for he rounded out our little party —

Perhaps there will be another, before long — now that the Pres. is in again for 4 more years —

. . . Here we are on the train: The Pres., Polly, O'Connor, Amb. McCarthy, & I, in the Pres.' car — Besides us, there are: Mr. Hassett & a sec., Miss Tully, Mrs. Brady, Miss [Antoinette] Batchelder, Miss [Alice] Winegar [secretary to William Hassett] and who-knows how many other necessary people!

. . . The Pres. looks very thin and tired, but is relaxed and having a wonderful time, talking along, joking, telling old stories. If he continues as he is tonight, this trip will do him a world of good. Polly finds it hard to relax & "do nothing" — It's good for her, too! To bed!

[Warm Springs]

❧ *Nov. 28 Tuesday. 3.15 p.m. central time* on the sunny porch of the Little White House at *Warm Springs* Ga. A perfect day — Mr. O'Connor is talking to F.D.R. about the Foundation, at the south end of the porch. I have just gotten settled. Polly is getting her dog's food ready — Arthur, the valet, and Charlie Fredericks are getting the Pres.' things settled. Daisy [Bonner] the cook is "hostess" to all of us. Fala wanders around, in the house, out to the porch in again, hoping to get free out of the house and into the woods —

The train was just about on time, quite a crowd at the station. Mr. Fred Botts was sitting in the Pres.' little blue car, ready to hand it over. The Pres. was taken off his train on the little elevator & carried into the little car. Mr. O'Connor got in front with the Pres. Polly, Amb. McCarthy, the two dogs & I got in the back & the Pres. drove around by the main building where the patients were assembled & clapped & waved & smiled — Up the hill to the Little White House, and — here we are . . .

❧ *Nov. 29 Wednesday.* Sitting in bed waiting for my breakfast — frozen! It has rained all night — a cold clammy, penetrating rain which goes through my three heavy blankets and my warm grey sweater —

The dear Pres. is having trouble with a back tooth which has been loose for a long time. It ached yesterday afternoon and evening. We had cocktails by the fire and at about seven we all drove to the Founder's dinner. At the speakers' table, Mr. O'Connor presided — The Pres. on his left, Amb. McCarthy on his right — Bette Davis sat at the Pres's left. She looks like a little girl and everyone finds her very nice. Polly & I sat at the opposite end of the long hall, with the White House staff, Charlie Fredericks, Mr. Spaman, some officers of marines, some physiotherapists. It is hard to know who are the patients unless there is a wheelchair or a crutch, etc., for everyone is cheerful and happy looking. A *few* look rather pale & thin, probably those who have not been here very long.

An "entertainer" [Chief Petty Officer Graham Jackson], a coloured man, played the piano [and] led singing with an accordion while we waited for dinner.

There must have been about 180 people there, in all, 114 of them patients. We had a very good dinner, beginning with tomato juice, and then turkey, peas & mashed potatoes — ice cream & pumpkin pie. After dinner Mr. O'Connor made a good little speech, introducing the people at the speakers' table etc. & then the Pres. just "talked," in his usual friendly "man to man" way — and a "show" was put on by the patients. It was amusing & bright. We stood up, along the wall, to see it better.

I found myself looking at the Pres. at least half the time. He looked pale & thin & tired. I try so hard to make myself think he looks well, but he doesn't. His colour at times seems better than it has been, but he gets very grey when tired, and it shows so much when he is sitting under bright lights next to people with high colour, like Mr. O'Connor & Amb. McCarthy — He looks ten years older than last year, to me — Of course I wouldn't confess that to anyone, least of all to him, but he knows it himself.

. . . Lots of coming & going of the S.S. early this morning. There is no sound-proofing in this house, & I can hear people talking almost in a whisper in the pantry, with two closed doors between! Polly is in the room Miss LeHand used to have, on the other side of the living-room, with a bath. I am in the little double room on the other side of the Pres.' bathroom. It is an awkward arrangement for anyone not in the immediate family, for the Pres. *should* have his bathroom to himself. He told me to use it, but I don't like to — so I have to go through the front hall & the living-room & Polly's room, to *her* bathroom!

With S.S. in & out all night — ! Fortunately when I get to bed, I usually stay there until it's time to get up —

Monty Anderson [Daisy's young cousin Montgomery Anderson] is near Augusta Ga. in Camp Gordon. I told the Pres. I might go there to see him. I would have to spend a night there & the travelling would be at least 4 hrs. each way, the Pres. told me, & wouldn't hear of it. He thought a minute & then said: "Take this down," & dictated a telephone message for Hacky to give to Gen. Watson, in Washington. The wording was, as well as I can remember it: "Ask the Commanding officer at Camp Gordon to have Lt. Montgomery Anderson report to me on Friday evening. I want to speak to him about some phases of the South Pacific, where he has been for over a year — He can be back in Augusta on Sunday evening. This short assignment should not interfere with the course he is teaching." The message included his "CoC, 7th Battalion, Training Replacement Center."

It will be wonderful if he comes over for the two nights. Mrs. Rutherfurd and [her only child] Barbara are coming on Friday also, and it will be nice for two *young* people. Barbara, is, I understand, "interested" in a boy who is now recovering from a serious wound in Europe. When they come, Polly & I will go up to the guest house, where the *only* heat is from the fireplaces!

10.10. The heat has been coming up for about a half hour. The Pres. still asleep in his room. Polly has the radio going in her room. Here, in the living-room, I can hear *every* word — and wonder if it is too loud, but if I open the door to tell Polly it is too loud, there will be a sudden blast of sound which will *surely* wake up the Pres. . . .

✧ *Nov. 30 Thursday.* It was a horrid day all day yesterday — The Pres.' tooth bothered him — was getting worse by degrees, so Adm. McIntire telephoned to Fort Benning for a dentist. The Pres. ate a little lunch with little appetite, sat around afterward, played cards — "passed the time" by the fire until the dentist, Dr. Rubin came, with a tall, lanky, self-conscious assistant.

The tooth came out without an effort and the Pres. "healed up" with no extra bleeding, etc. They fixed up a comfortable chair with a good lamp in the Pres. room. Drs. McIntire & Bruenn "assisted"; the Pres. continued his joking except at the actual moment of extraction. Polly & I listened from the living-room, and shortly the Pres. emerged, with his mouth closed on a bandage, which he was instructed to hold for 15 minutes. He managed to continue talking, however, without disturbing the bandage. He looked forlorn & made the most of *that,* and had us all laughing as usual!

. . . Today, the Pres. feeling a good deal relieved — The tooth inflammation practically gone. It is quite cold, but he put on his fur coat & drove us in his open car to the Knob where we sat in the sun for a while. The view is beautiful. This is the southern end of the Appalachian range so that the land gradually slopes down to the Gulf of Mexico.

We spent a quiet evening, the Pres. reading & at the last showing us a new game of solitaire. We were just settling down for the night when there was a sudden explosion in the cellar!! The Pres. called out to know what it was, Polly appeared with her flashlight & went off to investigate! Between the outer rim of Marines and the inner rim of S.S. it finally appeared that Arthur [Prettyman] had put on the night's coal supply too far forward in the furnace & that the gases formed there had blown open the door! No harm done, & we all settled down again, to a peaceful night — I must say I didn't worry much, for the only danger is fire, and in a one-story house like this the Pres. could be taken out of a window, if necessary.

✧ *Dec 1 Friday.* We have had an unbelievably peaceful time, but tonight a social weekend begins in the form of Mrs. Rutherfurd & Babs [Barbara Rutherfurd] & Monty Anderson. Amb. McCarthy comes for dinner too. A beautiful day, but quite cold . . .

The Pres. had his breakfast at 9, received Mr. Hassett & signed a lot of letters and appointments. Among the latter was that appointing [Edward R.] Stettinius Sec. of State. I was called in by Mr. Hassett to help handle these big appointments — for they roll up if not held flat. The ink must dry naturally on them, rather than be blotted. Then came the doctors for their look-over of the Pres. & then GGT with the morning mail. The Pres. finally came out of his room at about 12.30, and now sits in the chair with the rollers, ready to be moved to the dining table when it is time for lunch. Polly is packing up for our move to the cottage after lunch. It is something of a nuisance to have to move, but *I* want to see how comfortable the guest house can be. I have an idea we can keep it warmer than this house at night, as we can control the open fires!

Lizzie McDuffie arrived last night, & has taken charge. There is a great difference in the service, for she knows what is to be done & orders Tommy the Filipino around — This morning, instead of having my breakfast 20 mins. *late*, I had it ten minutes *early!* I saw her in a new light when she came in to the Pres. after having been in Johns Hopkins for months. She was just a "friend" for 5 minutes, told funny stories, laughed unrestrainedly & gestured most amusingly & even poked him on the shoulder on one occasion, to press home a point! She then resumed her position as maid. This is again an example of the Pres.' "humanity."

At lunch, the Pres. seemed tired and listless, didn't talk as much as usual — He ate a pretty good lunch, however — Afterwards, he went to his room for an hour of sleep. It was a pity he was waked, for he needs rest so much & was half asleep when he came out of his room. The sun was lovely on the porch & he decided to go out there for a while. He did a crossword puzzle, read the paper, & we talked a little. His back bothers him when he moves & he just doesn't feel up to anything. He stayed out for almost an hour, then came in & settled down in the leather chair and worked at the day's mail — reading it so as to be able to just say to GGT: "File," or "Tell him it can't be done" or whatever the answer may be!

At 6, the Rutherfurds arrived, minus the very old French maid we expected — The Pres. had described her as very, very old, & we visualized a thin, grey, timid little old lady, who couldn't speak English — The Pres. got me to call up Hacky & tell her & GGT to take care of her, see she was properly housed & fed, etc. Hacky said: "Tell the Pres. not to worry, we will take her under our wing." Mrs. Rutherfurd says she is enormous! Apparently Barbara just decided they could not bring her along & she would have to stay alone in the house at Aiken.

Mrs. Rutherfurd is perfectly lovely, tall, stately, & with the sweetest expression. She is much worried by the Pres.' looks, finds him thin and tired looking. I don't dare acknowledge that I feel the same way about him, for reports spread so rapidly from one person to another — Barbara is quite pretty, with dark arched eye-brows, tall, too thin. She is quiet and looks serious for her age —

Monty turned up a short time after the Rutherfurds, thrilled with the experience of coming here, & looking well — He is being put with Dr. Bruenn in Mrs. James Roosevelt's little cottage. Amb. McCarthy came for dinner at 7. We were just settling down to conversation when all the lights went out! When anything like this happens everyone wonders in the back of his mind if there is anything sinister in it!! All the S.S. are alert, the Marines peer into the darkness of the woods, we all watch look & listen — Candles are lighted, the Pres. jokes, cocktails are brought, the Pres. mixes them by the light of one candle which stands on the opposite side of the glasses from him. He peers through them to pour in just the right amount . . .

I have my sherry — Mrs. Rutherfurd has an old fashioned, made half-strength, but is given two, I notice, against her wishes! She says she never took one until she was fifty, & can't get used to seeing Barbara taking them — An hour & a half goes by. They discover that a fuse was blown out just above the cottage — all lights come on — there is no sabotage — The dinner starts cooking again on the electric stove — in a while we move to the table, . . . have a good dinner & delightful conversation & at a quarter to eleven the Pres. decided to send us all to bed — Polly & I to the guest house.

✧ *Dec. 2nd Saturday.* A *beautiful* day. . . . Arthur said he had orders to wake the Pres. at 9.15 — He wished the Pres. would sleep through the morning — I went down to the main house, found Mrs. Rutherfurd with her furs on over her wrapper, trying to get warm in Barbara's room, where B. lies in bed with a sore throat!

I found the Pres. sitting up in bed with a sweater on — feeling very cold. I got his grey coat & put it on him, also an extra sweater around his shoulders, while he ate breakfast. He feels more chipper this morning, after a good night's sleep, though the back still bothers him somewhat. Monty came with Dr. Bruenn about 9.30. Mr. Hassett came about 10. Miss Tully came about 11.

Monty & I, so afraid of "missing something," sit in the living room over near the dining table. Monty's eyes going up & down the columns of a very uninteresting paper, both ears taking in all that is happening. The Pres. sits near the fire in the leather chair, the card table in front of him — "doing" the day's mail. GGT works with him. Once in a while he makes a note himself, on a letter to be answered. He seems completely absorbed in something when suddenly: "Margaret, what is happening about our drive?"

I say that Monty will be there whenever the Pres. wants him.

"All right, in a few minutes then," & back to his work —

At about 12 he is carried out & bundled into his fur coat in the back of the big car with glass windshields on the sides, and the top down. Mrs. Rutherfurd climbs in & sits next to him. I am half hidden in the corner next to her — Polly & Monty Anderson sit on the little seats — In front, Monty the chauffeur & Charlie Fredericks & Fala — It is very cold for an open drive, but the sun is wonderful, and the wind & cold air & sun are just what the Pres. needs to stimulate him, just so long as he is warm. We drove to the Knob again, all the way in bright sun & the Pres. was relaxed & cheerful and seemed to enjoy every moment. Barbara has a bad throat & stayed in bed —

Lucy Rutherfurd is a *perfectly lovely person,* in every way one can think of, and is a wonderful friend to him. She worries a lot about him, as I do. There is so little one can do — I am so thankful that I can *sometimes* do a *little* for him in the way [of] taking care of him.

We had lunch as soon as we got home sitting at the table until 3.30 — The Pres. loves to sit & talk & smoke a cigarette. In the morning I asked him about daily plans, thinking that the only way for him to get the full benefit of this trip is to plan a little. But he said no, that was just what he does not want to do. At Washington, every minute is scheduled all day — Down here, he wants to feel free to do what he feels like doing at a moment's notice — He is not even planning on the day he will return — He is quite right, and is just now beginning to show some benefit . . .

֍ *Dec. 3rd Sunday.* . . . I had a little chance to talk to Lucy Rutherfurd. We understand each other perfectly, I think, and feel the same about F.D.R. She has worried & does worry, terribly, about him, & has felt for years that he has been terribly lonely. Harry Hopkins told a friend of hers that when he was living in the W.H. there were evenings after evenings when Franklin was left entirely alone, but for H.H. She thinks it is better now, for the last few years, since I am there a good deal and specially since Anna has been living in the W.H. We got to the point of literally weeping on each other's shoulder & we kissed each other, I think just because we each felt thankful that the other understood & wants to help Franklin!

We had lunch at 12.30, & at two, the Pres. took the Rutherfurds in the open car. We followed in the Rutherfurd car & we drove about an hour toward Augusta.

On the way, we ran over a pig, for which the S.S. paid the negro family $5.00 — much to their surprise, for no one ever pays them anything when pigs, chickens etc. are run over by car!

The Pres. then turned around; we got into the car with him, & the Rutherfurds proceeded on their way — We miss them for Mrs. is particularly lovely . . .

Franklin was "let down" after the visitors had gone, and I was glad when he went off to bed.

~ *Dec. 5 Monday.* The Pres. had a good day, and seems to me to be definitely better — He needs *rest* & *rest* & *rest,* interspersed with fresh air & cheerful conversation.

. . . We had a peaceful day, taking a drive in the open car after lunch, then a nap for the Pres. & then a walk for the dogs while the Pres. worked with D.B. & practically emptied one basketful — When he gets the other emptied he will be able to relax still better, for these are accumulations of work, and hang over his head until disposed of.

At dinner, he told us the story of the two beautiful spy ladies in Switzerland, when he & [Harvard classmate Charles B.] Bradley were 21 and on their own with $1,000 apiece for the trip. His story should be taken down word for word, but this is it in effect:

[Roosevelt and Bradley] were [in evening dress?] and saw two very attractive young women in black, at the next table — *evidently ladies.* By the most gradual & proper steps they picked up an acquaintance with them, and found by strange coincidence that they had planned exactly the same schedule.

They found themselves at the Hôtel Beau Rivage in Geneva, where Mr. & Mrs. Franklin Delano [the President's enormously wealthy great-uncle and great-aunt] always stayed, & the Mâitre d'Hôtel knew F. from several occasions when F. had visited his uncle & aunt. B. was particularly taken by the younger one, who looked 15 & was probably around 26. F.D.R. doesn't say he was "particularly taken" by the older one, but he naturally seemed to be thrown with her, since the other two kept together — The four had a very good time, taking the various trips arranged for tourists — up the Lake of Geneva on a boat, etc.

At dinner the 2nd evening, I think, the waiter came up & asked F. if he would be kind enough to speak to the Mâitre d'Hôtel in his office — it was very important.

F. was worried — thought it must be some bad news — excused himself & went out.

The M d H began somewhat like this: "Monsieur, I am an old man, I have known your uncle & aunt for a great many years, & I have known you since you were a child — you will forgive me if I speak frankly to you — What do you know about the two ladies with whom you are travelling?"

F. explained how they had met . . . , how their plans seemed to coincide, that they were the Baroness so & so & the Countess so & so, aunt & niece, very attractive and evidently ladies, etc. The M d H then proceeded to tell him that they were *not* the Baroness & the

Countess so & so, they were not aunt & niece, they were *not ladies!* But they were the best known pair of international blackmailers in Europe! Their game was to "be" whatever their victims were (they *were* good actresses!), in this case gentlemen & ladies — maneuver the victims into a compromising situation & then get the young man to send home for $10,000!

F.D.R. was *scared!* He asked the M d H what he should do — and proceeded to do it. He went back to the table with a long face, told B. & the ladies that he & B. would *have* to leave for Paris on the earliest morning train instead of the evening train, as planned. He had had bad news from home, didn't explain what it was, even to B. who was so crazy about the young countess that he might want to stay on with her! — Right after dinner R. & B. excused themselves "to pack." The ladies had planned something for the next day, & would take their accommodations for Paris the next night, as arranged, & would see the young men in Paris, etc.

In the meantime, the M d H had packed R & B's bags & taken them to the night train on which he had secured accommodations — the young men were spirited out of the hotel & off to Paris with advice of the M d H not to go to any of the usual haunts of Americans. They spent 4 days in Paris, before sailing for home, and had a far more interesting time seeing really French places than if they had done "the usual thing." It was a narrow escape, however!

∾· *Tuesday Dec. 6.* The Pres. was weighed today, and is definitely on the up-grade — He himself feels definitely better, which is half the battle . . .

∾· *Dec. 7, Wednesday.* A very good day for the Pres. It has been cloudy, but without wind, so he decided to go swimming. Mrs. Pearson [a long-time patient] was in the pool when we got there, it was warm in the enclosed pool, but the water was only about 83–84, instead of the 89 it is where it comes out of the ground. Dr. Bruenn, in charge, felt the responsibility keenly & wanted F. to be in the water *at the most* 10 minutes — But F. got talking to Mrs. Pearson about old times & then about his muscles; and he tried to walk & discovered his hips are stiff, and unless he loosens them up he will not be able to stand for his inauguration. So now there is a new problem of loosening the President's hips! He thinks he can do it by lying flat on a board, with his legs hanging, to stretch the front hip muscles. The Pres. seems to know as much about his muscles as the doctors — probably more!

I was watching the time & Dr. B. was wondering how to get him out — It was 20 minutes before he finally came out. We all combined to keep him warm on his way back to the fireplace, & to our joy, he has only had *good* reactions. He ate a *real* lunch, with *real* appetite, taking two helpings of everything and after lunch he was completely relaxed, & had a sound sleep until almost 4.

D.B. came then, and he worked on the mail until 6.30 — too long entirely. The Irwins & Dr. Bruenn came to dinner. The Pres. did all the talking as usual, and looked tired when they finally left. It was just a little "too much & too long," but I don't think the one social day will harm him, if it isn't repeated . . .

⟜ *Dec. 8th Thursday.* . . . When the Pres. was just about finished his breakfast I went in to say good morning — He had a slight headache, said he felt "executive," but didn't want to *do* anything. With these contradictory feelings, he decided to stay indoors & get some accumulated work off his mind — It poured all day — Polly took the dogs out, in my Sears Roebuck raincoat & my half-rubbers — and her tan & red umbrella . . .

Anna telephoned from Wash. with some political items & family news — Her John expects to get back from abroad this coming weekend — Buz comes from school; later, Sistie, so she won't be able to come down at all — Polly has her accommodations to return to New York, on Sunday, so I shall be left in charge of the Pres. for the whole week. There are uses for single old ladies who don't *have* to be at any particular place at any particular time. How fortunate it is that Mama is well and strong and doesn't need me at home . . .

The [Cason] Callaways & Haugheys were asked "to tea."

I said something to the Pres. about what would be given them with the tea . . . "Oh," said F.D.R. "if I gave them *tea,* they would never come again!"

The long table was set with glasses & bottles — Polly in charge. The folding table, which we use for meals, was set with the tea tray, two plates of sandwiches, and a beautiful plum cake, made at the hotel & sent to the Pres. by Mrs. [Ruth] Stevens, the Manager.

There is much talk about the Warm Springs Hotel. Some 5 yrs. ago, the owner, Mr. [Frank] Allcorn, was passing through W.S. & had to spend the night in the only hotel. He was shown into a room that was beyond description, dirty, and dingy & unattractive. The sheets on the bed had been used for at least a week — He asked the maid if there were not a better & cleaner room. She said no — this was like all the rooms — no clean sheets, etc. He decided to do something about a situation which was dangerous to public health, & bought the hotel. Judging from the dining rooms & the one room & bath we saw — it compares favorably with the best. The bedroom was as fresh, attractive and comfortable as any room at the Waldorf — They tell us the food is delicious and the service excellent —

But to return to the Little White House! The guests arrived promptly at 5.30. Mrs. Haughey was delighted to have tea, & took three cups — The Pres. took two cups & I took three — I think we pretty well emptied the pot between us — Everyone else had tall drinks served by Polly. It was a nice party — The Callaways are typical southerners. He has just been put on the board of the U.S. Steel (???). He has done a great deal for agriculture in this state & raises ducks, chickens, turkeys etc. in huge quantities, freezes them & ships them all over the country — The Pres. says he is quite a remarkable person.

Mrs. Callaway is tall and slender & has charm. When she had had her second drink she became over-"sweet" and proceeded to drape herself on the arm of the Pres.' chair & around his shoulders! — I haven't decided whether it amused him or made him uncomfortable — probably a little of both! He says it's just typical southern! I must say for her that she did her best not to take the second glass, but Polly insisted. I am afraid that I & my tea are always a drag on people who enjoy getting loosened up with a couple of drinks — that is — if they notice me at all! In the White House, no one *would* notice, but down here, and in the presence of the Pres. they are self-conscious . . .

ᐧᐁᐧ *Dec 9 Friday.* . . . A quiet evening by the fire. I think the Pres. looks a little better, but he needs a lot of quiet and sun. Just one week more.

He spoke very seriously at dinner about the German menace. He has just had a secret report from a German source which has been quite reliable in the past, to the effect that the Germans have a V3 bomb which will kill by concussion everything within a mile. They are planning to use it on New York for morale purposes — again, not seeming to realize that it will have the exact opposite effect to that which they expect. The entire Atlantic seaboard has relaxed all its dim-outs and air-raid precautions, etc. & the Pres. sent word to the Gen. staff that all previous preparations of that sort should be reviewed on the chance that the report about the V3 may be true. He said that in the next war, the side which first uses these new explosives will undoubtedly win. The Germans are way ahead of us in that direction, though we are doing a lot of research trying to catch up to them. We found one of their V1 robots, unexploded, & are improving on it.

[The Nazis struggled to forestall defeat with what Hiter called "revenge weapons," first the short-range V-1 pilotless drone aircraft and, after their bases on the Channel coast were overrun, mid-range V-2 rockets. These continued to rain down on London, with much loss of life, until Allied troops finally overwhelmed the launching facilities, in March of 1945. And there were plans on the German drawing boards for a still more formidable weapon that, using the V-2 as its second stage, was intended to reach targets twenty-eight hundred miles away.]

How unbelievably horrible it all is. In those mysterious books & reports about "Shangri-Las" in the Himalaya Mts. it is all prophesied. I keep wondering if they may not be entirely true, those reports, and that the human race is out to destroy itself. Only the few [who] live in isolated places may survive.

[Lucy Mercer Rutherfurd to Daisy]

Aiken, S.C.

December 8, 1944

Dear Margaret — Still no letter from you which you said was on the way so I shall quickly send this off and not wait for it any longer! I still want to thank you for the nice letter you wrote me on September 7th, and to tell you what a very real joy it is to me to know you and see for myself what an angel you are — I knew it must be so as I had heard it from the Source I Do Not Question — as you know as well anyone in the world the warmth of his praise and of his love. I felt badly to have been the cause of evicting you — but you can imagine how very wonderful it was for me to feel myself under the same roof and within the sound of the voice we all love after so many, many years.

I don't want my pen to run away with me — So, quickly, dear Margaret, I send you my love — I hope Monty [Anderson] will come to see us — If you send me his address I could send him a line — and if you come to see him you will let me know, won't you? I would so love to tuck you away here — and perhaps when the great meeting [the Yalta Conference] takes place you might feel like a little rest here & I could take care of you. I lead a completely quiet life & you need no clothes — you could work on your beloved papers & perhaps I could help you!

Do say you will come.

> Affectionately,
> Lucy Rutherfurd

∾ *Dec. 10 Saturday.* A beautiful day, and Polly has to leave tomorrow. She is such a vital person, so alive and attractive, we will miss her terribly — I think the holiday here has done her a great deal of good, in forcing her to be quiet at times. This is such a lovely place, on the hillside, with not a sign of human beings in any direction.

In the afternoon, we drove over to the Callaways'. They have 32,000 acres which they are evidently "working" in several ways: woods, turkeys, chickens, ducks — The house is a glorified log cabin, furnished in excellent taste but with nothing in it which has any associations. It seems strange to Polly & me, whose houses are full of family things — But, as the Pres. said on the way home: a new civilization is growing up down here.

The Pres. told Mrs. C. he would like to have *tea*. When we were seated in front of the fire, a maid & butler (coloured) brought in a tray with silver teapot, etc. and had it set on a long table in the middle of the room. Another table to the side was set with necessaries for cocktails etc. Mr. C. began telling F. of some wonderful brands, & F. said he would try them instead of the tea — I said I would take the tea anyway, since it was ready — Delicious sandwiches, enormous ripe olives and nuts. Mrs. C. then confessed that she had never made tea in her life, neither had her cook! They had had to consult a cook-book!!

∾ *Dec. 11th Sunday, 3.30 p.m.* Polly got off with Sister at 10 this morning. We shall be awfully quiet without her . . .

Now, F. is supposedly reading a detective story but though he is still holding the book, he hasn't turned a page in 20 minutes and I am quite sure he is fast asleep. I can't see his eyes — but — the book has just slipped to his lap! We are sitting on the porch in a delicious sun, with Fala curled up between us!

I feel very luxurious in my room & bath, vacated by Polly — I won't have to wind my head in a scarf to hide the combs when I go to take my bath! The S.S. who sits in the hall at night is tactful, and vanishes every morning before I come out of my room, but I am never sure, & this morning Tommy the Filipino was fixing the fire when I came through. Not that *they* care!

The only thing that worries me a little is that I am far from F.D.R. in case he should want anything in the night. But am going to leave my door [open] a crack, & can hear him if he calls — What a privilege to be *really* taking care of F.D.R. for a whole week —

Charlie Fredericks sees things just as I do, & we are the great "connivers." We are, I think, equally devoted — Col. Killen tells me that many of his men have never seen the Pres. & that he is detailing them to the pool, or to the gate, etc. as far as possible, so that they will be able to see the Pres. at close range, at least once . . .

A most restful day for F.D.R. He did stamps and signed some mail, then, after dinner, we played a couple of games of Chinese checkers . . . He got really interested & said he would get excited & not be able to sleep!! I was quite excited myself, for I was giving him a good game, instead of being beaten right off at the beginning, as usually happens!

[Lucy Mercer Rutherfurd to Daisy]

Aiken

Sunday [December 11, 1944]
Dear Margaret — Your letter came soon after I had mailed mine — and I was glad to get it and to hear the good news from Dr. [Bruenn] — It is only a week ago that we left you but to me it seems months — or years — & I have been hoping for word from F.

You who live within the radius of the arc lights do not know how hard it can be when one is beyond their rays. Yes, of course, every-thing is *naturally* "off the record" — It never occurred to me that needed to be said.

As to the valet, I don't know of a suitable one — though you are quite right & I might so easily have one up my sleeve! I have a man that has been with us for years & was wonderful with my husband when he was ill as he is very strong & very gentle & very loyal — but he is very lazy, too, & getting old and not very fond of work. There are lots of [indecipherable] — some good, some bad — but on the whole I know he wouldn't do. Aren't there some good Pullman porters? Such a nice one on the train that brought me to Aiken last year (private car). He spoke to me at Allamuchy that day you were there and I was struck with his respect and sympathy and nice man-ners. F. probably knows the one. Of course, he too might be a poor valet & have a difficult family. I shall keep my ear to the ground. There is another one on the Aiken train who has taken care of us for years & is very capable, too, but I should think anyone, even the Pullman Company, would give their best so gladly to F —

With my love and in haste. I thank you for all you say in your letter, with which I agree —

Lucy

It is pouring here & gloomy — I hope it is not so with you — 32 — so we fear an ice storm —

Please God, F is still gaining. It seemed too awful that 3 people remembered 3 different weights —

These State Department & British episodes must be exhausting and oh, oh why couldn't the Republicans produce something worth a hill of beans! And how can one help worrying, especially when one does not know what goes on from day to day?

[The State Department "episodes" had involved Eleanor Roosevelt. The new secretary of State, Edward Stettinius, had appointed two assistants whom she believed to be reactionaries and she had written FDR two sarcastic letters of protest, at which he had evidently shown his irritation to Daisy and Mrs. Rutherfurd.]

☙ *Dec 12 Monday.* A perfectly horrid day outside, blowing hard & actually "flurrying" with snow most of the day — So I took Fala for two walks, but otherwise stayed in with F.D.R. I went to the village with Fala, bought a cotton nightgown for $2.00 and some pecans. D.B. came in the morning & they actually *emptied* a wire basket! It was cold all day and everyone concentrated on keeping the living room warm. We decided that the "dining-room" (the middle part) was rather chilly, so, after dinner, the Pres. decided we had better sit in the "library" (sofa in the corner near the fireplace). He put his feet up and was very comfortable with some pillows and a detective story. I sat on the stool (coffee table?) and he dictated some reminiscences of the last war — while he puffed a cigarette in his long holder — I will type these reminiscences of his and he will then sign them. [FDR dictated to Daisy several of his favorite dinner-table stories, which he hoped one day to use in his memoirs.]

☙ *Dec. 15 Thursday.* How can I have missed these last 2 days! The weather is just hopeless and we hug the fire. The Pres. didn't go out of the house the 12th or 13th, but seemed quite cheerful and content — I once asked if he wouldn't like to have someone in, for a meal. He said: "You won't believe me when I tell you that I *like* to be quiet and I *don't want* anyone to talk to. Thank the Lord, I don't *have* to talk to you or entertain you"! Of course it *is* true, for the rare occasions when it happens like this, and it is true then, just because he hardly ever has a moment to himself.

The night before last, he was dictating to me from the sofa when Dr. Bruenn, Geo. Fox and Dr. [Robert] Duncan [a chest specialist from Bethesda Naval Hospital] came in at about 9.30. Dr. Duncan has come down to look over the polio hospital &, I suspect, primarily to see the Pres. & see how he is getting along — Well, before they came in, the Pres. was entirely quiet and relaxed, and dictating between puffs of his cigarette, looking toward the ceiling, & entirely unconscious of anything but his story — The minute the three men came in, he became the charming host, laughed & joked & told them stories, teased Bruenn, etc. He looked remarkably well, after the 2 long quiet days.

Yesterday, it seemed warmer, so we went to the pool for a half hour. The Pres. was carried into the water and just stood quietly with an attentive "court" paddling around him. He looked well then also. We went from the pool to the Marine Mess Hall for lunch. The Marines were drawn up at attention & their drum & bugle corps piped an appropriate greeting —

A coal stove in the center of the room is the only heat, but is quite sufficient, if kept going! A long table was set along one side of the room for the Pres.' party . . . The place cards were tents made of real army canvas — little pup-tents for us & a special, large tent for the Pres. His is an exact replica of the tents the marines are using, even to the little red bucket, which Col. Killen says is made out of an army thimble! It has been turned over to me for [the Roosevelt Library].

Lunch was very good, and the young officers at our end of the table, *such* nice boys. Some of them have been overseas, in the South Pacific — There is a deep sadness in their eyes — and they must feel lonely with civilians who just *can't really* understand — I imagine that they can feel much closer to, for instance, Cornelia Dewey [a patient], who is a living skeleton & has suffered for so many years — The Pres. was tired when we came home & went to his room for a nap.

I went with Fala to see Amb. McCarthy & to ask him for dinner. The Pres. & I sat quietly reading until 7, when the Amb. arrived. He is a dear person & the Pres. is devoted to him & enjoys talking to him, but the Pres. was already tired & the 3 hrs. of talking, until 10, was just too much & he looked awfully tired when he went to bed a little after ten. As usual, the doctors arrived at 9.30, & seeing a visitor, slipped in to the Pres. room through the bathroom, to wait.

I am *hoping* to get a little closer to the doctors, so that they will talk more freely to me. But they put on, or rather, *keep* on, their doctor's manner and tell you nothing. They seem to be concentrating on the Pres.' heart. He himself said it was a "cardiac" condition, and *that his muscles are "deteriorating,"* and *that they don't know why.*

This is where I am hoping Lenny can do some good, even if we can arrange only periodic treatments — From the little I *know* and from what I have observed for the last year, I am afraid the trouble is the Leukemia from which the Pres. suffered in 1939(?). No one has mentioned that word, but they said at the time that his illness was from a lack of *white* corpuscles in the blood. I have looked that up & can find only the one disease, & that is considered fatal, over a period of time. [As explained above, FDR never had leukemia.]

I hope & pray I am wrong — and I hope & pray that if it *is* this disease, Lenny will be able to arrest it. As far as I can find out, the Medical Profession have nothing to offer — Again, I *hope* I am wrong.

The weather bureau offers warmer weather in a day or two, so it may clear & be lovely when we leave on Sunday night!

Fred Botts & Miss [Alice] Plastridge [the chief physical therapist at Warm Springs and the woman who helped teach FDR the simulated walk he used so effectively while campaigning] got into the car, and poured their troubles into the ears of F.D.R. F.D.R. understands the situation very well: There is no "moving spirit" here. The [chief surgeon] attends to the medical and has no interest in the general picture. Old patients come down for a few weeks to find the swimming pool closed & no community feeling in the place — The buildings, even, are not kept in proper order, and the food, though well planned & perfectly good, is served cold —

We came back to the cottage for an hour before going to a cocktail party at Hacky's house (the Lovett Cottage). There were just Hacky, Tully, Brady, Bachelder, Winegar, Dr. Duncan, Bruenn, Hassett, Long, [John McMullin, of the White House communications room], Fox.

The Pres. told me to tell him when it was 6.30, but everyone was sitting adoringly around him, very quietly too, and he was reminiscing along in an effortless way, so I just didn't feel I *could* say anything. They might, too, resent it, if I did, so we stayed on until 7.20 — I was surprised that it was such a *quiet* party — Hacky made old-fashioneds behind a curtain & the two doctors did most of the passing around of little [hors d'oeuvres] to go with the cocktails . . .

They are a friendly happy group of people, all of them devoted to the Pres. Hacky in particular is very vital, very quick witted & very understanding. She carried the conversation most of the time, "opposite" the Pres. who is, of course, *the center.* We got home in time for dinner. At dinner we discussed spiritualistic experiences.

ↅ *Dec. 15 — Friday.* . . . [FDR] just started his message to Congress when Mr. [Robert] Hannegan [of the Democratic National Committee] arrived for lunch. The Pres. was going to keep him one hour, to two o'clock, but it was 3.15 before he finally left — The more I see the Pres. the more convinced I am that the *only way he can live* is by having *shorter* sessions, and repeated rests in between — It is probably the heart, for he gets so tired-looking & grey, but looks 100% better after a rest —

It is Amb. McCarthy's 75th birthday today, and he is giving his own party — We took a little drive, ending at [his] house at 10 to 5. The Pres. didn't want to get involved in a big party & asked me, early in the day, which I thought would be the best time for him to go: at the beginning or at the end! From *my* point of view the answer was obvious: the *beginning* of a cocktail party is gay and amusing — the *end* is childish and maudlin. I didn't say this to the dear Pres. but suggested that it might be less tiring to combine it with a drive, than to make a special trip just before dinner — He agreed, and it was *very* nice —

. . . The Pres. & I came home, had a good dinner of red snapper & string beans, & chocolate cake, etc.

We stayed at the table, talking until about 8.30 & then he got on the sofa. We have done a little "moving" . . . It looks more comfortable, & when the Pres. is on the sofa, it brings him nearer the fire. Mrs. Callaway gave me, for him, a book & he got right at it, read it aloud to me, sitting in the chair in the corner — He needs some chintz covers on that sofa & chair & some hangings. He is planning to come down in the spring, & says he will bring Polly & me again. It is *so* wonderful that he wants me and that I can be of this little use to him . . .

ↅ *Dec. 16 Saturday.* A perfect day for our last day here — Hassett at 10, Tully from 11–1, lunch 1–2, a drive in F.'s little blue car, to the Knob & back through the fernery, where the road in places consists of a ditch on one side, and a mountain on the other — You find yourself quite surprised at the fact that you remain upright sometimes!

. . . Dinner at Amb. McCarthy's, just us three — This is F.D.R.'s 2nd house, built by him for the express purpose of getting other people to build also. We sat by the fire for ½ an hour, with sherry & cocktails, then moved to the little table at one side & had a perfectly delicious dinner: fresh lobster on toast, broiled chickens, creamed celery, then a delicious dessert flavored with sherry or something & covered with whipped cream. Mr. McC brought out a bottle of delicious champagne — and we ended up with coffee. I was supposed to get the Pres. away at 9.15, but it was near 10.15 when we finally moved. The Amb. is a charming and interesting man. The Pres. enjoys talking to him & will miss him, now that he is retiring to Canada on Jan. 1.

When we got back home I tried to persuade the Pres. to go right off to bed — he looked tired & was yawning, but insisted on resting on the sofa for a while and kept right on talking through his yawns — even after the doctors arrived! Finally, he went off to his room with the 3 following him, & I could hear him telling them funny stories & their appreciative laughter — 11.15, and the doctors have gone, but Arthur is still fussing around in there —

We telephoned Lucy Rutherfurd & she will drive up to Atlanta from Augusta, & return [to Washington] with us on the train . . . It will be lovely to see her again.

❧ *Dec. 17 Sunday*. Atlanta, Ga. We are having a servicing stop — Lucy has just come on board and I have left her with the Pres. so they can have a little talk without an audience. I told the Amb. that she wanted to talk to the Pres. about something, so he has vanished into another car.

We got packed up very quietly this morning without hurry or worry — while the Pres. attended to his correspondence. He is definitely better though he hasn't put on much weight. What he needs is this sort of life as a regular thing, instead of just for a couple of weeks once in a while. He drove himself to the station with Fala & me next to him, stopping at Georgia Hall where all the patients were drawn up to wave goodbye to him. Among them was Alain Darlan [the son of the Vichy Admiral Jean Darlan, who became head of French North Africa and then was assassinated], who is being treated for a bad case of polio. He is in a wheel chair and repeated to the Pres. that he was getting steadily better, "Thanks to you, Mr. President."

It was a cheering warm farewell to the Pres. who told them he hoped to be back again in March . . .

I hated to leave the little house, with its cheerful fire burning day & night, its large windows looking out over the valley of pines. To be in a position to see F.D.R. every day for three weeks, to wait on him, to be at hand when he wants anything, whether it's a cigarette or just some one to talk to, is the greatest privilege in the world, and an education in itself. I am a lucky, lucky person.

[The White House]

⌒ *Dec. 19th.* . . . This morning, I had an example of the way the Roosevelts "play the game"! First, though, to just put down everything, the Sec. of State came on board to greet the Pres., found him looking much rested, & told me it was really up to the President to let him & all the rest do the mass of paper work there is, to relieve himself. The Pres. promises to *try* to not get overtired. We drove from the station, with me sitting between these two important men, & taking it all in the most casual manner! *That* is the amazing thing, that *I* am quite casual in the august presence of the biggest men in the world today! I don't understand it myself, except that F.D.R. is so much bigger than all the "bigness" — Books will be written about this for many years to come.

Well — at the W.H. Sistie stood, shivering & very pretty, in a red dress — Buzzie looking very well in his grey military school uniform, with a young school friend. Anna came dashing out just as her father got out of the car. The Sec. went off to his office — We all went up to breakfast in the West Hall. Anna put me at the end of the table opp. the Pres. On the Pres.' right, Sistie & Buzz: on his left the new daughter-in-law, Faye [Emerson, the actress], & Elliott.

They came in from the Lincoln room, Elliott evidently embarrassed. The Pres. put out his hand & pulled down Faye for a father-in-lawy kiss on the cheek — Everyone acted casual, & breakfast was gotten through with general talk about Elliott's dogs, his children, plans for Xmas, etc. The first meeting is over, and the worst — But *why* F.D.R. has to have these *family* things, on top of everything else — *I* don't know . . . [Privately, the President had little faith in the future of this marriage. Dr. Bruenn was in his bedroom the morning Roosevelt read about it in the newspaper. "*That* won't last," he said and flung the paper to the floor.]

I had quite a talk with Anna about her father's health. It is a very difficult problem, & I am entirely convinced that he can *not* keep up the present rate — he will kill himself if he tries, and he won't be so very useful to the world then . . . [Daisy was determined to do something. On the way back to Rhinebeck, she stopped to see Lenny at his New York hotel.]

✒ *Dec 20, Wednesday.* . . . I discussed at length [with Lenny] the question of F.D.R. I told him: The Pres. has high blood pressure, feels that his muscles are gradually weakening, has had a lump in his left side which is supposed to be weak muscles which cannot keep the organs in, at that point, but there is no pain or even discomfort.

Lenny said he had watched F.D.R.'s pictures on the screen and has diagnosed his case thus, plus what I have told him: the spleen is the organ that is making most of the trouble — in combination with others. The doctors admittedly know very little about the spleen. The Pres.' spleen has been gradually atrophying — When any undue exercise stirs it up, the blood pressure is temporarily better, instead of higher, as might be expected. When the Pres. has been particularly quiet, as he usually is during the night, the spleen practically stops functioning & the blood pressure goes down — but the general condition is a little worse, whenever *any* organ is not functioning.

Lenny says he believes F.D.R. is also deficient in either red or white corpuscles — He says his present condition is very dangerous, if his "absentee" diagnosis is correct. The danger is a thrombosis.

Lenny added that of course he may find an entirely different condition when he sees the Pres. I told him of my plan: When the Pres. can fix an afternoon, I will telephone Lenny & he will take the 2 P.M. from Grand Central. He will be smuggled into the library & the Pres. will come up "for tea" with the family [at Wilderstein]. Just as soon as the S.S. have gone out of the front door, the family will leave the library and Lenny will start working on F.'s feet — I am almost *afraid* of this meeting, for so *much* depends on it —

[On Christmas Day the President gave the go-ahead. Daisy called Lenny, who said he'd be happy to come up and see the President on the twenty-seventh.]

[Hyde Park]

✒ *Dec. 26th, Tuesday.* The Pres. arrived in H.P. Sunday morning, has had a hectic 2 days — He called me up at lunch time yesterday, having had the entire household in his room opening stockings, all the morning — He said he felt quite hoarse and would be worse after a long afternoon of opening the library-full of presents!

On Sunday afternoon, his Xmas message was beautiful, as always, & everyone remarked on how well his voice sounded — so strong and clear. ["We will pray," he said, "that with victory will come a new day of peace on earth in which all the nations of the earth will join together for all time."]

At the house are: 5 Boettigers, Elliott & new wife, Ethel & 2 little boys. While F. was talking to me on the phone, he interrupted himself to say: "I hear Jo (Franklin III) coming — He's grand — He's getting to be such a *big* boy." He said it with real pleasure — I suppose it must mean a little more, how one's *namesake* turns out —

Without warning, the Pres. arrived at the Library at about a quarter of twelve — I was at my desk when Charlie the Faithful suddenly appeared in the doorway — He is the *nicest* man — a heart of gold, and a good head on his shoulders — I wish he could be on duty 24 hrs a day!

The Pres. looked better than I would have expected to see him after the hard work in Wash. since his return from W. Springs & the excitements of Xmas . . . I gave him a bottle of garlic pills which he put in his pocket & promised to take 3 times a day (if he remembers!)

We talked about Lenny & planned for them to meet at our house tomorrow. I called up Lenny who promised to come. I pray & pray that this will work out for the good of F.D.R.

Mrs. R. sent word for me to go to lunch, which I did, with her & the Pres. She appeared just as he was starting. They both thought the decorations lovely in the Pres.' room, including the tiny Xmas tree on the table. At lunch were Sistie & Buzz, Ethel & I. At a side table the 3 little boys: Franklin 3rd & Chris, and Johnny Boettiger. Franklin 3rd is a charming very good looking little fellow. He gave his "Papa" a hug & kiss twice, in a most spontaneous way, which pleased him terribly. F. 3rd is evidently a very affectionate little child. He & his mother seemed very close. Ethel was sweeter & more attractive than I have ever seen her —

After lunch, the Pres. went up to rest & told me to return at 3.30 & help him unpack & list some of the 40-odd presents he still has to undo! I came back to find a completely silent house: Mrs. R. & Sistie reading by the fire, the Pres. still asleep . . . I settled down with the paper & read of our reverses on the French battlefront — an unhappy situation which we pray will not last. [The Germans had launched the massive counteroffensive in the Ardennes Forest that led to the Battle of the Bulge.]

After a while the Pres. came down & got to work — Some beautiful books from Bernard Baruch, a 10 lb. bag of cornmeal from me (from Warm Springs — to bring back memories of Daisy the coloured cook's delicious corn bread). Geo. Fox brought in the afternoon eggnog which took upon itself to upset all over the table, the parcels and the rug! Great excitement: I poured it off the wrappings to prevent its soaking through while Ethel flew for some towels, & GGT rang the bell for the servants. (That is rather amusing: "GGT rang the bell" for the servants, while Ethel & I did all the mopping-up we could!)

All was clean & clear again & I left GGT in my chair, making the list, while I went home. I took with me the Pres's *real reading* copy of his Xmas message — GGT will be annoyed (as usual) that he has given it to me, and will make a duplicate copy for the files, which *I*, however, will know is *not* the original reading copy! The Pres. knows these will eventually come to the Library —

⟋ *Dec. 27th Wednesday.* 10 mins. of 3 P.M. In my usual state of mental uncertainty when I have not had any direct word from F.D.R.! Lenny arrives at 4.05 at Rhinecliff [the nearest railroad station to Wilderstein]; Arthur to meet him & take him to the house. Buzz came in this morning at noon, with the news that Hassett & GGT had but just come, the Pres. had slept late — Mrs. R. came in to attend to various details — I am dining there, but before that, the Pres. is supposed to come here, & drive me home, and have his session with Lenny — I am quite sure he will turn up — but — *"en attendant . . ."*

Well — The Pres. came at about 4, and after doing a little work in his room, we got into the big car & drove through a real snowstorm to our house. Mama, Arthur & Lenny & the tea-tray were all "set" in the library. As soon as the S.S. had gone out, Mama & Arthur retired, and Lenny got to work on the Pres.' legs, right over his trousers & while he sat with his feet on the floor. Lenny was delighted & surprised at how much good circulation there is in those thin useless legs — After a while he got the Pres. to lie down on the sofa, & took off his shoes and stockings — Began to work on the feet — Suddenly, he looked up at the Pres. with a smile & said: "President, you're going to walk!"

I can't describe the hour & a half during which Lenny sat at the end of the sofa, working on the Pres.' feet, and carrying on an easy flow of conversation, mainly on the nerves, the organs, the glands, interspersed with a funny story, or a joke.

The Pres. lay there, relaxed, terribly interested, believing & not daring to believe. Those two complete contrasts: Lenny, simple, child-like, uneducated, but deeply conscious of a Power which he can't explain, but which he knows comes from God, for the benefit of human beings. The Pres., the product of the best education, cultivated, man of the world, but with a deep knowledge of God which makes him capable of believing in a person like Lenny who has a "gift." Those two could talk together and understand each other —

Lenny told the Pres. that his main trouble is the spleen; that it is very much congested; that the spleen is not making the blood which is its function; that therefore the Pres. has been losing weight since last April. As a corollary, the liver, pancreas and kidneys are also *partly* out of order — I *think* he said that, as yet, there is no definite crystal-lizing of the deposits — The deposits are still soft, & therefore the more easily removed —

Lenny got the circulation going in both the Pres.' legs, so that even 3 hrs. later, they were still "tingling," all the way up to his hips. He had had no such feeling since he had infantile, 23 years ago.

At six, we put the shoes & stockings on, brought in tea & sand-wiches & Mama & Arthur — The Pres. said he would see Lenny tomorrow, again.

We got into the car, took Lenny along, dropped him off at the Beekman Arms for the night, the Pres. sending Charlie Fredericks in with him to be sure they gave him a room for the night.

The Pres. then drove me back to Hyde Park; the snow swirling around, driving very heavy — We had cocktails in his study; Mrs. R., Miss Thompson, Buzzie — Then to dinner & the party at the Library for the M.P.s. The Pres. enjoyed it, but as the evening wore on, he seemed to me to be terribly tired & to be making an effort even in ordinary conversation. I got very worried, for fear the treatment might be having some reactions, but he said no, he felt all right, & felt this way every night. I helped Mrs. R. & Miss T. & Mrs. Stoller to distrib-ute the cornucopias & handkerchiefs to the M.P.s & then went "home" with the Pres. — not waiting for the end of the party. He went right off to bed — and so am I, in the middle east room, with the big bathroom.

⌖ *Dec 28th Thursday.* . . . The news from Europe is a *little* better this morning — or seems so, from the headlines. Mrs. R. & Miss T. left for the 9 o'clock train after Mrs. R. asked me to be with the Pres.

for lunch today & tomorrow. I said I "am always at his service," which did not surprise her —

I then went up to see the Pres. while he had his breakfast of hot cakes. We planned for the day: Lenny arrives by bus at Hyde Park at 12.50 — [William J.] Nichols & I pick him up & bring him to the Library — I go over for lunch at the Big House . . . The Pres. will come over right after his nap & will have *his* treatment.

Lenny will then drive back to Rhinebeck with Nichols & give him a treatment, and return to New York.

At the Pres.' breakfast, he told me he will arrange to have Lenny give him regular treatments in Wash. It *can't do any harm,* & may do untold good. It is now 12.10 — a beautiful day, with the sun shining on last night's snow fall.

Later — It has all happened as planned! A miracle in itself —

Lenny found Polly's hand in bad condition from deposits which have already crystallized to a certain extent — He connects the trouble with a broken toe which she says she set herself; it gives her a lot of trouble, in cold weather particularly, and at other times also. I hope she will have the treatments, though she seemed a little skeptical about results — it seems almost fantastic — but — the proof of the pudding!

Lenny worked on the Pres. for about 2 hrs. & was overjoyed to find far more improvement than he had hoped for — The Pres.' legs have not stopped tingling and he *wants* to move his muscles which are too weak to move! He has had no such "feelings" since he had infantile. Lenny says his organs are badly congested & should have treatment every other day "for a time." Lenny found a "stirring" in them today, much more than he expected, and especially in the spleen, which is the one in the worst condition. As the creating of white & red corpuscles in the spleen is *essential* to life, the function of it *must* be restored. This all ties up with what I have thought, in connection with the Pres.' illness three (?) years ago.

[Some years later, Lenny set forth his own reminiscences of his meetings with FDR in a clumsily typed manuscript, a copy of which is at the Franklin D. Roosevelt Library. When he had finished the first treatment, he wrote, and was putting the President's sock back on, FDR shouted out to Daisy, "I can move my little toe!"

"What a thrill I got when this great man said that, how I felt . . . [H]e turned to me and said, 'There is hope, isn't there?'

"I said, 'Prez, you bet . . . it won't be long before . . . I will have you doing a buck dance.'

"He . . . said, 'Who can tell what any man can do.'"

This has an authentic Rooseveltian ring, but it is difficult to believe that even so steadfast an optimist as FDR could really have believed he would ever walk again unaided. More likely he thought the treatments could do him no harm, might even make him feel a little better, and would, in any case, please his dear friend Daisy.]

I am torn between the fear of being *too* hopeful, and the fear of not having faith enough! But I know that this is my *reason* working, and that, at bottom, I am *sure* that F can be tremendously improved in health if Lenny has a chance to work on him. I am staying over at the Roosevelts' for the night.

∾ *Dec. 29th Friday.* I came down to breakfast with Buzz at 8.30. Charlie was in the hall afterwards & said, "Even Geo. Fox confesses that the Pres. looks so much better." I went up to the Pres.' room and found him just starting his breakfast. He said Geo. Fox was "alarmed" at the improvement in the blood pressure!! that is, last night. He did not turn up at all, this morning — probably thought the Pres. so well, he did not need to have it taken again!

. . . The Pres. looks pretty well, but says he is "all tied up" & fears a headache if something doesn't happen — I wish he had spoken to Lenny about that —

The Pres. felt relieved when he came to the big room, to be ready by the fire when "Martha" & Mrs. Ostgaard arrived. He looks definitely better to me, and feels the tingling in his legs. I wrote a note to Anna about Monday's massage & pray for nothing that will interfere: six treatments in the next two weeks, before he goes to the Black Sea to meet Stalin, right after Inauguration.

[Daisy to Anna Roosevelt Boettiger]

Dec. 29th 1944

Dear Anna

The miracle of 1945 is already happening! Your Pa is going to be massaged!

———

Yesterday, Polly was here with a masseuse who has rubbed various people from Damon Runyon in California to Thomas J. Watson [head of IBM] in New York.

He — your Pa — liked the sample rubbing on his legs so much, that he has "ordered" Mr. Harry Setaro (Italiano descent) [Lenny] to appear at the White House at 9 P.M. on this coming Monday, Jan. 1 1945 —

Mr. Setaro will call *you* up between 6 & 7 on Monday evening, and you can arrange how he is to get through the gate & up to your father's room, where your father is theoretically (!) supposed to be settled for the night (9 P.M.!)

The plan is that for the next two weeks there will be a massage Monday, Wednesday & Friday nights — I am writing this with your father's knowledge-approval, as he expects to plunge into speech making the minute he reaches the White House tomorrow — & may forget this most important item!

Much love to you all,
Margaret

* * *

❧ This is the end of my Diary for 1944, for I won't hear from F.D.R. until 1945 — I am full of hope for him, through the hands of Lenny, who says he is just a tool of God.

1945

There Is So Little
One Can Do

[Wilderstein]

↣ *Jan. 2nd Tuesday.* The roads are a sheet of ice, quite impossible for the Nash to attempt, so I stayed home & did a full day's work on old family letters. Mr. Nixon & I talked over the possibility of just such a day and he thinks it quite legitimate for me to work on old letters in *this* house, as well as in other people's houses — which is part of my Dutchess County Research work. [The President had assigned Daisy the task of collecting material on the history of Dutchess County for a special room in the library set aside to house it.]

. . . But the IMPORTANT THING today is a telephone call from F.D.R. at 9 P.M., just up from quite a big dinner: Everything in connection with Lenny last evening went off exactly as planned — not a hitch — and the blood pressure, though taken at once, after the treatment, was quite all right.

Anna did just the right thing: got Geo. Fox to be there, "to be sure (Lenny) Mr. Sebaro didn't do anything that could possibly hurt" F.D.R.

Geo. Fox said it was all new to him, but evidently gave a good report to Dr. McIntire.

F.D.R. said he had his fingers crossed, but when he was having his nose done this evening he said casually to the Dr., "I've got a new thing in massage, have you heard?"

The Dr. said, "So I hear."

The Pres. continued, "It's all right, too."

"So I hear," says the Dr.

Non-committal! But one can't blame him — and very possibly there is a *slight* hurt feeling that he wasn't consulted. The Pres. sounded really elated about it, his voice strong & almost "excited."

I was ready to burst into tears from sheer relief that it had gone so well.

Thank God.

F.D.R. said they have it all planned: 3 treatments this week &

next. Then, after the Pres. returns from his trip, two treatments a week for 3 or 4 weeks, & then an X-ray to find out if the gall stones have *really* disappeared, as Lenny will claim.

F.D.R. is taking his lemon & honey in hot water before breakfast every morning. Started it that morning on the train — Saturday — I'm responsible for that too! I've just though of a good description for me: the *Anonymous Seventh!* I don't want any credit for anything, quite literally — except from F.D.R. himself! — All I want is for F.D.R. to be well —

He says he thinks he has lost a little weight since returning from Warm Springs. Lenny said of course he was losing weight — the spleen is "eating him up." When Lenny gets that functioning, together with the other organs, the appetite & the weight etc. will all become normal again —

I am so overflowing with thankfulness for what has already happened — My prayers haven't been said on my knees but they have been said from the depth of my soul, most of the day & night — I think that sort of praying is the real thing — and God will answer it — always with the understanding that He knows best —

[Hyde Park]

◌ *January 8 Monday.* Saturday at 9.15 P.M. F.D.R. called me up just before going down for newsreels & excerpts from his message to Congress at 10.

He feels Lenny is getting somewhere with his treatments. He had the three planned for Monday, Wednesday & Friday nights, and the *blood pressure has been better after the treatments* than when he has not had them. So there is no difficulty with the doctors, and no discussion on the subject.

[There was a good deal of discussion among the President's staff, his secretary Dorothy Brady recalled many years later, and a fair amount of hostility toward Daisy. "We all turned against her when she got that strange fellow onto the scene. We were scared of him, messing with the President's treatment like that."]

On Friday, Lenny said he would give only *two* treatments *this* week, to give F.D.R. more time between them to "do their work." The treatments are to be today (Monday), and Friday, here at H.P.

The Pres. said he was so glad to get that message off — it is a tremendous one; would take 1½ hrs. to read, to be read on the radio, under a half hour — he was a little tired, & sounded so, later, when making the speech. He had also had quite a discussion at dinner, which "put my pulse up." He is *not* looking forward to the big trip he is taking after the Inauguration. It will be a great effort — and there is always danger, at best. He had been to see Cordell Hull that afternoon & found him improved, "though his wife is still there"! Mrs. Hull is evidently one of those nervous worriers, who thinks more of how terrible it is that she has to worry so much, than of being cheerful & buoying to the sick person.

I listened to the speech & at 10.30 P.M. [Nineteen forty-five, FDR told his listeners, "can and must see the substantial beginning of the organization of world peace . . ."]

Xmas called me up from N.Y. with a message from Lenny: He is very happy over the response he is getting from F.D.R. in the treatments. "Everything" is going well, & "beginning to work" as it should. He would like to be able to talk freely to F.D.R. about just what he is doing to him, but cannot in his guise of "masseur," in front of Fox, etc. So he asked Xmas to ask me to telephone F.D.R. to this effect, & to ask F.D.R. to eat no sweets, no starches, no liquids, & no citrus fruits for the 24 hrs. before Monday's treatment. The "no liquids" is hard to understand, but he has his reasons. If F.D.R. got (when he gets!) *very* thirsty, he can put a slice of lemon on his tongue.

Sunday morning, I telephoned F.D.R. to this effect & he promised to "try to remember," though he didn't think the no liquids & no citrus fruits sounded right — I agreed — but it was only for 24 hrs. . . . He said he would do it.

Lenny will explain at the very first opportunity — either to F.D.R. or to me, for me to tell F.D.R. So much for that — and now, for Friday & the week-end — And I go to Washington with F.D.R. Monday night, & stay over for the Inauguration . . .

❧ *Jan. 10 Wednesday.* How long the days seem between the exciting periods of seeing F.D.R.!

. . . This morning, at the library, I received a letter from Mr. Morgan at M.G.M. suggesting a movie short of Fala on the Pres.' forthcoming trip to see Churchill & Stalin if I will be there *to "manipulate"* Fala! I answered that I fear even Fala won't be along on this trip! . . .

Why don't I know Russian, so as to go as an interpreter!

❧ *Jan. 12, Friday.* . . . The Pres. arrived at the usual hour this morning, and finally came over to the Library a little this afternoon. Lucy [Rutherfurd] (my new "cousin") came up on the train with him, so he had a nice long morning in which to talk with her — She is *such* a lovely person, and a very real "old friend."

She & I have one very big thing in common: our unselfish devotion to F. He got on his chair & I wheeled him around, while he showed Lucy a few things she had not seen before — then she & Fala & I got into the little car, in the back, F in the front next to Charlie at the wheel & we went over for lunch. I think the Pres. looks a tiny bit better, though, as usual, he is very tired when he comes from Wash. [After lunch] . . . I took myself off as soon as I had finished my coffee, so they could talk . . .

Lucy goes down on the 3.27 from Pksie. & Lenny arrives for a treatment at 4. Polly will come down at the same time for her treatment. Fala is a *rag* after his two weeks' honeymoon at Dr. Sheldon's. I do hope it is not all for nothing. In any case. I won't bother the poor lamb again, if it doesn't work this time.

Lenny's treatment lasted for almost two hours, & included Polly. Then F & I went to the library in the big house & are now ensconced comfortably near the fire. F discovered that he could move his little toe & Lenny says this muscular gain is extending to the calf muscles, but that the total gain in the whole body will of course take a long time. F says his feet have not been cold for two weeks, or since the beginning of these treatments — He also says he feels in general that his circulation is much better —

In any case it is remarkable & gives one *so much* hope for constant improvement of the Pres.' health. While Lenny works away at the Pres.' feet, Geo. Fox sits, watching — As soon as he is finished, Fox takes the blood pressure. It has been good ever since Lenny started & today was a record "low": 190/88. F thinks I am wrong about the 88, that it was 98, but I think I am right — I will ask Fox.

Another treatment next Monday, here in the Library — It is easier for Lenny to come here than to go to Wash., but I hope there will be two more down there, before the trip.

◦ *Jan 13, Saturday.* . . . I am feeling a little hectic between income tax, work, spending the time with F when he is tired of working on his daily mail, planning for Church & a visit to A. Frost [ill and in the hospital] tomorrow, & going to Wash. Monday night. F hasn't a soul to be with him except the secretaries, & seems to want me; I of course want not to miss a single possible moment — but I *have* to do a dozen other things too!

. . . I think he looks *really* better. Another sign, besides his looks & feelings, is that he seems to be relaxed on today, the *2nd* day of his visit, whereas, since last April, it has always been 3 or 4 days before he seemed to *begin* to relax —

꙳ *Jan 14th Sunday.* A snowstorm blew hard all day . . . F.D.R. called up at 5 minutes of two — He had mistaken the time on his clock & had just come downstairs for his lunch — GGT waiting to do some work with him! He said he must give up the planned visit to Alan Frost at 4, & the planned visit to Polly & the 11 "beautiful new puppies" at 4.30 [Laura Delano raised Irish setters], and he would send a SS car for me at 4, so as surely to get me down before the snow was too heavy to get out of our place — (*We* have no "army" to plow us out, and have to wait until all the public roads are done before the county plow will come through to our house.) It was a beautiful snowstorm — blowing just enough to start drifts & without any question I would never have been able to get out from our place this morning if the storm had continued —

As it happened, the snow stopped at about 10 P.M. I packed in a hurry, sat with the family for a half hour & then the SS came for me. We went through Fisherman's Bridge road & found it pretty heavy, but quite passable, still. The car began to act strangely, got weaker & weaker, & when we got to Vanderbilt Hill it just couldn't get up. After a few trials, the SS called for help on the radio & before long, Monty, in the Pres.' car, & another SS car came to our rescue, their special lights blinking at us as they approached — I got in behind Monty & was taken safely on to my destination. Charlie Fredericks was laughing at the front door: "He really is something — the President — he told me to send two cars, but I laughed at him — and now it's taken *three* cars!"

. . . He had worked steadily, all the afternoon, & was tired. He had a typewritten summary of what is going to be a story of his life by a Mrs. Bernie Babcock of Arkansas. We both read through about 50 pages I should guess, & he looked up and said it was *awful!* I agree with him. Mrs. Babcock has evidently read & re-read a half-dozen books about him, until she feels she knows the family, how their minds work, how F.D.R. was brought up — his relations with his family etc. She has written imaginary scenes & imaginary conversations — pure fiction, most of them. The conversations are the worst for they are written in language which *never* was spoken by Mr. & Mrs. James Roosevelt, or F.D.R.! Slang — slurring of letters — omission of letters etc. — Mrs. Babcock probably doesn't know *how* Roosevelts & Delanos talk — and it is a pity for the future, to have her idea handed down, when it is so completely at odds with the truth. I am writing about this just because this book will probably be published, & will inevitably be considered a "source book" if it is. The Pres. remarked specifically that his mother & father *never* talked to him in the vein of this writing. The story of Mrs. R. getting a ladder from which to look in on F.D.R., in the infirmary, *is* correct!

[When FDR fell ill with scarlet fever at Groton in 1898, Sara Delano Roosevelt hurried home from Europe, raced to his bedside, and spent the better part of several days perched on a stepladder outside his infirmary window, reading aloud to her boy. Her husband thought this excessive. She did not. "Franklin loved to see me appear over the window ledge," she told her biographers, "and at the first sight of me his pale little face would break into a happy albeit pathetic smile."]

After dinner, we went down to the fire in the Library, & F.D.R. did his stamps for a while, before going off to bed — He has his inaugural speech on his mind at the moment. It is to be less than 5 mins, so it has to be particularly carefully written —
 . . . A Lenny treatment which lasted until almost 7. Lenny says F is definitely better — The spleen, the liver, the kidneys. He worked on the nerves affecting the digestion. The spleen, he says, is at the root of the trouble, but it has reduced in size already, & is begining to function. One more treatment before the trip, Thursday. 9.30 P.M. It is now getting towards the end of *this* visit, for he shall go to the train in half an hour — F is playing solitaire, the fire is crackling cheerfully, & I am writing on the corner of the card table — F looks tired, but not exhausted. His colour is good. He looks a little thin, but I think he has turned the corner with Lenny's help.
 Lenny does not think he will lose what he has gained during the treatment, while he is on the trip. Geo. Fox will take the vibrator along and give massage every evening and so hope to retain the circulation that has started —

[The White House]

⬿ *Jan. 16 Tuesday*. On the train, after a rather restless night. It is not yet 8 A.M. & the car is moving faintly, probably to pull into the station. F & I drove down to the station together, with Fala on the floor. We had orange juice & went off to our rooms without seeing GGT & DB, who have the other two rooms. It feels very warm after the cold air of the River.

Later at the W.H. Raining & melting all day — Mr. Byrnes' new rules on heating are keeping the temps. down to 68. That is the rule at any rate — some rooms are comfortable, but others are frigid — Mrs. R. says (in the paper) that her bedroom is an ice-box, and I can appreciate that, for I am in the corresponding room, back of The Lincoln Room! Mrs. R. called it the "Little Lincoln room." It is a most cheerful comfortable room with two huge windows & a fireplace in which I have a dozing fire burning, just to take the chill off!

. . . Upstairs, Mrs. R. was at the elevator from breakfast in the West Hall with a young couple. She had told the Pres. he & I had better have breakfast in his study — The couple were just leaving — He didn't quite like that! It sounded a little like keeping him out of some excitement, and though he gets awfully tired & bored having to meet so many Toms, Dicks & Harrys, still, he likes to be able to get out of meeting them, himself! I told him Mrs. R. was just being very thoughtful & considerate of him! I have noticed at different times, that just because he can't get up & go & find out what is happening, he is awfully afraid of "missing something"!

[Sometime that day, Dorothy Brady and Grace Tully were working on a speech with Judge Rosenman and Robert Sherwood and the President when FDR suddenly broke off, looked around the office, and asked, "What in this room reminds you the most of me?"

Grace Tully named a naval print.

Dorothy Brady picked a little French portrait of John Paul Jones that Louis Howe had bought for FDR for $25.

FDR — who called her "Child" — stopped and dictated little notes beginning "In the event of my death . . ." and had them put in the safe. When Mrs. Brady got back from Warm Springs after the President's death in April, she found the Jones portrait — which now hangs on her wall — waiting in her office.

Daisy got a painting, too, a rendering of the Statue of Liberty, the sight she had seen each day as she came to and went from her nursing job on Ellis Island during World War I. She hung it in her bedroom at Wilderstein.]

. . . Anna had a young couple for dinner, and we were almost through "cocktails" when the Pres. finally came in, looking completely exhausted after a very hectic day. [He had found himself at cross-purposes with Secretary of War Henry Stimson, who was not convinced of the need for a new National Service Act to replenish recent losses in the Army and Navy and to ensure that war production would not slacken as victory neared.]

We had dinner in the dining-room & then went down to a movie "Henry V" [with Laurence Olivier], sent to the Pres. from England via the Ambassador. It is very beautiful in coloring, and an entirely new thing — Shakespeare in the movies! I think Shakespeare *any*where, and *any*how is an education — and this was well done — the film is dedicated to the Commandos & airborne troops . . .

~ *Jan. 17 Wednesday.* "Fair & cold." I went in to say good-morning to F.D.R. and found him in the midst of his breakfast, and looking perfectly fine! He is getting back his recuperating powers, and I feel sure it is Lenny who is doing it. Someone may say it is purely coincidence — Perhaps it is — but the doctors have had a year to bring about this "recuperating power," & it has started to grow only since Lenny has been working on him — This is the third week, and tomorrow night, the last treatment before the trip.

At lunch . . . Lord Halifax is a charming person; very quiet, but quick & sympathetic. The Pres. told him various stories, but they did not discuss anything very much. They touched on the coming trip and the present situation in general. They talked about Mr. Churchill, both of them devoted to him & fascinated by his wisdom, his "boyish puckishness," the strange & contradictory elements in his character. The Pres. told the story of the name "United Nations." It has probably been written down elsewhere, several times, & perhaps I wrote it down too, but I'll repeat it here, for it should not be lost to posterity — It is too good a story:

W.S.C. & F.D.R. had discussed & thought about, & discussed again, the question of a name for the new League of Nations. W.S.C. wanted simply to revive the old, name & all.

F.D.R. said there was too much prejudice against the League in this country . . . etc. They broke up for the night, W.S.C. having the big S.E. room.

F.D.R. got into his bed, his mind working & working . . . Suddenly, he got it — United Nations! The next morning, the minute he had finished his breakfast, he got onto his chair & was wheeled up the hall to W.S.C.'s room. He knocked on the door, no answer, so he opened the door & went in & sat on a chair, & the man went out &

closed the door — He called to W.S.C. & in the door leading to the bathroom appeared W.S.C.: a "pink cherub" [FDR said] drying himself with a towel, & without a stitch on!

F.D.R. pointed at him & exploded: "The United Nations!"

"Good!" said W.S.C.

W.S.C. told F.D.R. at their next meeting, that when W.S.C. returned to England & was telling the King about it, he said: "Sir, I believe I am the only man in the world who has received the head of a nation without any clothes on!"

. . . I went out and tried to find some little odds & ends to make up a little birthday package to be given to F.D.R. on the 30th [his birthday], wherever he may be on that date — The stores are remarkable for their emptiness — You can't find a thing you look for & have to fall back on any little thing available. I got some cheap little cotton lunch napkins, because there were no nice ones, for the Warm Springs cottage, which I am giving him on Sunday night at the dinner . . .

[Daisy and Lucy Rutherfurd had also joined forces to make up a gift package for FDR's birthday to be opened aboard ship; it included "a lot of little gadgets," FDR told Anna, including not only the napkins, but a pocket comb, a room thermometer, and a cigarette lighter that worked in the wind.]

❧ *Jan 18 Thursday.* The numerous grandchildren are arriving today, so I move out, general excitement & confusion, though everything is *orderly* confusion — Chanler & Tony & David [Elliott's children] arrived about lunch time — the Pres. came from his office at 2.05 for lunch, looking very well & cheerful — His inaugural speech ready.

At lunch, he told the Struwel Peter stories to the children who loved them . . .

The Pres. showed me a copy of his inaugural address, which I read on the way out to Betty's house.

. . . I am feeling so very happy about F.D.R.'s health, for he looks so definitely improved, & his spirits, & his pig-headedness are much more visible! When he "gives in" too much it is a sign that he is just too tired to fight, & I worry! Nothing of that sort today!

❧ *Jan 19 Friday.* I came to the W.H. about 1.30, to find a large stand up lunch going on, for some political unit, I think — F.D.R. was sitting in the room, talking, & Mrs. R. was near the door — Various daugh-

ters-in-law wandering around, making themselves agreeable. I slipped
up to the North Hall & spent the afternoon working. The Pres. appeared in his room about 6.30 & we had dinner in the West Hall with
Sara, Kate, Chanler & Tony, the little girls very gay and full of laughter.

Tony rather boisterous & noisy with a sympathetic audience. A
few mild attempts were made to calm him down, by the Pres., but he
was loath to stop. The fun & roughhousing continued after dinner in
the Pres.' study, with Tony turning somersaults over backwards on the
Pres.' couch! All the other young people had gone to dinner with Mrs.
[Warren Delano] Robbins [whose late husband was a cousin of FDR's
and had been his ambassador to Canada and El Salvador], and Mrs.
R. was somewhere out, also. So, "we" signed a pile of letters, which
means I take the letter from the Pres. & blot the signature. I went off
home, to the Hambleys' at 10.30, with the promise of the Pres. that
he would go right off to bed . . .

～ *Jan 20th 1945, Saturday*. A memorable day. The *4th Inauguration
of F.D.R.* — that in itself is unique history — It was all very simple,
& impressive & quite wonderful.

. . . The Pres. didn't come out of his room until a little before 10.
He had tried on his braces & found he could stand on them all right.
He looks fine — everyone speaks of it — his colour good & a healthy
vigorous manner & not very tired though he has had *no* rest during
the day this week — The service was lovely, as it always is, & really
inspiring — Frances Watson & I, and others like us, get emotional &
are ready to burst into tears!

After the service, we all went up to the 2nd floor — (That is, the
family who are staying here, and Polly & I) Jimmy & Rommey had a
sleepless trip by air from California, had arrived at 11.30 last night &
did not get up for the service. They now came out of the blue room
and the two children were thrilled at seeing them — They are evidently perfectly devoted to him, & he to them. Rommey is a sweet
person, very sympathetic. I feel a little *de trop* with these family reunions & went down to the red room to join the Norwegians who were
waiting around between ceremonies.

The Crown Prince & Colonel Ostgaard arrived without warning
from London just the other day so the Cr. Prs. and Mme. O. are very
happy. After a while people began to arrive. At 20 of 12 the grandchildren & the nurses were taken out to the two circular stairs. Off in
the green room the Justices of the Supreme Court were collecting, with

their wives — also 2 or 3 Senators in wheel chairs — they moved out to the portico, to the left. Mrs. R. came, on the right, through the red room & started those of us gathered there out onto the north side of the portico. In the blue room, the V.P. & the incoming V.P. & the committee on ceremonies gathered.

The Pres. came in, pushed by Arthur Prettyman and with Jimmy, who has been at every inauguration by his father's side.

When I went out onto the portico, I found out at once that I would see *nothing*, for I would have to stand behind a large group, all of whom were, as usual, taller than I. So I went back & stood in the doorway between the red & blue rooms.

The signal came and the Pres. moved out to the porch behind the Chief Justice & the 2 V.P.s, old & new. After him went the committee, followed by me! I stood just at the corner of the porch door with a perfect view of the Pres. down to the waist.

. . . [T]wo men, I *think* C. Fredericks & G. Spaman, lifted him out of his chair to an upright position. He held on to the handles on the desk with both hands. During the first part of the speech, it looked as though his right arm was straining a good deal, it was trembling. But that all stopped, and when he had finished, and Jimmy asked if he wanted the chair, his answer was, "Oh no, I'm very comfortable!"

It did all of us good to see him standing there, straight & vigorous, thin but with good colour — All the sentimental ladies who love him were ready for tears! . . .

When the ceremony was over, everyone came in & Mr. Claunch begged Polly, & [Sara Delano's older sister] Mrs. [Price] Collier, and me, to go into the dining room & start lunch. The entire table the length of the State dining-room was covered with plates, already prepared, with chicken salad, a roll & a piece of cake — [The President had asked for chicken à la king, but the imperious Mrs. Nesbitt had overruled him. She then failed to thaw enough frozen chicken for the chicken salad, so the celery content was spectacularly high.]

At the west end of the table was a coffee urn. We filled our cups & put them on our plates next to the salad & looked for chairs. Mrs. Collier was the only one of her generation at the Inaugural, for Mr. [Frederic] Delano is not well enough to come. It must have been a terrible disappointment to him . . .

After a while, a butler, Fields, came for me to go into the Red Room where the Pres. was having his lunch, with all the Norwegians sitting around him! It was a nice party, with other special people coming in now & then to greet the Pres. & congratulate him. Polly came to tell me my family were asking for me. I answered firmly that I had been "ordered" *into* the room, but *not yet out* of it!

. . . [Later] I went to the Hambleys' for the night, stopping off for a little visit with Lucy Rutherfurd in Q Street [where she was staying with her sister], to tell her all about the *"inside,"* which she could not see from the lawn.

☙ *Jan 21 Sunday.* . . . I came to the W.H. at 11.30 & found [FDR] sitting up in bed; told him my message & started to leave.

"Do you want to save my life?"

"I would always be glad to save the President's life."

"Well then, stay & have lunch with me on a tray — the so & sos, and so & sos are coming — there'll be a crowd, and I just don't want to see them!"

Having been asked to lunch at the Marburys', with Lucy Rutherfurd, I jumped into a taxi & spent an hour with them before lunch — then Lucy brought me back to the W.H. in the Marbury car.

The Pres. was interviewing Jesse Jones, and as he afterwards told me, was having a very disagreeable time of it. Mr. Jones was very angry, and wouldn't take the suggestions offered him by the Pres., even though they offered him a still larger sphere of influence in the business of the world.

[The old quarrel between Henry Wallace and Jesse Jones still raged. When FDR asked his former vice president what cabinet post he would like, Wallace said he'd prefer to replace Jones as secretary of Commerce. Roosevelt promised the job to him, then offered Jones his choice of ambassadorships if he would gracefully relinquish the Commerce job. Instead, Jones angrily resigned from the government.]

. . . The family collected soon, the Pres. came from his room, & we went down to the Red Room where cocktails were set. The outside guests then came from the Green Room — the remains of the Cufflinks Club, Olaf & Martha from Norway, the Morgenthaus, two couples, friends of F jr & Ethel, Sistie, Bill, Chanler & Tony, his only grandchildren still here, who are old enough to come to dinner. I sat between Jimmy & John Boettiger, in a splendid position to see the Pres.

It was the same kind of a dinner as last year — very personal, and with an atmosphere of love & affection — A dozen toasts were made, all sweet, full of feeling. The Pres. made a double one, to the Norwegians: That they should be at *all* his birthday parties in the future, and also, that they should be home again, at this time next year —

Olaf answered with a nice little speech in his rather heavy way, looking at his plate most of the time, moving his glass a little to the right, & back again, to the left. The Norwegians brought the Pres. a large print of the Hudson River, and some glasses for old-fashioneds. Someone — I think Mrs. R. — gave him lunch napkins for the Warm Springs cottage — Ethel gave him a lovely photograph of herself & F jr and F 3rd (Jo) & Christopher — those little boys both look very much like their father and are full of charm. It is very touching to see how Jo adores his grandfather, and how very happy it makes F.D.R.

At our places were little square boxes containing copies of the Jo Davidson medal, struck off for the occasion. It is *dreadful* — makes F.D.R. look at least 90, and it doesn't even look like him. I shall look at it without my glasses — and try to think it's good! It is a beautiful present to have — with "MLS from FDR Jan. 30 1945" on the outside of the box —

I gave him lunch napkins, also for Warm Springs — but I gave them to him early in the day, and upstairs. He was delighted with them, so I tied them up in their box and marked them "for Warm Springs," and left them there on the bench in F.D.R.'s study — I hope he gets them safely when we go down there again. Incidentally, F has already set the date for March 28th.

We had champagne in which to drink the toasts. There was a note of seriousness, for one toast was "To the absent ones" — The Pres. looked tired, but not *too* tired . . .

Jan 22 Monday. I came down to the W.H. at about 9, went in to say good morning to the Pres. who said he was only half awake. They all played poker until quite late, then went to the Monroe room and sang all the old songs until about 2. The Pres. loves these simple parties that allow him to relax, even when he is tired.

This reminds me of my conversation with John Boettiger at dinner. I don't often have a chance to talk to anyone at the W.H. for we all concentrate on the Pres. when he is there. So I took this opportunity to tell him that I thought it so wonderful that Anna can be with the Pres. and be of such help to him, in a business & official way, as well as in a personal way. We agreed then that the Pres. needs help in many ways, and that several people do help him, each in his own way, though it may be also a *small* way.

Much to my surprise John said: "You, Margaret, contribute probably more than anyone, in allowing him to relax, and think of completely different things. He is under such a constant strain . . ." I was ready for tears; for it is very wonderful to feel I *am* of some help, small as it may be. John himself is quite a wonderful person — a really *good* person. It is the greatest tribute to him, that Sistie & Buzz both adore him . . .

I returned to the W.H., got my bags packed and went over to GGT's office. The secretaries are all very tired & nervous — The Pres. has been rushed to death, getting ready for his departure — and everybody is tired, including him, for it is just one thing after another, all day, & often into the night. At last, at 1.30, the Pres. sent for me to come in to lunch in his office. He was, he said, thoroughly *mad* about this affair of Elliott Roosevelt having his wings removed, etc. He feels it is obviously "politics" on someone's part. He mentioned some man on whose toes Elliott had stepped, etc. I don't blame him for getting mad, and I get furious myself, that his energy should be wasted on all these small personal things.

[Elliott, whose qualifications to fly high-performance aircraft was often questioned by senior officers because he had not undergone air force flight training, had been recommended for promotion to brigadier general. Republicans in the Senate had vowed to block confirmation.]

He doesn't relish this trip at all — thinks it will be very wearing, & feels that he will have to be so much on the alert, in his conversations with Uncle Joe & W.S.C. The conversations will last interminably & will involve very complicated questions . . .

I just hated to leave him — Poor dear! Another thing he has to think about constantly is not to hurt the feelings of all his adoring friends — like me, for instance! He had to slip in 2 or 3 other "goodbyes" beside me, during the afternoon — and was to leave at 10 P.M. for his train, to get on inside the Bureau of Engraving. He said it was *so* secret, that even the usual porter, Fred, was not to be there — the car was waiting inside; and at another point, the Potomac mess crew were put on another car, with no idea where they are headed for — An engine will back in — take the P's car out, attach it to a train somewhere or other, where the mess crew are also attached, & they will start off into the night. Before daylight, they will go to the station on the pier, at Newport News . . . The Pres. will shave and then will be wheeled off the pier into the destroyer & they will get under weigh at once, and be out of the harbor before the sun comes up — (I mention his "shaving" because he made a point of it when telling me about the places — that "it is so much more comfortable to be shaved," even so early in the morning.)

The Pres. said he would get into the elevator, go up to his cabin on the upper deck, have breakfast & then go forward on the deck & get the sea air and spray — if the weather is all right. I have two thoughts about the weather: he will *enjoy* the trip if the sea is smooth & the air is warm. On the other hand, if it is rough, there will be less danger from submarines — what a terrible thought, ever-present, even though one doesn't put it into words.

In the same way, there are two thoughts about Anna's going with him: she will be *such* a help & comfort to him. But how terrible if anything should happen to her — the mind goes round & round — pro — con — pro — con. But there is always the same conclusion: F.D.R. is of *world* importance — the rest of us, as individuals, are *not* important, except in as much as we can be of help to him. Without wishing to bring up the subject in this diary, I may put in here, that I have argued to *my*self & with members of the family as to whether whatever gossip about us there may be, is justified. Since there is nothing but good in my desire to help him, & since he seems to feel I *do* help him, I have long since made up my mind that *that* is the important thing. Only those who wish to find evil in our friendship, will do so — and I, for one, will not have my life ruled by that sort of person —

If good wishes and prayers could carry F.D.R. along, he would be floating very high today!

✎ *Jan 23rd Tuesday.* I . . . went to see Lenny for a treatment. He found my gall-bladder much improved & "gave me the works" as he puts it. He says that another year and I would have had an operation.

We talked a lot about F.D.R. Lenny says he got at him just in time, that from the waist down, everything was getting or already atrophied. That only F.D.R.'s heart kept him going. Lenny, in his ignorance of book knowledge, is a psychic.

He knows nothing of numerology but knows that he himself is a "9" — an instrument of God. F.D.R. is the first person he has come across who is also a "9." Lenny gave him the first treatment on Dec. 27th: 2 & 7 = 9. The last treatment before the trip, on the 18th of Jan.: 1 & 8 = 9. Lenny feels these are all signs that point to one thing: That he will make F.D.R. well — *Without* the signs, I feel it also —

Lenny told me to send word to F.D.R.: "When you sit between Churchill & Stalin, & they are talking & talking — hold the crucifix in your hand, in your pocket, listen to them & listen to God, & you will know what to say — and they will not be able to go against you." I went down into the hotel lobby & wrote this & mailed it to GGT to be put into the first pouch, on Thursday . . .

◦ *Jan 24 Wednesday.* F.D.R. is already a day and a half out to sea.

At breakfast this morning, I was petting Button, when Mama said, out of a clear sky & with eyes sparkling: "Dear little Button, she'll be having puppies soon."

"Well," I said, "you can't tell so soon — It's only two weeks you know —" "Oh," says Mama, as quick as a flash, "I have felt them"!!

For a person who has lectured me at length about not telling anyone about it — not even letting the President know that his own dog is to become a father, etc. — it was a little astonishing, to say the least — But if there *are* puppies, no one will be more thrilled than Mama! So I cross my fingers — and hope —

The F.D.R.L. [Franklin D. Roosevelt Library] is getting emptier & emptier — Mrs. Dean has now retired to private life, for she found she was always tired & couldn't do justice to either her home or her job. Nichols says he may have to leave also, just to get a better paying job — now that another baby is on the way. The great trouble, of course, is that Dr. Buck won't promote people without degrees — what hope have I, with only two years of college?

◦ *Jan. 31.* GGT called up . . . and told me there is no news as yet from F.D.R. That is natural, since no radio messages are sent out from his ship, & the first news will be by plane which may arrive at any time, without previous notice. If he is on schedule, I think he arrives in Yalta today.

Fala has all his old pep again, & has a beautiful time running in the snow with Button.

GGT said she would forward anything that might come, or, if [there] is nothing to forward, she will write me a note!

At last, a short letter from F.D.R. in the form of a diary, beginning the night he left Washington on the train.

[FDR's own account of the Crimea Conference, from a typed version. The original seems to be missing.

Jan 22	On the train: I am in bed at 11 P.M. after a hectic departure
Jan 23	We all arose at 7:30, though I am going in the wrong direction! We came on board & had breakfast, and by the time we were through we were out in the stream & heading out. The sea is almost smooth. Tonight we had a movie & we all dine & lunch in my cabin . . .
Jan 24	The routine of the voyage has settled down. I nap for a hour in the P.M., take another nap after breakfast — movie in the P.M.
Jan 25	ditto
Jan 26	ditto
Jan 27	ditto
Jan 28	ditto church service added
Jan 29	ditto. We located a submarine. She fired no torpedo. It gets smoother.
Jan 30	Birthday
Jan 31	Passed through Gibraltar — 5 A.M. Anna got up & got a sight. I slept!
Feb 1	A lovely smooth day. We get in tomorrow morning. All well.
Feb 2	In safely at 10 A.M. & WSC is on a nearby cruiser & came on board at once. Ann & Sara [Churchill] are getting on well. An awful day ahead & tonight at 10, we are off by air for the final destination. The voyage has been fine.]

He sounds a little tired & let down, which perhaps is natural — but I don't like it when he seems to have no particular *zest,* whether it's for the weather, or food, or whatnot. I *hope* he's all right. The trip was evidently pretty good as a whole, only slightly rough. They detected a submarine which did not fire at them. There must be more to the story than that! Something to find out about. The last entry is made on the day he meets W.S.C. and they all head for the conference — by air, Feb. 2nd. The envelope is dated Feb. 6 in Wash. & I received it the 8th by air-mail.

[That same week, Daisy got a letter from Lucy Rutherfurd.]

Aiken, South Carolina

Friday February 9th, 1945

Dear Margaret,

Such a nice letter! One of the world's best correspondents seems now in communication with one of the world's worst — who will, however, try to improve. It is a curious thing that great sorrows and shock leave one with a tremendous incapacity or fear of thinking. I feel as though I could scrub this little house from garret to cellar (if it had any) and do any physical thing — but my desk frightens me — and I find it difficult to think anything through. There seems to be so much to be decided — What is right and what is wrong for so many people & I feel myself incapable of judging anything.

Yes — it is difficult when we must speak in riddles but we have spoken to one another very frankly — and it must rest there — One cannot *discuss* something that is sacred — and even simple relationships of friendship and affection are sacred & personal.

Oh I am so glad that Fala is well — and that you think this time puppies are on the way — What fun and excitement! Has your Button got the charm of Fala, or at least ½?

It is disappointing that Lenny relieved you for only two or three days — but no matter how difficult you should make yourself go to town once a week — and give him a trial, no? Or is the weather so bad that you will lose more than you gain? — As to heat — I should think hot water bottles at night would be efficient & inexpensive. I am sorry I am not near you & could do it for you. I would prefer to die of the cold, I think, than take care of myself!

I have written my sister to ask if her husband still believes in injections for sciatica. If and when she answers I shall let you know — I remember Miss Tully told me he had helped her after a grim time. If I get no answer I will call them up & let you know *your orders.*

I was delighted with the description of sorting the prints & your trip to the attic to sort photographs, cartons, etc — How I should love to be there to help you. You could do all the brain work & I could do the reaching and dusting —

With very much love — and hoping that the sciatica is better. You should wear warm undies, if you don't already! The broken furnace didn't sound too helpful — and your room looked highly Franciscan. Hope you use F's room & have a blazing fire! Write soon

— and tell me whatever news you have as you are in official touch & I am not.

Dear little Margaret — goodnight —

Lucy

Enclosing the porter's name I spoke of — He is not as gentle and polished a type as the one on F's train & on investigation might prove all wrong — He works on the Southern RR and perhaps could be put on F's train sometime to see if he liked him. He does seem efficient and looks strong. If you follow this up, would *not* mention my name at all — at all —

∽ *Feb. 13.* Back at work in the Library. Yesterday, at 4.30, the 1st announcement was made on the radio, about the results of the Yalta conference — It was very thrilling to realize that, again, F.D.R. has accomplished so much that he is striving for.

∽ *Feb. 15.* I am really worried about F.D.R. Even the papers say "his aides are worried about his health." In all the pictures that have come out, he looks really sick, even when he was at Malta. The C.C. [Crimea Conference] must have been a terrific strain, for I am sure he never spared himself.

∽ *Feb. 19th.* I have been more & more worried, for no word has come *from* F.D.R. & there is nothing about him . . . Churchill has just returned to London. I don't *think* he would, if F.D.R. were critically ill.

How terrible suspense is. One can only do nothing but hope & pray. I called Polly who also has heard nothing, & is equally worried.

[From FDR to Daisy]

Feb 12   I'm in the last stretch of the conference — & though the P.M. meetings are long and tiring I'm *really all right* & it has been I think a real success. I either work or sleep! I am in the Palace of the Czar.

∽ *Feb 20th.* On coming home at 5, I find a little note from F.D.R. written on the 12th "in the Palace of the Czar"! I feel better, though it doesn't cover the eight days since then — However, the radio tells us this afternoon that F.D.R. & W.S.C. have been in Alexandria & Algiers meeting Haile Selassie, [King] Farouk [of Egypt] & Ibn Saud [of Saudi Arabia]; so my fears seem to be groundless! — and I am much relieved! F.D.R. must be on his way, definitely, and we have only the ocean & the submarines to fear, now. "Only"!

~ *Feb. 21 Wednesday.* All my fears seem to have been groundless! — The photograph of F.D.R. taken off Alexandria made him look well!

This evening Mama told me the W.H. had called up to say that they had a message for me "by air": I must call up to get it as tomorrow is a holiday, & no one will be on hand to give it to me. I called up the W.H. but it was too late — no one knew anything about it — I shall have to wait until Friday — to have to wait for a message from F.D.R. for two days — when you know the message is there!! waiting — probably locked up in a drawer — even if it is only to say that he is all right!

[From FDR to Daisy]

Feb 18   Algiers. We got away safely from the Crimea, flew to the Canal & saw King Farouk, then emperor Haile Selassie, & the next day, King Ibn Saud of Arabia with his whole court, slaves (black), taster, astrologer, & 8 live sheep. Whole party was a scream! Then, the way back, I saw WSC to say goodbye.

All goes well, but I still need sleep. I hope to get back Feb 28.

[Two days later, aboard the *Quincy,* General Watson suffered a fatal cerebral hemorrhage. Roosevelt was deeply affected by his loss. One by one, the President's closest companions had fallen away: Louis Howe, his mother, Gus Gennerich, Missy LeHand, now Pa Watson. And Harry Hopkins was so ill that he had disembarked at Algiers.]

~ *Feb. 23rd Friday.* The "message" turns out to be a final little note from F.D.R. dated at Algiers, the 18th. He hopes to get back to Wash. the 28th. He "sounds" all right, though his writing is poor. That may be due to the stiff right thumb. [Roosevelt's right hand had been mildly affected by polio and when he was tired, toward the end of his life, he sometimes had difficulty holding the pen steady.]

— GGT is certainly considerate & nice to send these letters by "special delivery!" She knows I am just waiting for them!

∾ *Feb. 26 Monday.* The W.H. has issued a statement that the Pres.' health is excellent, from the latest reports that circulated after the Crimea Conference.

Yesterday, Dr. Sheldon saw Button, & is pretty sure there are puppies — probably two.

∾ *Feb 27th Tuesday.* 9.15 P.M. He is safely back — sitting in his corner chair on the train, he telephoned me from where the train is standing on the dock at Newport News. Anna was on the ship again, while they were taking "Pa" Watson's body off. Franklin feels his death very much, & will miss him dreadfully — He always leaned on him, both figuratively and physically — "Pa" was a Rock, the only one of the aides who gave a feeling of security to F.D.R. when he stood with his braces — Always cheerful, ready with a joke, and completely & unselfishly devoted to F.D.R. "Pa" had a stroke & would have been paralyzed if he had lived — so his death is a blessing. He would have felt so terribly at not being able to be on duty — I am so sorry for Frances, they were a very happy couple — Interment in Arlington, tomorrow at noon.

Apparently F has been all right — He says the conference turned out better than he dared hope for; he is happy about it. He hopes to get away from Washington on Friday night, & spend three days at Hyde Park. It *will* be good to see him again. Let's hope for clear warm weather!

∾ *March 3rd Saturday.* At 3.20, F.D.R. called up to explain that he has had, & is having, an exhausting time seeing people — "fixing" things which have gotten out of hand during his absence. Everyone waits around for him to "lead" & guide. F.D.R. will arrive in Hyde Park Sunday A.M. I will get Lenny for Monday P.M.

∾ *March 4, Sunday.* At 2.30 F.D.R. called me up — very tired and sleepy — He had worked all the morning, had just finished lunch & was going to sleep for an hour before starting to work for the rest of the day. He has letters to answer from Jan 6th & hopes to get it off his mind, as far as possible, during these three days.

∾ *March 5th Monday.* . . . 2.30 P.M. At the Big House — F.D.R., in one minute, falls fast asleep on the sofa. He is to get up at 3.30, and we will take a 15 minute drive before going to the Library for a Lenny massage.

GGT stayed for lunch, & Polly came in for a few minutes on her way to the train in Pksie. We are all much excited over the hoped-for puppies next Monday, the 12th — and over the trip to Warm Springs, leaving Hyde Park on the 27th. F is asking Polly & me to go with him to the San Francisco Conference in April — How *can* such exciting things be happening to us all the time! [The opening session of the United Nations was to be held in San Francisco in late April.]

But the best of all, is that F looks so much better than anyone can expect — his colour is good & his blood pressure is pretty good. Lenny will bring it down a few more points.

I brought Fala over here at and went in to F with his breakfast tray — I was so thrilled to find him looking as he does, & he said he was fine throughout the trip — not a sick day. All the fears & worries for nothing, thank God!

Later. At 3.30 the Pres. woke up & we got into his little car & drove out the road, in through the Rogers place & back to the main road. When we reached the Morgans, the H.P. Fire Dept. caught up & passed us. F.D.R. was a little worried, as they don't go below his place. However, we continued on through the Morgan place to his door at the Library. Just at that moment the radio car got the message that one of the cottages at Mrs. J.R.'s was on fire! Fala & I were just out of the car: "Get back in," said F.D.R. and off we went to the fire, which was just on the roof, & practically out! "Much ado about nothing," but a little excitement for the place . . .

Back to the L. where Lenny gave the Pres. a good two-hour "massage." He found him a little improved, if anything; I was thankful that he had not lost the good effects of the first 9 treatments. F thinks he has lost more weight & after looking at him for a while, his hands, etc. I think he may have, though at lunch & in the morning after a good night's rest, his face seems to fill out a little — His colour is definitely good —

He said he gets so very tired after a long day, & it rather worries him, I think, for fear he won't be able to keep up the heavy routine . . .

After the "treatment," Lenny went off to the train with Com. Fox, & I went for dinner with F.D.R. It is lovely to be quietly with him — He makes no effort with me, which makes me realize I am of some real use to him — and of course, *I* am perfectly content in realizing that. It is the greatest privilege to be of even the *slightest* help to F.D.R.

❧ *March 6 Tuesday.* Very much the same sort of a day for me! I went over for lunch. DB was there instead of GGT. F.D.R. teases her the entire time & gets fun out of it! After lunch, he saw Mrs. Halprin for an hour, about the [James Roosevelt Memorial Library] in H.P. The village expects F.D.R. to continue supporting it, as his mother did; but he does not feel he can do it, or impose that obligation on his children — If the village won't accept it as a gift, with a small endowment, F.D.R. may sell the books, turn the building into a two-family house, & rent it. It would serve the village right, for they don't appreciate having a library — It is something like the situation of our Church of the Messiah, which has always depended on a few "rich people." Now that it has to stand on its own feet, it is coming to life & health & activity . . .

The Pres. took an hour's sleep, from 3.30 to 4.30, & then came for me at the L. We went to Top Cottage for a good two hours, with a large folder of work, half of which we got through. It was cold up there so I put my coat & an Indian blanket around him, & I sat with my back to a fine fire!

As usual, on these trips to H.P., when he comes more or less alone, for a real rest, it takes him 2 or 3 days to get relaxed, so he has now reached the *relaxed* stage, & feels rather let-down toward evening. He has had *no* cold feet since Lenny's treatments, & though during the trip he gradually lost the "tingling" feeling, his blood pressure stayed down pretty well.

↷ *Mar. 7th.* I went over for lunch, as usual — GGT was there. F. seemed tired & listless & had to make an effort. I am worried about him again. He slept after lunch, then came to the Library . . . He looked very thin and tired and didn't sit up straight — but his colour is good. We then came down to his room & stayed there until 6.30, talking a little & disposing of more things, which have been here for months — I tried to make him take a drive, but even that was an effort — However, before going into the house, we did drive down the road to the gate of the State Hospital and back. After dinner, we went to the big library & sat by the fire. I left at nine, much worried . . . I pray he's all right. Mackenzie King [Prime Minister of Canada] is coming on Friday — F. said he thought he would spend the weekend in bed . . . it will be much less tiring to see Mr. King quietly in his bedroom than sitting up & having to talk to a lot of other people, too.

↷ *March 9th Friday.* Button had two little puppies this morning — It took half an hour, with no help from Dr. Sheldon — they are healthy little things and everything seems to be completely normal. Dr. Sheldon called me up & said: "Miss Suckley, you are the godmother of two lovely little girls!!" I called up F.D.R., who is delighted. They are to be called Meggie & Peggie McFala. [It was later discovered that Meggie was really a male, and he was duly renamed Fala McFala.]

~ *March 12th Monday.* The puppies came home today, because Button is so nervous over them that she won't leave them to go out in the yard.

[The pages on which the next two entries appear were pulled from Daisy's diary but found elsewhere among her papers.]

~ [Hyde Park March 14?] . . . The Pres. called up this morning [from Washington] to know if all is going along as it should. He feels tired and wants to get off to [Warm Springs] on the 26th or 27th from here so that he can "sleep & sleep & sleep" — and not plan for *anything* at *any* time!

~ *March 15.* The Pres. called up this evening. He said he was sitting at his desk in his study (alone for a change!) & would go to bed in a little while after cleaning up a pile on the chair. Those everlasting piles that are replenished as soon as removed! He said he was "suffering from exhaustion" and hasn't much let-up on work to look foward to until he leaves Washington Saturday night.

The schedule is, for him:

Lv. Wash	Mar 24 P.M.
Arr HP	25 A.M. have tea at Suckleys to see the puppies!
Lv HP	28 P.M.
Arr Wash	29 A.M. spend the day
Lv Wash	29 P.M.
Arr WS	30 A.M.

This week he has Juliana, and next week the [Earl and Princess of Athlone].

~ *March 25 Sunday.* A Big Day! The Pres. and Mrs. R. came for tea at our house, to see the puppies . . . Mrs. R. drove her open car with the Pres. by her side & Fala in the back seat. We had tea in the enclosed porch, the puppies fast asleep in their box, at the President's feet. I took them out to be seen by the SS. When Charlie Fredericks petted them, Button would have flown at him if I hadn't been holding her collar! Fala came up with great interest, to see his offspring, & Button flew at him & ran around with him for a while.

Mrs. R. was very sweet & charming, as always. The President looks terribly badly — so tired that every word seems to be an effort. They stayed for about ¾ of an hour, Mrs. R. doing her best to get him started home to see some people at six — more people for dinner — He just can't stand this strain indefinitely. Thank Heavens he gets off to WS on Thursday night after another long day in Washington.

❧ *March 28th.* I am starting off tonight on the President's train. We spend tomorrow in the White House, leaving at four, for WS. These three days the weather has been lovely & warm. Monday the Pres. worked with DB until lunch. I had lunch with them & sat working in the big library while he took his nap on the sofa. We then came to the Library — Mr. Lenny came at four & I left for home at 4.30.

Tuesday about the same, except that Lenny was not here and we did some work in the L, including picking out things to be exhibited in the War Exhibition they are working up at this moment for the National Archives.

The President looks perhaps a tiny bit better each day, but he needs 2–3 months off-duty entirely to get back on his feet. He says he can't take the time off, and one wonders just how long he can keep going this way.

Today he worked with DB again up to lunch — took a little drive down to the river after lunch. We found Major Stowell down there with a military inspector and talked to him for a while about the future of the Rogers Place [now filled with troops assigned to protect the President] . . .

[A note added later in Daisy's hand: "March 28 F.D.R. made his last visit to the F.D.R.L. from 3–4.30."]

❧ *March 29.* En route to Warm Springs. We came down from H.P. to Wash. last night. From 8.30 to 4 P.M. the Pres. was on the go, ending with a half hour of nose treatment & tooth cleaning. By the time we got on the train he look completely exhausted. Amb. McCarthy & Basil O'Connor joined us on the train & are both alarmed at his looks.

This afternoon, he looks really ill — thin & worn — but joking & laughing & carrying the conversation on as usual. He has agreed to take gruel, besides his meals, as an experiment, and I can only hope it will help him as it has so many others . . .

[Warm Springs]

~ *March 30 At Eight*. . . . A crowd was at the station as always . . .
Fred Botts, Mr. Haughey, etc. etc. Charlie Fredericks drove the car,
F.D.R. on the front seat with him. Mr. O'Connor, Fala, Polly, Sister &
I in the back, more or less on top of each other! We drove slowly past
the front of Georgia Hall, where a large group of patients were collected to clap & wave to the Pres. in welcome — From there on up
the hill to the Little White House, where Daisy [Bonner] was at the
front door to welcome the Pres.

Dear F — He is completely "let down," which means that he is
relaxed & able to rest. He sat in his chair, without the energy to go to
his room & rest, reading a book — Finally, he said he would go — He
had a sound sleep, while Polly & I moved furniture & fixed things up
in general — "the woman's touch" is much needed!

We unpacked a set of glasses — tumblers & "old fashioned" glasses
given as a birthday present by the Morgenthaus. Also a breakfast set
for F.D.R., from Mrs. R. Also three sets of napkins, doilies etc. also
given for his birthday. Polly had sent him a "nest" of maple tables for
the living-room — they turn out to be mahogany, but one doesn't
quibble about a little detail like that, *these* days!

[That evening, Bill Hassett, gravely concerned about the President, took Dr.
Bruenn aside. "He is slipping away from us and no earthly power can save
him," he said. He was weary of maintaining the "bluff." So, he said, was
Basil O'Connor. Bruenn admitted that his patient's condition was "precari-
ous" but did not agree that it was hopeless, provided the President eased up
still further on his schedule.]

[Lucy Mercer Rutherfurd to Daisy]

Aiken, South Carolina

Saturday [March 31, 1945]

Dear Margaret,

It was nice to find your letter here when I got back and the card
announcing the birth of the heirs apparent — or rather heiresses.
What fun! I loved the sketches of the 2 dogs with their good and bad
points — You are a great artist! . . .

I am glad that the trip [to Yalta] is over & that happy, peaceful
days lie ahead — Please God they will be beneficial in a big way &
that nothing — not even Germany's collapse — will interrupt.

How is the sciatica and has Lenny helped you or Laura? He is a very interesting character — and it will be wonderful, indeed, if he proves his point.

You probably catch cold every time you go out with the pups in winter, regardless of the [indecipherable] dressing gown — Shall I point out that we are getting older even if you are nearly a year younger than I and can't take the liberties with such things we used to take.

Much love dear Margaret — and I must rush & thank you so much for writing —

Lucy

∽ *Warm Springs Ga. March 31st.* In my same little room — Polly is settled, with Sister, in her room, with a bath which I share with her — Having to walk "down the hall" to the bathroom, at home, it is not much of a hardship to have to cross the living room — but I do appreciate the "bed & bath" at the W.H. when I am there!

. . . I have just had a long talk with Dr. Bruenn about F. I am a little happier about it for he confessed to a feeling of frustration in trying to help [him]. The doctors work out a program of hours which it would be possible for F. to keep to without getting over-tired. The program is kept for 3 or 4 days & then abandoned completely, etc, etc.

Dr. Bruenn started by saying: "Miss Suckley, to begin with, you realize that like all people who work with this man — I love him. If he told me to jump out of the window, I would do it, without hesitation." We discussed the difficulties in the way of properly taking care of F. — his duties, obligations, people crowding to get a moment with him. Also the irritation where some individuals, which are valuable to him in other ways, think more of whether he is giving them enough attention than of serving him. These last are the "prima donnas," and I am sorry to see that Mr. Justice Byrnes is one of them, nice as he is. [On March 24, James Byrnes had handed the President his resignation as director of War Mobilization and Reconversion, and on March 31, FDR wearily accepted it.]

Not really knowing whether I am justified or not, I told Dr. Bruenn that he, or Dr. McIntire, or *some*one, should put it very plainly to F.D.R. himself: F.D.R.'s one really great wish is to get this international organization for peace, started. Nothing else counts, next to that. That is the means by which they must make him take care of himself: "You want to carry out the United Nations plan. Without your health, you will not be able to do it. Therefore — take care of yourself."

He *must* reduce his hours of work & *not* break the new schedule. He *should* take 2–3 months off to get well, but if he can't do that, he can & must fit his workday to his strength — if he is to live through these trying days — It has come to that point, and I think the doctors believe it though they have not said it to me.

Later still. The day has been a good one — lovely balmy air, so we could have the doors wide open. Mr. Hassett was here until about 12, so I suggested to Mr. O'Connor that the drive *after* lunch would be better. F. got dressed & had his bath without hurrying and came out of his room at about 1.30. We had lunch at once, & he ate well — He had a cup of gruel, which he finished to the last drop, then a plate-full of cheese soufflé, creamed carrots & canned peas — He finished all but two little scraps which he left for "Mr. Manners" [Fala] — A half a grapefruit for dessert.

After lunch, we all went for a drive in the big car [Monty Snyder was at the wheel now; F.D.R., who had taken such pride in driving his own car, no longer felt up to it], down to see the foundations of the new building & then to the Knob & back the short way, through a lovely but rough wood road — lots of azaleas in bloom & some dog-wood trees. The country is beautiful in its new spring dress —

When we got back F. wouldn't go to rest at once, but got to work on a box of books. [He had recently begun calling these big wooden crates of books and manuscripts, sent to him for sorting, "coffins."]

After a while he went off to his room for an hour before dinner. He looks depressed, both physically & mentally, and it hurts one not to be able to do much for him but to be ready & waiting if anything turns up.

At dinner, he looked better, his voice clear & less tired — He ate without much appetite, but he had had enough at other meals. By the time dinner was over, he had had just enough of talking, & when Mr. O'Connor began talking seriously, it was an obvious effort to F.D.R. to concentrate intelligently. I was thankful when he said he would go to bed at 9.15.

~~By ten he was settled for the night, & I took a coffee-cup full of gruel. I knew that if I took in even a tea-cup-full, it would probably look too big & he wouldn't take *any!* So much for that! It worked!~~

[Long after she had written of these last weeks of FDR's life, Daisy evidently went back through her diary and scratched out passages that suggested an intimacy with the President she did not wish any outsider to misunderstand. At the same time, these memories were among her most precious, and so, since she could not bear to efface them entirely, she drew a single, unwavering line through them so that they could still easily be read.]

ᐟ᷾ *Easter Day April 1st.* F looks a little better & has had a good day, on the whole. [He] woke up about 9.15 & had his breakfast & Mr. Hassett appeared with a batch of letters to be signed. Dr. Bruenn came at the same time & took the blood pressure which does or does not mean anything!

Polly, Bruenn, Charlie Fredericks, Mr. Hassett — all of us discussed whether F would go to Church or not. We decided he would probably not want to make the effort. At 10 we went in to him & suggested that Polly & I would go to Church — why didn't he just stay quietly at home. With a smile, he said perhaps he would get up, now, anyway — Mr. Hassett left —

We read the papers . . . At 5 minutes of 11, F's door opened & out he came looking very spick & span in a light grey suit — No idea of staying home!

F pinned 2 periwinkles with green leaves on his lapel & we got into the car & off to Church, veils flying in the wind. The congregation were all seated, many in wheel chairs. We went up the aisle, F's chair going ahead. He transferred himself into the 3rd pew on the left & Polly & I followed him in & sat down. The little chapel is charming, so simple in line, with plain glass windows, a white altar with a cross, two candles and Easter lilies on it. A local choir did very nicely.

Fred Botts sang a solo with much feeling. To me, Fred Botts rather typifies Warm Springs. He came here as a patient & has an important position here . . . in spite of his crippled condition. His face is thin & hollow, but his expression is deep & happy & alive. He is part of Warm Springs & a very important part of it.

The service was Presbyterian — very nice — except that the clergyman went on & on! *and* on! F said afterwards that he couldn't hear a word, which was just as well, for it was a series of quotations and much more suited to Good Friday than Easter — The seats were as hard as rocks, as I knew too well — not being very well "cushioned" by nature, & I knew that F would find it even more so, with his thin legs — Also, his back was bothering him —

After the service we came quietly out ahead of the congregation, & got away without speaking to anyone.

We took a good ¾ hr. drive through the woods road & then almost to Manchester (that great shopping town where there is nothing to buy!) F sat in front with Monty — Polly & I in the back. The air was good for him, but by the time he sat down to lunch, he was so relaxed & tired that he could eat almost nothing . . .

He ate a little better at dinner & told us several stories of his youth . . .

⤳ *Monday, Apr. 2.* After storming all night the skies are clear & we have the promise of a beautiful day — F. slept badly, being awakened by the lightning. Once, in the night, I heard him having quite a bad coughing attack — but this morning, he seems to be all right, though not rested as he should be . . .

Later. It has turned out to be a "good" day — F worked quite a lot, but did not *over*-work — he ate a pretty good lunch, had a nap & we took an hour's drive toward evening. Polly, the dogs & I — So far, he doesn't *want* anyone else . . .

⤳ *Tuesday, April 3.* A beautiful day, which promises to be *hot,* at 11.30 A.M.! F improves, slowly but steadily. Mr. Hassett had only a handful of letters to be signed — GGT is now working with him. Polly out with the dogs — I have been up for hours, through misreading my watch. It's the only way I ever get anything accomplished however!

p.m. We had all the Venetian blinds down this afternoon, for it was hot. F went for his nap at about 3.30, had a good sleep, and at 5 we went for a drive in the big car. We had the extra windshield in front of us, to keep the wind from our hats & hair, but F pushed the little shield at his end aside, to *get* the wind! Also he took off his cap.

The *drive* was lovely, with the sun, warm, but not hot, and the country so beautiful. The peach trees are covered with fruit, the size of walnuts, already — the season is a month early — F enjoyed it thoroughly — We got "lost" at the beginning of the drive, headed toward Atlanta, and shortly after, arrived mysteriously in Warm Springs! So much for my lump of locality in Warm Springs! It is usually good — elsewhere!

F told us stories at dinner, sat in his chair, reading, afterwards — until the Dr. came at about 9.45 — a little later than usual. The Dr. is pleased with F.'s improvement, but *hopes* he can put on a few pounds. I do, too. He is taking his gruel between meals — at 5 P.M. & at bed time, and seems to like it. I should *like* to give him two *more* cups-full, but am afraid to press the question, for fear of his getting tired of it, or the Dr. thinking it may interfere with his eating other food. "Well-enough" is better than not-at-all. If he doesn't get tired of it & it seems to agree with him, he *may* take more of it of his own accord & he may keep it up permanently.

✎ *Wednesday — April 4*, 11 A.M. A perfect day; every door & window wide open. F has coughed three mornings in succession — about 5 A.M. The Dr. examines his chest every morning & finds it entirely devoid of congestion. The coughing is a clearing up of accumulated mucus, & only occurs in the early morning.

The Dr. & I have long talks about how to regulate F.'s day at the W.H. — Let's hope a *little* improvement *can* be made — enough to allow F. to get steadily better instead of steadily worse —

Later. He took a full tea-cup of gruel at noon, and ate pretty well at lunch, though we had a salad which he doesn't care about. We had a wonderful prune soufflé with whipped cream for dessert. F.'s day is strenuous even here:

9 A.M.	breakfast & newspapers
10	Hassett & some 50-odd letters to sign, a good many of them having to be thought over & requiring extra work — information, etc.
11	GGT or DB for correspondence — signing & dictating new letters —
12	get up — gruel
1	lunch
2.30 or 3.00	an hour or so, later. Rest —
4.30 or 5	Out for a drive of two hours — gruel
7–9	Dinner & conversation
9	to bed —

This is the "ideal"! We have kept to it pretty well — down here — with changes and interruptions and the set hours being stretched sometimes almost an hour — the point is that what we are accomplishing is enough near the ideal so that F is steadily improving.

DB was waiting around for some time, while Mr. Hassett stayed over with some unsettled questions, so F had her stay for lunch.

Pres. [Sergio] Osmeña of the Philippines is coming to see F tomorrow. He has been asked for a 3-hour conference, *including* lunch — and he hasn't grasped the fact, to this day, that the Pres. *will not* see him beyond that point! He has taken quarters at the Warm Springs Hotel, though he has been told in definite words, that he is expected to return to Jacksonville after leaving the Pres. Mr. Hassett is handling this little job. He says there are so *many* people who take advantage of F.D.R.'s politeness & kindness and won't leave him even when someone is obviously standing in the room, to usher them out!

Polly & I will keep out of the way for an hour or so, & then join the party.

We had a beautiful drive, wandering on unidentified roads — Even F. entirely lost! Finally, in the huge *6,000 lb* open car, we came to a long covered bridge over the Flint river, with a capacity of *4,000 lbs!* It *probably* would have held us, but we couldn't risk it, so turned around & came back for several miles, the way we had gone — We *did* know by then where we were! The bridge would have taken us to Thomaston.

[In later years, Daisy loved to tell of this drive. FDR had been willing to venture onto the bridge, she remembered. But Monty Snyder was not, and neither was the Secret Service. As a sort of compromise, Daisy suggested that the President's car back up several hundred yards, then race forward so that even if the bridge did collapse, the car would make it to the other side through sheer momentum. Roosevelt roared and promised her a commission in the Army Corps of Engineers.]

Mr. McCarthy came for dinner . . . He has taken a great fancy to Polly & is planning "12-mile walks" with her . . .

The "Drs." (Bruenn & Fox) came about 9.30 & the Amb. (ex) left. The Drs. love this little time with F. for while he is getting ready for bed he tells them stories — We can hear the laughter from the living-room. When they have all gone, & when Arthur comes out of the Pres.' room, it means he is settled for the night, except for a newspaper or two which he reads before putting out the light. I get the gruel & Polly & I take it to him. I sit on the edge of the bed & he "puts on an act": he is too weak to raise his head, his hands are weak, he must be fed! So I proceed to feed him with a tea spoon & he loves it! Just to be able to turn from his world problems & behave like a complete nut for a few moments, with an appreciative audience laughing with him & at him, both!

Polly & I had a rather heart-to-heart talk afterwards, in her room. We agree about F. — his greatness & seriousness & the remarkable sense of fun which hardly ever leaves him. When he can't smile & joke, he is really pretty sick — we are *so* happy over his improvement in less than a week. Polly confessed that when she saw him last Thursday, she didn't think he would live to go to the San Francisco Conference. She feels entirely differently now, for she sees he can still "come back" in a remarkable manner.

ᔕ *April 5th Thursday* — From being unseasonably hot, I awoke this morning to find it *cold;* the wind blowing around the house & through the doors which Polly insisted on leaving open last night! — Polly was buried under extra blankets, every window & door tight closed — Sister also.

Fearing that F might be cold, I went in & closed his window — He also asked me to pull up his blanket: he was using only a sheet. His circulation is really amazingly good for a paralyzed person & as I have written before, he has had *no cold feet* since Lenny started treating him, in January.

. . . 12.45 Pres. Osmeña arrived at the dot of 11, as scheduled — F was not quite ready yet. I was just placing a last vase of flowers, and got caught in the hall & shook hands with Pres. Osmeña. I had the impression of a slight, grey little man with a pleasant expression, a quick smile & a sense of humor —

Polly came from her room, around by the porch & through F's room & bath, & my room: and out we went for a marvelous walk with the dogs — The air is cool & bracing, so different from yesterday, when we could hardly drag ourselves along! We came in the front door & were slipping into my room, when F called "Margaret" & F. introduced us both & asked me to telephone "Hacky" to have the three men of the Press [pool] & Mr. Hassett come at 2 and get a story to be released the day F leaves for Wash. We will be having lunch in a minute or two.

F looked up at us with a smile: "We are getting along very well!" That means a lot, specially that there is no strain, and that they must be in general agreement. The 11–2 is already broken — but we hope it won't be more than an extra ½ hr. — *On verra.*

3 *p.m.* Pres. Osmeña . . . has left. The "planned" schedule was only ¾ hr late, and that, because F.D.R. called the three members of the Press and had a Press Conference. F did all the talking and gave them a very clear statement as to what he intends to do in respect to the Islands — He wants to give them their independence before the deadline next year, when the subject could easily become a political football.

F was in fine form, & looking *so* much better than a week ago, that I forget, almost, that he is still not his old self — He looks as though he had put on a little weight — His face is a little fuller — or it may be that he just looks less tired. In any case, he certainly looks *better* & we are *so* thankful.

Pres. Osmeña is a sweet person, apparently very refined. He showed us a letter from his 9-yr-old boy, who says he doesn't want anything Japanese, but would like some American candy! The conference of the two Presidents was apparently without effort and covered the whole list made up by Osmeña beforehand — At lunch, conversation was general and easy — Pres. Osmeña ate his steak with relish, and at two o'clock was prepared to leave. However, F had arranged for the . . . Press to come up . . . Mr. Hassett brought them in, and DB took down all that was said.

F . . . didn't appear to be making any effort — It lasted until about 2.30. Everyone left & the Pres. went to his room for a nap — It has been a beautiful day, but cold & windy, so F decided not to go out. He worked on the "coffin," as we call it . . .

I could see the conference with Osmeña had tired him. It shows most in that he loses his buoyancy & his sense of fun. He took his gruel at 5, & ate an excellent dinner at seven: a very rich mushroom soup, scrambled eggs & bacon, peas, stewed peaches & cream. Off to bed at about 9, ~~& we could hear his cheerful laugh after he got flat on his back & relaxed.~~ The Dr. told us the blood pressure was up a little, as might be expected, & we will try for a very quiet week.

~~Lucy [Mercer Rutherfurd] will be a pleasure, but another interruption in the routine we are trying to keep — She will probably come on Monday. Polly & I took him his gruel, as usual, and he put on his little act of helplessness! It amuses him to be fed, and I love to feed him — so "a good time was had by all." I think that the gruel that he takes at night relaxes him & probably makes him sleep more soundly — In this house, one can hear when the person in the next room turns over in bed — I have heard less from F's room each night — His coughing, too, is much less.~~

◦ *Friday April 6.* Cold & raw — some rain during the night. I have Arthur's little radio set up by my bed & find there are three stations here in Georgia that come through very clearly. When my breakfast came in, brought by Lizzie, she had two pitchers of "top of the bottle" for my coffee & cereal. She explained that they were short on cream & holding it back for F. "He needs it so much; Daisy keeps it for him," she said.

In came Sister & Fala for a morsel — Sister had three bits of buttered toast, & departed — Fala is curled up on the rug —

The news in Europe continues the same — the Allies advancing continuously . . .

F. said [last] night that he thinks he can retire by next year, after he gets the peace organization well started — I don't believe he thinks he will be *able* to carry on. Polly reacted to his statement very much as I did, the first time he mentioned it to me: that he couldn't do such a thing — It had never been done etc. I remarked that no one had ever before had a fourth term, either!

On thinking further, one realizes that if he cannot, physically, carry on, he will *have* to resign. There is no possible sense in his killing himself by slow degrees, the while not filling his job — Far better to hand it over, and avoid the period of his possible illness, when he wouldn't be *able* to function.

From a personal point of view — he can then take care of himself and have perhaps years of useful, happy life, when his influence for good can continue — perhaps on the Peace Organization.

✌ *10.15 p.m. A stamp issue* was born ½ hr. ago: F was working on his stamps by the fire. Polly & I sitting reading on the sofa. Suddenly, F looked up: "What do you think of this? A simple new stamp without engraving: '3 cents 3' on the top line, 'United States Postage' on the bottom line, and in the middle, 'April 25, 1945; Towards United Nations.'" To be issued on the 25th as a means of telling the country what the San Francisco Conference is all about!

He called for Frank Walker, Postmaster General. Word came back that he was at the theatre but would be back in half and hour. Dr. Bruenn came in & was told about it. He is a philatelist also.

Ting-a-ling . . . The telephone rang. Frank Walker was told — The design will be sent down for approval by next Tuesday or Wednesday — So can people in high places sometimes get things done in a few minutes!

F worked a little too long today, & his b-p was a little higher than it has been . . . He shows signs of a little cold in his head — these extreme changes of weather are not too helpful, in an open-air house like this — When F was ready for the night, I got his gruel & took it to him. He lay on his back, & began to pull the covers up to his chin shivering & saying he felt so cold. A moment before he had been sitting up reading a detective story, so I knew it was another "act" — to get *himself fed* the gruel! On paper it sounds too silly for words, and it *is* silly — but he's *very* funny and laughs at himself with us.

~~Polly says all the men in her family are like that — And those who have accomplished the most in the world can be the silliest & funniest! It is wonderful to be able to be that way — A great safety valve for a man to whom the whole world turns.~~

He took half his evening gruel & then decided to smoke a cigarette. He talked seriously about the S. Francisco Conference, & his part in World Peace, etc. He says again that he can probably resign some time next year, when the peace organization — The United Nations — is well started —

~~He then relapsed into babyhood for the rest of the gruel — and then I kissed him goodnight & left him relaxed & laughing —~~

∾ *Sunday, April 8.* . . . He is very slowly improving each day. It shows in different ways: He sits a little straighter in his chair, his voice is a little clearer and stronger, his face less drawn & he is *happier!* He is, normally, such a consistently cheerful responsive person, that one hates to see him making an effort to talk — and of course, everyone is always looking to him —

We are now looking forward to Lucy Rutherfurd's visit. She comes tomorrow, bringing Madame Shoumatoff, for another portrait of F.D.R., and a photographer — Lucy & Mme. S. go into the guest house, & Polly & I are going to get flowers to make it look attractive. Lizzie the maid has been busy cleaning for two days — and it *will* be very nice. F. has never gone in there to see it.

I don't believe I have described the household: There is Daisy, the cook; Lizzie, the W.H. maid, who takes charge of everything outside of the kitchen, [Joe Esperancilla] one of the Filipinos, who cleans, and waits on the table with Arthur, carries firewood — a general factotum; Arthur is valet to F and also butler.

Charlie Fredericks is general supervisor of anything pertaining to F. There is no one really in charge of the house, but each is trying to do his best, and we all make suggestions when we think of them, so everything runs remarkably smoothly. Polly, of course, is the one everyone looks to next to the Pres. Also, one tries not to bother him about details.

As the Pres. feels better, it is more difficult to get him off to bed early! His tendency is to stay up late & then get up later in the morning. The Dr. would like to have him do just the opposite: get up a little earlier & get through the worst of the work in the earlier part of the day, when one is stronger . . . It is difficult to change one's habits, however —

❧ *Monday April 9th.* Beautiful weather. F. looks splendidly — ate two Finnan Haddie, a cup of gruel, and a glass of milk, with relish, for his breakfast. It is 11 A.M. and Polly has been busily telephoning her arrangements about many things to be done while she goes west. Two carpenters have nailed wall-board inside the north fly-screened porch, as a windbreak, so F can sit in the sun on the porch. Mr. Hassett came for 5 minutes; Lt. Collins for 10 minutes — ~~I read my papers in F's room while he read his, and the living-dining room was being cleaned.~~

Monday morning there is no pouch from Washington so Monday is as near to a "do not work Sunday" as F. ever gets to.

F wants to sit in the sun. I have a brown envelope for him to put on the *top* of his head, as the sun is too hot to sit still under, for any length of time —

Later. F came out of his room towards 12.30 and sat under the awning on the porch and worked with DB. There wasn't much, as no pouch had come on Sunday — After lunch he went for his nap. He ate a good lunch, without the gruel, and had an hour & a half sleep — but he always has himself waked, so that he never gets enough rest.

Polly & I got flowers from the woods, & roses growing over the porch & she stayed home to fix the vases for both this cottage & for the guest house, while I went with F. in the car toward Macon, to meet Lucy & "Shoumie" [Madame Shoumatoff]. It was a beautiful evening for a drive & we enjoyed it tremendously — on & on, away from the sun, scanning every car that headed towards us, imagining it was slowing up . . .

Finally, after driving 85 miles, we turned around & started toward the setting sun — It got quite chilly & F put on his cape & I my rain coat which, though not warm, is a good windbreaker. We stopped in front of the drugstore in Manchester, for a "Coke" & at that moment Lucy & her party also drove up to the curb! Lucy & Shoumie got into the car, I on the little seat, & we drove home to this "Little White House." The drive was too long, and F was chilly and looked awfully tired all the evening and his blood pressure was up when he went to bed. However, he took his gruel.

❧ *April 10.* Another beautiful, warm day. F had his usual morning, ~~with me reading the paper by his window, while he had his breakfast~~ [and] read all the war dispatches in 2 or 3 papers — He has the whole western front in Europe in his head, knows exactly where each army is at any one moment. He says he *has* to, for sometimes he has to make

decisions about operations. I was surprised at this, thinking that Eisenhower would have the final say about such things, but F explained
it this way: Some time ago, Eisenhower made a forward movement in
the southern part of the line. Winston Churchill promptly cabled F a
protest, asking that those troops be sent to help out some British
troops in the northern section — F, knowing what the plans were, sent
an explanation to W.S.C. backing up Eisenhower.

Lucy came down from the guest house to be on hand when F
should appear — He got up at about 11.30 & appeared some time
after 12, was photographed by Mr. [Nicholas] Robbins, who came
with Mme. Shoumatoff, & got to work on the porch, with GGT, Lucy
sitting in a corner, watching him. Polly & I went off for a walk, with
the dogs [and] Mme. S.

We came back from our walk at one, met Mr. McCarthy at the
gate & walked down to the house. F went on working for another
half hour or so, Daisy getting perfectly distracted in the kitchen, because the meal was getting spoiled from over-cooking! Nothing can
ever be done about that, however!

The lunch party was awfully nice. Everybody was cheerful, &
responsive & F told stories to his heart's content until 4 P.M.!! He
looked tired, but was having a good time. He went off to rest at 4,
came out at five, looking more tired than ever, & went out for a drive.
He took Lucy & Fala with him, to the Knob — the best thing he could
do. They sat in the sun, talking, for over an hour, & he came back
with a good tan —

Dinner was nice again, & the Dr. came about 9.20 & F very soon
went off to his room. The blood pressures were below the 100–200
marks, & we hope will stay there — Gruel again, before putting out
the lights . . .

❧ *April 11*. . . . 11 A.M. Another perfect day. F. with four women on
his hands & Mr. Robbins who wants to get another picture of F for
Mme. Shoumatoff.

I have just had another long talk with Lucy — and also with
Mme. S. about the new portrait. Lucy & Mme. S. had their breakfasts
at 8.20 this A.M., but are just now getting up out of bed. F had a good
night, and though the pressure is a little up this morning, he seems
pretty well — The doctor said "Keep lazy, Sir"! which I repeated to
Lucy, as she wants to cooperate. So today *should* be pretty quiet —
though Sec. Morgenthau comes for dinner.

Lucy brought some dextrin which she used to give to her husband [to help sustain his weight]. I spoke to Dr. Bruenn about it. He advises keeping it in reserve if F should keep on losing weight. He thinks it best not to run the risk of having F. not like the gruel with the dextrin in it, & he says it has little in it that sugar has not, from a fattening point of view — I have doubts about that statement, as I know that "baby foods" are what run-down people need — However!

Later. F came out of his room at about noon very smiling and handsome in a double breasted grey-blue suit and crimson tie — Mr. Robbins took a couple of photographs, with and without the navy cape — Then F went out on the porch with DB, and did the day's mail and worked on his speech for Friday night.

[After FDR had finished dictating to Dorothy Brady, she remembers, he said, "I want you to stay for lunch and be my hostess." He needed her, she knew, because Mrs. Rutherfurd and Cousin Laura (Polly) and Daisy all had rival claims on that position.

FDR knew that she and her husband had a farm that was too far from Washington for her to visit as often as she liked, and during lunch he said to her, without any explanation, "I think you'll be able to visit that farm more often now."]

We finished lunch at 2

At DB's suggestion, F went out on the porch & worked on the speech & also read the draft for another speech he has to make. At quarter to three he went to his room for a good sleep, leaving orders for the car at 4.30. In the meantime, DB left, and Mme. Shoumatoff went off to work on her pictures & Polly & Lucy & I talked & knitted . . .

Lucy is such a lovely person, but she seems so very immature — like a character out of a book. She has led such a protected life with her husband, who was much older than herself, always living on a high scale, that she knows little about life. Now, she faces a very different future, rather alone, for even her own Barbara wants to marry a boy of a very different background, & Lucy will be left entirely alone. Also, she isn't very well and that makes it more difficult to face life & make decisions.

F says she has *so many* problems & difficulties that she brings to him. She has no other person like him — a friend of such long standing — to whom to go for the kind of sympathetic understanding which he always gives — I cannot blame her, but at the same time, I can't help feeling that she should face her own life & not put too much of its difficulties on *his* shoulders — But, I must add, that he is always happy when he feels he is helping others & making others happy. Polly said that one reason he is taking us to S. Francisco, is that he knows how much we will love to go — It is true. Another reason is that if he has his private car filled with us, there will be no other *less relaxing*(!) people for him to have to talk to! At any rate, we are going!

At 4.30, F came out of his room. Polly & I planned to take a walk with the dogs, & let Lucy go out with him for his drive, but he announced that he wanted some of us to go with him, so I was delegated — I threw on my hat & my Sears Roebuck raincoat over my rather messy dress, jumped in, & off we went for a two-hour drive in warm, wonderful air — little Fala on the little seat, so he could look over the side once in a while. Most of the time he just lies on the floor with, usually, his head on his master's foot — It is very sweet the way he settles himself . . .

Lucy is so sweet with F — No wonder he loves to have her around — Toward the end of the drive, it began to be chilly and she put her sweater over his knees — I can imagine just how she took care of her husband — She would think of *little* things which make so much difference to a semi-invalid, or even a person who is just *tired*, like F.

Sec. Morgenthau came at seven, looking much worried over his wife who has been quite seriously ill with thrombosis &, just lately, a heart attack. After dinner, we 4 women left the P. & the Sec. for a half-hour conversation . . . The Dr. came shortly & F went off to bed . . .

After F had his gruel he was very tired, as he lay in bed, with gruel pouring slowly down his throat, he said, "Now I'm all relaxed again!" As I have told him *several* times he needs to lead as dull a life as possible, until he gets his strength back — The trouble is, that just as soon as he gets a little better he feels full of pep, and proceeds to use it up all over again. It's next to impossible to stop him at just the right moment between his having a happy interesting time, and his getting over-tired.

❧ *April 12th Thursday*. Another beautiful day, with the promised heat — F woke up with a slight headache and a stiff neck, which probably comes from being over-tired. Dr. Bruenn rubbed his neck for a while and ordered a hot water bottle as soon as breakfast was finished.

With two sofa pillows and his reading tray holding the newspaper

~~at an angle, he looks half asleep, upright in bed! I am reading the~~
~~newspaper in his room. The pouch from Washington, including the~~
~~morning Atlanta papers, won't arrive until after 11, but he is reading~~
~~more of yesterday's papers.~~

At the moment, everything is peaceful, at *10.20 a.m.* Charlie Fredericks is on a stepladder, putting new cords in the Venetian blinds — Two have broken just from age — Sister lies snoring under the desk in F's room. Polly is taking a bath — I must go up to the guest house & ~~report to Lucy~~ . . .

Midnight. This morning, I went up to the guest house and told Lucy the morning "bulletin" — F would probably get dressed earlier than usual, because of the delayed pouch. Lucy said she & Mme. S. would come down to the house before noon, & we would be ready, when F appeared, for Mme. S. to start painting . . .

F appeared just about as planned — Mme. S. had her easel set up, we put the Pres.' chair at just the right angle, so the light would be good. We were fussing around, getting things fixed. He came in, looking very fine in a double-breasted grey suit & a crimson tie. His colour was good & he looked smiling & happy & ready for anything. He sat down in his chair while I explained why the chair was facing toward the light, instead of in its usual position, toward the room. . . .

Mme. S. exclaimed: "Mr. President, you look so much better than yesterday, I am glad I did not start working before today." He looked so good looking; much as some of his earlier pictures show him — his features, at once strong and refined.

Mr. Hassett brought some papers to be signed. F. had his feet up on the wicker stool and the usual card table in front of him. He signed everything — Mr. Hassett laying them "out to dry." Mr. Hassett left, leaving the folder of signed letters on the Pres.' table. He began to look over some of them; Mme. S. began to work.

At about 20 mins. of one, the little tray with the cup of gruel and a small pitcher of cream was brought in & put on the table at his right hand — I got up from the sofa and went around to pour the cream for him, mix it a little, & get him started on it. He interrupted his reading for a moment & took some gruel, continued his reading, took more gruel. He enjoyed the gruel, always — he said it seemed to increase his appetite if anything —

Once, I remember, he said, "Wouldn't it be strange if this gruel should be the one thing to put weight on me!" Just a passing thought, of course, but he had his weight on his mind, & he realized that you are failing if your weight continues to *de*crease when you & your Drs.

are trying hard to *in*crease it. Arthur Prettyman also brought in his "green cocktail" which was supposed to increase his appetite, & he swallowed that without interrupting his work.

Mme. S. has given *her* version of what happened after this. He *did* say: "We have fifteen minutes more to work" — We all heard it.

My version is as follows: I was crocheting on the sofa, constantly looking up — at him — at Mme. S. — anxious to see the progress of the picture. However, Mme. S. didn't want us to look just yet. I got up for a moment or two, & stood in front of the fireplace behind F's chair. I discovered that from there, I could see the portrait in the little oval mirror which hangs nearest to F's bedroom door — I couldn't see very well, however, & went back to my crocheting on the sofa.

Polly (about 1 P.M.) went into her room to put water in a bowl of roses — I glanced up from my work —

F seemed to be looking for something: his head forward, his hands fumbling — I went forward & looked into his face. "Have you dropped your cigarette?"

He looked at me with his forehead furrowed in pain and tried to smile. He put his left hand up to the back of his head & said: "I have a terrific pain in the back of my head."

He said it distinctly, but so low that I don't think anyone else heard it — My head was not a foot from his — I told him to [put] his head back on his chair — Polly came through her door at that moment. We tilted his chair back, as he was slumping forward, & with Polly & Lucy holding the chair, I took up the telephone & said to the operator . . . "Please get in touch with Dr. Bruenn & ask him to come at once to the President's cottage," and put down the receiver.

Mme. S. in the meantime had called in Arthur Prettyman & Joe the Filipino. They picked up F. but found him a dead weight — not at all the way he usually put his arms around the men's shoulders & carried his own weight on them — Polly took F.'s feet, & somehow, between us all, we carried him in to his bed, and laid him on 3 pillows. [After FDR's death from the cerebral hemorrhage, Laura Delano would say that as they struggled to carry the President into the bedroom, she heard him say, "Be careful."]

We did not dare give him the internal stimulant or move him. I was cold as ice in my heart, cold & precise in my voice — I opened his collar & tie & held up the left side of his pillow, rather than move him to the middle of it. I held his right hand. Polly was on his left, her hand on his heart, fanning him. Two or three times he rolled his head from side to side, opened his eyes. Polly thinks he looked at us all in turn. He may have, I could see no signs of real recognition in those eyes — twice he drew up the left side of his face, as if in pain — But it was only a question of 3 or 4 minutes, for he became unconscious as far as one could see — His breathing was rather heavy but his heart seemed to be steady & strong, though quick —

Lucy brought some camphor and held it back & forth before his nostrils, Arthur & Joe stood by. I knew that I had little consciousness except for him. One must not do anything wrong. It was better to do nothing — the Dr. must have come in 15 minutes or so. It is hard to know about minutes in times like this, for one doesn't have the chance, or the thought, to look at a watch. When the doctor came, he asked us all to leave the room so they could get F. undressed & into bed. He was without question unconscious at this time & never regained consciousness —

After a while, the Dr. came out, asked us all what had happened, and telephoned Dr. McIntire in Washington.

Polly telephoned E.R. saying simply: "We are worried about Franklin, he has had a fainting spell. Dr. Bruenn will call you back."

She, of course, knew something serious had happened — Two hours went by — Lucy & Mme. S. left in the auto with Mr. Robbins within an hour.

Polly, Mr. Hassett & Charlie Fredericks & I stood around, tried to be calm. The Dr. came out & went back in again. Geo. Fox, the Dr, Arthur & Joe were in the room almost constantly — At first they were putting hot water bottles & blankets to warm F. Then, the blood pressure, which had gone way up, was brought down somewhat by an injection. F. ceased to be cold.

About 3.15 [Central War Time] F's breathing became *very* heavy & labored — I had a distinct feeling that this was the beginning of the end —

Dr. [James E.] Paullin was on his way down from Atlanta. He came in the door. Dr. Bruenn was talking on the phone to Dr. McIntire. He was saying: "If anything, he is a little better."

At that moment the breathing suddenly stopped in F's room, someone opened the door & called Dr. Bruenn.

Polly took the telephone from him & asked Dr. "Mac" to hold the wire.

Dr. Paullin was hurried into F's room. I looked at my watch: 25 minutes of 4. It was the end —

3.35 p.m. Franklin D. Roosevelt, the hope of the world, is dead — What this means to me, and to all who knew him personally, is impossible to put into words — What it means to the world, only the future can tell.

From then on, there seemed to be nothing to do, and at the same time, everything to do. Mr. Hassett notified whoever it was in Washington — Mr. Truman had to be sworn in at once —

Polly & I packed our bags to have the rooms ready for E.R. & whoever might come down with her — We moved to the guest house — we were both dazed — couldn't think what to put in the bag — Charlie Fredericks, strong & faithful, got to work with Arthur & Joe getting all F.D.R.'s things packed & marked. No one knew what would happen. Would we get on the train tonight — or wait 'til the morning? We must wait for whatever E.R. would decide.

Daisy [Bonner] & Lizzie both came into my room at different times, & we wept with our arms about each other. *Everyone* is crushed — It would be hard to say who feels it most. Of course, those of us who have been nearest to him: Charlie, Arthur, Mike Reilly, Guy Spaman, the Secretaries.

E.R. came, I think, before 11 — she, Hassett, Reilly, Dewey Long, Early, etc. decided what to do: The undertakers were waiting around. We leave at 10 tomorrow morning.

E.R. sent us off to bed, for some rest — even if we don't sleep —

Poor E.R. — I believe she loved him more deeply than she knows herself, and his feeling for her was deep & lasting. The fact that they could not relax together, or play together, is the tragedy of their joint lives, for I believe, from everything that I have seen of them, that they had everything else in common. It was probably a matter of personalities, of a certain lack of humor on her part — I can not blame either of them. They are both remarkable people — sky-high above the average.

What *I* have been able to contribute was a complete lack of "strain." He told me once that there was no one else with whom he could be completely himself. Even with 2 or 3 others, who meant more to him than I, he couldn't completely relax — That is why, in these past years, as he has been getting more & more tired, he would have me around half the time paying no attention to me, working on his stamps, reading, or working. I was somebody nearby, so he wouldn't be alone — And we understood each other.

◌ *April 14th.* The White House. This is the last time I shall be in this building, in which F.D.R. has always made me feel so completely at home — I want to wander in his study & look again & again at all his things, from the paintings on the wall to the silly little toys on his desk. Every item speaks of him & when the thought crosses one's mind that he has permanently left them in other hands, it is almost unbearable.

All during last night's trip from Warm Springs, crowds were standing silently at every station. Along the route small groups stood or sat on the grass, just to see our beloved Pres. go by for the last time. The shades in the observation car were up so they could see the flag draped over the casket; the four servicemen were standing guard, & a few beautiful wreaths given by organizations & cities along the way —

Polly & I had adjoining rooms in the car with the casket — dear little Fala knows something is wrong — He is depressed, he wanders around — In the Pres.' car he feels at home, but he knows his master is not there, and, as at Warm Springs, he did not once go into F.D.R.'s room.

We got into Union Station at just 10 o'clock as planned. The Supreme Court & their wives & the Cabinet & their wives came on board at once, to pay their respects to E.R. She never for a moment loses her poise, says just the right thing, etc.

Polly & the dogs & I went into the first stateroom off the observation car, to make room for the family who came on first. There were Elliott & Faye, & the 3 other daughters-in-law, and dear Anna & her John — It is pathetic to see all the little wives without their husbands —

As soon as the Cabinet had left, Mrs. R. & the "children" went out, then Polly, Harry Hooker & the dogs & I. Mr. Baruch was put in the car with us — The slow procession to the White House was very moving & impressive. I forgot I was part of it. The casket on the caisson was pulled by 6 white horses & the rate was a steady walk which did not seem to overtax the WAVES walking in front of it . . .

Mr. Baruch told us something about his trip abroad: the terrible devastation of German cities; there is at this moment *no* organized German resistance to speak of; he is hopeful that we really *are* going to make a workable peace this time; he told Churchill just what this country will do (and no more) and that "so much" is expected of Great Britain. Churchill was terribly crushed by the news of F.D.R. I remember F.D.R. telling me that W.S.C. told him, "I simply can't go on without you" when it was a question of F.D.R. running for a fourth term, etc. This was all while we were on the way to the White House, sad & solemn crowds lining the streets.

I *knew* it was F.D.R.'s body that was being taken on its last journey, but I also knew that F.D.R. was no longer in that body & that in all probability he was seeing this mournful procession & all us sad people, from his newfound freedom, and he is wishing he could tell us not to be sad, but to tighten our armor of faith & carry on the great fight which he has been waging with such courage & faith. Perhaps his death will tie together the millions of people who were depending on him. As E.R. said, one man alone couldn't do it — "All of us" have to do it, and F has shown the way — We *must* carry on —

Arrived at the White House. There was a [Navy] band . . . drawn up beyond the portico. The caisson & several cars drove in through the gates —

We got out & stood behind the members of the family. The casket was lifted off, & slowly carried into the house while the band played the National Anthem. The family followed, then a few special people like Frances Watson & Mr. Baruch. I couldn't look around very well, so I don't know just who was there. Polly & I with the dogs followed in through the hall, down the red carpet to the East Room. The South Wall is a bank of beautiful flowers & in the center stands the casket on a stand draped with grey velvet.

It is beautiful, the entire thing, the dignity & simplicity of how everything is done — Just as Franklin would want it, if he *had* to have any sort of a public burial — Of course, as he told several of us, he never even wanted to be embalmed. He wanted to be wrapped in a sheet and laid next to the ground. But that is hardly possible under the circumstances, & I am quite certain that he is not worrying about that at all where he is . . .

 April 15th Sunday. [Hyde Park] A perfectly beautiful day, just as almost every day was, at Warm Springs . . . Fala came with me, & stood with Polly, Mrs. J. R. Roosevelt, Mrs. Douglas Robinson & me. When they fired 3 volleys into the air, Fala gave a sharp bark after each. An unconscious salute of his own, to his master — Everyone is so sweet to me, & so sympathetic — I become reduced to tears without much encouragement. On the other hand, sometimes, I lose all sense of feeling — It is too much to grasp.

Polly & I have had some talks which have brought us very close, I think. We are both "lone wolves," though we are outwardly rather gay — She is always talkative — I only on occasion, & more easily so with strangers than with people I know. Fala & I joined the family after the service & drove home . . . I don't see how any loss could be worse than to lose the kind of a friend F.D.R. was —

◇ *April 19th, Thursday, at F.D.R. Library.* One of the hardest things I have had to do was coming to this Library on Tuesday morning, with the realization that F will never be seen here again, and that his body lies at rest in the garden — that tired body which he kept going by sheer will-power. Any other man would have gone to bed a year ago — but F. had his hopes & plans for world peace, and he couldn't give up until he had done everything in his power to get that peace started. He was working against time, and against his failing strength, and I think & know that all those who worked for him & with him for that goal will carry on as best they can. F. himself did not have too much faith in Stalin, but he thought that he & Stalin looked at things in the same *practical* way, & that for that reason, there was much hope that Stalin would follow along — Perhaps, now, Stalin will *lead,* along the lines of F.'s ideas. There are no words adequate to express the feelings of us all — for me, it is a *personal* loss, beyond anything, but for even the humblest workman on this place and in this Library, it is also a "personal" loss in a very remarkable way. When F. once smiled a greeting or shook a hand — he became a "friend." Millions all over the country feel that, even those who have never seen him.

On Tuesday, the mass of flowers was still standing by the grave, but fading & drooping.

Wednesday, Mr. Plog had removed them.

Grass has been put over the grave, & two large baskets of flowers at the head & foot. An M.P. walks slowly up & down the pathway, gun on his shoulder — I go over at lunch time, pick the pansies & fill a glass with them — Mr. Plog has received 14 boxes of orchids from S. America to be put on the grave. We consulted about them, and decided to put one box-full on the grave now; put half the remainder in the ice-house, unopened, the other half in water, & keep them until Sunday, so Mrs. R. can see them. I told Mr. Plog that I will pick the pansies every day, & keep a bowl of them on the grave as long as they last. Someone put a little bunch of forget-me-nots there, but without water, so they are faded — I will get some containers from Mr. Plog.

The people in the Library are *so* nice. They realize what this means to me, & want to show their sympathy . . . The most interesting period of this Library is over, the period of the President's association with it. What *we* must try to do is make it the kind of place the President wanted it to be — His spirit is here, & when I get a sort of helpless, "what's-the-use-in-doing-anything" feeling, I can feel his thought that no matter *what* happens, one must never give up — that was *his* motto, & the reason of his greatness.

"The President's Room," I hope, will remain as it is, always — for he fixed it this way, placed the furniture, had the pictures hung, etc. . . .

☙ *May 1st.* This morning (we hear) the Roosevelts turned over the "big house" to the government. Mrs. R. will live in her Val-Kill cottage.

I was alone [at Top Cottage] during lunch & the tragedy came over me as it does many times a day, the tragedy of my personal loss of a perfect friend — And then I realize that I *must not* "give up" — I must go on — stronger than ever — as he would want me to do. I believe that my friendship with F.D.R. was one of those very rare relationships (outside of marriage), which is so simple, so completely clean & straightforward, that only a person who has experienced it can believe it and understand it. I never felt any self-consciousness or embarrassment, or any inhibitions, when with him. I could say or think what I wanted — He never needed to worry about hurting my feelings — He answered, or did not answer, my questions without my insisting on an answer or without my feeling hurt when he didn't answer. He knew that I knew there were many things he could *not* answer . . .

Up at Top Cottage I was mentally saying farewell to just another chapter in F.D.R.'s life for it is probable that when I have finished this inventory, I shall never again see that lovely room *as it is.* Such happy hours have been spent there by F.D.R. — relaxed and peaceful; sometimes with one person, or two, or three, or even 6 or 8 — but always people with whom he did not have to make an effort — who did not demand anything of him, & always loved every little joke . . .

☙ *May 7th.* The grave in the garden looks so sweet with pots of ivy and the fresh bowl of roses Mr. Plog puts there every day, and my birdbath full of pansies and forget-me-nots — *and* bees!

I love it just as it is now, without any stone — just nature, helped a little. I think he loves it as it is now, because it has been fixed by the hands that love him . . .

Afterword

Daisy went on quietly working at the Library until her retirement in 1963, identifying in her neat, tiny hand hundreds, perhaps thousands, of people in family letters and photographs who would otherwise have remained forever mysteries to the biographers of her great friend.

One by one the members of her family died, until she found herself alone at Wilderstein. Ceilings fell, plaster cracked, water poured through the roof, but she soldiered on until, in 1980, friends eased her burdens by establishing Wilderstein Preservation, dedicated to maintaining her father's handsome but costly legacy.

I visited Daisy at Wilderstein one day in 1987 while working on my second book on Roosevelt's early career. She was ninety-four then, but her affection for the President had not diminished, her memory of those early days was still sharp, and, perhaps because no one else seemed ever to have asked her much about them, the interview seemed to go particularly well. She was especially glad, she told me, that I hadn't probed her painful memories of the President's last days at Warm Springs.

Finally, just as I was about to leave, she said she had something she felt she had to show me, something she had kept from every other writer. She rose from her chair and searched through the dark clutter of the dining room, in which we'd been having tea, until she found her small black purse. From it she drew an ancient, dog-eared envelope.

"I *always* keep this near me," she said, opening the envelope and carefully smoothing its yellowed contents on the tabletop. "It's very important."

I held my breath as she began to read aloud.

It was a newspaper clipping that someone had evidently brought to her attention. It seemed that an Irish medium had been in touch with FDR. The President reported that he was having a "perfectly *grand* time" on the Other Side.

"Doesn't that sound *just* like him?" Daisy asked, hugging the clipping to her bosom and beaming.

It did sound just like him, and now that I've read the letters and diaries she always avoided disclosing but made sure she kept, I think I understand the special delight she showed that afternoon. Surely, the article and the promise it held out suggested to Daisy that there might still be a way to reach Top Cottage, after all.

Most of the proceeds from this book will go to Wilderstein Preservation to help maintain Daisy Suckley's beloved Rhinebeck home. Readers who would like to help and scholars who want to consult the Suckley papers may write to:

Wilderstein Preservation
P.O. Box 383
Rhinebeck, New York 12572

Gifts to Wilderstein Preservation are tax-deductible. Visitors are welcome. For dates and hours, call 914-876-4818.

Acknowledgments

Whether Daisy Suckley ever intended for her papers to be published is impossible to say, but certainly she could not have foreseen how many people would eventually find themselves involved in getting them ready. I am grateful to all of them.

First I'd like to thank the members of the board of Wilderstein Preservation, past and present — including Raymond Armater, Joanne Lukacher, John McGuire, Al Vinck, and Duane and Linda Watson — who found and assembled the Suckley papers and then sought me out to edit them. Special thanks go to Daisy's friend and executor, J. Winthrop Aldrich, without whose vast knowledge of the Suckleys, their neighbors, and their rarefied world this would have been a very different book. Whenever I wonder how an intensely private person like Daisy Suckley would feel about having her intimate friendship with FDR made public I comfort myself with the knowledge that the primary beneficiary will be the old house that came to mean everything to her.

I'd like to thank Margaret Nyhof of the Franklin and Eleanor Roosevelt Institute, who saw to it that typed transcripts were made by Michelle Butler, Alison Nyhof, Keith Nyhof, and Sarah Augusta Johnson, as well as all my friends at the Franklin D. Roosevelt Library, especially Elizabeth Denier, who read over many of the transcripts with her practiced eye.

Old friends and fond relatives of Daisy's helped me understand her better, and I owe a considerable debt to all of them: the late Deborah Dows, Joan L. Aitken, Montgomery Anderson, Catherine Hambley, Margaret Hambley Hendrick ("Roly" in Daisy's diaries), and Mrs. John Maury.

And then there were those who knew best other members of the cast who were kind enough to look over the manuscript on my behalf, answering questions and clearing up mysteries: the President's secretary Dorothy Brady, his grandson Curtis Roosevelt, and his physician

Dr. Howard Bruenn; Eleanor Roosevelt's great friend Trude Lash; Mrs. Lucy Mercer Marbury Blunden, who shared her warm memories of her aunt; Mrs. Curtis Read, who gave me insights into the elusive, prickly personality of Laura Delano; and former Secret Service agent Milton Lipson, who recalled for me the special demands of caring for an immobilized President.

My old friend William Emerson has once again rescued me from a host of errors of my own making; none of my work on FDR would have been possible without his encouragement and wise counsel.

I'd like to thank my agent, Carl Brandt, who made it possible for me to take on this project. And, since it took twice as long as we all thought it would take, I also owe a special debt of gratitude to John Sterling of Houghton Mifflin for his patience and his enthusiasm for the manuscript. Finally I want to thank the manuscript editor, Frances Apt, for the special pains she took to ensure that Daisy's authentic voice would be preserved for readers who never got the chance to know her. "I just like her so much," she told me as the manuscript went off to the printer.

So do I.

Index